THE
NEW
STATE

THE
NEW
STATE

Etatization of
Western Societies

◆

SZYMON CHODAK

Lynne Rienner Publishers ◆ Boulder & London

Published in the United States of America in 1989 by
Lynne Rienner Publishers, Inc.
1800 30th Street, Boulder, Colorado 80301

and in the United Kingdom by
Lynne Rienner Publishers, Inc.
3 Henrietta Street, Covent Garden, London WC2E 8LU

Library of Congress Cataloging-in-Publication Data
Chodak, Szymon.
   The new state.
   Bibliography: p.
   Includes index.
   1. State, The. 2. Capitalism. 3. Welfare state.
I. Title.
JC325.C48   1989   320.1   88-18552
ISBN 1-55587-107-0 (alk. paper)

British Cataloguing in Publication Data
A Cataloguing in Publication record for this book
is available from the British Library

Printed and bound in the United States of America

The paper used in this publication meets the requirements of
the American National Standard for Permanence of Paper for
Printed Library Materials Z39.48-1984

To Yurek

Contents

Part 3   THE CONTEMPORARY INDIVIDUAL AND
THE HISTORICAL INEVITABILITY OF ETATIZATION

Tables

Preface

Societal development today tends to be organized by the state; consequently, theories of societal development and of the state converge. This book is concerned with such an amalgamated theory.

Because this book is intended as a study of the contemporary condition perceived from the complementary perspectives of divergent social science theories, works by Marx, Weber, Durkheim, Simmel, Schumpeter, and other classical theorists constitute the departure points for analysis. While I wanted to preserve the original interpretive intentions of these writers, I sometimes replace old terminology. For instance, instead of "division of labor"—the term used by Adam Smith, Emile Durkheim, and, sometimes, by Karl Marx, who employed the concept in relation to class division—I employ "differentiation" and "specialization." "Interdependence" is employed instead of Durkheim's "solidarity"; "interdependence of coexistence" instead of "mechanical solidarity"; "complementary interdependence" instead of "organic solidarity." These terms are defined in *Societal Development* (Chodak 1973). Initially intended merely to modernize terminology, these changes broadened the actual scope of the theory. A third level of solidarity/interdependence, engendered by growing state control and regulation in etatized societies, was discerned.

Modifications in theoretical expression reflect changes both in thinking and in actual processes of societal development. They are not unique to my approach. By including intermediation in the traditional concept of class conflict, Marxist and other academic theorists have significantly modified the theory of class relations.

I started work on this book at the Institute of International Studies, University of California, Berkeley, during a sabbatical leave in 1978-1979, continued at Concordia University in Montreal, and returned to it at the Institute of International Studies during a second sabbatical leave in 1985-1986. I owe my deepest gratitude to Carl G. Rosberg, the director of the institute, for invitations to Berkeley and for assisting my endeavor in many ways. I am deeply indebted to Alex Inkeles for encouragement and valuable advice. Kenneth Westhues read an earlier version of the work; it is in response to his question, "Is etatization inevitable?" that I wrote Chapter 15. I am grateful to him for his incisive comments. My gratitude goes to Aaron Wildavsky for his opinions and advice. I owe special thanks to Dennis S. Ippolito for making available a copy of his *Hidden Spending: The Politics of Federal Credit Programs*, before it was published.

The initial versions of Chapters 1, 2, and 3, were read (under different titles) to annual meetings of the International Society for Comparative Study of Civilizations. I wish to thank the participants in those sessions for comments. I owe particular gratitude to Carroll Bourg, with whom I discussed a number of the concepts in this book during its incipient stage. In March 1986, I was invited to discuss what later became Chapter 5 on the typology of etatized societies, and some concepts of etatization theory, at a special meeting at the Department of Political Science, the University of British Columbia, Vancouver. I would like to express my strong appreciation for the stimulating discussion during that meeting.

My gratitude is due to the Social Science Research Council of Canada for a grant and fellowship that made possible necessary travels and the completion of this work. I would like to thank the Hoover Institution for its invitation to Stanford, California, for six weeks of study. I also wish to express gratitude to P. J. Albert, vice-dean of research and space, art, and science at Concordia University in Montreal for a grant to prepare the manuscript for publication. My book is not representative of any position of the institutions that supported my research or of any particular ideological orientation.

My wife, Nina, has sacrificed a great deal of time to read chapters of the manuscript over and over again and to involve herself in my research, instead of her own work in linguistics. My gratitude expressed here is but a token of recognition of this sacrifice, and of the support and sound counsel she gave me.

I owe many thanks to a number of students who assisted me in the project: Robin Golt, John Curran, Athanasias Antoniou, and Gillian Kraniefs.

Finally, I would like to express my gratitude to Pamela Ferdinand for her innovative advice, her patience, and particularly her skilful copyediting.

Szymon Chodak

Introduction

For some time now, Western societies have been undergoing a major transformation into state-controlled and state-regulated systems—in short, into etatized societies.[1] In the past, the state performed two essential functions: the external function of defense, and the internal one of maintaining law and order or policing the community. In more recent times, however, the state has acquired numerous new functions.

Typical of the new condition is state management and regulation of the new, mixed-market economy, composed of private and state-owned sectors, and of the whole society, equipped with service and welfare systems. As in the past, people are motivated by material interests. They strive for profits and larger incomes. Yet, they also seek to preserve a higher level of economic and social security, equity, and equality maintained by state institutions. And they like to keep society as or more open to free expression, association, and private entrepreneurial initiatives as in traditional capitalist society of the past. The state provides vehicles for attaining these objectives.

Capitalism is not metamorphosing into a more capitalist or a socialist condition, as was predicted. The new equity, which presupposes entitlements—rights and welfare systems—can be characterized as containing some ingredients of socialism, but it cannot be seen as implementing the socialist ideals advocated by great thinkers of the past and pursued in rebellions, revolutions, and large scale reforms. Capitalism continues. Yet, this is a different society.

While persisting under old names, realities inevitably change. Consequently, difficulties arise in distinguishing the old reality from the new. For a long time, the new development was difficult to distinguish from the old capitalist economic and social structure. Currently, more and more writers are realizing that this new society—complete with a new class, new poverty, new economic and social structure, and new state—is distinct from the capitalist society of the nineteenth and first half of the twentieth

1

centuries. Some theorists, Dahrendorf for one, express the opinion that not only pre–World War II concepts have grown antiquated, but that "political paradigms of the fifties and the sixties are dead."[2]

Old theories are still valid; if not for other purposes then for seeing how much society has changed. I agree with Dahrendorf and those others who say we cannot anymore discuss effectively this rapidly changing reality by using old names and concepts. New theories and new concepts are needed. The new situation must be examined from an interdisciplinary perspective, not as a fixed but as a developing condition, and free of biases and conceptualizations of capitalist or socialist schemes. This book is designed as a modest attempt in this direction. In it, transformation of society and economy into state-controlled and state-regulated structures is called *etatization*.[3]

This term was first introduced by me in *Societal Development* published in 1973. The concept was independently used by a number of writers discussing developments in Eastern Europe.[4] Etatization consists of a complex intertwining of economic, organizational, social, value, and other changes advancing differently in the nations under consideration but generating everywhere more state control and regulation. The concept denotes not only an established structure, or other fixity, but a process in which growth, change, and multiplying interactions and conflicts are molded by the state's newer functions.

Since the West has been regarded not only as capitalist, but also as democratic, the meaning of democracy must be amended. Contemporary Western societies are democratic not only in the sense of having two or more political parties, competing for political rule; not only because of the division of power and checks and balances built into their political systems; not only because they provide citizens with legally guaranteed rights and liberties. They are democratic in a new sense: The state provides all citizens with certain essential economic entitlements. In other words, the state maintains a "safety net," which protects citizens from economic and social disasters that might otherwise adversely affect individuals or society as a whole. There are two simultaneously operating systems of sharing: the redistribution of some portion of the national income through taxes, and social insurance programs aimed at resolving social problems.

At the same time, in the new condition, the family, other primary groups, and many secondary associations and organizations diminish in importance; some actually disintegrate. The atomized members of society are forced into situations in which they as individuals, and not as members of a family, community, or association, have to rely on the state, now operating as a *super-family*. Because it performs so many new functions, and acts as a super-family, the state is actually a much changed state still operating within the old structure. In this book it is called the *New State*.

The term etatization derives from the French *état* (state). It must be pointed out, however, that etatization has a different connotation than *étatisme*. *Étatisme* is employed in works in French and other languages, including English, that discuss the system of centralized administration instituted by Jean-Baptiste Colbert, the minister of finance and controller-general under Louis XIV in the seventeenth century, and in later systems of centralized government in France. The interpretation of etatization differs from that implied by *étatisme*. The two are related perhaps, but differ.

Colbert's activities and *étatisme* are discussed in Chapter 6. Here, I would like only to contrast etatization with *étatisme* by quoting Cole. He is author of several books on Colbert and the mercantilism of his time, and often employs the term *étatisme*. In *Colbert and a Century of French Mercantilism* (1964, 1: 25–26), Cole writes:

> On the practical side *étatisme* meant the extension of royal authority as against the feudal rule of the nobles and the power of the provinces. . . . On the theoretical side it meant the belief in the absolute sovereignty of the royal government, its complete power to act unhampered by the interference of other bodies, its right to legislate on all subjects, its irresponsibility to all authorities save God. Mercantilism represented the economic counterpart of political *étatisme*.

Other writers list *étatisme* among principal traditions in French political culture.[5]

I employ the anglicized etatization not to denote an outlook, but rather the process of transformation of Western societies into new, postcapitalist systems.

Etatization can be well interpreted within a framework employing Durkheimian conceptualizations. From this vantage point, proceeding transformation from "mechanical solidarity" to "organic solidarity," engendered by increasing division of labor, produces a new condition in which individuals, social sectors, and corporate orders become linked in a complex and continuously growing interdependence. This condition, which I call complementary interdependence, generates many benefits, according to Durkheim (1984, 208–215, 304), but produces, also, frequent breaks "in the equilibrium," lapses into disorganization, "societal sicknesses," anomie experienced by individuals and seen in the market economy and other spheres of societal interaction. As he points out (293), "at the same time as specialization becomes greater, revolts become more frequent." Conflicts multiply; industrial and commercial crises, "partial breaks in organic solidarity," erupt more and more frequently. Bankruptcies multiply; "hostility between labour and capital" intensifies. In our time, we see this happening not sporadically but continuously. Under such conditions, Durkheim anticipated that the state would regulate economic and societal interdependencies more pervasively than ever before. New aspects of the state's regulation allow some alleviation of the consequences of this periodically experienced anomie. As the state acquires new functions, it provides a new form of superintegration. More succinctly: "mechanical solidarity," transformed into "organic solidarity," manifested in complementary market interdependencies, evolves into an even more complex structure of interdependencies and solidarities, engendered, controlled, and regulated by the state. Etatization defines this new stage of societal development in the current practice. Whether such a stage is inevitable in historical evolution is an issue of controversy. This book addresses it in Chapter 15.

Early in the nineteenth century, de Tocqueville (1969, 691–692) envisioned many elements of the general contours of the etatized society now developing:

> I am trying to imagine under what novel features despotism may appear in the world. In the first place, I see an innumerable multitude of men, alike and equal, constantly circling around in pursuit of the petty and banal pleasures with which they glut their souls. . . . Over this kind of men stands an immense, protective power which is alone responsible for securing their enjoyment and watching over their fate. The power is absolute, thoughtful of detail, orderly, provident and gentle. . . . It provides for their security, foresees and supplies their necessities, facilitates their pleasures, manages their principal concerns, directs their industry, makes rules for their testaments, and divides their inheritances. Why should it not entirely relieve them from their trouble of thinking and all the cares of living? . . . Equality has prepared men for all this, predisposing them to endure it and often even regard it as beneficial. . . . It covers the whole of the social life with a network of petty, complicated rules that are both minute and uniform, through which even men of the greatest originality and the most vigorous temperament cannot force their heads above the crowd. It does not break men's will, but softens, bends and guides it; seldom enjoins, but often inhibits action; it does not destroy anything, but prevents much being born. It is not at all tyrannical, but hinders, restrains, enervates, and stultifies so much that in the end each nation is no more than a flock of timid and hard working animals with the government as its shepherd.

Nonetheless, there were many aspects of the new reality that de Tocqueville could not foresee. Although guided and supervised by omnipotent and omnipresent tutelar governments periodically elected by the citizenry, contemporary society is split by antagonisms and divergent strivings. It is not only divided by class, but also by the conflicting interests of the corporate structures on which it depends. Society is divided into interest groups, each trying at the others' expense, to get more rights, more protection, and more control over available means.

De Tocqueville could not foresee that individuals would suffer inner conflicts between their various interests and their many selves. He did not foresee that, as the state became to all appearances omnipotent, it would also become more inept, ineffectual, and overwhelmed by the affairs of its citizens and by providing them with the necessities and security to which they would claim entitlement. He did not envision that with the introduction of more scientific management, econometrics, and leading-value indicators (once regarded as sure reflections of economic trends), scientists and experts running the affairs of the economy would no longer know what to make of all the equations and figures before them. He did not expect the men of the future to rebel against tutelary authority and the imposition of bureaucratic organization.

Max Weber, discussing developments prior to and during World War I in Germany, the United States, and Russia, envisioned a future resembling de Tocqueville's scenario. In his early writings, Weber perceived the emergence of capitalism as a process of growing rationality. Later, he discovered that capitalist rationality required the development of bureaucratic hierarchies. He foresaw such hierarchies mushrooming throughout the new capitalist economy—pervading society from the top, imposing numerous governmental, civilian, and military administrations—and pushing up from the bottom as scaffolds of democracy. As de Tocqueville had before him, Weber wrote that capitalism, under which individuals are allowed to strive for functional rationality and in pursuit of personal wealth, begets a new condition. While certain individuals engaged in capitalist activities turn into innovators and entrepreneurs, those involved in bureaucracies are transformed into mindless functionaries, devoid of any initiative save the bare minimum necessary dutifully to implement orders and instructions and satisfy crude desires. Weber feared that the bureaucratization he saw was prodromal of even greater bureaucratization; he described socialism and communism as but other versions of domineering bureaucracy.

Weber was skeptical that democracy might neutralize or alleviate the oppressive nature of an imposing and overwhelming bureaucratization. He argued that the possibility of direct democracy was exclusive to small communities, direct government by the people within a large mass society being practically impossible. Mass democracy, wrote Weber, is in danger of falling prey to demagogs. He wrote that in the future, as in the past, mass democracy would unavoidably engender authoritarian, caesarist rule. "The future belongs to bureaucratization," despaired Weber, again and again, in his works. He envisioned societies composed of gigantic hierarchical structures, informed by compulsive associations of consumers, organized and manipulated by the state. The state would institute mandatory professionalization and absorb corporations, unions, and every type of "compulsive organization" that could be invented and developed, into one huge structure—"*Verstaatlichung und Verstadtlichung*"—to wit, etatization (Weber, 1971, 63; see also Gerth & Mills 1967, 17–18). The process was imminent. Worse, Weber could offer no way to prevent it.

What these men feared was not so much socialism or bureaucracy. They feared that, under a future collectivistic regime, the individual would be forbidden his creativity, his thought, and the opportunity to express himself freely; he would be totally subordinated to the collective will, which governments would claim to represent.

In the 1930s, George Orwell, Franz Kafka, Emil Lederer, William Reich, Hannah Arendt, and others recognized the shift in this direction in the new societies of Stalin's Soviet Union, in Germany, Italy, and other European nations under Fascist and proto-Fascist regimes. They warned that unless action were taken to reverse such developments, Western civilization would cease. Humanity could look forward to a gloomy future under the regimented ordering and oppressive command of elite rule.

At about the same time, Adolf Berle, Gardiner Means, James Burnham, and a few other writers tried to link economic processes with these visions. Berle and Means limited their analysis primarily to the United States, discussing processes in the capitalist economy, and were quite circumspect in their prognoses and conclusions. Burnham was much more radical. He offered a sweeping, though not so carefully substantiated interpretation of the present, and a controversial vision of the future. Burnham claimed that the world would be composed of neither capitalist nor socialist, but managerial societies. Both Berle and Burnham concluded that in the world's most capitalist and democratic society—the United States—the consequence of economic growth will be not revolutionary takeover but a socioeconomic order similar in certain regards to that developing in Europe. They believed that the increasing concentration of capital in large finance corporations, the growing dispersion of stockholding, changes in the structure of private property and in the administration of business (such as the growing trend among managers to administer both large private corporations and the state) were bound to produce an entirely new socioeconomic structure. They, and Schumpeter, wrote that capitalists, as a class, were becoming redundant; managers now assumed many of their functions. Both Berle and Burnham believed that capitalists would become less and less involved in entrepreneurial decisions and more and more subject to the direction of managers; in turn, managers would become the ruling elite.

In retrospect it is clear that, though these writers were keen observers of capitalist development, they, and particularly Burnham, exaggerated the consequences of the power attained by managers and underestimated the resilience of the capitalist economy and capitalists as a class. Capitalism has demonstrated an exceptional ability to thrive under changing conditions. More important, Burnham wrongly predicted that most capitalists would withdraw from active decisionmaking, and even from managing their own financial affairs, to live in leisure. In fact, without neglecting leisure activities, wealthy capitalists have acquired managerial expertise. Without giving up their capitalist positions, they have assumed positions as politicians, top executives, bankers, university professors, and experts. Some, of course without giving up their incomes, have even become champions of alleviating poverty and eradicating underdevelopment. There is some semblance in this change to the transformation of Western European nobility in the past. Yet, we are only at the beginning of the transition from capitalist to postcapitalist structures.

Reinhard Bendix (1968, 1977a, 1977b), masterfully employing the Weberian art of analysis of the evolution of citizenship, class relations in an age of continual change of social contract, the structure of new civil rights, the administrative authority of the state, and the age of continual modernization, presents a discussion of still other aspects of this development.

What has emerged in Western Europe and North America is a social structure highly controlled and regulated by the state. Under this new condition, everyone in society, and all units of economic organization, depend more and more on each other and the social system as a whole. Because relationships are increasingly complex and interwoven, operations involve and affect more people than ever before. However, the system, while imposing greater restrictions and control, also provides more choices, allocates more freedom in certain regards, and institutes a greater degree of equity and equality. How real such choices and freedoms are is subject to disagreement.

I share Durkheim's and other sociological theorists' (e.g., Smelser, 1968) perception of development, which defines societal evolution as an ongoing process of specialization and differentiation of institutions and roles, producing increasingly complex interdependencies. I see etatization as a novel extension of these processes, one which involves the state. My understanding of this new stage of societal development can be summed up as follows:

1. Etatization advances when the state gets involved in instituting a two-sector mixed (private and state) economy, instead of the one-sector free-market economy; when the state acquires responsibility for economic growth and employs regulatory practices to implement its management function. Under such conditions, private investors finance both private and public corporate sector ventures; capitalists become managers and state managers evolve into capitalists.

2. Etatization advances when society develops state-maintained services and institutions and redistributes a portion of its gross national product (GNP) in entitlements, to procure economic and social security, equity, protection of the environment, and other social and political objectives.

3. Etatization advances as the state assumes certain functions formerly performed by primary groups such as the family, community, and other traditional institutions. This transformation has progressed throughout the twentieth century. At present, the state alone is capable of maintaining

institutional structures to assist needy citizens, collapsing industries, and underdeveloped areas, and to deal with various other social and economic problems.

A great many books and articles on the state have been published recently by social scientists. Skocpol, in her introductory section to *Bringing the State Back In* (Evans et al. 1986) reviews these works exhaustively. She discerns several topical interests and corresponding schools of thought. *The New State* may be included under the section she names continental European. I, however, would rather include it in the school of classical sociological tradition, to which many U.S. and Canadian scholars have contributed.

Classical sociological theorists analyzed the evolution of traditional into modern societies by employing dichotomies. Durkheim (1984), as mentioned, developed the mechanical-organic solidarity scheme. The *Gemeinschaft-Gesellschaft* dichotomy, designed by Toennies (1957), became the sociological telespectroscope through which both Toennies and Weber looked at society of their time. Weber employed other sociological tools, such as ideal types and comparative analyses with other societies. Cooley (1956) introduced the concept of primary group. His students completed his vision by adding the concept of secondary groups and secondary relations. *The New State*, concerned with contemporary society, introduces a third element of analysis. I see societal evolution as advanced in three formations: the first being mechanical solidarity, *Gemeinschaft*, primary groups; the second, organic solidarity, *Gesellschaft*, and secondary groups; the third, anticipated by some of the classical theorists, etatization, *Verstaatlichung und Verstadtlichung*, tertiary statal formation, and control of relations by the state. In this book, I predominantly employ etatization, but those other terms are quite equivalent. I hope that this supplementation does no damage to the clarity of classical schemes and allows us to employ these schemes more effectively in discussions of current evolution.

I found strong inspiration in the writings of classical sociologists, Durkheim and Weber in particular. I was also strongly influenced by Schumpeter's vision of development. I often employ Weberian concepts to illustrate and argue my point. Because of this, and other concerns that I share with Weber, one might classify this book as an analysis of the changing functions of the state attempted from a Weberian perspective. This book is not, however, a straight elaboration of any theme discussed by Weber; it is not intended to advance his teaching. It is Weberian only in the sense that it recognizes the method of comparison and *Verstehen* as an important sociological tool. This book attempts an undogmatic application of complementary approaches to structural and developmental processes focusing on the changing structure of conflicts as they determine the character of societal structure.

The approach advanced in this book is developmental, but not speculative. I strive to interpret the new interplay between economic forces, changes in value orientations, demands to extend social and economic security, and deliberate governmental policies undertaken to meet current needs. The final outcome of these processes cannot be predicted. My only assertion is that with this historical evolution there emerges a more state-controlled and state-regulated society. The magnitude of change involved in this process is comparable to the development of capitalism from precapitalist formations, two or three centuries ago. Both processes include successions of rapid economic changes and vast social reforms. In trying to comprehend the process of etatization, I had to concern myself with issues discussed in a large body of literature and documentation not directly on societal development and like theories, but rather with the current activities of governmental agencies, with social problems, and changes in social values and lifestyles.

PART ONE

TRANSITION TO THE NEW STATE: GENERAL THEORY OF ETATIZATION

CHAPTER ONE

State Functions

Eight processes are discerned in etatization. These processes are conceived as covariations (in the Durkheimian understanding of that concept) of general etatization theory. They are:

1. Multiplication of state functions
2. Monopoly control over economic management, education, and other selected areas of social activity
3. A new stage of societal development: old and new interpretations of development
4. State responses to social and economic problems, including services for the populace at large and welfare systems for the needy and unemployable
5. Transformation of the stratification structure
6. Emergence of two-sector mixed economies and systems of direct and indirect regulatory practices
7. Spread of a bureaucratic mentality and appearance of a new double morality
8. Change in the conflict structure of society[1]

Classical academic and Marxist literature discusses the state as an institution developed by society to perform two principal functions.[2] The external function of the state is to defend society against foreign encroachment; the internal is to maintain law and order (as defined by academic theorists) or to maintain class domination (as defined by Marxists and other nonconformist thinkers). Lenin—especially in *The State and Revolution*—referring to Marx and Engels, claimed that the state exists only where there is class antagonism and struggle. Under such conditions, wrote Lenin, the state acts "as an instrument for the exploitation of the oppressed class." Some Marxist writers believed that class society would disappear with the abolition of capitalism; the state would then wither away.[3]

These definitions are obviously no longer adequate. At present, the state performs many other functions. Alfred Stepan points out (1978, xii; see also Skocpol 1986, 7–8) that the state "must be considered as more than the 'government.' It is the continuous administrative, legal, bureaucratic and coercive systems that attempt not only to structure the relations *between* civil society and public authority in a polity but also to structure many crucial relationships within civil society as well."[4] Since the state also operates as the super-family and largest conglomerate of the nation, it must be defined in broader terms. The state, absorbing many functions formerly performed by independent societal and economic institutions and acquiring certain new functions not formerly performed by any system, evolved into a bigger structure—the New State. In the course of this evolution, and by substituting for previously existing institutions and relationships of the civil society, the new state engendered many new systems of organization and a vast bureaucratic hierarchy. Nowhere in the world are there signs of the state withering away. Everywhere, under socialism, capitalism, peoples' republics, or any other systems, the state grows stronger, acquiring new functions and dominating society more than ever before.

Perhaps because the West did not repeat a cycle of political revolutions like those of the nineteenth century; perhaps because it was involved in intensive growth, industrial development, and capitalist expansion raising the overall standard of living; perhaps because the state became involved in maintaining welfare organizations and service systems and in preventing the economy from running into depressions like that in the 1930s, contemporary Western society evolved into a condition that, while it continues to be capitalist, has acquired features that are neither capitalist nor socialist. The most apparent change consists in numerous new functions of the state and the multiplication of sub-systems involved in implementing its new obligations. Most discussions of the contemporary condition or the contemporary state recognize and record this distinction. Abraham, for instance, analyzing the functions of government in regard to what he calls big business in Great Britain, uses the term "the new disorder," and enumerates the roles of government in contemporary society as follows (1974, 23–27):

> As a *regulator* the government's aim is to apply rules so that companies, trade unions and others conduct themselves without too much damage to the interests of their customers. . . . As a *communicator* the government is a major publisher of statistics. . . . As a *protector* of people, the government prescribes what is permissible across a wide field. . . . As a *peacemaker*, the state can provide money, facilities, and staff. . . . As a *major buyer,* sometimes even *monopoly purchaser* . . . the state has an enormous leverage.

Abraham also lists other functions of the contemporary government, such as entrepreneur, shareholder, planner, and manager.

Von Beyme (1985) writes that through implementing fiscal and monetary policies, the state determines (among other things) how the national income is consumed, how much of it is spent on public services, and how much is reinvested to generate new development. Society no longer exists independently; it is controlled and developed by the state. Andrain (1985, 8–20), Wilensky (1975), Janowitz (1976), Flora and Heidenheimer (1984), and Friedman (1981) outline how the state, as manager of the most important national economic and social affairs, organizes welfare systems to assist the needy. Others, (e.g., Gersuny & Rosengren 1973) portray the new condition as a service society, providing "intangibles," such as transportation, health care, education, and recreation services on which everyone now depends.

The state has emerged as sole provider to an increasing number of people. Transfer payments from the government constitute the principal livelihood of a large sector of the population. In the United States, for instance, according to the 1985 report of the U.S. Census Bureau, one in three households relied on benefits from one of five principal programs: medicare, medicaid, food stamps, school lunch, and subsidized housing. In Canada and Western European nations, an even larger percentage depends on transfer payments. Even in Japan (Woodsworth 1977; *Facts and Figures of Japan* 1982, 97; Fukutake 1981, 45–55), where until recently only a small portion of revenues went toward social programs, the state now disburses significant amounts on such services. The population depends on schools, medical services, transportation, electricity, and water supplies, as well as other services that the state provides either at no cost or well below maintenance costs. In addition, more people have become indirectly dependent on the state through employment by state agencies and institutions maintained by governmental budgetary allocations. In Western Europe and Canada particularly, a significant part of the labor force is employed in state-owned or mixed (state- and privately owned) industries. Still more are employed in industries that depend on state funds or government contracts. Rose, in a book on state employment in different nations (1985), writes that in Sweden, France, Great Britain, West Germany, and Italy close to a third (or more) of the labor force is currently employed by the state. In the United States less than 20% is so employed; in Sweden close to 40%. More than half the population of some nations depends on wage or salary, pension, unemployment pay, or other income from the government. In 60–70% of families, at least one person receives an income from some level of government. At the same time, however, income tax and social security payments as a percentage of gross income have been raised from year to year. In 1980–1981, the average (for employees of large manufacturing companies) was: Sweden, 52–56%; Canada, 33–35%; the United States,

30.1%; Great Britain, 29.9–31%; Japan, 22.5–25%; France, 18–20%; and Italy, 13–16%. From partial data available for subsequent years (1981–85), it appears that the tax increased by 5% to 8% in these years. Great Britain's government is the only one that reduced income tax in the last few years. Governments of other nations have either increased taxes directly, or shifted from income to other taxes.

A comprehensive list of New State functions does not exist in the available literature, partially because new functions are continually added, partially because of the difficulties of cataloging present involvement in an intelligible way. Let me note, however, that, in addition to a number of systems maintained by the state in the past and listed in the classical literature in this connection, many new systems have been developed under etatization. *Traditionally maintained systems under the old state include*:

a. Defence forces protecting the nation against foreign invasion
b. Administrative apparatus and bodies maintaining law and order within society
c. Revenue-collecting agencies

The list of new systems established under the New State would have to include:

d. Direct and indirect regulatory agencies and (in nations where the state owns sectors of industry) management systems
e. Service agencies benefiting society at large, such as education, environmental protection, health and safety administration, medical services, certain research and development agencies
f. Social security, welfare, and other rescue systems established to assist individuals, groups, corporations, and needy sectors of the economy
g. Institutions to regulate social and economic problems and to assist individuals facing such problems (e.g., programs dealing with minorities discrimination, affirmative action, and the consequences of the destabilization of families, drug addiction, and juvenile delinquency)

Some newer agencies, such as those involved in central planning or in formulating industrial and other policies, can be added to this list.[5]

The difference between the old and New State is not only that the traditional state performed fewer functions, but also that the old functions, in one way or another, were enacted as practices of coercion. While continuing these practices, the New State, and particularly the institutions that compose the New State, is strongly involved in providing greater economic and social security to citizens, protecting of human and civil rights, and in providing services to the populace. The new functions require the use of certain measures of coercion as well, but, as Offe and other writers notice, the nature of class and other interest is changing.

Not only does the contemporary state perform more functions and comprise many more bureaucracies, apparatus, regulatory agencies, and systems of organization; not only does it appropriate a much larger share of the gross domestic product (GDP) to cover its expenses, maintain services, and distribute transfer payments; the state assumes responsibility for the entire condition of contemporary society—the condition of the air, the food and water, the relationships its citizens must be involved in, the habits they develop, their education, their health, and their ability to make a living.

The state maintains a welfare system for the poor and a service system for all. It also subsidizes, protects in various ways, and in time of adversity bails out both state-owned and privately owned large corporations. It is the largest consumer, the only consumer for some industries. So it can be argued that the state maintains two welfare systems, one for the poor, the other for the rich and corporations. Furthermore, the state (e.g. the United States) not only furnishes loans and loan guarantees, and rescues failing banks (e.g., First Pennsylvania Bank, the Continental Bank of Illinois; Cargill & Garcia 1982, 2–3, 41; Melton 1985, 157–165; Greider 1987, 523, 592–4, 517–520, 632), large corporations (e.g. Penn Central Transportation Company, Lockheed, Chrysler), and even cities (e.g., New York City). It is also engaged in international financial aid and loans (e.g. the United States to Mexico, Brazil, other Latin American, Asian and Eastern European nations). All this activity not only allows corporations to engage in new profit-generating activities and provides relief to corporations and governments in trouble, it preserves jobs on which vast sections of the population, directly and indirectly involved with these corporations or governments, depend.

Paradoxically, each function results in initiation of a new activity, which eventually evolves into more new functions for the state. Social security, welfare, and general services are sustained by taxes. By collecting taxes and transferring revenues back to society, the state becomes involved in redistributing a portion of the GNP. While engaging in partial redistribution (see Janowitz 1976; Friedman 1981, 49, 202, 205–206—she calls it "oblique redistribution"), the state not only continues to represent the interests of the dominant old and new classes but, to an extent, also represents the interests of the deprived and needy. One could argue that by maintaining the welfare system, the state does what it has always done: preserves the status quo dear to the wealthy and powerful. But now it employs a shrewder method. It pacifies the poor, while the main elements of their condition do not change. While this is true to an extent, it does not correctly reflect current reality (see Cawson 1982, Ch. 4). First, it is unreasonable to argue that by assisting the poor, the state actually acts against their interests. Second, when class struggle is replaced by intermediation, the entire character of class relations changes. A large army of politicians, theorists, and negotiators is now involved in permanently ongoing intercession. It claims to be a third, neutral, force representing not only the principal classes, but even more the numerous groups concerned with specific interests: the peace movement, environmentalists, feminists, pro- and anti-abortion groups, etc. This third force is not the state, but interest groups, lobbyists, institutions, and movements that exert pressure on the state in the name of justice, equity, and reason; in some instances acting as though they are extensions of the state. In the introduction to Offe's *Contradictions of the Welfare State* (1985, 25), Keane affirms that:

> this state has become irreversible in the precise sense that it performs functions essential for both the capitalist economy and the life chances of many social groups. In the face of whatever remains of the blind optimism about the future of the welfare state, Offe nevertheless seeks to theoretically determine its *limits*.

Offe (1985, 149–157) addresses the issue by pointing out that the Right rejects the welfare state by claiming that it is "the illness which it pretends to cure." He condemns as absurd the Right's arguments that the welfare system "amounts to a *disincentive to investment* and *disincentive to work*." He also points out that the Left criticizes the welfare state as "ineffective and inefficient; repressive; conditioning a false ('ideological') understanding of social and political reality within the working class." Furthermore, Offe (119–120) rejects as "gravely misleading" the argument that the contemporary state is "an instrument for promoting the common interests of the ruling class." And he refuses to accept that the state "seeks to implement and guarantee the *collective* interests of all members of *a class society dominated by capital*." The etatization theory does not advocate either the rightist or the leftist view. From the perspective of etatization theory, the New State has to be considered as: (a) a platform of conflict and intermediation between divergent interest groups, corporate and institutional orders, and single issue movements; and (b) as Crozier and other theorists (see Rueschemeyer & Evans 1986, 51–53) have convincingly demonstrated, as a self-transforming fortress of bureaucracy and new class domination.

Another example of how state engagement in one activity simultaneously prepares the ground for engaging in yet another activity can be found in the field of education. "Postprimary education is perceived" in the United States and Western Europe, writes Heidenheimer (1984, 269), "as an instrument for the realization of states' concern with equality and security goals, and hence the emphasis on education and social security programs are viewed as the cores of alternative strategies pursued by emerging welfare states." While developing educational opportunities and providing easy access to education, the state not only provides still another entitlement but simultaneously subsidizes research, supports diverse areas of cultural activity, and, in fact, indirectly regulates general cultural development. Similarly, the state maintains medical services, is involved in drug testing and licence issuing, checks medical practices and remedies, restricts smoking areas, and in many other ways engages in general health-care activities benefiting both young and old.

Under certain conditions, institutions established to serve societal entities (associations) develop a separate, independent existence, sometimes dominating the structures that created them. This seems to be the case with the state. The state, in a sense, is now in the process of superseding class and the other societal structures that brought it into being. The conflicting interaction between society and the state under these new conditions is difficult to characterize. Society exists, more and more, through the state, which increasingly determines all aspects of social existence. At the same time, as always, society also exists for itself and apart from the state; regardless of state domination, society retains a separate identity. Although it retains its capitalistic nature and many of the structural and cultural features of the past, contemporary society operates under a different capitalism, one not only engendered in the market but also promulgated under state tutelage.

One does best to paraphrase Marx: The new grows in the womb of the old. Moreover, it continues to develop without separating from the old. The state acquires new functions because society, while remaining capitalist, develops new needs and evolves into a new condition in which it can only retain a free-market economy and preserve its old existence through increased state management and regulation. The New State has come into being not through negation, not through a political revolution proclaiming the overthrow of an old regime and the enactment of a new order, as was the case when the bourgeois state was first proclaimed in the nineteenth century. Rather the New State is engendered within the old, hatching from the existing shell of the political organization of society.

CHAPTER TWO

Principal Features of Etatization

Monopolistic Control in the New State

Discussing the "modern state" at the turn of the century, Max Weber (1978, 56) defined the state as a "system of order" that exercises binding authority and monopolizes the legitimate use of coercion within its jurisdiction. Weber's widely accepted definition must be modified when applied to the postmodern, contemporary condition. In an etatized society, the state not only possesses the sole right to maintain law and order, but acquires new monopolistic rights to regulate and manage the economy, to own certain branches of industry and the economic infrastructure, to control education, health, and a variety of other services. The state's monopoly is more imposing in some nations than in others. Under the type of etatization maintained in Western nations, liberties are preserved and room is left for private initiatives within the limits of state controls. Certain individuals, groups, and corporations are exempted from subordination to certain controls. Nonetheless, in whatever field—as, for instance, in central economic management or education or in ownership of certain branches of industries—the state acts, it establishes a monopoly. It may involve the private sector in certain operations; however, it does not tolerate competition.

As with the monopoly of coercion (which under different guises appears in all political systems, from democracies to extreme forms of authoritarianism), new monopolistic rights are currently exercised by the state in varying degrees and by varying economic and social orders. The kind of economic control, regulation, and management and the proportion of the economy that is state-owned, determine, in turn, other aspects of conditions of etatization. In this regard, as will be discussed further, one can distinguish several types of etatized societies, ranging from those wherein the state manages the economy to a great extent indirectly and directly regulates the observance of commodity service standards and conditions of work (as in the

United States and Japan) to instances (as in Western Europe and Canada) where the state not only performs those functions but also sets specific developmental objectives and directs their implementation, and owns certain branches of industries and directly intervenes in production and trade. There are also instances (as in the Soviet Union and other Communist nations) where the state owns most or nearly all economic assets and where all aspects of economic life are under central planning and direct command. A more detailed typology and analysis of these types will be found in Chapter 5.

Etatization as a New Stage of Development

Although relatively new, the processes discussed in etatization theory constitute an extension of the societal development that directly concerned classical sociological theorists.

At the turn of the century, social scientists began to notice that small primary groups and various community structures, which had once formed the principal (if not the only) spheres of interaction for the majority of individuals, had begun to lose significance. Certain functions of these structures were absorbed by the larger, depersonalized organizations, associations, and bureaucracies, representing specific interests, which emerged. In the *Communist Manifesto*, Marx considered some of these changes as manifestations of the ongoing transmutation of precapitalist into industrial and capitalist societies. This became the theme of classical sociology. Each of the master sociologists writing at the end of the nineteenth and the beginning of the twentieth centuries was concerned with some aspect of this preeminent transition. Toennies was particularly alarmed by the declining role of *Gemeinschaft* "sociations," exemplified by kinship, neighborhood, community, and friendship, and the spread of *Gesellschaft* associations, "artificially" established to represent, not individuals or groups as such, but certain of their specific interests. Durkheim described the process as a transmutation from "mechanical solidarity," which prevails in aggregates of analogous social units, into new, more complex associational structures constituting wide and complex interdependencies of "organic solidarity." Cooley was concerned that the transmutation evident within U.S. and other societies would result in a decline in the role of primary groups and an increasing dependency on organized agencies, and what were later called secondary groups. Weber discussed the change in value orientation caused by the spread of the Protestant ethic, specific conditions in European cities, and other factors that engendered new lifestyles under capitalist domination. He predicted that all such changes would lead to more rapid transformations. He was concerned about the decline of vocation and charisma and the rising domination of soulless professionals, functionaries, and demagogs. Weber envisioned a time when all economic, social, and intellectual life would be subordinated to schematic bureaucratic rules and dominated by centrally directed hierarchies.

I see etatization as succeeding the tendencies discussed by classical theorists. I consider it to be a new, in a sense third stage, after the *Gemeinschaft-Gesellschaft*, mechanic-organic solidarity stages analyzed in classical works. However, not only has the importance of family and other primary groups continued to decline, and many forms of small groups and communities become extinct, but some of the middle-range, secondary associations, and larger organizations established to represent specific interests, have begun to lose their initial importance to the masses of their members. In certain situations, they are evolving into large bureaucracies of the emerging corporate structure controlled by the state.[1]

Small structures, such as families, small businesses, church congregations, small schools and colleges, communities, clubs, and small- and medium-sized groups, associations, and organizations are being engulfed by super-businesses, super-associations, super-institutions, super-corporations, and by the state. Atomized members of society are forced into situations in which they must face the state and its apparatus, not as members of a family, community, or group, but alone.

Societal evolution, as understood in this book, and etatization as an evolutionary stage, does not necessarily entail progress, ongoing improvement, and the emergence of a more substantively moral and rational society. From a neodurkheimian perspective (see Smelser 1968, 125–46; Chodak 1973, 55–76), growth and development are perceived as processes that engender a growing complexity of specialized, differentiated units, agencies, and roles under an intricate and widening network of interdependencies, engulfing communities, nations, and the world.

In the terms earlier developed by classical theorists, societal development may be characterized as a movement toward more advanced stages of specialization, differentiation, and interdependence, resulting in the transformation of society into more complex systems.

It is interesting to note that more recently, theorists concerned with economic development have been focusing on these transformative processes. Their interest is in the developing economic and social condition of the state in accordance with set objectives. Schumpeter (1936, 63–69) was the first to differentiate between circular flow, change, and development in the economy. Development was defined as the "carrying out of new combinations." "Development," he posits, "is a distinct phenomenon [from growth or change] entirely foreign to what may be observed in the circular flow or the tendency towards equilibrium." Perroux (1983) refines this conceptualization, attributing to it certain system-theory connotations. He reserves "growth" for increases in scale. "Development," he writes (32–34), "presupposes dealings between people in the form of exchanges of goods and services and of information and symbols." In economic context: parts of a whole are organized into subgroups, branches, industries, enterprises. The whole is reorganized in a way that directly causes and indirectly induces action, interaction, and feedback. "Economic structures are thus bound up with the mental structures and social structures of groups in organized society: the former and the latter interact." And finally, as the "economic and social machine" is developed, it yields more and more sophisticated economic, social, and intellectual products. Sociologists characterize such processes as differentiation and specialization engendering more complex interdependencies. At the current stage of societal development, the state is charged with the responsibility of controlling, managing, and fostering growth and the entire, hitherto unrestrained, automatic evolution of society. Development schemes are set forth that aspire to mold the socioeconomic condition according to certain values, certain ideological and economic objectives. In these terms, etatization imposes directions "from above" on an evolutionary process "from below" and on the spontaneity of market processes. During two decades of experimentation, it has been established that state efforts to mold and direct societal and economic development can only partly succeed. It seems that the optimal solution is a combination of free growth through market expansion with a certain degree of control and management, varying from nation to nation.

Corporate theorists and writers discussing corporatism (see Schmitter 1975; Schmitter & Lehmbruch 1979; Pike & Stritch 1974; Berger 1983; Jessop 1982; Cawson 1984; Offe 1985; Heydebrand 1983; Lehmbruch 1984; D. Cameron 1984; Harrison 1980; T. Smith 1979; Katzenstein 1984; Cox 1988) address a different aspect of this transformation.[2] They are concerned with the dynamic of interest representation. They recognize that society has undergone a historical transformation, and they discuss the ideological, political, and economic parameters of diverse interest groups facing each other in societies increasingly controlled and regulated by the state. The concern of etatization theory is with the causes and consequences of increased state control and regulation. This theory does not dispute the correctness of the corporatist theorists' analyses; it discusses a related but different theme.

In the past, particularly in the 1930s, corporatist visions were mostly propagated by social conservatives. Landauer (1983), Gregor (1969), Lombardini (1969), and others trace the origins of the idea of the corporate state to doctrines advocated by: von Ketteler, Hitze, Frantz, and their Catholic disciples in the pre–World War I German Center Party; Rathenau, von Moellendorff, Wissell, Spann, and Nazi doctrines later; de La Tour Du Pin La Charge and a number of other Catholic thinkers in France; and Maurras of the L'Action Française, in the 1930s. Social conservative corporatist doctrines were adopted as part of their ideological arsenal by Mussolini, Spirito, Dollfuss, Pétain, Salazar, and Franco. Hitler developed his own version of these ideas into a theory of the "folkish state."

Landauer (1983, 38–58) and T. Smith (1979, 10–16, 50–78) also discern the left-wing brand of corporatism, represented by guild socialism, Russian Soviets, and certain Labor Party theorizing in the 1930s. This group involved G. D. H. Cole, Finer, and a number of others.

The prevalent social conservatives called for the restitution of "natural cells" and reconstruction of healthy "national organisms"; in a sense, for a return to *Gemeinschaft* structures. Under the "alternative ordering" envisioned by these theorists, the revitalized society was to be composed of "intermediate associations, such as professional or regional bodies, to stand between the individual and the state collective discipline." They believed that such a society would generate unity, harmony, and collaboration between classes, instead of the disunity engendered by different forces at the time. Kuisel (1981, 103), discussing the French variety of corporatist doctrines in pre–World War II France, writes that these people wanted

> to revive such cherished values as hierarchy, family, discipline, class conciliation, religion, and work. . . . Individualism, Marxism, and étatisme were equally reprehensible from this perspective. Economic liberalism bred disorder, selfishness and materialism. . . . The corporatist association was also an antidote to the Marxist poison of class hatred that destroyed social solidarity.

Class conflict was to be ameliorated by lenitive incorporation into hierarchical structures through which every individual would be rewarded with a fitting position. Political parties, seen as promoters of discord and disunity, were to be abolished. Society was to be cured of the vices of individualism and the anarchy and marasmus engendered by it.

Cole and his associates argued that the only result of implementing corporatist organizations would be "the completion of the present tendency towards State Sovereignty by the piling of fresh powers and duties on the great Leviathan." The guild socialist proposed to reorganize the system of democratic representation in such a way that each individual would be allowed to elect "a representative for each of his several major interests" (T. Smith 1979, 11).

Contemporary corporatist theorists are, for the most part, oblivious of the ideological postulates of their predecessors. At present, a great many corporatist theorists—Jessop (1982), Klein (1974), Panitch (1977; 1979), and, in part, Offe—employ predominantly Marxist conceptualizations, with admixtures of "pluralistic theories." They perceive the growth of the state as a form of the state-monopoly variety of capitalist or late-capitalist societies. Some can only be called "corporatist" because they address the issues of corporatist structures, which they subject to devastating criticism. Others employ a combination of traditional corporatist approaches with Marxist, Weberian, and other perspectives. In his book discussing British economic ideas in the twentieth century, Trevor Smith (1979, 163) reports that "the 1960s saw the effective changeover from an essentially pluralist system of functional representation to one that was to a greater or lesser extent corporatist." In his opinion, the transition to the new system of mixed and directed economy occurred because the pluralist system of representation seems to have experienced a crisis. Others maintain that the welfare state is experiencing dilemmas and contradictions and can even be regarded as on the verge of collapse. Offe (1984, 139), a leading exponent of the corporatist perspective, while he presents the gist of the corporatist idea, explains that applications of such perspectives "require a *dual* or *combined explanation* that relies exclusively neither on the social class nor on the pluralist paradigm." From the perspective of etatization theory, this interpretation is quite apt. Offe considers the welfare state as better than earlier forms of capitalism, but still not adequate. One may ask what could replace the welfare state? Adding functions to the state seems to be the only available alternative; even conservatives advocate more direct state control; not nationalization of industries but greater state involvement in protecting the economy and in maintaining its equilibrium. Liberals argue that the welfare state needs to be strengthened. Few writers venture to suggest any way to run contemporary society with less state control.

In the mid-1970s, the principal interest of corporatist theorists was in Spain, Portugal, and certain Latin American systems, which Pike (1974), and Newton (1974) characterize as "passing populism." In the early 1980s concern turned to Western European nations. Katzenstein's (1984) work is representative of this interest and of the more recent, principally pluralistic interpretation of the "democratic corporatism" in the small states of Austria and Switzerland. Katzenstein writes (1984, 135) that these governments, by "relying on broadly based, centralized peak associations to limit the public agenda" and by creating a durable internal consensus, "leave the state relatively passive and lacking in autonomy." He points out that in these countries the political process emerges in the outcome of a consensus that "incorporates virtually all important sources of potential opposition." Katzenstein (1987) characterizes West Germany, in which the state is highly active and displays a great degree of autonomy, as a typical corporatist state. Schmitter (1983), who redefined the corporatist concept and the idea of "intermediation" developed in the 1930s, is now employing that idea to discuss the United States. Offe writes (1983, 136): "Corporatism is a concept that does not describe a situation, but rather an `axis' of development. In other words, political systems can be more or less corporatist." He characterizes the West German state's activities, whether under the Social Democratic or Christian Democratic party, as highly interventionist.

Other corporatist theorists—Schmitter, Lehmbruch, Berger, and others—also apply bifocal, dual analyses comprising both class and interest-group considerations. They prefer to regard contemporary society as late capitalist. For analysts of societies in transition from capitalism to post-capitalism containing elements of both old and new structures, this is an appropriate method.

I am concerned here with a different analysis, complementing that of corporatist theorists. I think that political, economic, and social systems can be more or less etatized. Furthermore, the degree of etatization can be estimated by taking into account the extent to which society and economy are regulated and controlled by the state; extent of state ownership, dependence of individuals on incomes and services provided by the government, and so on.

State Responses to Social and Economic Problems

Etatized societies evolved through organized efforts to address multiplying social and economic problems; i.e., as a response to spreading alienation, poverty, unemployment, decline of family, and other related problems.

Alienation

Where the state, while retaining responsibility for defence and law and order, takes charge of the nation's economic performance, provides services important to all, and distributes social security benefits and assistance to those who declare themselves needy, the individual is able to exist alone, outside family, primary group, secondary associations, or class. All one needs is the state. Unfortunately, in practice this is no happy symbiosis. Although the state relieves citizens of obligations to family and fellow citizens, thus allowing them ample opportunity to enjoy individual freedoms, never before have so many felt alienated, forsaken, and lonely as at present, under the depersonalized guardianship of the state. The causes of alienation differ. Some feel alienated because they are subordinated to machines, self-organizing mechanical systems, computers, and the daily routines of desk work; others by absurd rules and excessive bureaucracies; still others because they have no family, no real friends, and no primary group. It was assumed, in the past, that workers, the unemployed, and people affected by major crises were most vulnerable to alienation.[3] Yet now, regardless of cause, individuals of all classes and occupations, at all levels of organizational hierarchies, in capitalist and socialist societies alike, experience isolation, self-estrangement, and alienation.

Alienation has become the principal theme of contemporary arts. The most celebrated post–World War II philosophers, writers, and playwrights—such as Heidegger, Sartre, Camus, Niebuhr, Tillich, Lukács, Marcuse, Beckett, Wolfe, Miller, Ionesco, and Orwell—declare that ours is a time of universal alienation. The protagonists of their works are haunted by ghostly, nameless images, by absurd rules and regulations; are put on trial by unknown authorities, for never-committed crimes; are lonely and unable to find others willing to share the warmth of true intimacy. They experience their social surroundings as a vacuum or a web of incomprehensible absurdities. Their lives are spent making futile attempts to overcome the dissociation that envelops them. While some writers portray their heroes as egotistical and narcissistic, devoid of concern for their fellows, others create protagonists who are forced into a competitive rat race devoid of real purpose and happiness. The message is clear. People are alienated, not because they are evil nor because they do not wish to associate with others in common human pursuits, but simply because they have become isolated by the same networks of social relations that were created to ensure their well-being.

We live in a time of rapidly accelerating developments and changes, in a condition of continuously changing norms and values and, in Durkheim's terms, unceasing anomie and moral anarchy. The very same growth and development that requires the state to assume more functions and become the New State, is also the principal cause of spreading alienation. In the past, the family was not regarded merely as a unit of companionship, to be discarded at will when it became too obtrusive or whenever a more attractive companionship could replace it; livelihood was dependent on the family. The individual was under normative pressure to live up to its expectations. One was important to society as a representative of family, not as an individual. One was addressed usually by one's family name; only family and close friends used the personal name. In 1879, revolution transformed France, bestowing the franchise and other rights on citizens regardless of family and estate. What was subsequently described as progress consisted of an increase in individual freedom (first to men and then to women). The role of the family declined. The expanding democracy meant extending equal rights to pursue happiness, self-fulfilment, status, and achievement outside the family. More recently, such rights are bestowed under the tutelage of the state's welfare and employment agencies. The process was, and still is, one of liberation from traditional dependencies and controls, from family control particularly. It advances liberties and, more recently, entitlements but also generates estrangement from the family and other traditional associations.

Today, with the exception of Japan (and even there the situation changes), belonging to a family, community, locality, or church is of more private than public importance. In legal terms, contemporary society does not comprise families, communities, or groups, but is a system of roles occupied by individuals whose affiliations with such groups are incidental. One must belong, of course, to unions or associations within hierarchies of corporations, and everyone who works acquires specific occupational associations. These affiliations, however, wherein the individual is but an easily replaceable member, provide a poor substitute for membership within smaller structures, in which each individual is unique and irreplaceable.

Major processes of societal evolution cannot be reversed at will. Consequences of technological development are even more difficult to reverse than changes in attitudes or customary practices. And, since the decline of the role of the family and other traditional groups is largely the result of technological developments, unless we decide to follow the example of Ayatollah Khomeini, a sudden and rapid return to traditional ways of life is not feasible within technologically advanced societies. Men and women who have joined the labor force to make a living, to achieve, and to attain self-fulfilment through careers in industries, administrations, professions, and politics will not relinquish their lifestyles to return to the ways of traditional family living.

"The individual alone," wrote Durkheim (1958, 210), "is not a sufficient end for his activity. He is too little. He is not only hemmed in spatially—he is also strictly limited temporally." Under contemporary conditions, the individual alone constitutes the end of his and the state's activity. The state, as the new super-family, is provider and educator. It cares for the young, sick, elderly, and disabled. It maintains standards of health and safety. It even intervenes in family conflicts. Nevertheless, the state cannot produce a true substitute for family and societal membership. It cannot generate intimacy, love, or trust. It is unable to provide the emotional refuge that lonely individuals crave.

The War on Poverty

In the 1960s, when Western societies declared themselves affluent (and progressively becoming more affluent), poverty was touted as the major social problem. With more people benefiting from technological innovations, cheaper travel, increased availability of goods, and billion-dollar technological projects (such as space exploration), the persistence of poverty became a bleeding sore on the conscience of rich nations. Galbraith wrote (1969, 292):

> An affluent society, that is also both compassionate and rational, would, no doubt, secure to all who needed it the minimum income essential for decency and comfort. . . . A poor society . . . had to enforce the rule that the person who did not work could not eat. And possibly it was justified. . . . An affluent society has no similar excuse for such rigor. It can use the forthright remedy of providing income for those without. Nothing requires such a society to be compassionate. But it no longer has a high philosophical justification for callousness.

Presidents Kennedy and Johnson felt that a large part of society had closed its eyes to poverty, but that solutions could be found by organizing social assistance programs. Furthermore, they felt that even if solutions could not be found, it was the obligation of a civilized, decent, humane society to care for those unable to care for themselves. Johnson, engaged in war in Vietnam at the time, declared another war, on what was then named "new poverty," at home. Numerous programs were instigated to win that war. Western European governments, which had instituted welfare programs earlier, also undertook massive efforts to eradicate poverty in their domains. And everywhere, the state was charged with the mission of rescuing the poor. It was expected that, with the disappearance of poverty, all other social problems would abate. After more than two and a half decades, the effectiveness of rescue operations remains disputable. Some statistical estimates claim that in most Western capitalist nations poverty has been nearly eliminated. Others say it persists. Still other estimates find that poverty has, in fact, increased. According to the most convincing accounts, when the war on poverty was waged in the United States, 17.3% of the population lived in poverty. This subsided to 11.1% in 1973. But in 1983, after having spent over $100 billion (in 1980 dollars) annually in the late 1960s, and over $200 billion annually since the mid-1970s, the figure rose to 15.3%. The 1987 figure is above 16%. Considering population growth, the number of those living in poverty has increased. "America Still Haunted by Problems of Black Poor" ran the headline in the *New York Times*, January 17, 1988; "The Hidden Poor: There Are 9 Million of Them, Mostly Working. And Their Ranks Could Soon Grow" ran a front-page statement in the *U.S. News & World Report*, January 11, 1988. There are more homeless people in the United States now than there were when social-welfare programs began. According to press reports, a million or so people have no home. Many among them suffer from severe mental illness. There are 50,000 unemployed and homeless in London, reported *The Economist* (December 20, 1987). In Canada, where the official poverty line is drawn higher than in the United States, various agencies give different estimates, but again poverty is estimated to be at an only slightly lower level than twenty years ago: between 18 and 25 percent.[4]

In 1984, Harrington, author of *The Other America*—which in 1962 had catalyzed the declaration of war against poverty—published *The New American Poverty*. He begins: "The poor are still there." He recapitulates most of the arguments he raised in 1962, and writes that new poverty is intransigent and that not enough efforts have been made to eradicate it. It has come to afflict new categories: the homeless; mentally ill; new immigrants and undocumented workers; families headed by women; unemployed steel workers; the young who face difficulties entering the labor force; the new "Okies," who travel from place to place searching for work and a way to survive; and other groups of the growing underclass. According to Harrington's count, 40 to 50 million U.S. residents live in poverty. His views are representative of those who believe that programs to combat poverty have not gone far enough. He blames the system—the social condition—for the existence of poverty. He and other writers and activists call for further development of programs maintained by the state.

Murray's *Losing Ground* (1984) represents the opposite, conservative position. Murray includes figures (242) that in 1950, the U.S. federal welfare expenditure consumed $36,014 million (in constant 1980 dollars). In 1960 the expenditure was $69,277 million; in 1970 $163,822 million; in 1980, the sum had drastically risen, to $303,345 million. He writes:

> Using constant 1980 dollars as the basis of comparison, we find that during the five Johnson years (fiscal 1965–69), the federal government spent a total of $66.2 billion on public aid. This was $30 billion more than was spent during the five preceding years—a major increase. But in the five years immediately after Johnson, public aid spending rose by $80 billion. In other words, the increase in the five years after Johnson was 2.7 times larger (in constant dollars) than the increase from Eisenhower/Kennedy to Johnson.

Welfare's objective, he claims, was to eliminate dependence on public assistance. Yet, as the availability of money for public programs increased, claims for money and assistance in kind rose even faster. The idea was to give a hand (22), but the hand became a handout. Murray analyzes program after program; in his opinion, all ended in failure. According to this critic (82) "the problem with [this] new form of unemployment was not that young black males—or young poor males—stopped working altogether," but that counting on unemployment benefits, they moved in and out of the labor force, neglecting to obtain skills and work habits. They worked sporadically and randomly, in order to be eligible for assistance but did care to find permanent employment. Welfare for unwed women resulted in a massive increase of single teenage pregnancy: "In 1980, among black young women aged 15–19, 82 percent of all births were illegitimate" (127). "Babies having babies," laments Murray (1985, 27–28). "Poverty breeds dependency"—states John Moore, one of the leaders of the Conservative Party in Great Britain. "As living standards rose, the definition of poverty changed, and the poor 'felt' just as poor as before, though their real incomes had risen," points out Paul Johnson (1983, 640). Other conservative critics of the war on poverty programs argue that though some are poor because of the conditions they live in, many stay poor because they neglect to improve their condition and correct personal faults, which no program can rectify. But, as Vendi Hudd, a student in one of my courses, wrote, "Welfare doesn't solve the problem, but it does keep people alive."

The opposing views expressed by Harrington and Murray reflect a profound opinion split in U.S. society. Both views have merit. Poverty is a major calamity. The problems associated with the old poverty, such as how to find a job or get a higher wage, still exist. Hypothetically, an expanding economy should solve these predicaments. The new poverty, however, is in some instances engendered by the decline of family and the inability of individuals to cope with difficult problems alone; in others by failure of the poor to improve their own condition, or inability to acquire skills needed for jobs in increasingly high-technology industries. Most of the new poor are unable to work or make enough money to move up. The new poverty is only partially work-related and cannot be blamed on the rich accumulating wealth. Many of the new poor, especially the elderly, the chronically ill, and women with many children, have no one to care for them. They are frequently characterized as belonging to the underclass. Regardless of economic development, this type of poverty will not disappear. These people usually are dependent on supplementary benefits and other transfer payments from the state. Their problems cannot be dealt with by anyone else. No business, or charitable institution, regardless how much money it would make, would take care of the poor. The problem can only be handled by the state. The controversy is over how much should be spent on social programs.

Every major development produces new categories of poor. Those who become superfluous because of new technological developments (workers too old to acquire new skills; fishermen and seal hunters who cannot make a living anymore in their trade) are included now. As reported by Goldman Leventman (1981) and others, they are even joined by some highly qualified scientists, engineers, and other professionals (such as those who worked in the industries along Route 128 in Boston or in Silicon Valley) who suddenly lost their qualifications when new technology was developed. The new poverty is augmented by immigrants arriving from the Third World, which suffers poverty to which no one has solutions. And now, under *glasnost* we are beginning to hear more about poverty in the Soviet Union and Eastern Europe.[5] The new poverty can be reduced or alleviated but not eradicated. Solutions that would lead to complete eradication of poverty are not in sight.

I am portraying a conflict. On one side are those with altruistic attitudes or plain compassion, who feel that our duty is to rescue the poor and all those who cannot help themselves. They want the state to redistribute income to a greater degree and allot more money to the needy and to collective needs. On the other, are those who fear that such policies will destroy the prosperity the West is enjoying, destroy their way of life, reduce the potential of the economy, and actually not help the poor. They say we are obliged to assist those in need, but the poor must try to help themselves more. My concern with the issue here is not with the merit of these arguments, but as one problem at the roots of etatization. We want social problems to be solved by the state. We want the state to run the economy and keep it in balance. We want more security and we want more freedom. But every problem the New State undertakes to deal with becomes consolidated into the permanent condition. Poverty is an exemplary case: Evidence to date proves that the state is unable to eradicate poverty. But it also is an issue that cannot be eliminated from the state's agenda. The war on poverty constitutes now one of the permanent functions of the New State. While relieving certain groups from destitution, the state is also a factor in transforming poverty into a static condition. The state, as the super-family of the nation, must continue to provide sustenance for the new poor. The issue is how big a part of the GNP is to be spent on maintaining the poor in a developed society. Because of the decreasing role of the family, there are no effective ways of dealing with the matter without involving the state. Yet, the state is able to find only remedies that arrest and to an extent alleviate growing social problems. It must be repeated: The state, regardless of whether it is capitalist or socialist, is evidently unable to find solutions that will eradicate poverty completely. Poverty, even when drastically reduced, can grow back rapidly, if not because of old, then because of new causes.

Unemployment

Governments in Western societies have been more successful in reducing unemployment, the other major calamity of the 1930s. They are more successful only because, after a period of rapid nationalization—as in Western Europe—and intensive regulation of the daily activities of industries, governments withdrew from many such policies, in some instances associated with socialism. Large-scale privatization coupled with reduced obligation to cover losses of state-owned industries, and the stimulation of consumption and entrepreneurial activities by tax reductions in the mid-1980s, improved economic conditions. Unemployment was reduced to one-digit percentages in the United States and Canada, and to a lesser extent in Western Europe. Great Britain was not successful in this regard until 1988, but is beginning to see an improvement now.[6] Again, the state can only control the situation and implement policies to reduce unemployment. It can organize programs that would employ for some time large numbers of people. As the situation in France, Great Britain, the Netherlands, and Canada demonstrates, the state usually experiences great difficulties in attempting to reduce a two-digit percentage of unemployment; it cannot satisfactorily handle the situation when more than 15–20 percent of the labor force is unemployed. The Swedes maintain a very low percentage of unemployment at a high cost to the public. A number of nations have enacted full-employment laws but are unable to counteract sudden declines in labor demand.

In short, the economy and society of highly developed Western countries cannot exist anymore without state control and management but also cannot grow and develop freely under excessive supervision and state interference. The state is being transformed into a universal rescue organization. Funds are scarce, however. Allotments to certain interest groups restrict the state's ability to assist others. The system of universal assistance and universal dependence, maintained by the New State, is also a structure inevitably divided by deep antagonisms and conflicts.

It is well known that large, centrally managed organizational systems could be highly effective in attaining desired results, provided that all elements of the system operate exactly as anticipated. When they are successful, they are successful in a great way. However, they frequently fail when confronted by an unanticipated condition, requiring variegated initiatives from below. Even with built-in mechanisms for eliminating malfunctions, large, complex systems can be easily affected by disruptions, discords, or diverging self-interests both within the organization and in its environment. And when they fail, they fail in a large way, producing major disasters. Societies can be transformed into centrally directed organizations. They cannot be made conflict- and problem-free.

As centralized state systems grow more complex, and are required to perform more and more functions to fulfil frequently conflicting objectives, they inevitably become overrun with bureaucratic routine, factional interests, patronage, nepotism, misuses, and conflicts. The short history of etatization is a history of state systems turning dysfunctional, inoperative, and too costly. Instead of providing solutions, state bureaucracies breed new impediments to social change and development. According to Crozier (1964; 1973; 1982) and other French writers, under state management and control, developed at first by de Gaulle and his conservative successors and then by Mitterrand endeavoring to expand the scope of socialism, France became a "stalled society." British writers, considering parallel developments in their nation, described the resultant conditions as "British sickness."

Transformation of the Stratification Structure

A fully developed analysis of the new social stratification emerging under etatization cannot be included here. A sketchy comment seems, nevertheless, worthwhile.

As in the past, the degree of control an individual, group, institutions, or organizations exert in society is, to an extent, a function of the power, wealth, or prestige that the individual or group represents; i.e., the position one holds within a hierarchy. However, it is also determined by the changing importance of that hierarchy in society. The degree of control exercised by an individual or group cannot be measured in pecuniary terms, or by counting subordinates or followers, or by estimations of popularity. Ownership provides the privilege of control, but other forms of control, derived from occupation and status, allowing certain people to influence the course of society and social attitudes, are equally important. One's position within the social strata still tends to be assessed by one's manifestation of wealth and power, but another criterion is acquiring importance. An individual is evaluated according to his or her job within a given organization and by the organization's place within the more general network of the national structure.[7] Although apparently related to occupational role and class, one's job represents a rather different criterion. Its value lies not only in how much money it generates, but in the kind of activity it requires and the scope of information access it provides, and the scope of social and private contacts it offers; in sum, the value of the privileges and entitlements it brings.

Under all-encompassing etatization, the class division typical of capitalist societies intertwines with growing hierarchical orders of official and unofficial power positions engendered by corporate and state organizations. Linked at some points, but divided and running parallel at others, the two status structures complement and conflict with one another. Contemporary stratification comprises the following elements:

1. The elite, occupying controlling positions and deriving its power and rewards from ownership of financial assets, high salaries, royalties, and other incomes, as well as from high positions in the political, managerial, legal, professional, media, or artistic sectors
2. The middle echelons of contemporary social structure, occupied by two middle classes: the well-to-do individuals of the old middle classes, procuring middle-sized incomes and engaging in private entrepreneurial activities, and the growing salariat of the governmental and corporate bureaucracies
3. The numerically dwindling working class, represented by well-entrenched unions, still in conflict with the old capitalist establishment, but also frequently at odds with the management of corporate structures and, increasingly, with the state
4. The large and growing underclass, dependent to a great extent on services and transfer payments provided by the state

Mills' (1956, 9, 13) concept of power elite is quite applicable to the controlling elite of this new structure:

The higher circles . . . are often thought of in terms of what their members possess; they have a greater share than other people of the things and experiences that are most highly valued. From this point of view, the elite are simply those who have the most of what there is to have, which is generally held to include money, power, and prestige—as well as all the ways of life to which these lead. But the elite are not simply those who have the most, for they could not 'have the most' were it not for their positions in the great institutions. For such institutions are the necessary bases of power, of wealth, and of prestige, and at the same time, the chief means of exercising power, of acquiring and retaining wealth, and of cashing in the higher claims for prestige. . . . The elite who occupy the command posts may be seen as the possessors of power and wealth and celebrity; they may be seen as members of the upper stratum of capitalist society.

Mills included in the power elite the rich, chief executives of corporate establishments, leading members of the two main political parties (the difference between Democrats and Republicans and between those in government and those in opposition was then not as great), and high-ranking soldier-statesmen in the military. He portrayed the ruling elite as a fairly homogeneous, mostly WASP class, linked by a common lifestyle, social connections, and marriage, and educated in elite universities. Portrayals, patterned on this study, of similar elites in other Western nations soon appeared in England, Canada, and elsewhere. Mills' power elite consists of individuals who are both wealthy and in control.

Although Mills' concept is still valid thirty years after it was introduced, the controlling elite is quite changed now. It is obvious that the old moneyed classes are still part of the elite. Whether they play as important a role as in the past is debatable. At present, the elite includes many more of those who have recently attained positions of power and influence—the new class who have made money in professions, in the stock market, by developing new high-tech and information industries—and the upper echelons of the managerial strata of society, involving administration, financing, and other industry. According to other analyses, the elite encompasses the upper part of "the new class" (Bruce-Briggs 1979, 2–18), top bureaucrats, members of governmental committees, who are said to be motivated by ideas and ideals; experts; important personalities in the media; the upper ranks of the professoriat and the rest of the intellectual elite who, as consultants and authors, shape the image of society and the issues of concern to politicians and society at large.[8] Successful lawyers often shift back and forth in top political, financial, management, and corporate positions within the power structure. Celebrities of the *beau monde*, highly paid artists (frequently with political ambitions), and certain religious leaders are also part of it. Prominent members of the antiestablishment have to be included in the new power elite as well. Not only do these people share the wealth, prestige, opportunity, respect, and lifestyle of the power elite, but, as self-appointed or actual representatives of the poor and the minorities, they exert a profound influence on the decisionmaking process, and most of all on the ethical values and attitudes of society. The chiefs of the military staff are still part of the establishment, but in spite of the increase in military spending, their role in society has markedly declined.

The new power elite cannot be described as homogeneous, nor is it linked by a shared value orientation, as was the power elite of the 1950s. It shares the high-class "good life," but consists of people from different social groups and educational milieux and various ethnic origins, who have attained their peak positions by climbing different ladders. It is less frequently connected through family networks, but more through ideological affiliations, the web of common acquaintances, top executive positions, and high-class party connections. The elite of the etatized society thus comprises a mixture of groups that may share some status holdings but are divided by the ongoing enmity of distinctive interests and ideologies.

In *Political Man*, Lipset (1981, 127–137) analyzed the composition of the "traditional" and "modern" middle classes in Western Europe in the 1930s. The difference has become now more evident. In fact, two middle classes now occupy the center of the social structure of contemporary Western societies. A comparison of *The Entrepreneurial Middle Class* and *The Real World of the Small Business Owner* (Scase & Goffee 1982, 1987)— portraying the traditional middle class—with *Men and Women of the Corporation* (Kanter 1977) provides a most appropriate illustration of distinctions between these two middle classes.

The old middle class is made up of people who own property, by which they sustain themselves. They earn a living in the marketplace. When they retire they depend primarily on accumulated savings. Their chief concerns, therefore, are ownership rights and the preservation of free enterprise. Interest rates and other credit conditions make them anxious because they directly affect their well-being. With the return of conservatism, their condition has recently improved to an extent. But many still feel threatened: farmers by foreclosures, small and middle businessmen by the growing power of big corporations and the possibility of sudden, rapid inflation or an unexpected economic recession like that in the 1970s.

The new middle class depends on salaries, promotions, fringe benefits, and other supplements derived from contracts, and on individual and collective agreements with employers, corporations, and—increasingly—the government. These people are joining unions to defend the benefits of such contracts; they are concerned about adequate salaries, work facilities, promotions, and retirement schemes. In contrast to the old middle class, these people care more about job security than about credit and other conditions in the market. To be sure, they too desire low interest rates, but they need these primarily for mortgage and credit payments, not to run their businesses.

The two middle classes have different taxation concerns; the old resents excessive property and business taxes; the new fears that certain services will not be maintained by low taxes. In fact, the two classes pay different kinds of taxes. Members of the old middle class fear higher taxes on business and professional operations, because these threaten the very maintenance of their businesses, often forcing them to resort to tax shelters, bartering, and withholding income information, or other escapes such as involvement in the underground economy. (This behavior is described by the Laffer curve). Business people fear inflation because it raises interest rates on business loans, reduces market demand, and wipes out the value of retirement savings.

The salariat and the working class are in a different position. They experience inflation as a loss of purchasing power, and demand compensation from employers.

The old middle class adheres more to traditional values; the new middle class tends to follow more liberal than conservative norms in personal life (Lavau et al. 1983; Ross 1987; Elliot & McCrone 1987; Goldthorpe 1982; Scase 1982; Scase & Goffee 1982). The two middle classes share a lifestyle, but not necessarily a taste for commodities, housing conditions, or recreations. One can deduce this from Mitchell's (1983, 55) findings on U.S. lifestyles. In Mitchell's terminology: one part (the old middle class) includes many other-directed "emulators" and "achievers"; the second (the new middle class) many inner-directed, "I-am-Me," and "experiential" individuals. His study contains a table (180) reporting what percentage of individuals with such attitudes belongs to different middle classes in six Western nations. Because both groups comprise people considered to have "mid-sized" incomes and because both groups to an extent share a lifestyle, they can be regarded as constituting a middle class as a whole. But, it is a divided middle class, whose two halves have different interests and at times become completely incongruent.

The middle classes comprise the majority of the population of Western nations. They constitute the core of bourgeois society. At present, this core, encompassing most of those employed in tertiary industries and the better-paid members of the working class, is in the process of changing into a salariat. Presently, around 5 percent are employed in primary industries in most Western industrialized nations. Secondary industries, like manufacturing, account for less than 25 percent. Between 73 and 78 percent work now in tertiary industries—administration and services.

Individuals operating at this level of societal structure do not express as strong a class or group solidarity as in the past. They share a dissatisfaction with current conditions and expect the state to improve the situation and provide them with higher incomes, more security, and protection against emerging adversity. They strive to preserve traditions to which they are attached, but they also like to embrace new values and ideals advocated by the media. They give vacillating support to institutions and causes represented by single-issue movements, rather than to organizations acting on behalf of class interests. They vote for parties but expect parties to advance causes postulated by environmentalists, peace activists, consumer crusaders, feminist advocates, defenders of the rights of ethnic minorities, religious fundamentalists, leaders of taxpayers' rebellions, and so on. The two halves support different single-issue movements.

If we regard the working class in a traditional sense, as a class providing manual labor for wages and salaries, then it is shrinking. But if we consider unionization as a criterion of working-class membership, then this class comprises most of the population and includes some highly paid experts and the unionized professoriat.

The underclass, defined (Auletta 1982; Vercauteren 1970) as a strata of mostly unemployed old and new poor, dependent on transfer payments and other assistance schemes organized by the New State, currently engulfs growing numbers of people. It is no longer regarded as part of the proletariat (Briefs 1937; Lipset 1981b), nor as a "lumpenproletariat" or an agglomeration of "dangerous people" (Chevalier 1973, 363–367). It is sometimes characterized as having a "culture of poverty," or as the marginal strata of contemporary society.

Two-Sector Mixed Economies

Managerial Capitalism. The economic history of the United States, Western Europe, and Japan from the end of the nineteenth century is marked by the transformation of family-owned businesses to modern, large-scale, multi-unit enterprises, which dominated the economic scene up to the 1950s. Small and mid-sized enterprises multiplied at the same time, but unless they grew, most of them did not last long and were soon replaced by new, small, family businesses popping out of the fertile economic soil of capitalism. Chandler (1977, 6–8) writes that the modern multi-unit business enterprise absorbed smaller traditional enterprises and dominated the market "when administrative coordination permitted greater productivity, lower costs, higher profits than coordination by market mechanisms, . . . and when the volume of economic activities reached a level that made administrative coordination more efficient and more profitable than market coordination." What began with old-style entrepreneurs developing family businesses into empires (see Berle & Means 1968; J. Burnham 1962; Herman 1982, Chandler 1977) was continued by the professional managerial elite, who not only continued to expand the enterprises they were entrusted to run into large corporations but developed new management practices and established their own kind in a new controlling position, distinct from that of owners and shareholders. This managerial takeover was accomplished after World War II, and though the processes were parallel throughout Western Europe and the capitalist world, U.S. companies acquired the role of pattern and pacesetter (Mirow & Maurer 1982). The leap into economic modernity brought about a major, two-sided transformation. One side involved the appearance of oligopolies acquiring control over large areas of market activities; they set the pace of growth, established standards for commodities, and governed market prices. The other side of the transformation took place within the structures of business organizations; money-making by financiers was separated from the management, marketing, and production levels of corporations.

Capitalism transformed into managerial capitalism continued to advance under its own steam, engendering bigger and bigger corporations. Managers took control of financing, production, and marketing; they also became active in running state affairs. They administered state-owned enterprises. Along with these changes, a new, highly significant phase of the economic and societal transformation began to manifest itself. Regulatory agencies came into being, and the state began to interfere in various aspects of market activities. The government's aims were multifarious. It felt impelled to interfere in order to prevent spreading unemployment, to assure economic stability, to enhance growth, to establish industries in areas the private sector neglected, to prevent monopolization and protect the market economy, to defend national industries against foreign competition, to develop a system that would protect the natural environment, to assist the poor and sick, and so on. Keynes and many economists after him have argued that the developed and increasingly interdependent units of modern large-scale economies, and the market itself, require state interference and supervision. Interference and regulation evolved into management of national economies. In some nations, as for instance in the United States, the state imposes very loose managerial control and employs predominantly indirect regulations to attain its ends. In other instances, the state administers the economy through systems of agencies that directly intervene. This sometimes involves day-to-day monitoring activities. Now, in fact, the market economy requires state supervision.

Rueschemeyer and Evans (1986, 44–46) list "a number of theoretical arguments as to why state intervention should be necessary for economic transformation in a capitalist context." These can be summarized as follows:

a. The market cannot function well without a strong set of "normative underpinnings." Such "normative underpinnings" are provided at present in the form of regulations. This was also Durkheim's idea and has been pointed out by such contemporary leading economic theorists as Perroux, and by system theorists.

b. They believe that: "The state apparatus is likely to become an important element in the struggle to initiate a process of accumulation." (Good examples of such cases are discussed in R. Cameron [1972].)

c. National economic objectives, as expressed by the state, frequently collide with those of privately owned corporations, operating in pursuit of profit and disregard of national interests.

d. Even in an ideal market economy "collective goods will be inadequately provided" whenever "negative externalities [are not] controlled, and the rate of accumulation will suffer correspondingly in the absence of some institutionalized mechanism for imposing a less atomized rationality."

e. The need for state intervention and control increases as economies become dominated by oligopolies and large corporate organizations.

f. "The state may have to intrude in order to interject entrepreneurship." Yet, one may add, excessive control and regulation is resented by businesses and frequently becomes an impediment to economic development.

The history of growing state control in the last forty years can be adumbrated as follows: The state took over most of the economic infrastructure of industrialized nations—transportation and communications; coal and steel industries; and energy-generating facilities. In some nations, governments developed brand-new industries. The state also engaged in establishing mixed enterprises. In certain instances, the private sector was invited to finance government undertakings; in others, the state financed private undertakings. Thus, the contemporary state-supervised, mixed economy came into being. In the capitalist United States and Japan, government does not get involved in profitable business but practices policies that produce optimal conditions for some corporations. In capitalist West Germany, government representatives sit on the boards of many private businesses, shares of which are held by the state; in capitalist Italy, government-owned corporations produce not only cars, petroleum products, and complex machinery, but even ice cream and shoe polish. In some nations, the market economy is more strictly, in others less strictly regulated. The state incurs deficits year after year. But everywhere, under state protection, large corporations, whether privately or state-owned, are now more secure against foreign and internal competition, internal economic disruptions, recessions, and the consequences of mismanagement or faulty decision policies. The contemporary condition never escapes conflicts among state representatives, private entrepreneurs, managers of private and state-owned corporations, large unions, consumers, environmental advocates, and other interest groups. State management is a process of continual mediation.

The essence of the economic transitions discussed above can be summarized thus: from a condition guided by the invisible hand of self-interest (as characterized by Adam Smith), the economy evolved into a system of modern enterprises managed by a quite visible hand—professional managers (as described by Chandler). From this, under etatization, the economy is transformed into a system of production and transactions still geared to the market, but managed, regulated, and partially owned by the even more visible conductorship of the New State. The full meaning and consequences of this evolution are still difficult to grasp. However, its importance as an aspect of etatization processes cannot be underestimated.

The two principal elements of this transformation have been already identified: (*a*) The structure of economic ownership was radically amended by the development of two-sector, mixed economies; (*b*) the state engaged in various regulatory activities and in fact took charge of the economic management of the nation. Services and the welfare system were developed simultaneously.

TNCs. A third issue is the current role of transnational corporations (TNCs). Autarchy and self-sufficiency are outdated concepts. No nation, not even the

United States, the Soviet Union, or Japan, not even the European Economic Community (EEC) as a whole, can presently operate comfortably without foreign trade. As Japan's and the United States' success and troubles prove, the prosperity of nations now hinges on maintaining a positive balance of foreign trade. As a result, today's international market is dominated by TNCs. Assessments of TNCs' role in the world are conflicting. On one hand, they are seen as agents of a new form of stateless (or U.S. or Japanese) economic imperialism; as instruments of foreign capital that restrict the internal development of smaller nations. TNCs are also criticized for excessive power, which neither national governments nor the public can control effectively. This has been proved to be an exaggeration. At present, the prevailing opinion (Negandhi & Welge 1984, 77, 113; Vernon 1974, 1977; Madden 1977; Savary, 1984) is that TNCs constitute another form of the state's external activity.[9] Castells (1980, 73) points out "they are not placed above the state institutions of the different countries. On the contrary, they are joined to them in a specific manner, playing one against the other and organizing in a different way their ties to the `internal bourgeoisie' of each society." Evans (1986, 193, 207) characterizes TNCs in a dualistic perspective. He writes: (*a*) In view of the new role of TNCs, "it is obvious that the state as an economic actor becomes an anachronism"; (*b*) on the other hand, however, "the economic power of `home' transnationals may even be seen to be an extension of national sovereignty rather than a challenge to it." Some experts in business schools (e.g., Leontiades 1985) recognize only subsidiaries of multinational corporations at the national level and write as though the state is truly an anachronism that does not count in world markets anymore. But the perspective that TNCs extend the state's power seems to reflect reality more accurately. It is true that to avoid control, and, even more, taxation, some TNCs have established subsidiaries in Liechtenstein, Bahrain, the Bahamas, and the Caribbean islands. It is also true, however, that TNCs cannot operate effectively without the backing of powerful state protection. Western European TNCs are mostly mixed enterprises, partially owned by their respective states. Those who believe that TNCs are stateless must at least provide an example of such, successfully operating without any state support and permission from the government of the given nation. U.S. and Japanese TNCs operate under strong protection from their governments. As Negandhi and Welge's research demonstrates, though the host countries' attitudes toward TNCs is frequently indifferent, ambivalent, and sometimes restrictive, they are generally welcome and are encouraged to invest more. World interpenetration of TNCs must now be regarded as the economic environment in which all national states must compete in order successfully to run their economies. Those who take a protectionist stand usually advocate restriction of foreign-based TNCs, but protection of "ours." Antiprotectionist free-trade advocates argue that TNCs bring foreign investments and introduce a stimulating competition with national industries, which benefits all involved.

Objectives and results in mixed-sector economies. Governments of different nations are motivated by different objectives in involving the state in economic activities. The British first nationalized coal and other industries to prevent major unemployment and to rescue some industries facing bankruptcy. The Italians built brand-new industries in a major effort to industrialize their economy. Scandinavian nations aspired to develop extensive social services and a semisocialist social structure. The French, under de Gaulle and his successors, and the Germans, under the Social Democratic governments of Willy Brandt and Helmut Schmidt, nationalized some of their industries and developed large TNCs under the tutelage of the state to meet the competition of U.S. and, eventually, Japanese TNCs. Under Mitterrand, French socialists enhanced the development of TNCs and their operations in order to advance socialism. Regardless of initial motivations and objectives, the two- or three-decade experience of state engagement in managing economic affairs produced certain general experiences.

In contrast to privately owned enterprises, which operate with the single objective of generating profit, the state-owned sector pursues at least three objectives: (1) to provide society with essential services; (2) to produce jobs; and (3) to generate profits that will supplement tax revenues. Because of these multiple and often conflicting goals, state-owned industries frequently fail to meet their objectives; they generate deficits, poor services, and products of lower quality than those produced by the private sector. The state rarely succeeds as an entrepreneur and owner of industries. The massive nationalization efforts of the 1970s, for the most part, ended in failure and deficits. Most European parties, including left-of-center parties, presently advocate reduction in state-ownership and increased privatization. The state succeeds better when it cooperates in mixed enterprises. It succeeds better as a general manager of the economy, especially when it has flexible policies involving both the private and the state sectors, winning a position in international markets. The economic success of modern, highly industrialized nations is strongly dependent on their ability to win these markets.

In all contemporary Western capitalist societies, the state owns large portions of the economic infrastructure. In most of these nations, a large part of the banking, insurance, and other branches of the finance industry have been nationalized. In Western Europe, states own many principal industries (see Table 8.2), such as mining, transportation, aerospace, oil exploration, and petrochemicals, which have been nationalized or developed at one time or another. States also hold shares of mixed or even privately owned industries. By maintaining some industries, states are able to provide energy, transportation, and communication services at relatively low prices. This type of ownership can be regarded as integral to the infrastructure maintained by the state. Other industries are used to serve state objectives and social policies, such as combating unemployment.

According to Von Beyme's (1985, 18–21) and other estimates, the state appropriates, at present, between 20 and 40 percent of GDP in industrialized Western nations. These monies are acquired through taxes, profits from state-owned enterprises, stockholding, lotteries, and other financial operations. Part of these funds are expended on collective needs, from defense to building infrastructure and public utilities, to preserving the natural environment and constructing low-cost housing for the poor. Other funds are allotted to maintaining and developing education and medical services, and to subsidizing private and state-owned industries. Still another portion, varying between 40 and 50 percent, is spent on social programs. The state is also required to bear the cost of deficits incurred by state-owned industries and to provide them with new investment funds.

Governments not only redistribute that part of the national income they appropriate in taxes and profits but, to further economic and financial objectives and to generate adequate revenues for growing needs, manipulate numerous fiscal, credit and other financial regulatory mechanisms that regulate investment and spending propensities. More generally, governments oversee the financial flow of that part of GDP that they do not appropriate, but which equally affects the economic stability, growth, and industrial development of the nation.

Four distinct patterns and, correspondingly, four types (further discussed in Chapter 5 and graphically depicted in Table 5.2) of development can be discerned regarding etatization in Western societies.

1. The United States still maintains a one-sector corporate market economy. At present, the federal administration not only directly regulates economic and consumer behavior but increasingly employs the system of federal institutions—the Federal Reserve and the cash and credit budgets, the fiscal system and export–import controlling agencies to supervise its capitalist economy. The subordination of society and the economy to direct and indirect varieties of regulatory practice and management is the chief cause of etatization.

2. In Western Europe and in Canada, where the state owns a significant part of the economy, governments, while managing their own industries, are also involved in the overall management of the national market economy. Furthermore, some Western European nations, such as France during the earlier period under socialist rule, attempted to shift toward more centrally planned economic growth and development. Rocard, the present prime minister, was then in charge of this development. So far, however, in France and in other Western nations, only a limited number of select industries are subjected to centrally planned development. The implementation of planned targets is mostly induced, not enforced. This development differs from abstract models of central planning and from that practiced in the USSR. It aims to bring about certain social as well as economic solutions.

3. In Japan, the state owns only those industries that the private sector regards as unprofitable to operate, but which are, nevertheless, necessary, such as railroads and other services. Through its Ministry of International Trade and Industry (MITI), the Bank of Japan, and other institutions, by initiating major entrepreneurial activities, and by conducting and disseminating scientific, market, and other research, the government directly supports large corporations. It also sets national economic and developmental objectives. The state involves the Bank of Japan and other banks in providing expertise and credit to businesses, in acting on behalf of the private sector, in job-creating activities, and generally in strengthening the national economy.

4. Simon, in *The Smaller Democracies* (1939), discerned peculiarities characterizing small nations under democratic systems of government. Switzerland, Sweden, Denmark, Norway, and Finland came under this heading. Katzenstein, more recently, discusses two of these small nations, Austria and Switzerland, under the heading "democratic corporatism." According to Katzenstein's (1984, 27) definition:

> The "democratic corporatism" has three defining characteristics: an ideology of social partnership expressed at the national level; a relatively centralized and concentrated system of interest groups; and a voluntary and informal coordination of conflicting interest objectives through continuous political bargaining among interest groups, state bureaucracies, and political parties.

Actually, other small democratic nations, such as Israel and, perhaps, Denmark, could be characterized in similar terms. This group of nations is here discerned as a separate, fourth group of Western nations undergoing etatization.

The four patterns of etatization apparent within Western nations reflect distinct peculiarities of the bureaucracies and technocracies of specific nations, as well as cultural differences. In this book, with a few exceptions, analysis ends in 1985.

The Bureaucratic Mentality and the New Morality

No analysis of society is complete until it considers not only the character of the social structure and institutional orders, but also the culture and value orientation. Societies currently considered as Western (including, to a degree, Japan) share some essential features manifested in lifestyles, moral concerns, and various material, social, and cultural needs. This similarity stems from similar processes of industrialization and economic development, certain cultural properties derived from the Judeo-Christian ethos, and the sharing of technological and cultural achievement. During the twentieth century, normative and value orientation structures of Western societies changed fundamentally in several ways. These changes began in the Western world and later affected nations under Soviet-style government and in the Third World.

Early in this century, European and North American value orientations evolved from standards set by the family, the community, and the church. Norms instilled by these institutions determined the actions of individuals through inner processes of consciousness orientation, characterized by Riesman (1955) and others as inner-directed. Since the 1930s and particularly after World War II, the traditional value orientation metamorphosed into a new value orientation advocated by educational institutions and the mass media. The peer group, the school, and the mass media (particularly television) began to play a critical role in shaping individuals' behavior and ambitions. Generations of achievement-oriented individuals emerged, who set for themselves objectives that had been attained by others. These individuals have been characterized as other-directed. During the late 1960s and in the 1970s, the value orientation began to change again. Bell (1978) and others characterized these newly emerging attitudes as hedonistic. Lasch (1979), Sennett (1978), and Hougan (1975) saw them as narcissistic. Yankelovich (1974; 1981) called these attitudes the "New Morality" or the ethic of self-fulfilment. He wrote that the younger generation, and some groups in the older generation, attracted to this new ethic, were strongly motivated by such concerns as the preservation of the natural environment, self-fulfilment, the absurdity of the rat race, and ethical satisfaction through creative lifestyles, equity, and equality instead of material success. Yankelovich, among others, expected this value orientation to proliferate and become dominant in the United States and elsewhere.

Changes in value orientation produced not only new attitudes and lifestyles but brought forth a change in the public's expectation of the government, and therefore turned into an important factor of etatization. The public wanted to have more services, more protection against unemployment, more social and economic security and equity provided by the state.

The 1980s, however, brought a return to and new development of a conservative world outlook and value orientation. This currently manifests itself in patriotism, the rejection of liberal and socialist ideals as unrealistic and unattainable, and tax revolts. In the United States, certain groups have become active in the anti-abortion movement and other programs calling for the restoration of traditional institutions and ways of life. Criticism that the government is too big, too costly, and is involved in too many aspects of life in which it was not supposed to be involved became widespread. Yet at the same time the electorate was not willing to give up services, welfare institutions, and the newly established equity developed in the 1970s. Large sectors of the electorate in the United States, France, Great Britain, and other nations have supported conservative candidates. Religious fundamentalism has gained popularity. Intellectuals, including former liberals and socialists, have become increasingly concerned with alienation and other moral, psychological, and social problems resulting from the declining role of family and community, disrespect for authority, growing budget deficits, public programs, and excessive state intervention. Again, with the turning to conservatism, attitudes and expectations of the state changed. In response to new expectations, these intellectuals have adopted varying postures of neoconservative theories in their work. Governments, including the French, Italian, and other socialist governments, have begun to employ supply-side and monetarist economic concepts developed by these scholars. In spite of the election of conservative governments in many nations and the widespread adoption of conservative perspectives, however, the return to the morality, worldview, and lifestyles of the past was not complete. Today, individuals who vote conservatively, stand for traditional values, and express opinions on internal and international matters from a conservative perspective, often embrace certain aspects of the self-fulfilment and liberal ethic at the same time.

Society is irreversibly changing in another respect. Computers, automation, and other high-technology devices are being applied to all areas of production, distribution, management, and consumption. As the postindustrial information society emerges, new technologies are transforming value orientations and lifestyles. New forms of organizational structures affect organizational practices. These developments engender new career patterns and achievement goals. Contrary to expectations voiced in the late 1970s by Yankelovich, Inglehart, and others, who predicted that altruistic, postmaterialist, and self-fulfilment attitudes would prevail, most people today are highly competitive, aggressive career seekers, and corporate-ladder climbers. These people value power, for its own sake and for the influence and material wealth it procures. Most of them are also concerned with high salaries, office "perks," and fringe benefits. They value "the good life" and also strive for self-fulfilment.

The mentality of the individual in etatized society differs from that of individuals at earlier times, when one's life was directed primarily toward one's family, one's business, and the market in which one made a living. Under etatization, individuals depend on the state; also the state provides some of the principal ladders of mobility. The new morality, reflecting etatization and the life objectives newly enhanced by the media and academic literature, is still in the making. It contains some values of the self-fulfilment, egotistic ethic, but is governed predominately by an achievement-striving morality and more traditional values, with a strong bureaucratic attitude. People primarily employed by and dependent on bureaucratic institutions naturally develop a bureaucratic mode of thinking. Although concerned about nuclear war, ecological disasters, poverty, and starvation in their own nations and elsewhere, they also feel a strong need to "make it" in bureaucratic environments.

CHAPTER THREE

Conflict over Socioeconomic Issues

Conflict and antagonism appear in any "sociation." In a certain sense, they are to be regarded as integrative forces without which unity cannot be imagined. In his classic work on conflict, Simmel (1966, 17) points out that: "A certain amount of discord, inner divergence and outer controversy is organically tied up with the very elements that ultimately hold the group together." He also writes that in any society one can discern a hierarchy of relationships and, correspondingly, of conflicts. One of the most effective ways to analyze society, in his opinion, is to study the central conflict of the social structure.[1]

Most classical political and sociological theorists discussed conflict and employed some variety of conflict theory to characterize social conditions. Marx, as is widely known, was primarily concerned with class struggle. He believed that newer conflicts between material forces and production relations, base and superstructure, and class antagonisms beget higher and higher, in a sense more perfect, social and economic structures.

According to Max Weber, social structure arises from continuous conflicts over scarcities and the resulting allocation of wealth, power, and prestige. His portrait of society consists of a complex interlacing of diverse class structures, status hierarchies, and power orders engendered by different forms of property, divisions along the lines of group interests, and jockeying for position. He characterized this structure as integrated by the very same interests that sunder certain groups and pit individuals against others, as well as by the value system reflected in religion. The state represented the national interest in wholeness. Perceiving authority or legitimate domination as the monopoly power of political groups to exercise coercion over legally controlled territory, Weber (1978, 56) defined the state as "a compulsory organization with a territorial basis." The state presides over the complex structure of conflicting and shared interests.

Pareto and Durkheim used a different terminology. Pareto dedicated a great deal of attention to what he called "ubiquity and normality" in the use of force. He was especially interested in the use of force by the ruling class and by those who, in the name of justice, equity, or other cause, strive to wrestle political power and control from the hands of the power elite.[2] Durkheim described society as a growing complexity of interdependent centripetal and centrifugal forces. He (1984, 291–328) addressed conflict in works on anomie, types of suicide, and changing forms of solidarity. In his wording, conflict generated "abnormal forms." Durkheim believed in solidarity, integration, and interdependence and, therefore, expected the state to provide centripetal forces that would balance the centrifugal forces of conflict. Conflict is a key concept, opening a wide variety of sociological analyses.

Classical sociologists were not alone in their concern with conflict. Historians, political scientists, philosophers, and most authors of serious *belles lettres* addressed this issue also. Kriesberg (1973, 3) points out that "many persons believe that conflict properly institutionalized is an effective vehicle for discovering truth, for attaining justice and for the long-run benefit of society as a whole." Conflicts on macrosocial levels are among the principal determinants of social and political conditions.

At each stage of societal development, in any period of the history of a nation, there arise certain principal (and many less consequential) conflicts over specific issues. By distinguishing principal conflicts, one can effectively differentiate stages of societal development and periods of history.

Assessments and definitions of capitalist relations refer to private ownership of the principal means of production as the chief cause of conflict in society.[3] Without such private ownership, capitalism is no longer capitalism. It is ownership that determines the character of all other relations in the free-market society. Other conflicts in capitalist relations are secondary, even the universal conflict between the elite and the masses. Conflicts of lesser scope, such as those that occasionally emerge in ethnic and majority-minority relations, are more obviously secondary. Secondary conflicts arise out of struggles to establish democratic institutions, freedom, and human rights, or as a result of divergent ideological orientations and lifestyles, or different attitudes stemming from contrarieties induced by religious affiliations. Secondary conflicts may or may not occur at any stage of development and can be regarded as situational. Any portrayal of capitalist society, then, must include an analysis of the conflicts inherent in the private ownership of the principal means of production. To the extent that contemporary society continues to be capitalist, it retains conflicts typical of capitalist structures. This book aims to demonstrate that contemporary capitalist society is metamorphosing into an etatized society. This claim has merit only if a new set of conflicts significantly different from those attributed to capitalism can be distinguished as characterizing the etatized condition.

New Issues, New Conflicts

The principal conflicts in etatized societies can be effectively compared and contrasted with those of capitalist societies by paraphrasing "Who gets what, when, how?"—the question once raised by Lasswell. Previously, the issue was: Who gets what out and how out of the capitalist ownership of the means of production? In etatized society, the central issue has become: Who gets what and how out of the state's control of the economy and its distribution of the national income? The old issue has not been removed from the agenda of public confrontations. Yet, newer controversies and confrontations concern the multifarious interest groups comprising present-day society much more and reduce the importance of past concerns. This shift merits a new perspective.

While many of the issues that spark conflict in capitalist societies persist, new and profoundly different issues have emerged in etatized societies. The new issues deal to some extent with property rights, but focus more on control than on ownership. They pertain to control over property, but increasingly to control over a mixed economy. More and more, in all Western societies, including the United States and Japan, conflicts concern control by the state, which has been transformed into the manager of the whole of the national economy. Increasingly, the principal issues are related to control of the state's budgetary allocations. This is quite apparent in current congressional and parliamentary debates, mass media discussions, and the actions of special interest lobbies. It is evident in party competition for power and in many other aspects of political life. Every interest group in contemporary society is fighting to get more out of state management and control of the economy, state distribution of benefits, and state protection. Conflicts over state control are more apparent, involving more groups, because more people and corporations depend on the state for their income, profits, and security, and because state policies can be influenced through the mass media, elections, demonstrations, and other forms of public pressure.

These new issues are not as universal as the perennial split between ruling elites and the masses. They are also not as peculiar to specific conditions in a given region and time as conflicts over regional, ethnic, and religious policies have been and continue to be. To an extent, the new conflicts are transformed old conflicts. Yet, they increasingly concern issues that did not exist or were not raised in the past, such as entitlements, budgetary allocations, rights to services, taxation to maintain public services, and the welfare system. These new issues will continue to be the principal issues for a long time to come.

Who controls what is an issue with many faces. In etatized societies, ownership, and especially exclusive ownership in the traditional meaning, is less socially important than the more specific question, "Who controls corporations?" The unique aspect of the new control of corporations, as

Berle and Means (1968) first observed (and as other writers have since corroborated), is that the controllers are not necessarily owners, yet their authority is as pervasive and decisive as that of owners in the past. The rewards to some individuals in control and management are comparable with profits to owners. However, managers are rewarded regardless of whether their operations are profitable, and for some time, whether they are successful. Political office under etatized conditions involves making decisions that affect large numbers of people, but also involves allocating funds. However, just as stockholders do not fully control the enterprises they own, politicians, government officials, and managers are not complete masters of the administrative and technocratic structures they direct. The bureaucratic apparatus controls a great deal of political activity. Those in control hold extensive powers and enjoy numerous privileges that enlarge their rewards. At the same time, however, they often feel they are no more than "cogs in the wheels" of the system. Control is rarely exclusive. It is, as a rule, divided and constantly challenged by competing forces. Control involves ongoing negotiation with superiors, subordinates, partners, clients, competitors, and with others who share the given type of control or exercise another kind of control in the given area. Exchange, cooperation, compromise, persuasion, and, of course, intercession and conflict, form a part of day-to-day life under such conditions. Each interest group practices whatever pressure tactics it can master in its efforts to manipulate a given situation. The state is frequently required to act as supreme intermediator. Conflict over control, which is essential to etatized society, specifically manifests itself in:

(a) controversies over budgetary allocations, distribution of rewards, and, more generally, income distribution
(b) conflicts over the ownership of means of production and the distribution of means of consumption, as affected by the mixed character of the economy
(c) disagreements over the meaning of equity and other ethical concepts, and the meaning of achievement
(d) schisms over the rights and obligations of those in managing roles and of the common people; in some situations, this is experienced as a contrariety between the public and private roles of the same person[4]

Income Distribution: Who Should Get What and for What?

Until recently, people derived income from wages, salaries, royalties, professional fees, profits, interests, and dividends. Although these forms of income still constitute most of the income structure in Western nations undergoing etatization, part of income also consists of services, transfer payments, and other government benefits. Not always perceived by the population as actual income, but merely as part of the available condition, such benefits can be considered invisible income. Special privileges associated with particular positions in the bureaucratic structure can also be equated with income. Thus, under etatization, three components of individual income, and, consequently, the national income, can be discerned:

Entitlements. Entitlements (E) come in the form of services provided by the state, such as public education, medical services, and cash transfers, food stamps, subsidized housing, legal services, etc. Entitlements, and funds provided specifically as entitlements, are designated either for collective or individual consumption. A recently published editorial in the *New York Times* (April 24, 1988), discussing entitlements in the United States, declared:

> "Entitlements" are open-ended Federal commitments to meet certain needs of specific groups. Welfare, food stamps and Medical limit benefits to the neediest people. Such "means-tested" entitlements account for only about 8 percent of the Federal budget. The great bulk of entitlements, everything from student loans to Social Security, are not means-tested. They are paid to anyone in the benefit category, regardless of financial need. Last year, these programs accounted for *38 percent* of Federal outlays, or about $383 billion.

The editorial advocated a new solution of the deficit problem: "to require of the affluent Americans to pay their own way." U.S. citizens do not have universal access to health services, enjoyed by citizens of other Western nations. Senator Edward Kennedy and other liberal congressmen have repeatedly called for the institution of such services. The editorial pointed out that, with rising expenditures on one side and reduced taxes on the other, the United States would do better to reduce non-means-tested entitlements.

Remunerations. Remunerations (R) include payment for work in the form of salaries, wages plus fringe benefits, profits, dividends, and interest. As in the past, these are rewards for individual initiatives and activities, such as labor, occupation of a position, ownership, investment, or participation in market operations.

Privileges. Privileges (P) (more accurately benefits from privileges), providing substantial gains, are derived directly in the form of "perks," such as executive expenses, luxurious accommodations, and travel; and indirectly in pecuniary and nonpecuniary benefits, generated by connections developed through holding executive governmental or corporate positions. In the past, when government, public-service, and corporate bureaucracies were smaller, the number of officials benefiting from such privileges was also much smaller. Consequently, so was the portion of the total national income they appropriated. At present, benefits derived from privileges constitute the spoils of a vast new class of top executives, experts, and the personnel working for them. Although the cash value of such benefits is rarely reckoned and cannot be easily estimated on the basis of bills and receipts, these benefits have substantial real and potential monetary value.

The analysis of income distribution that discerns these three components will hereafter be called the ERP perspective.

Entitlements, remunerations, and gains from privileges are all elements of legal income. A fourth income source can be included. Not perceived by the public as seriously criminal, this component represents significant illegal income generated in the underground, black-market economy. Illegal income derives from a broad range of activities, such as bartering, unreported business and profits, tax evasion, illegal drug deals, and favors-in-kind. Although it often involves substantial gains, (of between 5 to 15 percent of the actual GNP of the industrialized nations), illegal income is not included in ERP.

The literature on income distribution and its consequences in capitalist society is extensive. Most studies conclude by addressing issues of class relations. Recent studies (Kolko 1964, 48–50; Schnitzer 1974, 112, 113, 185, 228; Thurow 1980, 155–158; Blinder 1980, 435; Ross 1980, 11–41) portray inequality in income distribution, and its consequences, by employing quintile or income-tenth analyses.[5] While some authors focus attention primarily on income distribution to families and unattached individuals (as reported on tax returns), others prefer to consider income distribution per capita in a given society.[6]

Table 3.1 compares income distribution by quintiles in industrialized Western nations.[7] As evident in this comparison, 20% of the wealthy, i.e., those in the highest quintile, were apportioned 38% to 46% of the total national income. The statistics remain constant regardless of whether the economy comprises one sector, as in the United States, or two sectors as in Scandinavian countries, France, Canada, and elsewhere. The 20% included in the fourth quintile appropriated between 21% and 24% of national income. The 20% in the middle quintile gained between 15% and 18.5%; those in the second quintile, 10% to 12.6%, and those in the bottom, fifth quintile, only 3.8% to 7% of national income. Comparing annual changes in GNP appropriations by quintiles, from the end of World War II to the present, one must conclude that it has not changed significantly. Each nation has maintained a distribution that accords 35% to 45% of income to the top quintile, and 7.5% or less to the bottom. Some writers, discussing income distribution in the United States, claim that the higher quintiles presently appropriate a smaller share of the national income than they once did. Others find evidence to the contrary.[8]

Incomes of different quintiles are frequently portrayed by segmented

Table 3.1.   International Comparison of Income Distribution per Household in Western Industrialized Nations

Percentage share of household income, by percentile groups of households

	Year	Lowest 20 percent	Second quintile	Third quintile	Fourth quintile	Highest 20 percent	Highest 10 percent
Australia	1975–1976	5.4	10.0	15.0	22.5	47.1	30.5
Belgium	1978–1979	7.9	13.7	18.6	23.8	36.0	21.5
Canada	1981	5.3	11.8	18.0	24.9	30.0	23.8
France	1975	5.3	11.1	16.0	21.8	45.8	30.5
Germany (FRG)	1978	7.9	12.5	17.0	23.1	39.5	24.0
Italy	1977	6.2	11.3	15.9	22.7	43.9	28.1
Japan	1979	8.7	13.2	17.5	23.1	37.5	22.4
Netherlands	1981	8.3	14.1	18.2	23.2	36.2	21.5
Norway	1982	6.0	12.9	18.3	24.6	38.2	22.8
Spain	1980–1981	6.9	12.5	17.3	23.2	40.0	24.5
Sweden	1981	7.4	13.1	16.8	21.0	41.7	28.1
United Kingdom	1979	7.0	11.5	17.0	24.8	39.7	23.4
United States	1980	5.3	11.9	17.9	25.0	39.9	23.3

Source: World Development Report. 1985. Table 25. Income Distribution. (New York: World Bank and Oxford University Press).

circles, as in Table 3.2, portraying income distribution to U.S. families and unattached individuals per household, subdivided into quintiles according to 1977 data. This example has been discussed in a number of recently published books. Thurow (1980, 156) and Blinder (1980), for instance, discuss income distribution data for 1977 as reported by the *Current Population Reports* (1979, 45, 226, 227). According to these calculations, the U.S. 1977 income appropriation by quintiles was: 5.2% to the lowest; 12.7% to the second; 17.5% to the third; 24.2% to the fourth; and 41.5% to the highest.

Although instructive in certain regards, quintile analyses fail to reveal alterations in the composition of quintiles over time. This is important, since the composition, particularly of the highest and fourth quintiles, has significantly changed over the last twenty years. In the 1950s and early 1960s, the top two quintiles comprised, predominantly, owners of large property assets. At present, these quintiles include many new groups, not only those who are privileged because they are wealthy, but also those who have become wealthy because their positions have entitled them to privileges: executives, professionals, top bureaucrats, famous entertainers, artists, and other celebrities. One has only to glance at the article "Executive Pay" in Business Week (May 2, 1988) or at like publications to appreciate this phenomenon. "Executive Pay" contains tables listing 522 executives of major corporations and their compensation (salary and bonuses). Among these, 134 received, in 1987, compensations of more than $1 million. The top five are J. P. Manzi (Lotus), $26,297,000; L. A. Iacocca (Chrysler), $17,896,000; P. Fireman (Reebok International), $15,424,000; P. B. Roomey

Table 3.2 U.S. Income Distribution, 1977, by quintiles

(a) 1977 Distribution of family income in the capitalist United States

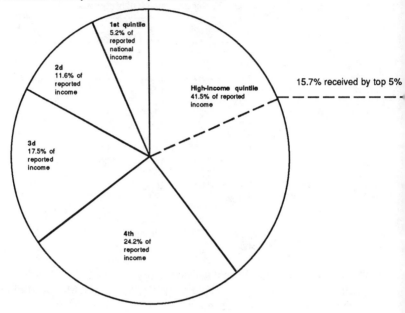

(b) 1977 Distribution of family income in the United States as seen from the ERP perspective

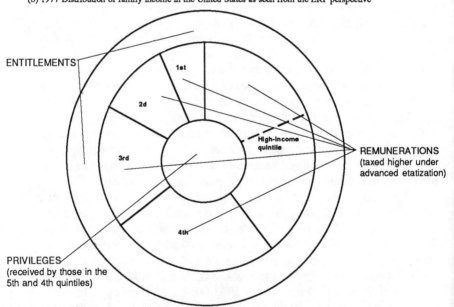

Source: Data from *Current population report: Consumer income 1977*. March 1979. (Series P-60, no. 118. Washington, D.C.: U.S. Bureau of the Census.)

(Waste Management), $14,276,000; and R. M. Furland (Squibb), $13,217,000. The smallest amount, from the top ten went to E. R. White (Amdahl)—$8,846,000. In 1985, just two years ago, (*Business Week*, May 6, 1985) T. Boone Pickens, Jr. (Mesa Petroleum), with much less—an annual total compensation of $4,223,000—was at the top of the list; Barry Diller (Gulf & Western), with $2,866,000, was second, and so on. The journal compared these business executives' compensation with that of Michael Jackson ($35 million), Clint Eastwood ($10 million), Marvin Hagler ($3.3 million in 1978), and Dan Rather ($2.2 million). Harrop compares (1980, 181) business compensations in what he calls "brass tacks jobs" with those of "glamour jobs" (professional sports, book publishing, journalism, entertaining, and the arts), tax-paid jobs in government, and elite professional jobs (medicine, law, and education); see also "Growing furor over pay of top excecutives," (*U.S. News & World Report*, May 21, 1984).

These best-paid executives, media people, anecdote makers, entertainers of all sorts are also recipients of various frequently untaxed P benefits. There are good reasons to speculate that people in these categories appropriate a larger percentage of the real national income than is reflected in quintile analyses on the basis of net tax returns. At the other end of the spectrum, individuals in lower-income categories receive more entitlements than those in other quintiles and do not report certain income. Thus, the real size of their income is not fully accounted for by quintile analyses, either.

In order to depict these new changes in income distribution, and the new conflicts arising from them, the quintile scheme needs to be amended. Table 3.2. offers a graphic depiction of the new income distribution in etatized societies. Instead of one circle (*a*), representing the national income pie divided into quintile segments, the new portrayal (*b*) consists of an outer circle, representing E; a segmented division, representing quintiles of R, and a center circle, representing volume P.

How large are the portions of the national income currently received under each component distinguished in the ERP scheme? Between 18% and 30% of the national income is currently appropriated in different ways by the

Table 3.3. Comparative Government Expenditure on Social Security and Welfare

				(percent of the budget)				
	1978	1979	1980	1981	1982	1983	1984	1985
Canada	33.79	32.50	32.71	31.74	34.87	35.62	33.47	27.25
France	43.99	44.14	44.39	43.89	44.19	43.96	n/a	33.92
West Germany	49.90	49.58	44.22	49.54	49.66	49.97	50.22	
Italy	29.14	28.91	28.39	31.08	33.02	32.76	30.59	29.05
Sweden	49.16	48.18	48.31	46.30	49.27	48.95	49.93	48.46
United Kingdom	25.49	25.47	26.37	28.23	29.79	28.55	28.62	28.55
United States	34.19	33.72	34.10	34.24	33.54	33.99	32.07	28.42

Data taken from *Government Finance Statistics Yearbook*. Vol. 8/,1984; 9/,1985; 10/,1986; 11/,1987 (Washington DC: International Monetary Fund).

New State. Of this, 30% to 50% (as portrayed in Table 3.3) is spent on social security and welfare. In short, 10% to 15% of the national income of Western societies is currently distributed by the state through social and welfare services. The current value of benefits derived from privileges, which have proliferated widely under etatized conditions, can only be speculated.[9]

The September 1987 (9, no. 10.) issue of *Inc.: The Magazine for Growing Companies*, contains the results of a survey on executive compensation conducted among 20,000 subscribers (1,582 usable returns). While the data do not seem reliable enough to be included here, the list of executive benefits and perks is illuminating. It includes: company car and expenses; supplemental life insurance; supplemental medical insurance; tax-return preparation; club dues and expenses; personal tax and financial planning; annual physical examinations; low- to no-interest loans; supplemental retirement benefits; deferred compensation; and first-class air travel. The magazine reports that 83% of the surveyed companies paid bonuses constituting 25% of base salary. In 58% of instances, bonuses were discretionary; in 24% they rewarded achievement of sales goals; in 30% they honored achievement of profit goals.

The Economist (February 21, 1987) contains another informative discussion. Let me quote only one paragraph:

> There is no simple definition of a modern business perk. Sometimes it is payment in kind (a house, a car, health insurance, a big lunch, even a Lautrec painting) in lieu of taxable cash. More often it is a way of offering or promising money (a super-pension, a stock option, a soft loan) in such a way that the employee voids paying as much tax as he would on an equivalent amount of pay. In either case "tax efficiency" is the key ingredient. Cash bonuses awarded to top managers for performance are not, strictly speaking, perks at all: they are a variable form of pay taxed at the same rate as salary. They show the way that perks should go. Perks are so unstructured and fickle that the international institutions which gather statistics, like the EEC or the OECD, do not try to keep track of them.

Apart from any other discoveries that large corporations can claim recently, there is one which saves them considerable money, about which they do not like to brag too much. They offer their executives a somewhat lower pay, which is also taxed at a lower rate, plus housing, a company car, travels, vacations, etc., which are not taxed, but which the company can claim as business expenses. This reduces the cost of the company's business as well. Good business is smart business. (I say this not to blame, just to express regret that universities do not have such provisions in *their* collective agreements).

Bonuses and perks comprise only part of privileges, which include a long list of prerogatives enjoyed by individuals in positions of power, such as connections and other nonpecuniary benefits, which may eventually bear monetary income. Unreported earnings of those on welfare and unemployment rolls are pitiful in comparison.

Income distribution in an etatized society is not determined only by the structure of ownership, class composition, and gains defined as remunerations. It is also, and to an increasing degree, structured by policies that effectuate the volumes spent on E and P benefits. The importance of E and P benefits as sources of income is rapidly increasing. Such benefits also become a major issue of conflict and intercession among interest groups. Differences in interests, ideologies, values, norms, and lifestyles determine what side of the conflict individuals and groups will weigh in on. Under capitalist conditions, the principal conflict was over income engendered by private ownership of means of production—surplus value, in Marxian terms. In the new condition, the conflict is over incomes engendered by different forms of control, some related, some not related to ownership. The new issues raised under etatization are: How much of the national income should be spent on entitlements? How much should individuals in high positions be allowed in P benefits? Should such benefits be taxed and, if yes, by what kind of estimates?

Another aspect of this changing condition needs to be pointed out: Under etatization, a significant part of the GNP is redistributed by the state, in money transfers, goods, and services, to part or all of the population. Under enactments instituting entitlements to such benefits, citizens acquire a *de facto* right to a portion of the national income, not in remuneration for work, merit, or contribution, but solely for citizenship. The institutionalization of entitlements is tantamount, in fact, to the adoption and legalization of a new principle in income distribution. This raises a new conflict: What amount of the national income must be redistributed in accordance with this new principle?

Funds that governments allot for E or P benefits—received by those in state employment—are raised by direct and indirect taxes on income and sales. One way or another, they result from R—income received in remunerations. Part of the profits generated by state-owned industries is also expended on E and P. Governments favoring collective consumption, social programs, and equalization expend larger portions of their national income on E than do governments advocating private initiative in a free-market economy and capitalist expansion. In any case, increased spending on E and P requires higher taxes and, therefore, occurs at the expense of individual R gains. For example: the Scandinavian nations increase the share of E to citizens by imposing higher taxes on R. The Soviet party-state maximizes spending on investments, particularly in heavy industries and the military, by instituting a policy under which both R and E of most citizens are maintained at low levels. In addition, a relatively large part of the Soviet national income is expended on rewards for the *nomenklatura* elite. Western European governments nationalized some industries specifically in order to appropriate more funds for growing outlays on entitlements and services. In order to protect the gains of the middle class and corporations, Reagan's economic policies have consisted of keeping taxes at a minimum, while maintaining the established proportion of spending on entitlements and administrative expenses. In all these instances, policies under etatization changed the proportions between E, R, and P in the structure of income distribution: E and P factors were expanded at the expense of R. Such changes can be characterized as typical of etatization.

Those advocating maximized entitlements not only believe that the poor deserve relief, but also that all citizens are entitled to a certain minimum of the national income, distributed in services and entitlements. The debate is no longer whether every citizen is entitled to such a share, but how large this share should be. This conflict over the size of entitlements addresses the division of only a part of the national income. However, it represents a fundamentally new value orientation and a new conflict structure, significantly different from the traditional perspective that recognizes market norms as the only factor determining income distribution in society.

New conflicts over the distribution of income do not eliminate the long-standing conflicts engendered by class divisions. A list of discords and conflicts over income distribution in the New State must include both new and old antagonisms:

a. Traditional conflicts persist; over inequalities of income and their consequences, which are manifest in the division of social classes. Current criticism of the structure of income distribution, mirrored by quintile analyses and other related studies, reflects these concerns.

b. New conflicts arise over the allocation of shares of the national income to E, R, and P, and related disagreements pertaining to the varying levels of taxation across income classes, allocations to defense and social programs, national budget deficits, and corporate taxes; in short, the issues reflected in daily debates between principal political parties in the congresses, parliaments, and chambers of representation of Western societies.

c. Disagreement, typical of etatized societies, concerns the propriety of privileges, which allow individuals in certain positions to enjoy the life of the very rich without receiving large incomes, by simply exploiting perks and connections.

d. Occasional discord surfaces between the interests of the old moneyed class and the new class. In some situations, the line between these groups is definite; in others, it is blurred and less apparent. Discords of this sort are secondary but, nonetheless, pertinent to this account.

e. Conflicting interests and disparity can be seen between worldviews of the old middle-class entrepreneurs and the new salaried middle class. These conflicts are also secondary.

The problem of conflicts over the allocation of goods becomes continually more complex. Because the number of new services and entitlements provided by the government increases, and the scarcity of funds persists, the problem has exploded into a number of overlapping conflicts. For example, modern medicine has significantly extended the average life span; as a result, government pensions and medical assistance to the old must extend over a longer period of time while remaining sufficient to adequately support the elderly. These necessary increases in allocations for pensions and medical care for the elderly inevitably conflict with the needs of other groups. More funding is required for education, to raise teachers' salaries and to make them proud of the job they do. Otherwise, children will not be educated well. But where to find enough funds for the increased needs of teachers, universities, libraries, and other educational institutions? What kind of fairness can satisfy all these expectations? The allocation of funds to medicine causes many controversies. Should funds be spent to satisfy the needs of the terminally ill (e.g., those suffering from AIDS)? Should money be expended on developing sophisticated medical facilities that only a small percentage of patients will need? Or should funds be directed toward ensuring enough hospital beds and other basic facilities? Elderly employees may be kept on the job because it costs less to keep them working; as a result, the young may be denied promotions, or even the opportunity to work. When only limited money is available, and more aid is given to the elderly, there is not enough money to combat poverty among the young.[10] If scarce resources are spent on highly talented children, helping them become great artists or mathematicians, or brilliant innovators, then less is available for the average child, or for the retarded who need special pedagogical care. When money is spent on sewers or environmental protection, less can be spent on developing an infrastructure to attract industries and generate jobs. As more is spent on defense, less is available for social programs, and vice versa. Priorities essential and justified to some are seen as unnecessary by others. The ensuing conflicts constitute a multisided predicament, which decisionmakers today can neither avoid nor resolve.

In the past, priorities were decided by families and small groups, within their limited budgets. As the New State absorbs the role of the family, it simultaneously inherits concerns over resources and priorities. Moreover, controversies over the allocation of funds intensify as members of society become more dependent on entitlements and privileges from the state. Conflicts that were not issues of public concern and discord a decade or two ago, have become major issues dividing society along new lines. Under present conditions of etatization in Western societies, only 20 to 35 percent of the national income is appropriated by the state and disbursed by budgetary allocations. Nevertheless, conflict over the distribution of this part sets many people at each others' throats.

Conflict over Ownership and Control

In the *Manifesto of the Communist Party*, Marx and Engels wrote: "modern bourgeois private property is the final and most complete expression of the system of producing and appropriating products that is based on class antagonisms, on the exploitation of the many by the few. In this sense, the theory of the Communists may be summed up in the single sentence: Abolition of private property." Not only communists and socialists regard private ownership of the means of production as the principal cause of exploitation and other evils in capitalist society. In the second half of the twentieth century, this feeling has become quite widespread. But it is a mixed feeling. Many people feel it is unjust that large property owners amass wealth while the majority, because they own little, remain poor. They also sense, however, that to expropriate property, or to end private ownership altogether, would not be right either. Western civilization has traditionally accepted property ownership as an elementary human right. It is also well known now that the division into rich and poor does not disappear with the abolition of private ownership. To reconcile these conflicting attitudes numerous solutions were practiced. They include: nationalization of certain sectors of industries, with adequate compensation to former owners; state monopoly in certain fields of economic activity, while maintaining market competition in others; two-sector economic structures; state control and regulation of private ownership; public services. Along these lines, each Western nation developed distinct institutional structures and solutions.

Since etatized Western societies are still capitalist, they retain private ownership of the means of production and continue to experience the conflicts thus generated. To the extent that they have become postcapitalist, however, these societies sustain new conflicts engendered by state ownership of enterprises and the dependence of individuals on a public sector with limited resources. Many conflicts exist between: public and private sectors of the economy; the state and the private sector; and even between the state as central authority and the subsidiary state-owned sector, which tends to develop interests distinct from those of the central administration. Some individuals own personal and private property and profit-generating investments, while others own little and depend on wages, salaries, and transfer payments to stay alive. Since the inception of capitalism, debates have arisen over the legitimacy and morality of the private ownership of the means of production. It is now evident that the abolition of private property does not automatically produce equality, justice, and ideal socialism. Furthermore, the nationalization of property does not lead to tangible collective ownership of the means of production, in which decisions would be made by all. Nationalization leads only to state ownership and bureaucratic management. Individuals in high managerial positions are rewarded with high incomes, comparable to traditional capitalist profits. In the meantime, lower-level workers are paid as little or even less than before. An average family with two children, aspiring to moderate consumption, cannot live on one income, as it used to in the 1950s and 1960s. Employees of state-owned enterprises and services are presently engaged in labor conflicts with the state, as employer, just as they were formerly in conflict with the capitalist.

The existence of a public sector or state-owned industrial sector may be regarded as beneficial to workers and the needy. In certain circumstances, however, the state can be just as exploitative of workers as was the private sector. Should the public sector be expanded, even if it does not serve society well, in order to deprive the wealthy of their riches? Opinions on the matter are as divided as on other central issues in etatized societies. During the 1960s and early 1970s, politicians, social scientists, the media, and large sections of the public were quite enthusiastic about the advantages of the public sector and a state-owned economy, over private industries and the market economy. The public and state sector developed under these conditions. In the 1980s, the situation reversed. *The Economist* (December 21, 1985) describes the change:

> The selling of state assets—from airlines to jute mills—is captivating politicians everywhere, even in socialist Spain and communist China. At its best, "privatisation" creates competition, efficiency and wealth. At its worst, it substitutes intensive privately-owned monopolies for intensive publicly-owned ones and feeds corruption.

The study discusses the efforts of governments, in Great Britain, Italy, France, and around the world, to sell and denationalize industries. In Great Britain, at the end of the 1970s, the state sector of industries, accounting for 10 percent of the GDP and 15 percent of total investment, had produced close to zero aggregate return on capital for more than a decade, at high expense to taxpayers. Thatcher's government, which claims to have an electoral mandate to implement major economic reform, is heavily involved in privatization efforts. Disagreement over whether to reduce, maintain, or expand the state-owned sector of the economy has become a prominent conflict in contemporary Western societies.

Arguments for Denationalization

Privately owned companies function better than state-owned ones, because they must be efficient, highly productive, and profitable in order to survive in the competitive market. For the same reason, the quality of services and commodities offered by privately owned companies is superior to those offered by state-owned companies. Also, privately marketed services and commodities are often offered at a lower price. State-owned companies, usually monopolies, do not go bankrupt regardless of inefficiency. They incur deficits year after year. By selling off industries owned by the state, the government not only obtains a substantial infusion of revenues with which it can remedy many current problems, but relieves itself from the need to subsidize inefficient and deficit-incurring industries.

Arguments for Nationalization and Against Privatization

Many private industries, large ones in particular, make profits and do well in the market only because they are de facto subsidized, through tax relief or government contracts, under which they receive higher than market prices for goods and services. Nationalized industries should be regarded as facilitating solutions to social problems, and not only as productive units of the economy. State-owned industries reduce unemployment more effectively than does the private sector, precisely because they are less concerned with profits. They are also part of the redistributive system developed to ameliorate the social condition. State-owned and state-subsidized industries can compete more effectively in the international market than can private companies with limited resources. Nationalized key industries provide essential services to the poorer population, and even the private sector, at lower prices than do comparable private-sector industries. Nationalized industries tend to generate low profits because low-profit industries were usually the first to be nationalized. In an economy with a larger nationalized sector, "cross-subsidization" would prove more effective, and the nationalized sector would be equally more efficient. Unions in Western Europe and Canada usually strongly support such arguments.

At present, those who fight to privatize and preserve the capitalist market economy seem to have the upper hand. But the controversy is not over. It is unlikely that any nation with a two-sector economy will change completely to a one-sector private economy, or to a wholly nationalized state economy. When a large privately owned company is in danger of collapsing, and thus destabilizing the economy by increasing unemployment or provoking any other major social and economic disaster, the state has little choice but to intervene. In the United States, the government shrinks from interfering in the market if it can possibly be avoided. Yet, in a crisis, it will interfere by providing the industry with loan guarantees or loans. For example, the government practically nationalized the Continental Bank of Illinois in such an occurrence. Again, in September 1987, the Federal Deposit Insurance Corporation pledged to provide the First City Bank of Texas with nearly $1 billion in aid; closing the bank would have cost the government twice that sum. Western European governments have nationalized many industries to rescue them from trouble. And no one, either on the Left or the Right, is protesting such decisions.

In etatized societies, optimum conditions can only be attained by an economy that is neither completely capitalist and devoid of state control nor under any form of socialist command management that excludes private entrepreneurship. The best solution is a balance between private and state-controlled interests. But such a compromise leaves both sides wanting. Even when society agrees to a mixed economy, debates persist over the proper proportion of each sector. There is never a resolution; as long as the economy comprises two sectors, increase in either private or state ownership is always a possibility. Nor is this debate confined to the West. What is to be left in private hands and what is to be completely controlled by the state continues to provoke disagreements in China, Hungary, Poland, and, currently, the Soviet Union.

At each stage of the historical evolution of Western societies, the idea of property and ownership, and related notions originally adopted from Roman law, have been reinterpreted in accordance with new requirements. One tendency was constant, however, until the onset of etatization. The Romans employed a complex structure of notions recognizing divergent forms of property, different for immovable and movable objects, different for slaves, chattels, wives, and children. They accorded three rights to the owner of any of these properties: the right to use (*ius utendi*), the right to abuse (*ius abutendi*) and the right to utilize the fruits (*ius fruendi*) of the objects.[11] Medieval Church jurists proclaimed that property constituted part of the divine ordination. Those born to own were accorded the three derivative rights as recognized in antiquity. Under capitalism, possession was modified into private property and ownership. It was not regarded anymore as a privilege accorded by the grace of God, but as a commodity available in the market. At first, during the nineteenth-century revolutions, private property was proclaimed to constitute "an inviolable and sacred right" of an individual—a right, indivisible, of liberty and democracy. Capitalism could not develop otherwise than through maximal economic privatization. During this early period of capitalist development, the law strove to enhance private property and to consolidate the rights of owners to use or abuse property and its fruits; to create a more homogeneous and exclusive right of the individual to own property, guaranteed by the state. But as time went on, a different stance emerged. Rights of individuals were accorded to corporations, institutions, cities, and the state. According to Schumpeter (1966, 142), property was dematerialized and stripped of "its visible and touchable reality." According to Bowles and Gintis (1986, 170), "property rights become depersonalized to the extent they are held by non-persons." Individuals could now hold minuscule investment shares in large corporations, which entitled them to no more than some expectation of any profit. While old forms of ownership continued, new forms—diverse types of equities, securities diversely defined and combined into complex kinds of ownership—emerged. Metamorphosed into investment, in its new liquified form, ownership evolved into a form of control. Under more pure forms of capitalist domination, the value of ownership, and correspondingly, the degree of control it provided, was determined in the market. But soon, the state would start to interfere with this exclusive market prerogative.

Under etatization, several tendencies can be observed. The three derived rights of ownership are in many instances separately accorded under supreme state control, superimposed on market control. Rights to abuse owned property are severely restricted. Rights to use owned property are limited in accordance with numerous codes designed to protect the rights of other users of the same or other property, rules developed to protect the environment, the public, and the interests of different levels of government. The right to the fruits of ownership and control is most fully recognized. Contemporary law and the mores of daily practice recognize other forms of control as valid, sometimes equally so or less, but valid, as are those derived from ownership. Many rights to control thus overlap. Other, more and less limited, rights to control objects of property not owned by the controllers are emerging as well: the public's right to determine, through environmental groups and the media, whether an object is put to safe uses; unions' rights to participate in the decisionmaking process affecting certain aspects of production; the rights of the entire hierarchy of public authorities in the territories where the owned object is located. The state has proclaimed its right of ultimate control, through which, as much as through the market, the eventual price-value of the object is determined.

Certain forms of control, ownership, management, and territorial rule, constitute a condition in which the controller—an individual or corporate entity—may earn pecuniary values. Other forms of control—as the right accorded to public institutions to restrict the use of private property because of safety or other concerns or the unions' rights to participate in corporate decisionmaking, may not yield direct monetary earnings to the controlling agent, but are as important as money.

Under etatization, not only is ownership increasingly transformed into a form of control and the rights of many other groups to control objects they do not own increasingly recognized, but certain forms of control are implemented through regulatory practices, which in turn, when conducted along with an objective of generating more values, evolve into a form of management. In this sense, the regulatory function of the state metamorphoses into management of the economy and society. Each aspect of such management is subjected to public scrutiny. Each is subject to ongoing controversy and conflict.

CHAPTER FOUR

Conflicting Philosophies

Equity

Common opinion holds that, though in the past capitalist society was divided by many conflicts, the social structure was principally determined by two conflicts: over ownership of the means of production and over income distribution in society. Class conflict reflected the division of political forces, first into conservative versus liberal parties, then into Right against Left. During the past two decades, however, numerous single-issue movements have appeared on the social and political scene. Some writers (e.g., Inglehart & Rabier 1985) think that, as a result of this development, current politics polarizes along new divisions, only loosely related to the traditional Left-Right axis. This is partly true. However, the ideological and party spectrum in all Western nations remains divided into a conservative Right and liberal or socialist Left. The issues dividing parties and the electorate are new. Contemporary liberals and conservatives raise issues and present programs significantly different from those advocated by parties bearing these names in the past; the new arrangement operates under old names.

Although single-issue movements are only loosely related to political parties and frequently act independently, they will often chose to support a party on the Left or the Right in order to achieve their objectives. Thus, two lists of single issue movements can be compiled. One list includes movements and groups linked with the liberals and the Left, the other with conservatives and the Right. The antinuclear movement, the environmentalist movement, a large part of the feminist movement, the limits-to-growth movement, certain unions in the United States, Great Britain, France, and elsewhere, various ethnic movements and Black organizations are quite closely linked with Liberal, Democratic, and Socialist party forces. Patriotic movements in the United States, Great Britain, and elsewhere, some veterans groups, pro-family and anti-abortion movements, fundamentalist and certain other religious movements, anti-tax movements, the Moral Majority in the United States, and, in Great Britain, the National Viewers and Listeners' Association, the National Federation of Self-Employed, and like organizations and business clubs, tend to associate themselves with Conservative, Republican, Tory, and Traditionalist party forces. Only the Green movement and party, in West Germany, stands significantly apart from this divided spectrum, and even this party-movement frequently associates with the Social Democratic Party. Single-issue movements and groups tend to be concerned with narrow issues. Yet, members of these movements usually have affinities with other groups and with a political party that they support. In some circumstances, these movements operate as pressure groups affecting party politics. In other instances, they recruit voters or act on behalf of their party. In still other cases, they independently foster the causes of their own group. The proliferation of single-issue movements has split society in many new ways, dividing it into large camps of associated groups and individuals. Each camp professes a common moral and ideological value orientation, and each espouses a different philosophy.

The old political split, with the conservatives and the Right on one side and the liberals and the Left on the other, was chiefly along class-interest lines. The new division, more vertical or diagonal, is incorporating individuals of all classes, all walks of life, and reflects differences in philosophies.

The outstanding philosophical issue exerting a determining influence on the position of parties, groups, and citizens concerns the role of the state. In some instances, this concern appears in combination with differences of opinion over matters related to equity and equality. Movements on the liberal, socialist, Left list generally believe that collective interests ought to prevail over individual aspirations. They may express dislike for bureaucracy, but they expect the state to implement their causes and generally favor greater state involvement in the affairs of society. Conservative parties and groups on the conservative, Right list, advocate freedom as the chief ethical principle to be upheld—freedom for private enterprise foremost. Oakeshott (1962, 43) expresses their attitude thus:

> Of the many species of liberty which compose the freedom we enjoy, each amplifying and making more secure the whole, we have long recognized the importance of two: the freedom of association, and the freedom enjoyed in the right to own private property. A third species of liberty is often set beside these two: freedom of speech.

Consequently, conservatives call for the reduction of the state's role in society, but not the "minimal state," writes Scruton, (1984), Elliot and McCrone, (1987, 499), and others. Conservatives call for a return to more traditional ways of life and the maintenance of a traditional market economy.[1] Only small minorities within each camp profess extreme views and demands on the subject of state control. Most members of society tend to be to a degree liberal or conservative; i.e., liberal or conservative in certain regards. Depending on their current concerns, they elect Left, liberal, or conservative representatives to legislative bodies and other authority structures. Economists are divided into monetarists and supply-siders on one side, neokeynesians and post-keynesians on the other, along corresponding lines of controversy. Nell (1983) illuminates the positions of the two principal economic camps. The controversy appears especially vivid perhaps not so much among philosophers but in the field of philosophy.

The liberal mode of thought, or rather, the principles of contemporary liberal philosophy, on income distribution and the state's role in managing society and the economy seems best reflected in John Rawls' *A Theory of Justice* (1971). If a liberal fundamentalism is conceivable, Rawls represents it. He does not discuss principles of actual practice or rules to be followed in daily activity. His treatise concerns principles of pure ethics. Rawls is the only philosopher to have come up with such a fundamental work on liberal principles. It is, in my opinion, a very important work, since it reflects on the orientation that other liberal thinkers and practitioners express and promote, though in less fundamental, more moderate, pragmatic, and pedestrian forms. Rawls' work proclaims ethical principles for a pure liberal society. It is not meant to be a book about the principles the actual society currently follows or should follow.

No comparable contemporary work representing the conservative mode of thought has yet been written. One can refer to Burke, Oakeshott, or William F. Buckley in presenting a contrasting conservative approach. I have chosen *Statecraft as Soulcraft* (1983), by George Will, to represent the conservative position. Will may be considered insufficiently representative of the conservative position, yet, of the currently available philosophical works representing the conservative mode of thought on income distribution and the role of state, his book is not only the best and most comprehensive, but thematically well matches Rawls' work.

In Rawls' writing, several philosophical traditions can be distinguished. Like philosophers in the eighteenth century, Rawls and other liberal and socialist thinkers of today call for a new social contract.[2] The first debate ever over this idea was launched on the eve of the emergence of capitalist economies and the new democratic political order. Hobbes, Locke, and Rousseau, the principal champions of the social contract theory, did not propose any concrete reforms. Instead, they philosophized over principles and ideals. They wrote about a "society of justice without which there can be no peace," "the restored ideal state of nature . . . in which all the power and jurisdiction is reciprocal, no one having more than another," the civil society in which "each would depend on the whole." Each of these thinkers was inspired by different motivations. Hobbes, in *Leviathan* (1969, 102–103) felt that, under the "Commonwealth" and "Distributive Justice" that he envisioned, a covenant would be instituted. He posited equality under authoritarian rule. Locke (Second Treatise, 97, after Gough 1963, 140; see also Locke, Hume, Rousseau, 1970) believed that all citizens are entitled to enjoy the natural rights of "life, liberty and estate." According to Locke: "On becoming a citizen, . . . a man surrenders all his natural rights, and `puts himself under an obligation to everyone of that society to submit to the determination of the majority and to be concluded by it.'" Rousseau insisted that, by enacting the social contract, people would agree that the "general will" was superior to their own "private will." His pronouncements can be interpreted as meaning that one ought to give up liberty in exchange for equality.

All three philosophers advocated an interactional structure of equality. They were preceded in this line by some Protestant religious groups, who had incorporated ideas of equality into certain community relationships as a foundation to their relationship with God. But these Protestants also believed that a true Christian equality would ensue only with the restoration of pristine rules of the religion. Mill, Locke, and Rousseau developed a secular rationale for a new order of equality. They constantly referred to "natural facts," "natural tendencies," and "the natural state of affairs." Rousseau recognized that people can eliminate only "moral or political inequality." Inequality resulting from what he termed "natural or physical . . . qualities of mind and soul" are impossible to countermand. Most social contract theorists employed the idea of contract metaphorically. Others believed that some kind of social contract must have been actually concluded between rulers and the ruled. They considered their societies to represent "the fallen state of nature," as Locke expressed it. These theorists felt that justice demanded the restoration of the old contract or reorganization under a reconstituted version.

Rawls writes in this tradition. His efforts to restructure the world are rooted in the concept of justice rather than in the intention to restore society to any imagined notion of its natural condition. Nonetheless, his argument simply rephrases the old contractarian concerns and demands, this time as an ethical quest for equity. In this sense, *A Theory of Justice* is a new proclamation of demands voiced in the past. But from the perspective of our analysis, it is more important that Rawls announces a manifesto of pure liberal ideals, and most of all represents an extreme but clear liberal position in the debate over entitlements, remunerations, and privileges, a position uncontaminated by mundane concerns, such as how to win an election. In the name of justice, Rawls presses his readers to maximize the allocation of entitlements, at the expense of remunerations, and thus maximize justice, as he interprets it. He disregards the obvious: Such a distribution could only operate under a bureaucracy, and in such an instance would engender a new system of privileges. Rawls neglects this problem because it is separate from the philosophical concerns preoccupying him. *Fiat iustitia, et pereat mundus* (Justice is to be done, and let the world perish)!

Published in 1971, Rawls' book was widely and emotionally debated in certain academic circles. The large list of books espousing its content or criticizing Rawls' position (Daniels 1975; Barry 1975; Wolff 1977; Schaefer 1979; Wellbank 1982; Rex 1985; H.G. Blocker & Smith 1980) testifies to the perceived importance of the work and the amount of interest it generated. Critics point out that Rawls' principles, postulated as elements for the foundation of a new social contract, are simultaneously too abstract to provide guidance in a concrete situation, and too reflective of the ideals of the New Deal, the Great Society, and the general dominant moral and ideological concerns of liberalism to represent such general pure principles as they are designed to represent. They criticize him for failing to formulate a reasonable, concrete plan of action for achieving the objectives outlined in his principles. As one critic, Schaefer (1979, 56–57), writes:

> His standards of a just political economy require nothing more than a competitive market system, government sponsorship of education to promote "equal chances of education and culture *for the person similarly endowed and motivated*," progressive taxation, and the guarantee of a "social minimum" through such devices as social security or a "negative income tax." . . . But Rawls has formulated no meaningful principles; he has merely endorsed the policies of the modern welfare state as appealing to his sense of justice. The fact that he has furnished no standards by which one could determine whether an actual inequality is or is not unjust according to his principles does not prevent him, however, from taking the opportunity to denounce "the injustice of existing institutions."

Other critics express similar opinions. These attacks are not entirely fair, however. Rawls is not a practitioner. Philosophers of the past who called for a new social contract and exerted an inspiring influence on the French Revolution, are not held culpable for lacking concrete plans outlining how to implement their postulates of justice. Still, though they were not blamed for lack of insight or practical acumen at the time they launched their ideals, they inspired many to revolt. A philosopher does not govern. He or she discovers and interprets the substance and purpose of that part of human creativity that is neither entirely godly nor entirely pedestrian, but has a separate, strictly human significance. Philosophers work to discover and adjure any special human meaning, such as a moral purpose extending beyond the individual, one to which only groups and nations can aspire. The import of Rawls' work consists in discovering and interpreting for practitioners the substance of liberal moral objectives and moral principles. Rawls should not be obliged to discuss concrete "ways of improving things." Besides, as his critics have noted, the status quo, universal suffrage, the welfare system, government- sponsored education, and progressive taxation do not satisfy Rawls. Therefore, he chooses an ongoing process toward a more fundamental distributive justice and equality, to be pursued until no one is entitled to more "primary goods" than others, and all the populace can enjoy life, property, happiness, self-respect, liberties, and other "goods" equally. Whether this can be implemented is another question. Rawls' concern is reminiscent of Rousseau's plea for the maximization of equality. The difference is that Rawls presents his argument in the form of a Kantian categorical imperative (Wicclair 1980). Rawls' general conception of justice for institutions runs as follows (1971, 303): "All social primary goods—liberty and opportunity, income and wealth, and the bases of self respect—shall be distributed equally unless an unequal distribution of any or all of these goods is to be to the advantage of the least favored."

The arguments raised in support of this postulate crisscross all of Rawls' book. At one point he implies: If you are honest and serious about what you say, if you have a morality at all, then you should adopt my principles and implement my philosophy in your daily practice.[3] Finally, Rawls (302) proclaims two uncompromising principles of his justice:

> *First Principle.* Each person is to have the right to the most extensive total system of equal basic liberties compatible with a similar system of liberty for all. *Second Principle.* Social and economic inequalities are to be arranged so that they are both: (a) to the greatest benefit of the least advantaged, consistent with the just savings principle, and (b) attached to offices and positions open to all under conditions of fair equality of opportunity.

According to what are rather complex "priority rules," the first principle takes priority over the second; and point (b) of the second principle supercedes point (a) of that principle. By asserting the priority of the first principle while emphasizing the priority of civil rights, Rawls raises the value of equal basic liberties above self-respect. Both these rights are proclaimed much more precious than other "primary goods," such as wealth and power. Both critics and admirers write that the rationale Rawls offers for his hierarchies is quite confusing, and not entirely altruistic. On one hand, he seems to predicate instituting a high degree of equality in respect to the less important "primary goods" through effective redistribution. At the same time, by proclaiming the priority of civil and political rights over other "primary goods," Rawls affirms, in Barry's (1975, 31) words, that civil liberties "are themselves the direct and immediate means to the realization of central goals in life held by (almost) all people." Then he announces the priority of equal liberties. The question of whether there could be true equality in civil rights and liberty without a preceding equality in distribution of other "primary goods" remains unanswered.

Critics agree, to again use Barry's words (164), that "Rawls does not suggest ways of improving things."[4] Moreover, in contrast to radical-left theorists, Rawls acknowledges that both socialist and capitalist societies could be just, if they were to redistribute to the general benefit of the least advantaged. He seems to believe that equity and equality are not fixed entities. Like certain revolutionary fundamentalists who advocate permanent revolution, Rawls believes in permanent redistribution, up until no one feels himself to be less equal than anyone else. In Rawls' opinion, only this striving deserves the name of Justice. The question persists: Can such equality exist in practice? But Rawls is not interested in practice; he announces pure principles. In view of all this, de Jasay (1985, 154) raises the following point:

> The irony of it all is that had Rawls not tried and failed to prove in the doing, that a theory of distributive justice is possible, it would be much easier to go on believing that universalist claim for democratic values, i.e., (in essence) that equality is valuable because it is the *means to the undisputed final ends* of justice or utility or perhaps liberty, too, and hence it is rational to choose it. Rawls had made it easier for non-democrats to cry that the Emperor has no clothes.

Justice is often portrayed as a blindfolded woman holding scales. Rawls' justice is no different. An observer of contemporary conditions can easily anticipate what would happen in a society governed under Rawls' new social contract. Rewards for work, prudent investment, creative activity, and innovations would not only transfer to the disadvantaged, but would be appropriated in the form of privileges, perks, and benefits of power by the distributors, regulators, lawyers, and other officials of this new justice. Such a system of advanced redistribution would reduce and eliminate incentives to produce more "primary goods," such as income and wealth, food and housing, liberty, opportunity, and, eventually, self-respect. It would eliminate the old inequality only to produce a new inequality. This has already become evident in the recent history of many nations that have attempted to establish a system of continuous redistribution, and one much less rigorous than the one Rawls proposes. Liberal practitioners do not go as far in their demands as Rawls does. They differ among themselves on how far to advance redistribution. Whether 10 or 15 percent of GNP is to be redistributed, as at present, or more, the state is to be involved in implementing this redistribution.

The other camp in the controversy over the role of the state in society is most adequately represented by conservative economists of the monetary and supply-side schools. As mentioned, *Statecraft as Soulcraft* (1983) by George Will, a work concerned with moral principles and philosophy from a conservative perspective, seems most suited for contrasting with the liberal viewpoint. Some conservatives find that Will "sounds like a closet liberal." Opposing such opinions, Goodman, in a *New York Times* review of the book, observes that Will still "remains a deep-dyed conservative, and his main strictures are directed at liberals who are quick to use the powers of the state to satisfy the hour's desires but not to enhance our moral condition, which he believes is gravely imperiled." Like Rawls, Will speaks of justice and moral dimensions. He posits that, under contemporary conditions, the welfare system ought to be sustained. However, instead of accepting the liberal perspective, he refers to the classical conservative rationale and conservative practice. This intertwines with a strong defense of liberty as a fundamental moral imperative. Will proposes no new principles of justice comparable to those introduced by Rawls. Will is quite pragmatic. He writes (138):

> A society determined to have rapid economic growth through predominantly private market mechanisms must provide the requisite rewards for the persons most proficient at generating wealth. That means inequality. A just society is not one in which the allocation of wealth, opportunity, authority and status is equal. Rather, it is one in which inequalities are reasonably related to reasonable social goals. Therefore justice, as well as elementary utilitarian considerations, requires a hierarchy of achievement. Furthermore, equality, when defined in terms of rights derivative from possessions, is not conducive to community. And questions as to how much equality of material condition society needs or morality demands of the economy can stand are less interesting than this question: How equal a distribution of ideas and sentiments is needed for social cohesion and all that derives from it? Such decisions depend on a revised sense of citizenship.

A new social contract? Not according to Will. Will pins his faith on self-interest. He believes in a society governed under the principle that (60): "Every individual can be a self-constituting creature, manufacturing himself by choosing purposes and values by whatever principle he wishes from the universe of possibilities." Of the many concerns voiced by Will, two predominate: freedom, and statecraft as soulcraft, understood as a moral dimension of governance. He acknowledges that the state is inevitably coercive; thus, freedom and the state's authority, in a sense, oppose one another. Will affirms the need for both, but only "up to a point."

Will posits (93-95):

> All politics takes place on a slippery slope. The most important four words in politics are "up to a point." Are we in favor of free speech? Of course—up to a point. Are we for liberty, equality, military strength, industrial vigor, environmental protection, traffic safety? Up to a point. . . . It is about the point up to which we want to go in pursuit of a good that may, at some point, conflict with other goods. . . . The aim is not to make society inhospitable to pluralism, but to make pluralism safe for society. . . . Although something calling itself conservatism has become known for its hostility to government, the hostility only underscores this conservatism's kinship with liberalism. . . . But it is a *non sequitur* to say that because the state has a monopoly on legitimate coercion, its essence is coercion, actual

and latent. . . . Proper . . . conservatism teaches that authority grows organically from the rich loam of social mores and structures.

Will represents the moderate conservative position. One can describe it metaphorically as follows: One ought to have the right to use fire, but not to the extent where one would set fire to one's neighbor's or one's own home, endangering the safety of others or causing damage to property. Next, Will explains his notion of justice (93). As one would expect, it differs fundamentally from Rawls':

> There is only one political good that we should not speak of wanting only 'up to a point.' It is the central political value, justice. But then, justice consists of pursuing other political values—such as freedom and virtue—only up to appropriate points.

Will recognizes that the conflict over greater equity and greater liberty may be unsolvable but, recognizing the importance of these strivings, recommends pursuing them *up to the point* where the maximum of each can be achieved. According to Will, man should be guided by both reason and passion, each *up to a point*. In striking contrast to Rawls and perhaps to extreme conservatives as well, he recognizes the need for passion in striving for freedom, equality, justice; for passion but for reason as well, so that passion does not become tyranny, a new form of inequality and injustice.

Whereas Rawls uses a single rationale—justice—to advocate the welfare system, Will advances several justifications. He recalls (126) Disraeli and Bismarck, who pioneered the welfare state, and points out that their initiative was driven by "impeccably conservative reasons: to reconcile the masses to the vicissitudes and hazards of a dynamic and hierarchical industrial economy." Will maintains that:

> Today, the conservative affirmation of the welfare state should be grounded on, and conservative purposes for the welfare state should be derived from, three additional considerations. They are considerations of prudence, intellectual integrity and equity. A welfare state is certainly important to, and probably indispensable to, social cohesion, and hence to national strength.[5]

Discussion of these two moralities and philosophies serves not only to report the discord within philosophical circles, but to portray the two principal philosophies at the root of the conflict structure of etatized societies. That this conflict focuses on entitlements, remunerations, and privileges—more generally, income distribution and the role of the state in administering it—distinguishes these works from others discussing the central conflict characterizing strictly capitalist societies. The fact that corporatist theorists, many still essentially Marxist, are shifting their principal concern from aspects of class struggle to aspects of intermediation within the state, or that they portray intermediation as the old class struggle still continuing, demonstrates the transition from capitalism to postcapitalism: Progress means advancing change and nothing else. How have they not noticed that a new class conflict is developing, that between "regular Joes" turned into salariat and "super Josephs" emerging as the new elite?

Equality

During the last hundred years, throughout the West, no cause was ever so widely supported as that of universal equality. Equality was inscribed on the banners of most European revolutionary movements as the principal condition for social justice; it was postulated in the programs of various political parties and proclaimed in the constitutions of many nations as an essential right. Equality was recognized not only as a fundamental ethical principal and, to an extent, the legal norm, but also as a most noble objective in the quest for human progress. At different times and to different people, the ideal carried different meanings and different interpretations. At the end of the eighteenth century, equality was seen primarily as necessary to the abolition of the privileges and birthrights of the nobility. People struggled to institute legal equality for all and to develop a democratic system, based on universal enfranchisement. It was hoped that equal representation would naturally foster other forms of equalization and economic progress. Later, the emphasis of the struggle shifted, becoming transformed into a striving against discrimination on the basis of creed, belief, race, or sex. Toward the end of the 1960s and during the 1970s, demands for equality fused with other issues raised by the anti–Vietnam War, environmental protection, feminist, various ethnic, and Black movements.

Two phenomena should be noted. First, though the struggle for equality abolished numerous concretely specified inequalities, this did not trigger the birth of any society practicing universal equality. While it did not eliminate various forms of inequalities in Western capitalist societies, it brought about a set of conditions under which a larger section of the population enjoys much greater equality of opportunity and in which individuals are, at least formally, treated without prejudice in public affairs. Simultaneously, it involved larger circles of the population in increasing competition for entitlements and privileges. Inequality continued, and society divided into those who feel that achieved equality is insignificant and those who assert that only a limited equality, in definite areas, or relative equality, can be achieved at all. Second, while the cause of equality was continually held up as an ethical cause, its significance gradually shifted from a predominantly political and social to an economic interpretation. The concepts of the original struggle for equality remain valid and are still fought for today. They are, however, superseded by struggles for specific entitlements, rights, goods, services, positions, and welfare benefits provided by the state.

People have always disagreed, still disagree, and will continue to disagree over the moral postulates of equity and equality. Under etatization, the state is expected to advance the cause of equality and equity. It is also expected to protect the market economy and other structures engendering inequality if not inequity. A great many of the newly acquired state functions have been developed to implement equity and advance equality. What results may we observe?

1. Conditions of greater equality, as under etatization, necessitate not fewer, but more conflicts and competition.

2. The practice of equality entails instituting laws, rules, norms, and standards that define the meaning and scope of equality and the entitlements of citizens in given conditions, specifically. Society must also create rules to regulate competition for goods and services and evaluate claims for entitlements from newly emerging groups. It must solve disagreements over the institution of equality and the allocation of scarce positions and goods that cannot be distributed equally to all.

3. The practice of equality, particularly in a large society with a variety of interest groups, requires that some people become regulators and intermediators. Consequently, equality engenders new forms of inequality. The new class of regulators who supervise the maintenance of equality also produces the cause of new inequalities, inherent in its own existence.

Contemporary society must strive to maximize equality and equal opportunity. However, growth and development advance through specialization, differentiation, and expanding interdependence. These and other improvement-generating processes simultaneously reproduce inequality. Furthermore, society is obliged to recognize and reward talent, effort, loyalty, and other virtues, again perpetuating inequalities. The present controversy among conservatives, liberals, and other ideological groups rests thus on different opinions and sentiments as to what type of equality is affordable, which entitlements are essential, and how to lower the cost of government—the costs of maintaining regulators, distributors, inspectors, etc.

Briefly, equality and inequality are dialectically interrelated; any system of equality includes actual inequalities and breeds new ones. Tawney, Wilson, and a number of other writers maintain that, though equality is a noble goal, to strive for anything more than the maximization of equal opportunities is unrealistic. In a real human society, full equalization of the populace is unattainable. To quote Tawney, (1964, 102; see also Wilson 1966, 40, 58, 83, 153; and Rees 1971, 19–22): "Rightly interpreted, equality means not the absence of violent contrasts in income condition, but equal opportunities of becoming unequal."

There exist other, more restrictive limits to particular instances of equality. The degree of equal opportunity a society may offer depends not only on the prevailing understanding of social justice and the good intentions of the populace, but also on the level of technological and economic development.

Obviously, only the wealthy industrialized nations are able to generate enough funds to sustain developed systems of services available to all, and to assist pensioners, students, the jobless, the ill, and other needy people, while maintaining the ability to create new jobs, develop new industries and resources, and offer a relatively high standard of living to the population at large.

Contrary to the assumptions of natural law theorists, people are not born equal. Nature does not create people equal or unequal, but alike. At the same time, it endows each human being with different qualities or potentials. Society attributes greater or lesser importance to qualifications, rewarding some and not others. Society further develops notions and conditions of inequality and equality. The public at large is generally appalled by poverty, and resents injustices, but does not necessarily believe in the dream of a society of equals. People develop different aspirations. They usually desire equality, particularly with those higher in the social hierarchy. But they also wish to retain their uniqueness and individuality. Thus, they detest the kind of equalization that restricts their uniqueness and distinctive individual development. Hirsch raises this issue in his *Social Limits to Growth* (1978, 5, 6, 106, 134–136, 188), where he stresses that:

> Opportunities for economic advances, as they present themselves to one person after another, do not constitute equivalent opportunities for economic advance by all. What each of us achieves, all cannot.

> What is possible for the single individual is not possible for all individuals—would not be possible even if they all possessed equal talent.

He defines these, and other, mostly psychological attitudes, as conditions that socially limit growth. He also admonishes the reader that the value of scarce items decreases as they become more widely available. New items of scarcity are then invented or recognized. Equally rewarding all raises the general level of satisfaction with conditions in society but "brings mass consumption to the point where it causes problems of congestion in the widest sense—bluntly, where consumption or job-holding by others tend to crowd you out—then the key to personal welfare is again the ability to stay out of the crowd." As a consequence, competition has crept to a higher and more important level. It now involves more and more people struggling over more and more goods and positions.[6]

The etatized society inherited from capitalism the now-traditional conflict over ownership of means of production. Conflicts over privileges and over excessive state control limiting initiatives and growth are principal in socialist societies. These conflicts, too, albeit to a much smaller degree, are beginning to be manifest in contemporary Western societies. Under etatization, conflicts over the role of the state in providing equity become cardinal. The Left advocates maximizing redistribution until ultimate equality is achieved. More moderate liberals set the limit at the point at which discrimination is erased, poverty is abolished, and the needy are provided for. The Right believes that equity entails inequality. It advocates improvement, through economic growth and development and through market expansion. The new contrariety over the role of the state in reducing and regulating inequality currently constitutes the fundamental conflict of the new condition.

Economic and Political Systems of Western Nations: Typology

The Soviet Union and Eastern European nations within its sphere of control were etatized by decree, under the grand Marxist plan aimed at transforming capitalist into socialist societies. The processes of etatization in Western Europe, the United States, Canada, and Japan have advanced by, among other things, applying Keynesian and neokeynesian remedies to social and economic conditions, developing social services, subordinating the national economy to state control, and transforming single-sector economies into mixed economies. These nations remain capitalist in that they continue to recognize the right to own private property and engage in money-making in the market, but also submit capitalism to control and regulation by the state. Western societies are also democratic, in that they are run under political systems that involve two or more political parties competing for control of the polity and votes of the electorate, and because governments in these nations are obliged to act according to codes of law that not only define the rights of citizens but limit the power of authority.[1] Currently, a new property of democracy has developed: Western societies have recognized the right of all citizens to services and some essential material entitlements, provided by society in instances when citizens are not able to take care of their own basic needs.

Characteristics of the New State vary from nation to nation. Expectations and developments have everywhere been similar, focusing on the control of poverty, unemployment, and other social problems, and the maintenance of balanced economic growth. But because of different initial economic conditions, diversity of cultures, and differences in objectives pursued by governments, etatization differs from one society to the next. The size and wealth of a nation are also important, because they determine the magnitude of effects from comparable reforms.

At present, Western industrialized nations are to different degrees capitalist, democratic, and etatized. This chapter attempts to develop a typological scheme accounting for the similarities, dissimilarities, and varying degrees of etatization measured by political authority and economic organization. A graded scheme seems to suit this objective best. I shall begin by discussing certain ideas to be employed as qualifiers.

Similarity and Dissimilarity

Inkeles' (1981) convergence/divergence theory provides an illuminating instrument to measure the aspect of similarity/dissimilarity of etatized societies. His theory (8–13) was intended as a tool for comparing converging and diverging nations across the world, but especially compares Western and Soviet-bloc industrialized nations. Inkeles' study discerns five levels of similarity/dissimilarity resulting from convergence/divergence processes:

1. Modes of production and patterns of resource utilization
2. Institutional arrays and institutional forms
3. Structures of patterns of social relationships
4. Systems of popular attitudes, values, and behavior
5. Systems of political and economic control

Inkeles (23) asserts that "divergence is most dramatically illustrated in the realm of production and the generation of physical wealth [and] of institutional patterns." He lists numerous other divergences, acknowledging (24), "Convergence toward a common point is not a guarantee that once two or more systems come to be alike they will continue to be alike."

Inkeles' convergence/divergence theory can be suitably applied to discuss the processes of convergence and persisting divergences among Western nations. His five levels, or points of convergence, are sufficiently comprehensive; no amendments are necessary for our purposes. The only difference between the present application of this scheme in comparing nations of the West and of the world is a question of scale. Convergence within the sphere of Western nations on one side, and within the Soviet-bloc nations on the other, is obviously stronger than convergence between the two blocs as a whole. Nonetheless, divergences persist within each bloc and are even greater between the two systems.

The history of convergence, while preserving divergences, stretches over two millennia in the West. Integration began under the Roman Empire, which allowed conquered territories to retain divergent aspects of their sociopolitical cultures. The Middle Ages produced another form of convergence with divergences intact, instituted by the Church. During the Renaissance and Enlightenment, a new platform of divergence within growing civilizational convergence was created. Throughout recent history, Western nations have retained divergent interests and cultures despite converging capitalist economic interdependencies.

The West, including the United States, Canada, Japan, and Western Europe, is currently experiencing a new stage of the continuing convergence/divergence process, manifest in the various similarities and dissimilarities of the evolution of state functions. Centrifugal forces are manifest in the widespread adoption of common values, and in similar patterns of economic development and interdependency, which became particularly evident during the stock-market crash in October 1987. TNCs can be considered as advancing convergence processes. Despite the Common Market, economic and military cooperation, and alliances linking Western nations, divergences have not been erased, however. Of the nations considered in this book, each has an economy based, to an extent, on different principles and subject to differing methods of state control. Our comparison commences with a typology that discerns certain principal subtypes and designs of etatization.

Covariation Methodology

The methodology of comparative analysis employed in this book was originally designed by Durkheim in *The Rules of Sociological Method*.[2] Durkheim distinguished this methodology from quantitative or empirical analyses that limit the plurality of questions and investigate only a select number of variables of construed hypotheses. To further delineate the difference and contrast it with methods employing quantifiable variables, Durkheim (1966, 133) described the method of comparative study as "one which studies co-variations" or "concomitant variations." In his own works, he employed both methods.

The present inquiry attempts a synchronic analysis of societies similar in many important respects but different in others.[3] Several factors are taken into consideration. Each society is classified as capitalist. Each operates a welfare system and has been subordinated to direct and indirect economic regulatory controls by the state. Each can be characterized as having a market economy under state management. In addition, each nation has both a public and private sector. In certain societies, such as Western Europe and Canada, the state owns a large part of the economy. Here, the public sector—in this study the concept is employed in a broad sense—consists of state-owned enterprises, services, and welfare institutions. In others, such as the United States and Japan, the state owns few industries. In small democracies, such as Austria, Switzerland (see Katzenstein 1984), and perhaps Israel and Denmark, state and society are closely integrated; the party in power and the opposition cooperate. Decisions of the state reflect more the continually changing national consensus attained in (135) "the intricate political bargaining between all forces in society, than the position of the party which won the majority of votes in the elections." Some Western nations to a greater, others to a lesser degree strive to develop a redistributive society. Each retains culture and traditions particular to itself. Thus, each experiences etatization differently.

The analytical study of the transmutation of capitalist into etatized societies can utilize quantitative and/or qualitative approaches.[4] Not all processes of change and transformation can be portrayed by statistical data, however. Certain aspects of development cannot be quantitatively analyzed and permit only qualitative conclusions. This book represents, mostly, the qualitative approach. Results of quantitative analyses are employed whenever available and applicable.

The typology below depicts some basic divergences between subtypes of converging Western societies. While recognizing the many similarities and distinctions in the etatization processes of Western societies, an attempt is made to portray the position of each within an arrangement delineated by two gradational polarities: one between *authoritarian regimes* and *polyarchy*, the other between *free-market economy* and *command-systems economy*, as in the scheme developed by Lindblom.

Typology of Etatized Western Societies

The two scales, represented by axes (see Table 5.2), employed in the typology of etatized societies must be explained: The horizontal (a—b) scale discerns the principal subtypes of Western etatized societies. This scale can also be regarded as a convergence/divergence axis. The vertical (x—z) axis presents the polyarchy-versus-authoritarianism scale and was adopted from Lindblom (1977). Comparing Western and Communist regimes, Lindblom points out that societies run under two systems of control: the market and the government. The current central issue, he asserts, concerns the degree of control exercised by the market versus the government. Any national system can be classified from either a political or economic perspective. Lindblom combines the two.

Lindblom (161) writes that, from an economic point of view, all systems can be divided into: (*a*) market-oriented systems (not exclusive of authority), and (*b*) centralized authority and preceptoral "systems" (not exclusive of markets). Certain political scientists distinguish between (x) polyarchic and (y) authoritarian systems of authority.

"Polyarchy," says Lindblom (132), "is not a social system. Nor, strictly speaking, is it a political system. It is only part of a political system: a set of authoritative rules, together with certain patterns of political behavior that follow directly and indirectly from the existence of the rules."[5] He remarks further (131) that "to these systems tradition gives the name liberal democracy." According to Lindblom, roughly thirty out of 144 nations belong to this category. Because Portugal, Spain, Argentina, and Brazil

Table 5.1 Lindblom's Politicoeconomic Systems

	Polyarchic	*Authoritarian*
Market-oriented systems (not exclusive of authority)	All polyarchic systems: North America, Western European, and others.	Most of the world's systems: including Yugoslavia, Spain, Portugal, most of Latin America, new African nations, the Middle East except Israel, and all of noncommunist Asia except Japan
Centralized authority and preceptoral systems (not exclusive of market)		Communist systems except Yugoslavia and perhaps Hungary; Nazi Germany

Source: Adapted from Charles E. Lindblom, *Politics and Markets* (New York: Basic Books, 1977), 161. Reprinted with permission of the publisher.

recently joined the ranks of democracies, roughly thirty-five nations presently constitute this group. Employing these criteria in a two-by-two scheme, Lindblom develops a four-block classification. But, because in practice no polyarchic structures operating under a centralized economic authority and preceptoral "systems" exist, he (161) distinguishes only three types of actually existing politicoeconomic systems:

1. "All polyarchic systems: North American, Western European, and others," considered the First World by some other writers
2. "Most of the world's systems, including Yugoslavia, Spain, Portugal, most of Latin America, new African nations, the Middle East, and all of noncommunist Asia except Japan"—in other words —the Third World
3. "Communist systems except Yugoslavia and perhaps Hungary [and] Nazi-Germany," called the Second World by some, totalitarian regimes by others

The present study modifies this scheme. The tripartite division of the first, second, and third kinds of nations is accepted, but instead of taut polarities, the polyarchy-versus-authoritarian axis is regarded as reflecting

ble 5.2 Industrialized Nations Under Etatization, 1985-1986: Typology

1	2	3	4	5	6	7
One-sector		Two-sector, mixed economies				One-sector
			Redistributive economies			
				Centrally planned economies		
Minimally regulated, free-enterprise, capitalist systems	State-regulated capitalist systems	State-managed capitalist economies with developed welfare systems	State-managed mixed economies developing redistributive systems	State-managed mixed economies with elements of selective central planning	Hypothetical state-managed mixed economites with a dominant state sector under central planning and state management	Command-system economies under central planning

Chile

Taiwan

South Korea

Brazil

Argentina

Mexico

Spain

Portugal

Japan

Italy

Norway *Austria*

United States *Canada* *West Germany* *Sweden* *Australia* *Switzerland*

Netherlands

Great Britain *France*

A B C D

Direction of change aspired to in Eastern European rebellions

USSR, Romania, Bulgaria, Czechoslovakia

Hungary *Poland*

Yugoslavia

Ideal advocated by some socialist theorists

gradational qualities of political systems. In other words, from our perspective, political systems are to a degree polyarchic or authoritarian. The *x—y* axis measures their proximal qualification. The other qualifier, the market-versus-central-management or command-control-economy scale is depicted by gradation on the *a—b* axis. Some Western nations retain a more traditional market orientation than others. But, since they are all to a degree etatized and maintain welfare systems and services, these nations are regarded as New States. In fact, no presently existing nation allows for a completely uncontrolled and unregulated market economy. Even the previous existence of such economies is now regarded as doubtful. The free-market economy actually implied economies with minimal state control. The ratio of state-to-market control in any nation, including Soviet-bloc countries, is presently in flux. During the 1960s and 1970s, state control over Western economies increased. In the 1980s, this process appears to have stalled. Despite denationalization and privatization efforts by some governments, there is no doubt that state control over the market, which was previously minimal, is currently significant. Account must be taken in new typologies both of the degree to which economies are managed and the degree to which they are owned by the state; these characteristics may not coincide. Extremes range from instances of market economies with no state control to completely state-controlled economies. Even in the Soviet Union, under the command system, the economy is not fully state-controlled. Under Gorbachev's reforms, which have decentralized control to an extent, the economy will remain state-controlled as before, but might comprise a dominant state sector and a small private sector, legalized after fifty years of formal nonexistence.

Seven subtypes of societies can be discerned, as seen in Tables 5.2 and 5.3. Five of these are etatized to different degrees and in varying regards. Not a single society is included under the heading of minimally regulated, free-enterprise capitalist systems.

The Soviet Union and Eastern European nations are listed under the heading of command-system economies under central planning. Yugoslavia is set somewhat apart. Indeed, I have been advised, with some merit, to exclude Yugoslavia from this heading altogether. The sixth subtype was reserved, however, for hypothetical or possible systems that have not yet emerged; Yugoslavia could not be positioned there.

The contemporary state has been transformed from a principally political to an equally strong economic force; it is as engrossed by economic and social matters as by political issues. In the Soviet Union and other Eastern European countries, the state is also involved in cultural matters. In Western nations, however, the cultural sphere remains nearly free from direct state involvement. Because of important changes in the functions of the state and the corresponding increase in the dependence of the economy on the political system, and vice versa, the division between polyarchic democracy and authoritarianism is no longer an adequate classification of the political organization of society. The classification involving political criteria must be complemented with the economic classification. Together, such a typology offers a tool for characterizing and comparing the political and economic structures of contemporary nations.

The seven subtypes of economies discussed by the typology are:

1. Minimally controlled, free-enterprise, capitalist systems (hypothetically speaking, non-etatized capitalist economies)
2. State-regulated capitalist systems
3. State-regulated/managed capitalist economies with welfare systems
4. State-managed, two-sector economies with developed services, social security systems, and welfare organization (some, particularly Scandinavian countries, have also attempted to institute advanced redistributive systems with the objective of reducing inequality)
5. State-managed, two-sector economies with elements of selective central planning and small nations under democratic corporatism
6. State-managed redistributive, two-sector economies with a dominant state sector under central planning (hypothetically, this is the future of certain Western European nations)
7. Command-system economies

It is assumed that etatized societies can operate under varying degrees of political authoritarian or democratic (polyarchic, in Lindblom's terminology) systems. The Communist nations, which maintain centrally planned and centrally directed command-system economies under authoritarian regimes, are listed in the top right corner of Table 5.2.

Western nations, which maintain state-controlled and state-regulated market economies, are listed in the lower, central part of Table 5.2. (Third World nations are not examined in this book. However, most of these nations would fit in different locations of the upper central and left corners of the scheme.)

Typological subtypes were discerned according to estimations of:

(a) State involvement in the management of national economy
(b) Size of the state-owned sector in relation to the private sector
(c) Dependency of the population on jobs, services, and transfer payments provided by the government
(d) degree of central planning in the management of society

Tables 5.2 and 5.3 illustrate this scheme; its limited use is recognized. It is hoped the tables in this chapter will serve as a visual reference, orienting the reader toward a comprehensive idea of the wide mosaic of etatized societies and where each stands. Yet, the accuracy of these estimates is by no

Table 5.3 Capitalist Economies Changing Into State-Controlled and State-Managed Economies: Characteristics of Etatization

	1	2	3	4	5	6	7
	Minimally regulated, free-enterprise, capitalist systems	State-regulated capitalist systems	State-managed capitalist economies with developed welfare systems	State-managed mixed economies developing redistributive systems	State-managed mixed economies with elements of selective central planning	Hypothetical state-managed mixed economies with a dominant state sector under central planning and state management	Command-system economies under central planning
	One-sector		Two-sector, mixed economies			Centrally planned economies	One sector
				Redistributive economies			
State involvement in management	None	Minimal	Increasing state involvement in regulating the economy by direct and indirect means; developed public services	Strong state involvement in the economy, both in directing the state sector and the economy as a whole — Direct and indirect regulation of the economy with the objective of attaining wider redistribution of income	Especially strong involvement in directing strategically important industries	Hypothetically close to complete control and direction of the economy by the state; small private sector	Complete state control over the economy; entire economy operates under central planning and management

Ownership of profit-generating assets	Private ownership of principal means of production and assets with certain exceptions	Most economic assets owned privately by individuals or corporations	Accelerating growth of giant national and multinational corporations		Two-sector national economies; state ownership of banks, key industries and services; in some nations of other industries		State owns entire economy; in some nations (Poland, Hungary) small privately owned enterprise; in Poland, privately owned farming
Property relations	Nationalization of some industries to avoid unemployment	Few, if any, state-owned, profit-generating enterprises	Large public sector, mostly in services; some state-owned enterprises	12–20% of the economy state-owned	18–30% of the economy state-owned		80–95% of the economy state-owned
Dependence on services, jobs, transfer payments from the state			Numerous services provided by the state; e.g., education, transportation, medical help; increasing dependency on transfer payments and welfare	20–30% of the population depends on transfer payments from the state; 25% of the work force in public employment	More than 30% work for state-owned industries or the state administration	Hypothetically 60–70% employed by the state	80–90% of the labor force employed by the state (USSR = 95% if collective farming included)
State planning	Nonexistent	Nonexistent or minimal	Certain targets within some governmental departments set in advance	Selective state planning	Extensive but still selective state planning involving important industries	Hypothetically most of the economy under central planning	Entire economy under central planning: growth, distribution, market exchange
State involvement in solving social and economic problems	Stimulation of economic growth and stability; reduction of poverty and unemployment			Stimulation of economic growth and stability; reduction of poverty and unemployment	Stimulation of economic growth; job-creating activities	Strengthening the position of strategic industries; support of social programs	Maximization of productivity; preservation of existing social and economic order

means definite.[6] Although this typology identifies stages in a unidirectional evolution, it is limited in its capacity to describe any particular tendency or inevitability in the direction of development. "The *constructed type* is a heuristic device," writes McKinney (1966, 12, emphasis added). And (7), "The constructed type as a conceptual device represents an attempt to advance concept formation in the social sciences from the stage of description and empirical generalization to the construction of theoretical systems." That is also the objective in developing this typology.

Some self-evident inferences can be drawn from the typology shown in Tables 5.2 and 5.3:

• "Free," minimally regulated enterprise—capitalist societies, in the classical sense of the term—no longer exists.

• Among the nations classified as state-regulated capitalist societies, those in the upper part of Table 5.2, i.e., Chile, South Korea, and Taiwan, are ruled by authoritarian or semiauthoritarian, rightist political regimes. Several years ago, when work on this book began, Argentina, Brazil, and the Philippines were also listed under this subtype. These nations have recently adopted a more democratic form of government. Spain, Portugal, and Mexico are listed at the polyarchic-democracy end of the axis. These nations are listed as state-regulated capitalist systems. These are nations that operate under multiparty systems (Portugal, Spain) or semi-multiparty systems (Mexico). They maintain a state-regulated economy with large sectors owned by the state. Having much poorer economies, these nations have not been able to institute as highly developed systems of services and public programs as have richer nations.

• Japan and the United States are in the same subtype. These nations do not own large sectors of nationalized industries. Japan developed a unique state patronage over the private sector under a fairly democratic polyarchic and multiparty system, with umbrella regulating mechanisms.

The United States is classified as a state-regulated, one-sector capitalist economy with a welfare system, administered through direct and indirect regulation. The state is also expected to provide the means of essential welfare, basic entitlements, and general services to the public.

• The rapid transformation of Great Britain from a state-regulated, capitalist society, with a developed welfare system, into a redistributive two-sector economy with a dominant state sector, was attempted under the Labour government in the mid-1970s. Thatcher's Conservative government is attempting to reverse this development, privatize the economy, and reduce state management. Great Britain is portrayed as standing apart from other Western European nations, which have not taken this course of action to the same extent.

The Federal Republic of Germany has a highly developed welfare system. The government has not resorted to outright nationalization policies and distributive practices to sustain this increasingly costly system, but has employed a wide variety of partial controls to generate necessary funds.

Italy, France, and Canada have been changing into redistributive economies with prevailing state sectors. Italy's evolution in this direction is being slowed, and even stalled, by the existence of a large underground economy, and thus a large amount of tax evasion. Canada belongs to the Western European type of societies in that it maintains a highly developed system of social services. Yet, the Canadian economy is strongly intertwined with the U.S. economy. U.S. culture also exerts a more profound influence on the behavior of Canadians than on Europeans.

Scandinavian countries are included in the group of strongly redistributive societies, because of their highly developed welfare institutions sustained by high taxes, especially for upper-level income brackets. Yet Sweden, the largest and most industrialized of these nations, has not nationalized its major industrial corporations. Most state-controlled, capitalist societies with developed welfare institutions do not impose high taxes with equity or equality as the principal objective, but merely to obtain funds for "common expenses," such as defense, maintenance of public services (roads, schools, etc.), and welfare institutions. These are costly activities requiring quite high tax collections. States that adopt redistributive policies tend specifically to tax high-income groups more heavily and, in certain instances (e.g., France), nationalize industries not only in an attempt to extract higher revenues and to reduce unemployment, but in order to implement specific ideals of equity ("The rich must pay"). In this instance, "in assessing the rate of tax on an individual" or restricting profit-making and property ownership, "the government is deciding not how much of his own income it will require him to pay, but how much of the society's income it will allow him to keep" (Plattner 1979, 31).

• Command economic systems have not emerged in any Western nations. The Soviet Union and Eastern-bloc nations differ from Western societies principally in the two regards adopted in this scheme. These nations are governed under single-party, authoritarian systems of government. They have developed command systems of economic planning within which all means of production are owned by the state. The 1956 Hungarian, 1968 Czechoslovakian, and the more recent Solidarity revolt in Poland reflect the desire by large parts of the population to reduce the rigidity of state control and provide room for small-business initiatives, some self-management of state-owned enterprises, freedom of expression, and individual initiative.

• In the 1930s, Schumpeter predicted the appearance of democratically managed, centrally planned, state-owned economies. Such economies have not emerged so far. Systems displaying these characteristics, if they appear, will possibly be those of Eastern European nations, after major reform or successful rebellion.

In conclusion, this analysis leads one to distinguish four types of Western etatized societies (see Table 5.2):

A, exemplified by the United States, where a capitalist market economy persists under general regulation by the state

B, exemplified by the larger states of Western Europe and by Canada, with two-sector economies and elements of redistributive systems and central planning

C, exemplified by Japan, where the state provides services to the capitalist economy, and enterprises still secure a large part of employees' welfare; currently the state is becoming involved in developing a more universal welfare organization on a national scale

D, exemplified by the smaller democracies of Western Europe, Austria, Switzerland, possibly Denmark, Israel, and other small democracies, where the state represents the consensus reached in intermediation involving, principally, the plurality of interest groups and unions as well as political parties seeking to advance their aspirations by means of consensus.[7]

PART TWO

COMPARATIVE ANALYSIS OF THE NEW STATE: THE UNITED STATES, WESTERN EUROPE, CANADA, AND JAPAN

CHAPTER SIX

Direct Regulation:
The United States

Rather than attempt to present a comprehensive history of etatization in each nation considered, this book focuses on selected aspects of each country's development that were, or continue to be, particularly generative of etatization and the New State. It is hoped that such an analysis will foster both the general interpretation of the theme, and the depiction of the varieties of etatization processes in the Western world. Regulatory practices, existing in all etatized nations, are best exemplified by U.S. phenomena. Discussing Great Britain, the analysis is focused on the decline of productivity, economic deterioration under increasing state-ownership and management, and partial recovery under privatization. France's case exemplifies stagnation, produced by bureaucratization, and futile attempts, under socialism, to overcome it. Italian material exemplifies the fusion between state and private sectors. Nationalization and the development of two-sector economies are compared in all European societies. Canada offers an example of a nation turning to etatization in order to build barriers against U.S. multinationals. Finally, Japan presents a unique case of indirect regulatory management of the private-sector economy under a variety of state umbrella mechanisms.

Direct Regulation

To stay balanced and grow, and simultaneously to change as required by internal and environmental needs, open systems must be regulated. This is congruent with the basic premises of the general system theory. Von Bertalanffy (1968), a leading theoretician in the field, posits that open systems—economic and social systems among others—"actively" tend toward higher organizational complexity (142): "The system remains constant in its composition, in spite of continuous irreversible processes, import and export, building-up and breaking-down, taking place." Such systems exist and grow by subjecting their structures to continuous self-transformations; they move from a "lower to a higher state of order" through "learning," i.e., absorbing information from the environment or reorganizing information already stored. Open systems are endowed with a variety of feedback and control mechanisms, which make ongoing reorganization and reintegration possible whenever needed. Yet, as they grow, such "organisms" face the danger of becoming "mechanized" and stagnant. This danger is overcome by developing internal control systems. "Primary" regulations involve the whole system from lower levels of organization to higher orders. "Secondary" regulations involve metabolic controls, which maintain structural arrangements intact by rebuilding and replacing elements of the system. Regulation and self-regulation are engendered within the structure in response to emerging needs and are maintained at "a distance from true equilibrium, typical for closed systems." As a result of employing both regulatory practices and feedback mechanisms, open systems (some more open than others) are capable of retaining their basic structure while changing and growing.

Most likely, von Bertalanffy and other theorists developing the foundations of general system theory were not familiar with neodurkheimian perspectives in sociology or with Perrroux's theory of economic development. It is, therefore, remarkable that within their own discipline, mostly by logical deduction, they arrived at similar conclusions as did both social scientists (concerned with macrostructures) and managers of the state and large corporate organizations (endeavoring to solve societal and organizational problems by propounding regulatory solutions). The following observations are derived from theories representing the three disciplines.

Societal and economic systems possess an inherent propensity to expand, grow, and turn increasingly more complex. Elements of their structures—such as firms, corporations, branches of government, small "empires" built by active entrepreneurs, politicians, and all kinds of people—display a similar proclivity. Under capitalism, each individual, group, firm, corporation, and industry strives to augment its sphere of activity, to increase its control of the market, and, where possible, to engulf the sphere of others. Conflicts thrive under such conditions. However, internal regulation overcomes recurring disarray and any imminent dangers to the system. The state equilibrates growth by instituting regulation. The etatizing state aims to regulate everything that can be regulated, which contradicts the intrinsic striving of organisms and open systems as a whole to maximize the freedom with which they operate. As the system grows larger, encompassing increasing numbers of more complex interdependencies, the state strives for more penetrative control over more relationships, both within and beyond the sphere of its management. Standards are set for courses of action, services, and commodities: for everything that can be standardized. Norms and rules are set for any recognized roles, positions, and activity. Societal and economic structures become increasingly more systemic in character.

In etatized societies, the state employs either direct or indirect regulation, and most frequently a combination of both. This chapter discusses direct regulations, but I must begin by pointing out the difference between direct and indirect regulatory practices.

Direct regulation, is effectuated by order, command, rule, instruction, requirement, or norm-setting, as well as by prohibition or restriction. It is meant to be coercive; noncooperation is deterred by punishment or threats of negative sanctions. Direct regulation employs "thou shalts" and "thou shall nots." Because direct regulation restricts freedom (the freedom with which business wishes to operate); because fulfilling direct regulatory requirements is costly to large corporations, smaller businesses, and anyone who is obliged to obey them; and because no one likes to be coerced, people who are forced to obey direct regulation perceive it as restrictive, excessive, oppressive, and often absurd. Whether serving political, economic, security, or ideological objectives, direct regulation affects daily practices, primarily because rules are "on the books." Whether orders issued in the past continue to serve the purpose for which they were instituted or have actually become detrimental to the current condition, is inconsequential to the acting bureaucrat; orders must be obeyed.

The practice of indirect regulation differs in many regards; different authors define it differently.[1] In this book, governmental activities involving inducement, manipulation, use of tax and other incentives, provocation of market decisions, and the dissemination of information to induce desired behavior, are classified as indirect regulatory strategies or practices. Instead of regulating specific behavior (as direct regulations do), indirect regulation usually effectuates many simultaneous and long-range objectives: maintaining the economic condition and financial stability in general; generating growth and economic improvement; raising revenues; and so forth. Most importantly, through indirect regulation, the administration strives to create a condition in which individuals, groups, corporations, and institutions behave, on their own volition, as the state would like them to behave.

Moreover, indirect regulation simultaneously pursues both immediate results and long-range objectives. Both direct and indirect regulation are employed by all contemporary governments. However, while some rely principally on direct regulatory means, others rely on both or try more often to mold conditions, to cause citizens to behave as the state believes beneficial for the system, rather than force them to act under orders and duress. The example of the U.S. federal government under Reagan's administration portrays such a strategy. That administration implemented its aims relying strongly on indirect regulatory means, such as fiscal, budgetary, monetary, and credit policies. Carter's administration relied also on indirect regulations but instituted a great many direct regulations that upset the business community and the public at large; the U.S. public, more than, for instance, the German, tends to dislike direct orders. Whether a government relies more on indirect or on direct regulations depends partly on whether it controls the legislative body, which enacts required regulation, what kind of control it can master, and other factors. U.S. presidents, facing congresses dominated by the opposition, tend to employ indirect regulatory strategies more frequently. Western European governments most often involve elements of both methods.[2] This occurs particularly where the state acts simultaneously as a government imposing rules, as an authority molding conditions, and as a major stockholder and owner of industries, and therefore a participant in corporate decisionmaking.

The literature on regulation contains diverse definitions and interpretations of regulatory concepts. Mitnick (1980), for instance, recognizes two types of regulatory practice. One chapter of his book is called "Regulation by Directive: Rules and Standards, Public Enterprise" (396–415); another, "Regulation by Incentive: Tax Incentive, Effluent Charges and Subsidies" (364–395).[3] In other chapters he discusses theories and practice of regulation and deregulation. In my book, the terms direct and indirect regulation carry a somewhat different emphasis,   facilitating the explication of the etatization theory. For instance, budgetary allocation and the activities of credit-budget agencies are regarded here as "indirect regulation."

Regulatory Practices and Étatisme

The origins of regulatory practices can be traced to ancient Babylonian, Egyptian, and Chinese times. Regulation had been widely practiced in medieval Europe long before the contemporary state-controlled and state-regulated societies emerged. In the medieval city, guilds and merchant organizations strictly regulated all organized trade, crafts, and any related social life. They sought to eliminate malpractice, to protect members against outside competition, to regulate the conduct of members in mutual relations, and to control social behavior in general. They had rules for everything: apprenticeship; employing journeymen and clerks; manufacturing materials; quality standards; sales commissions; fair play among competing guild members; assistance to fellow guild members experiencing adversity; ethics and the social obligations of members. Rules and regulations were commensurate with requirements set under corporate and canon law, and the expectations of kings, nobility, and Church. Medieval regulation, though pertinent to a wide range of activities, was, however, only as extensive as the given market, and, in those days, the market was predominantly local. Thus, most regulations were imposed locally, according to local standards, and served the authorities in specific places. Cities, courts, and, to some extent, the Church had the prerogative to conduct some regulatory practices; central authorities, however, were rarely involved in such affairs.

Things began to change during the sixteenth and seventeenth centuries as new concepts of economic administration by absolutist monarchies obtained wider currency. Adam Smith, who surveyed the conceptualizations and actual policies of the sixteenth to eighteenth centuries, described them as "mercantile." Eventually, the term mercantilism appeared. Kings needed more and more money to sustain enormously expensive courts and armies. The treasury of the state was the treasury of the monarch. The problem was that most of the time the treasury was empty. As Heaton writes (1948, 226), "even the most comprehensive money-raising policies could not meet the combined cost of luxury and pugnacity." European monarchs pursued money by any means. They waged wars over colonies or simply to destroy competitors in order to enrich themselves. They strove to increase revenues by imposing heavier taxes and by exporting more than was imported. In short (Heaton 1948, 228), "whatever the method pursued, the aim was usually to gain some profitable favor, privilege protection or monopoly at the expense of rivals at home and abroad, or other interest or sections of the community or of the consumer." Money could have been obtained by seizing the wealth of people in far-away foreign lands, by taxing domestic subjects more, or by developing manufacturing and trade. With the passing of time, the last solution gained popularity. The idea was to transform the monarchy from a system involved in robbing its subjects to a system that would husband them—i.e., take care of them and support their entrepreneurial initiatives—to increase national wealth and consequently the yield from taxation. Different nations pursued different mercantilist policies. While Holland's and England's policies tended predominately to reflect the pursuits of the trading classes, France conducted a mercantilist policy under state control and regulation—*étatisme*. Historians differ over the characteristics of mercantilism. Some follow Adam Smith, depicting mercantilism as a protectionist practice designed to raise revenues. Others, Schmoller (1967), who analyzed Prussian policies, and Charles W. Cole (1964), whose interest was mostly in the French, characterize mercantilism as a policy of economic unity, self-sufficiency, and built-up production in industry, agriculture, and commerce, conducted in pursuit of precious metals. Cole (1943; 1964) and others discuss mercantilist policies as laying the groundwork for capitalism, especially in prerevolutionary France. This is also the opinion of Webber and Wildavsky (1986, 237-247), who write on European mercantilism in general:

> The traditional prerogatives of local aristocrats merged with the market methods of earlier eras. Overriding both these influences yet sometimes interchangeable with them (for at times kings used market techniques to

recruit and reward state officials), was the central government bureaucracy. . . . Despotism shaded back to collectivism and accommodated growing elements of economic individualism. A working alliance between principles of hierarchy in the state and competition in the economy was in the making. . . . Individualism at first coexisted with collectivism. Soon enough, however, there would be attempts to separate the two orders by confining each to its respective domain.

At this point, our interest must be focused on French mercantilism, as conducted by those most egregious practitioners, Jean-Baptiste Colbert and his king, Louis XIV. Cole (1964, I: 25) writes that the French variety of mercantilism "represented the economic part of political *étatisme*," which eventually became widely regarded as the prototype for diverse *dirigiste* forms of regulatory policies as practiced in France and elsewhere. Although Colbert has no reputation as a theorist, he is nevertheless regarded as the founder of *étatisme*. His deeds are superbly documented by instructions, memos, regulations, and letters, contained in seven volumes edited by Pierre Clément (1861–70) and two volumes of documents assembled by Neymarck (1970 reprinted). His system of state management was subjected to incisive analyses in another two volumes by Clément (1892), two volumes by Voltaire (1926), four volumes by Cole, works by Pierre Boissonade (among which *Colbert: Le Triomphe de l'étatisme* is particularly outstanding), and in dozens of works by other authors (e.g., Trout 1978 and Goubert 1970).

Colbert's main preoccupation was finances. He tried to raise the state's revenues by reorganizing taxes and by other means. In 1661, the king's treasury managed to procure 31 million livres in revenues. Nine million of these had to be expended, however, on interest and other carrying charges. Colbert began by revising the *rentes* the treasury was obliged to pay. Against *rentiers*' protests, he tried to pay off as many *rentes* as he could and to reduce other debts of the monarchy. Then, despite nobles' and "false nobles'" protestations especially, he tried to abolish the offices of 4,000 financial officials and to reform the system of universal *tailles* (personal and real property taxes) in order to increase revenue from that source. He failed in this endeavor and discovered the effect that is now described by the Laffer curve: Imposition of higher taxes resulted in more tax evasion, bribery, and corruption, and, finally, in lower revenues. He was concerned that the misery resulting from excessive taxes would produce rebellion. Several such rebellions had to be quelled during Louis XIV's reign. Colbert reduced the *tailles*. Revenue from the *taille personelle* had declined from 42 to 34 million livres. But Colbert still needed money. So he increased the *aides* (sales taxes). This resulted in an enormous increase of lawsuits initiated by the state and taxpayers. This was too difficult a problem for the state to handle. Two centuries later, Reagan would introduce a tax reform with similar intentions, but much better results. Colbert tried then to increase the *gabelles*—the salt tax borne by people of all estates—but was obliged to alter the system of *grand gabelle*. Eventually, Colbert could claim some success in obtaining higher revenues, but he did not succeed in reducing the monarchy's expenses and its debt (which grew bigger when the king waged war on Holland and built a larger navy). He granted various privileges to those who increased productivity, which was expected to generate more taxes in the future. Subsequently, Colbert invented new devices. He (see Boissonade, 1932, Pt. 2) sought to develop royal monopolies on postal services, tobacco, public transportation, production of arms, munitions, saltpeter, and construction of naval vessels. He also established royal manufacturing of tapestry, mirrors, and some other commodities with high market demand. And he established a system of chartered companies operating overseas. "The East and West Indies, the North and Levant and Africa, each in turn was the object of his fostering care," writes Sargent (1899, 80). The British and Dutch took this path also. Yet, in contrast to the French, they merely granted privileges to private entrepreneurs to establish companies operating in foreign lands and promised to shield them with their might. Colbert's companies were established by royal decree. He employed "gentle methods of compulsion," forcing private investors to acquire shares. Yet, as in our times, he achieved little (84); "the companies failed, but not before they had produced the most deplorable results in the sphere of international politics." He also (44) conducted an "industrial policy." Colbert believed that foreign trade is warfare by economic means. He waged commercial wars on the rest of Europe. And when he failed to beat the Dutch in trade, he supported Le Tellier and Louvois, his enemies in court intrigues, in waging military war against Holland. His chief objective in this venture was to ruin Dutch trade and to destroy the Dutch merchant fleet. He supported colonizing New France in Canada and tried to expand colonies elsewhere as well.

The complex system of ordinances regulating many aspects of economic and social activities instituted under Colbert's regime was highly acclaimed by other governments and by his successors. It did not produce the results Colbert expected, but nevertheless was monumental. In 1664, Colbert instituted tariff reform. In 1667, he issued the Civil Ordinance and regularized the practices of courts. Cole (1964, 1: 312) points out that this ordinance later "served as one of the sources of the *Code Napoléon*." The General Regulation of 1669 regularized "in the most minute manner with all the details," operation of the textile and other industries. The same year, Colbert proclaimed the Criminal Ordinance and the Ordinances of Waters and Forests. The Ordinances of Commerce in 1673, of the Marine in 1681, and other regulations followed. Eventually, he prepared the *Code Noir*, which was issued in 1685, after his death. This code "sought to fix the civil and criminal status of slaves" in the French West Indies. "In the Codes of Colbert," writes Cole (1964, 1: 313), "there was a strong tendency toward increased uniformity and enlarged powers for the central government. In the field of general administration a similar trend was notable. Colbert sought ever to strengthen the central government and to create unity and order."

Among numerous other undertakings, Colbert pursued a policy of self-sufficiency and strove to maintain a favorable balance of trade. He believed in bullionism, tried to accumulate as much precious metals as he could, and tried to prevent such wealth leaving the country; in those days, gold and silver possession was the measure of prosperity. He built a powerful navy and a state-owned merchant fleet. He imposed heavy duties on foreign shipping and enacted many barriers and tariffs against foreign merchants. He built numerous modern roads and canals. He subsidized farming and other economic ventures. He induced and protected economic initiatives, which he expected to fill the king's coffers in the future. He established a national loan system (*caisse des emprunts*) by means of which he tried to administer *rentes*, and a state insurance system. An Academy of Sciences to foster economic growth was built on his initiative. His staff was small. With only 300 bureaucrats, without computers and other contemporary technology, how much could this man do? His objectives were unattainable. He could not undertake any major social reform. He had to watch out constantly for intrigues spun by his enemies. He was hated by aristocrats and merchants on whom he imposed strictures, regulations, tariffs, and more taxes; by financiers whom he punished for defrauding the state; by his own subordinates whom he kept under rigid control; and by the common people upon whom, against his will, he imposed a great deal of misery. No wonder he failed in most of his endeavors, except to enrich himself. But others were not deterred by his failures and again and again tried to solve problems by subjecting nations to etatization. Sargent, whose book was published in 1899, explores attempts by Turgot, Necker, and Napoleon to carry on affairs by Colbert's means. Those of his successors in prerevolutionary France who followed his ways also failed.

Cole writes (1964, 1: 351):

> He detested idleness in any guise, and approved of hard work with an almost Puritanical enthusiasm. He was anxious to see the "idle poor" all employed in some form of productive work. He wished to drive all habitual vagabonds out of the country or to put them to enforced labor in the galleys. He regarded monks, nuns, lawyers, and officials as unproductive idlers, and wished to reduce their numbers.

It is reported that Colbert was planning a monument in Paris. It would stand on a rock in the center of a pond. Upheld by several colossal statues, Louis XIV was to be depicted as hurling to earth discord and heresy. I think that such a monument is still needed, but not to Louis XIV—to Colbert, the *étatiste*. And in my opinion, the statues supporting it should be of Louis XIV, Napoleon, de Gaulle, and Mitterrand. And I am willing to donate the first, tax-exempted, of course, $100 to this endeavor, should anyone ever undertake to erect it.

The United States: From Old to New Regulatory Practices

Discussion of etatization in the United States must account for both direct regulatory practices based on rules, orders, and prohibitions, and indirect regulatory practices involving fiscal, budgetary, credit, and other economic, semi-economic, and social policies of the government, implemented by the state. In the United States, direct regulatory agencies are delegated power by Congress. Yet, they constitute part of the administrative structure of the federal government and therefore of the executive branch. Indirect regulation is practiced by involving the cash and credit budget; the fiscal system, and the Federal Reserve and other agencies. These agencies report to Congress; but the consequences of their policies cannot as easily be assessed by a congressional committee as can those of direct regulatory practices.

U.S. society became etatized mainly through extending regulatory control. By expanding the functions, powers, and structure of direct regulatory institutions, Johnson, Nixon, Ford, and, especially, Carter extended state control over the economy, market, and society far beyond any previously accepted range. Such changes were advanced as developing democracy, stability, and growth. Yet, large parts of the population became discontented, not with the new aspects of democracy, stability, or growth, but with what they saw as excessive commands and restrictions. Reagan was elected president because, among other reasons, he promised to reverse this trend and abate regulatory domination. At first, he attempted significantly to reduce the scope of direct regulatory controls. At the same time, however, Reagan extended the power of the Federal Reserve and of other federal agencies concerned with general management and indirect regulation of the market economy. Eventually, his administration had to issue more direct regulations. During the first years of his presidency, Reagan reported that the volumes containing federal regulations had shrunk by so many pages. While in his second term, he did not report on this aspect of presidential activity.

During the first part of the twentieth century, economic growth and policies pursuing national economic interests persisted as major concerns of both European and U.S. governments. A dual stance was adopted. On one hand, the dominant ideology upheld the free-market economy, and a free economy was to be kept unrestrained, as far as possible free of state intervention. The state strove to defend capitalism. On the other hand, the means it had to employ contradicted the ends it strove to achieve; to perform its task, the state had to arm itself with regulations restricting freedom in the free-market economy. Lowi's book, *The End of Liberalism*, has a fascinating chapter on the subject: "Liberal Jurisprudence." He lists (among others) the Sherman Antitrust Act, the Clayton Act, the Transportation Act of 1920, the 1914 and 1920 Federal Trade Commission Acts, and New Deal legislation as constituting the progressive institution of federal controls and regulations in the United States, under the pretence of defending freedom and the free-market economy of capitalism. He concludes (1969, 143–144) that

> there is an expansion of the scope of Federal Control in the sense of the
> number and types of objects touched by directly coercive Federal
> specification of conduct. . . . The movement seemed to be *from the*
> *negative to the positive, the proscriptive to the prescriptive* [in our terms,
> from direct to indirect regulatory control]. The latter did not replace the
> former but only supplemented them. . . . As *regulation moved from the*
> *denotation* to the connotation of what is subject to public policy, discretion
> inevitably increased; and *the process unavoidably centers on*
> *administration* [emphases added].

Although he mentions "private corporate, local and state regulations," Lowi
does not discuss the wider practice he indicates.

In a society based on the unrestrained exercise of individual interests,
ubiquitous regulations emerged through attempts to reduce and avoid
explosive conflicts. Regulation protected group interests and, in some
instances, the interests of the wealthy and of corporations. Controls and
regulations proliferated with the increasing complexity of societal structures.
In a society composed of individuals independent of family and community,
other intermediate institutional control and regulation is even more required.
The market alone cannot generate all the necessary standards for big and
small industries attempting to win larger shares, frequently with no regard to
the damage they do to the larger economic environment, market system,
culture, or anything important to the collectivity.

Some experts who discuss the recent development of regulatory
practices in the United States discern two principal periods of institution and,
correspondingly, two distinctive types of regulation: old- and new-style
regulatory practices. In *The Intellectual Development of the Regulatory*
Movement (1955), Bernstein, a regulation theory pioneer, distinguishes two
periods of regulatory practices in U.S. history: 1887 to 1920, and since 1920.
More recent studies (Herman 1982, 173; Wilson 1980; Weaver 1978;
Mitnick 1980; White 1981) are less precise about dates but regard most
regulations enacted until the late 1960s as traditional, i.e., old regulation
(OR); and the regulations enacted in the late 1960s and 1970s as new
regulation (NR). They also stress a different, more important, distinction.
OR, write Herman and other experts, was enacted against cartels, with the
objective of arresting the growth of monopolies. These regulatory activities
were introduced on the initiative, or at least with the partial consent of the
regulated industries. They were to regulate but mainly to sustain the
oligopolistic structure of the economy. Most strategic business
variables—notably, prices charged, allowable entry, and services
rendered—were very detailed. NR, in contrast, deals with different, mostly
social concerns. NR was enacted to: (*a*) protect the natural environment; (*b*)
guard the public against unsafe and unhealthy commodities on the

market—generally against the mistreatment of consumers by corporations; (*c*) enhance safety conditions at the work place; and (*d*) protect women, ethnic minorities, and certain other categories of people against discrimination. Herman points out that NR was costly and restricted businesses. Business executives considered many of the regulations enacted in the 1970s as antibusiness, oppressive, anticapitalist, and restrictive of free enterprise.

Principal OR agencies include: Interstate Commerce Commission (ICC), established in 1887; Federal Trade Commission (FTC), 1914; Farm Credit Administration (FCA), 1916; U.S. International Trade Commission, 1916; Federal Power Commission (FPC), 1920; Federal Deposit Insurance Corporation (FDIC), 1933; Securities and Exchange Commission (SEC), 1934; Federal Communications Commission (FCC), 1934; and Civil Aeronautics Board (CAB), 1940.

Principal NR agencies include: Environmental Protection Agency (EPA), 1970, established to reduce pollution and clean up the natural environment; Nuclear Regulatory Commission (NRC), 1975; Food and Drug Administration (FDA), 1931; and Consumer Product Safety Commission (CPSC), 1972, preoccupied with the safety of products and services and fair treatment of consumers (reorganized in 1974 with new objectives, the FTC could also be listed here); Occupational Safety and Health Administration (OSHA), 1970, and National Highway Traffic Safety Administration (NHTSA), 1975, meant to maintain high safety standards in the work place and on highways; Equal Employment Opportunity Commission (EEOC), 1965, and Commission on Civil Rights, 1957, which aim to eliminate discriminatory practices. The FDA is listed as a NR agency because, though its original scope was rather narrow, public concern during the 1970s and 1980s caused it to expand its regulatory practices considerably. All NR commissions, boards, and agencies possess administrative and license-granting rights. They were established in response to public concern, as voiced by the media. They were formulated to represent the interests of society vis-à-vis the new corporate structure.[4]

Under the Carter administration, these agencies evolved into an interlocked, centralized regulatory system. Their authority was so vast and, at times, so conflicting that some experts considered them part of a new, fourth branch of government. The time was ripe, these experts felt, for the establishment of a superregulatory agency to oversee the ever-growing number of commissions, administrations, and boards. A proposal of amendment the U.S. Constitution to recognize the new role of regulatory agencies was even advocated. Some who initiated this proposal wanted officially to endow one White House high official with the authority to oversee the work of all regulatory agencies. Certain of them (Noll 1971, 89), such as some members of the Ash Council, believed that this official, a regulatory "czar," should be recognized as a second vice-president. These people argued that regulatory agencies should report directly to the president.

From another perspective, critics saw most regulatory agencies as excessive and wasteful. In 1975, President Ford estimated the annual cost to consumers of unnecessary regulatory activities at $2,000 per family. Furthermore, it was determined that Washington's 63,500 regulators cost the public $130 billion annually. In 1976, responding to critical opinion that excessive regulation was one principal cause of inflation, Ford issued Executive Order 11821, requiring regulatory agencies to prepare cost-benefit analyses before introducing any new regulations.

The heyday of direct regulatory activities arrived with the inauguration of Carter. The number of regulatory agencies, regulations, consultants, and lawyers employed by agencies grew so fast that eventually senators, the media, and Carter himself grew uneasy; they took measures to arrest this tendency. Yet in 1978, the press reported that while more than fifty regulatory agencies, employing over 100,000 individuals, directed the United States from Washington, DC, the army of personnel was still too small to cope with their functions.[5]

In 1982, after initial deregulations by Carter, and more drastic ones by Reagan, the press reported fifty-four principal regulatory agencies employing 324,000 individuals, apparently facing even greater problems coping with their tasks. The problem, as then seen by critics, was not only too many regulatory agencies employing too many bureaucrats, who poked their noses into activities that, until then, had been regarded as private. The problem was compounded because many regulations were excessive, in some instances plainly absurd. They cost taxpayers and corporations a great deal of money, contributed to inflation, impaired productivity, and dealt with matters that did not need to be regulated. However, the snowballing growth of regulatory agencies could not be curbed.

What kind of sociological importance can be attributed to this developmental process? Weaver's (1978, 54–63) analysis excellently interprets the development of regulatory practices in a way parallel to the perspective of etatization theory. He contrasts OR objectives of "saving `free enterprise' from big business—i.e., of preserving competition (or at any rate competitors) to a greater extent than the `natural' dynamics of a free market would allow," and "helping to integrate a diverse, localistic, continental population into a single, interdependent society," with those of NR, "whose announced objective . . . is to promote health, safety, a cleaner environment, and a more open political process." More importantly, however, he explains the historical significance of the shift from the first to the second form of regulation. He specifies that the two types of regulation correspond not only to different social policies, but to different social classes professing different values. Weaver (57–59) well clarifies the idea and illustrates the specific aspect of etatization under discussion at this point; therefore, I quote him at length.

The Old Regulation, for the most part, is the social policy of *that curious class of reformers, professionals, politicians, and businessmen* around the turn of the century who blended the "populist" and "progressive" impulses into a body of political views that eventually transformed a traditional, bourgeois political economy into the mixed corporate order we know today. The New Regulation, by contrast, is the social policy of what is often described these days as the *"new class"—also largely professional and managerial,* like its turn-of-the-century counterpart, but committed to "humanistic" work in the not-for-profit and public sectors, and generally hostile to the economic accomplishments and political vision of the Progressive era. . . . The second managerial revolution is transferring power from the managerial class to the new class, and from quasi-public institutions to fully public ones—i.e., to the government [emphases added].

The classification of OR versus NR may appear ornamental, but it reflects a major change in societal development. It demonstrates that the institutionalization of direct regulatory practices advanced in two stages, at the bidding of different groups and different classes. This process corresponded with the economic transition from the free-enterprise market economy—which the OR was expected to defend—to the new, transitional economy that combines elements of the market structure with elements of a universal distributive structure—which is institutionalized and managed by means created through NR. The shift from OR to NR represents a major change in the value orientation of society: from an achievement-oriented, other-directed ethic to a new morality that links fairness to the preponderance of collective interests, as represented by the state, over individual interests. Thus, as Weaver puts it, "the OR was forged in the armory of the old ruling class; the NR comes from the arsenal of the state-managing `New Class.'" From the perspective of etatization theory: the OR represented the extension of the old state; the NR are evidently part and parcel of the New State. By checking the dates of the NRs' establishment, one can almost write the New State's birth certificate.

Although at first, NR improved the material conditions of the poor, it failed to increase security, safety, fairness, and equity as much as expected. It did, however, produce conditions under which general etatization could advance into an age of decline of small producers in industry and agriculture, stronger domination of the economy by oligopolies, and rapidly advancing dependence of megacorporations on the federal state. One can discern two sides to this process: The state serves megacorporations to a greater extent than before, while megacorporations progressively evolve into huge tentacles of the gigantic octopus-state. In Western Europe and Canada, many large-scale business enterprises are now incorporated into the state. In the United States, corporations are privately owned and represent different interests than does the federal government; but simultaneously, as part of the national economy, they are protected by and occasionally act on behalf of the state.

The Revolt Against Regulators

From 1977 to 1979, the media overflowed with horror stories about regulatory agencies. A new plague was afflicting the United States, they claimed: rampant regulation, sapping freedom and money. It compelled the financier, entrepreneur, and manager to engage in the Sisyphean task of filling out lengthy and numerous forms. They were also forced to engage in other unproductive activities—all requirements by regulators—that often drove them to bankruptcy. Examples of absurd regulations, and the even more absurd and costly activities involved in preparing regulations, were endlessly discussed in magazines and by TV panels. The FCC was reported to have heavily regulated cable television and smaller TV stations in favor of the three major networks, thus restricting access to information. The ICC enacted prohibitions and complex tariffs that restricted business dealings with new trucking companies. The ICC had allowed no new truck carrier to enter the market since 1938; this, in the critics' opinion, enormously increased the cost of transportation and commodities to consumers. The CAB, for a long time, prevented airlines from introducing cheap charter flights (Goldwater 1976, 96–111).[6] The EPA obtained a court injunction halting work on the 95-percent completed, $113-million, Tellico Dam, in order to save the snail darter, a newly discovered 3-inch fish declared to be an endangered species, but later discovered in other places. Arco Oil complained that it was forced to close its Anaconda Copper Mine because the cost of complying with government regulations made its operations uneconomical. The steel industry echoed this complaint when it was forced to stop operating dozens of mills for similar reasons.[7] In other publicized instances, new projects for improving the economic condition of numerous communities were halted. Entertainers and journalists ridiculed the lengthy (some of them several hundred pages) manuals developed by regulators, at a cost of thousands of dollars, to explain how to build mouse traps, the proper shape of ice for cooling beverages, and the best shape for toilet seat covers. They scoffed at worthless campaigns undertaken by regulators—for example, warning farmers to beware of slipping on manure. There was no question about it: Regulatory agencies engaged in a profusion of activities, many of which, to the average taxpayer, were absurd.

Experts focused on different areas of criticism: In many instances (see Huntington 1952), older regulatory agencies are eventually "captured" by those they are expected to regulate.[8] Since an agency's funding depends on the continued presence of the problem it was designed to reduce and eliminate, regulators become reluctant to kill the proverbial goose that lays their golden eggs. The agency begins to share vested interests with the regulated sector.

Others, Milton Friedman in particular, have argued that direct regulation of the economy is, in principle, wrong; that it adversely affects the market economy. Instead of enhancing economic freedom, direct regulation inevitably reduces it, stifling entrepreneurial initiative and imposing restrictions on activities that, under healthy conditions, would be tested in the marketplace. These critics claimed that, in the past, the U.S. economy improved and grew strong because business was forced to please clients in order to make a profit. Direct regulatory commissions, they argued, are forced to employ armies of lawyers and other experts to develop regulations. Corporations, too, deploy squadrons of experts to advise them on current regulations, in matters of safety, standards, packaging, labels, pollution, the filling out of forms, and legal defense if they are accused of breaking any rules. To compound this, the spate of regulations required an army of inspectors to supervise the observance of regulations. Even without corruption, which is bound to occur, the cost of maintaining battalions of lawyers and regulatory practitioners forces up the cost of products and services. Regulation is, thus, a major cause of inflation. And inflation causes a decrease in consumption and, subsequently, generates unemployment.

In another area, critics pointed out that businesses that know how to please regulators prosper: they get governmental contracts; they get licenses more easily and faster; they are subject to a lesser degree of control and are first to receive important information. As a result, instead of devoting their efforts to pleasing customers, these businesses spend time and money filling out forms and pleasing regulators. Productivity is adversely affected. In sum, critics agreed that, though regulation produces some benefits, it is not worth the cost.

The argument defending direct regulation makes the following points: A complex industrialized society with diversified interests and activities requires the balancing force and direction of experts and regulatory agencies. Without regulatory restraints, profit- and power-hungry corporations would run amok, devouring and wrecking one another, cheating the public, exploiting employees, and devastating the natural environment. Although costly, regulatory agencies are necessary.[9] Some of the rules and activities developed in the 1970s to implement direct regulation had perhaps been excessive and (see Bardach & Kagan 1982) unreasonable; however, the benefits of cleaner air and water, safer products, more security for the aging and for single-parent families, and less discrimination cannot be disregarded. The harm that might have been done without the watchful activities of the EPA cannot be estimated. Many unsafe and harmful products have been removed from the market and safety conditions at work and in public places have improved. Discrimination, though still present, has markedly abated.

One may ask, could these gains have been achieved more cheaply without the excesses and adverse consequences that regulation produced? The trade-off between benefits and losses generated by direct regulation are not easily calculated.

In the 1970s, particularly under Carter's administration, critics felt that direct regulatory practices were excessive, overly bureaucratized, and hostile to business. Although many of them accepted that regulation could be beneficial, they complained that most regulatory policies restricted growth and development, not because these were harmful, but simply because regulations were anticapitalistic.

In 1965, 10 percent of U.S. industries were considered regulated. By the end of 1970s, 30 percent were in that category. However, Weidenbaum (1976; 1979) and other critics of regulation felt that though some industries are more regulated and others less, virtually every aspect of production and marketing was affected by some form of regulation. According to Weidenbaum (1979), the effects of regulation fall into three broad categories: direct, indirect, and induced. As an example of the first category, he cites the approximately $665.87 increase in the cost of an average car, between 1970 and 1975, and the rise of construction costs for a new house by about $1,500. As examples of indirect effects, he considers the cost of excessive paperwork and the longer amount of time needed to acquire permits. Money spent on lobbying Congress for a tax system with ample loopholes and the enactment of special rules to exclude certain corporations from general rules, if added to the list of indirect effects, would even further increase the cost of regulation. As an example of the third category of cost, Weidenbaum refers to a study in St. Louis County, Missouri. Its authors found that a substantial number of individuals had given up trying to build houses because of the prohibitive costs anticipated in meeting regulations. In other cases, certain industries decided to cancel plans to build plants. Weidenbaum (1979, 25) cites cases of synthetic fuel plants, which allegedly were not built because of excessively harsh requirements. He maintains that "the rapid expansion of government regulation of business is also slowing down the rate of innovation and scientific progress in the United States."

On the surface, the debate over regulations appears as a conflict between critics fighting excessive bureaucratization and absurd rules, and those who believe business needs to be controlled, that unscrupulous money-making without concern for its adverse effect on the environment and the public must be curbed. Beneath these issues, however, lies the battle of two concepts, one advocating the preponderance of the market, the other favoring the state.

Toward the late 1970s, opposition to the bureaucratizing and regulating of the U.S. economy and society came to involve numerous leading senators and congressmen, certain economists, and administrative experts. Goldwater (1976), Wallis (1976), MacAvoy (1970), Weidenbaum, (1976; 1978; 1979), and a number of research institutes published studies in which they demonstrated that U.S. regulatory practices were harming society and generating inflation, were wasteful and frequently absurd. Some major corporations—Gould Inc., for example—became involved in publishing and distributing pamphlets within business and university communities, attacking overregulation as a principal cause of declining technological development and growth.

Opinion polls indicated that most people thought "competition is better than government regulation to make sure that the public gets what it pays for." At the same time, the public's trust of business was, on the whole, low. People favored a moderate form of public intervention, but felt that U.S. society had been regulated too far. Lipset and Schneider (1979), comparing a number of opinion polls conducted at that time, found that 26% to 36% of the public favored more regulation, 23% to 38% thought that the degree to which society was already regulated was about right, but 27% to 43% wanted to see less regulation. Analyzing a survey conducted by the Roper Organization in December 1977, in which respondents were asked questions about the regulation of specific industries, these authors estimated that 52% felt regulation of the automobile industry should remain as is, while 37% desired more government intervention; 45% were satisfied with the current regulation of the chemical industry, while 34% supported an increase; 44% wanted to "keep the present system as it is" in the steel industry, while 41% desired greater government involvement. However, for the oil industry, only 31% were satisfied with the present system; a 54% majority favored "stronger government action." Earlier opinion polls (*Public Opinion*, May–June 1978, 26) revealed that 72% of the public wanted stricter regulation of working conditions; 61% of handgun possession, and 57% of marijuana use. But only 48% approved increasing regulation of "dangerous" food and drugs, 44% of pornography, and 29% of saccharine use.[10]

Deregulation in the 1980s

Regulation ranked among the principal issues of the 1980 Republican election program. Reagan promised that, if elected, he would restore the economic growth and prosperity enjoyed by the United States during the two decades following World War II. He specifically promised to change economic policy and: (1) bring the rate of inflation down; (2) reduce government spending and balance the budget; (3) generally cut taxes, in order to stimulate investment and economic growth; (4) abolish oppressive regulatory enactments and reduce the effects of other regulatory practices; (5) reduce bureaucracy; and (6) stabilize monetary growth.

The merits or demerits of these economic objectives will not be discussed here. However, it should be noted that, during the first four years of the Reagan administration, the first objective was, to a significant degree, achieved. The annual rate of inflation was reduced to a level not exceeding 5 percent and remained low to 1987. A proper assessment of the administration's accomplishments or failures in reducing the cost and expenditures of the government requires a complex discussion. Nonetheless, the facts reveal that though the administration tried initially to reduce some government expenditures and, to a lesser extent, administrative costs, it could not reduce expenditures on social programs and chose to increase defense spending. Therefore, the budget was not balanced and the deficit grew even larger. Regarding the third point: Taxes were cut. The effects have been differently assessed, from various ideological and political perspectives. A debate on fundamental tax reform is currently in progress.

The bureaucracy grew bigger. According to data published by the *U.S. News & World Report* (October 18, 1982), 2,192,972 civilians were listed on the payroll of the executive branch in June 1982, 5,316 more than on inauguration day in 1981. At the time, Reagan declared again and again that bureaucracy would be cut by 75,000, but bureaucracy grew regardless. It is quite obvious that Reagan could not force the jinn released by Carter back into the bottle on his commands. The *Statistical Abstract of the United States* 1986 (294) reported 2,942,000 civilians on the federal payroll in October 1984 (and another 13,494,000 employed by state and local authorities). If this figure is accurate, it follows that under the president who declared war on bureaucracy, bureaucracy (particularly in the defense, interior, and agricultural departments) grew at a rate much higher than did the general population. The state failed in its war on bureaucracy as it failed in its war on poverty.

Our discussion at this point has to focus on the fourth point of Reagan's program: the abolition of certain effects of regulatory enactments and the reduction of others. Regulatory reform was undertaken as part of a declared intention to restore and enhance the free-market structure of the economy. In reality, something different happened. While removing certain abusive practices of regulatory agencies, reducing the number of contradictory regulations, lessening government interference in specific affairs of the corporate sector, and reducing supervision over consumption, the Reagan administration, by consolidating direct regulatory supervision under the Office of Management and Budget directors' command, and extending the role of the Federal Reserve, the credit budget, and the manipulatory function of the fiscal agencies, shifted U.S. regulatory practices from a lower, direct gear to a higher, more sophisticated, indirect management gear. Although criticized as "reaganomics," or "voodoo economics," these practices found unexpected popularity among heads of state in Europe. These leaders designed their own "voodoo economic" practices. The surprise was that it worked, and worked better than the "sound neokeynesian" practices previously employed. Some economists argued that it worked because Reagan's policy was actually based on some elements of keynesian practice. In mid-1980s, the United States and Western Europe again experienced a period of prosperity—a "mini-prosperity" with less rapid growth than the 1960s had witnessed, but a prosperity to be reckoned with in historical analyses, nevertheless. The stock market went up and up, unemployment in the United States was around 6 percent or even less, GNP growth moved from zero and below zero to around 2–3 percent. Then, in October 1987, the long-predicted, sudden crash of the stock market occurred. Experts list among the principal causes of this disruption, U.S. budgetary and trade deficits and loss of value of the dollar (the latter is also regarded as a positive phenomenon, which is expected to enhance U.S. foreign trade). Yet, the crash did not affect conditions, as predicted by "gloomers and doomers." The economy regained its strength and, although not thriving as much as before, moved on.

On January 29, 1980, immediately following his inauguration, Reagan ordered a sixty-day moratorium on pending government regulations. Vice-President Bush had been assigned to chair the Task Force on Regulatory Relief.[11] The president issued Executive Order 12291, transforming the Office of Management and Budget (OMB) into a superregulatory agency with the task of supervising reform and reformed agencies. The OMB became responsible for keeping the costs (to the government) of existing regulatory activities to a minimum and for weighing the effects of new proposals in order to establish whether the benefits of intended regulation outweighed its anticipated costs. It was announced that the government would award contracts and tax reliefs to companies with self-auditing systems. Critics of regulatory agencies, who had been vocal in universities, professional journals, and in a variety of private institutes and organizations combating regulation under Carter, were nominated to head regulatory agencies and fill influential positions in the management of the nation's economy. These individuals focused on reducing all direct interference by regulatory agencies in operations affecting a corporation's standing in the market; yet subjected the market to a greater degree to new, indirect regulatory practices conducted by inducement. At the same time, the regulatory importance of tax incentives, government subsidies, loans, and cooperation with the Federal Reserve was enhanced. Instead of regulating the behavior of corporations and consumers, instead of forcing individuals to obey rules and follow restrictions, the new program emphasized regulating the conditions in which corporations and consumers operate. Despite holding no explicit authority delegated by Congress to perform central economic management, the OMB, the Federal Reserve, and the revenue service *de facto* comprehensively regulated and managed the economy while performing other functions. Business forces tacitly consented to cooperate with the government, preferring Reagan's management style to that of his predecessors.

What exactly was the scope of the initial deregulation?

(*a*) New rules introduced by Carter's administration during its last month of power, and certain other practices in the process of becoming instituted, were suspended for an indefinite period. The rationale was that the federal government could not afford these services. Specific projects for enactments and rules, which would have established a Solar Energy and Conservation

Bank, a government-owned synthetic fuel industry (*de facto* establishing a two-sector economy), and the expansion of urban development, were also halted or cancelled.

(*b*) The government announced its intention to abolish a number of existing departments and commissions involved in regulatory activities: the departments of energy and education, CAB, and several other less important agencies. Later, this idea was abandoned.

(*c*) Environmental requirements and certain antitrust rules restricting some forms of takeover and merger of larger corporations were eased. In order to reduce production costs, the ailing steel industry was allowed to release more polluted water from mills; certain industries were allowed to discharge toxic wastes into local sewage systems; schools were released from the requirement to detect and remove asbestos from classrooms. Strip-mining rules and the labeling of chemical and food products were eased. Some rules of the EEOC were rewritten.

According to analysts of these changes (see Guzzardi 1982, 36), as a result of the abrogation of many rules and regulations, the number of pages in the *Federal Register* shrank from 86,406 in 1980 to 63,554 in 1981. (Since then, however, new regulations have appeared. No one seems to have counted pages in the register recently.)

(*d*) Budgets of most regulatory agencies, especially the EPA, OSHA, and the NHTSC were substantially reduced. These agencies, like others, were forced to reduce staff. Although this reduced interference by regulatory agencies in business activities, in some instances, it was perceived by corporations as detrimental to productivity; certain industries experienced substantial delays in acquiring assorted permits, inspections, and other necessary services. Eventually, staff was restored, though not in all agencies to the same degree. In the meantime, however, the amount of paperwork generated by regulatory agencies was significantly reduced.

Well-developed, comprehensive, expert analyses of these deregulatory activities are still not available.[12] It is quite evident that these policies arrested for some time the expansion of direct regulatory agencies, but the trend has not been significantly reversed. The new, complex economy of the 1980s required greater regulation than in the 1950s. Consumer groups and certain experts criticized deregulation policies. Some charged that business was relieved from its obligations to the consumer and for employee safety. Others claim that deregulation failed to create, as it had promised, increased competition, better products, cheaper services, and larger profits. Neither the advocates nor the critics got what they expected with deregulation. Increasingly, it is becoming evident that many established businesses can no longer operate in a deregulated market economy; nor can consumers live in one. For instance, while deregulating transport industries strengthened the position of some well-established firms, it also produced many adverse consequences. Like animals released from a long time in captivity, Braniff International, some smaller airlines, and many trucking firms were unable to operate efficiently under deregulated, "jungle-market" conditions; they were soon forced into bankruptcy. Many large and small corporations can no longer operate without subsidies, government orders, tax releases, and other protection provided under the state umbrella. At the same time, others suffer fatally under supervision and protection. The government cannot allow a business with a large work force, a large investment agency, or a bank to collapse. Frequently, the consequences would be seriously detrimental, not only to the companies and their employees and clients, but to entire industries and the economy as a whole. Knowing this, executives sometimes engage in risky operations, relying on a forthcoming rescue should there be a crunch. The list of giant corporations in the United States, Canada, and Western Europe that, without government subsidies, protection, and other forms of assistance, would no longer exist, lengthens steadily. The U.S. government helped Chrysler out of trouble; it nationalized the Continental Bank of Illinois to prevent a chain reaction of disasters in the banking industry. Deregulated transportation industries and the manufacturers of airplanes (e.g., Lockheed, McDonnell Douglas, and Boeing) accumulate deficits on sales of civilian aircraft and experience great difficulties competing with European state-owned or subsidized firms, but stay alive by making profit on military contracts.

The war over regulation continues. In the literature on the debate, one side is represented by those who (see, e.g., Poole 1982) believe in the principle, once declared by Coolidge: "The business of America is business." On the other side are those (see, e.g., Tolchin & Tolchin 1983) to whom "the rush to deregulate is tantamount with dismantling America." The conflict rages between these representatives of two distinctive, evidently incompatible, life philosophies and economic attitudes.

The first group says: We, like everyone else, value clean water, clean air, and safety in the working place. What concerns us is money: the amount we can afford to spend on regulatory management and regulatory practice. We must be economical to stay in business; yet regulatory agencies, such as OSHA, EPA, and the FTC do not recognize that costs matter. Their effect on costs have been uncontrolled for too long. The public is willing to pay for environmental protection and safety, but the costs must be worth it and affordable.

People of the second group say (Tolchin & Tolchin 1983, 22–23, 256, 276):

> Regulation is the connective tissue of a civilized society. . . . What had taken years to build was dismantled in the first twelve months of the Reagan administration. . . . The rush to deregulate is a return to the law of the jungle. . . . Regulations provide protection against the avarice of the market place, against shoddy products and unscrupulous marketing practices from Wall Street to Main Street.

Regulations protect us against environmental disasters, work hazards, and the unsafe use of technology, chemicals, and nuclear energy. To claim that benefits can be quantified by placing a monetary value on human life is ridiculous, impractical, and unfair.

Some combine both approaches. Wilson (1980, 366–367), for example, points out that "perception of fairness and unfairness of a policy" determines the outcome of its application. He believes policy areas can be classified according to "whether the costs and benefits are widely distributed or narrowly concentrated" from the perspective of those who bear the cost and those who enjoy the benefits. Kelman writes in the same book (1980, 266):

> Many of the benefits of social regulation have no ready dollar value because they are not traded on markets. . . . An obsession with . . . cost-benefit analyses would itself remove something of what is special about the social regulatory agencies as expressions of a desire to keep market relationships in their place. Still there is a point at which even the advocate of such a view would have to say "stop"—that *we cannot guarantee a right to a healthy workplace if it would cost half the GNP to save one life* [emphasis added].

Another pertinent observation can be made: Once introduced, direct regulations not only control activities intended to be regulated, they radically transform economic and social conditions so that state control becomes indispensable. The process cannot be changed without adversely affecting large groups and their vested interests. At most, it can be arrested at a certain stage, for a period of time. Weidenbaum—a highly vocal critic of regulation, who became chairman of the Economic Advisory Committee to the President—and others who fought regulations, eventually came to hold positions of control over regulatory agencies, but they managed only to reduce the excesses of certain practices and were not able to eliminate regulatory agencies or cancel many programs. Their attempts to abolish major programs were met by enormous and vocal opposition. As a result of these miscarried efforts, the system of agencies controlling the economy and society through direct regulation attained even greater legitimacy and became even more incorporated into the structure of the U.S. government and economy.

By restoring beneficial market conditions for small and medium businesses, and at the same time creating a market more conducive to mergers of large-scale corporations and financial operations involving billions of dollars, the government produced a situation in which the U.S. economy began to grow again. New foreign money was invested in the United States where product consumption had increased, but the strong position of the U.S. dollar meant that fewer U.S. products could be sold abroad. The United States faced increasing competition from Japan and the Europeans; its trade deficit became enormous. Under these conditions, the

United States' restored prosperity and growing market needed government protection and regulation more than before. The extensive system of indirect regulatory mechanisms developed under the Reagan administration suited these needs well, at least for some time. By regulating certain factors, the government can control market conditions; it cannot regulate the fears and thoughts of investors, however.

CHAPTER SEVEN

Indirect Regulation:
The United States

Indirect regulatory practice in the United States is implemented by several principal systems:

1. The OMB develops and implements the administration's fiscal and budgetary policies. It is well named; it is the central managing agency of the state's systems. Among its principal functions, it prepares and supervises the administration of both cash and credit budgets; formulates fiscal programs; keeps the president informed; and generally supervises interactions between regulatory agencies.

2. The Federal Financing Bank in cooperation with the OMB, implements the administration's credit policies, which determine the scope of direct loans and loan guarantees issued, by either on-budget agencies or off-budget (for budget concepts see *Historical Tables. Budget of the U.S. Government 1986*, 1–1) entities, to national agencies, corporations, and foreign governments.

3. The Federal Reserve System, the semi-autonomous central banking institution, conducts monetary policy concerning the availability of currency in circulation, influences exchange rates, determines the cost of credit, and manages other elements of the general financial condition of the market.

Taxes and the Budget

In a capital study discussing the budgetary process in the United States, Wildavsky (1984, 128–129) points out:

> The budget is the lifeblood of the government, the financial reflection of what the government does or intends to do. . . . The crucial aspect of budgeting is whose preferences are to prevail in disputes about which

activities are to be carried on and to what degree, in the light of limited resources. The problem is not only "*how shall budgetary benefits be maximized,*" as if it made no difference who received them but also "*Who shall receive budgetary benefits and how much?*" [emphasis added].

In the past, when revenues were collected principally to sustain the administration, military, police, justice system, and government, the budget was much smaller, and the wider public's interest in budgetary allocations exiguous. Today, both revenue collection through taxation schemes, and the distribution of outlays, including transfer payments from the government to society, profoundly affect the immediate social and economic environment and, over time, the entire fabric of society. Hence, budgetary conflicts greatly interest the media and public at large. This change, typical for etatized societies, represents an important feature of conditions under the New State. In a contemporary etatized society, everyone depends, not only on the market, but on the state budget as well.

The U.S. government presently appropriates (see Table 7.1) approximately 18–19 percent of the nation's annual GNP through federal taxes, excises, and other payments. Total government expenditure as a percent of GNP (*Historical Tables, 1986,* table 14.3) in 1984 was 23.5; at present it is close to 25 percent. It is expected that the government will requisition a similar or larger portion of GNP over the next decade and thereafter. European governments appropriate a somewhat greater share of their GNP, but spend a larger part of their revenues on social programs.[1]

In this chapter, our interest concerns only one aspect of budgetary and taxation activities: their instrumentality to etatization. Still, some general information must be included.

U.S federal taxes include two separate components: income tax and social security payroll tax (see Table 7.1). The progressive income tax system was introduced in 1861, during the Civil War, in order to generate funds for the military and other Union expenditures. Few nations, at that time, had a progressive income tax system. The introduction of this system was regarded as a new step in the democratization of society. The law underwent several amendments but the income tax system was not effective enough at first. It was abandoned in 1896, when the U.S. Supreme Court declared income tax unconstitutional. In 1913, however, after a two-year debate, Congress enacted the sixteenth Constitutional Amendment; the universal taxation of income was revived. Under this law, individual and corporate incomes are taxed at source, according to a progressive scheme. This scheme has been revised many times and continues to be controversial. Income tax remains the principal source of revenue for the U.S. government; it sustains administration, defense, and other services. At first, tax increases were regarded as expedient only in connection with war and major calamities. After World War II, however, and especially during the 1970s, the rapidly growing services and social programs maintained by the

Table 7.1.   Percentage Composition of U.S. Budget Receipts

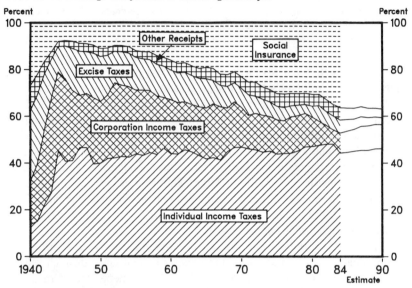

Source: Historical Tables: Budget of the United States Government. Fiscal Year 1986 (Washington, D.C.: OMB, 1985)

Table 7.2.   Budget Outlays by Superfunction as a Percent of GNP

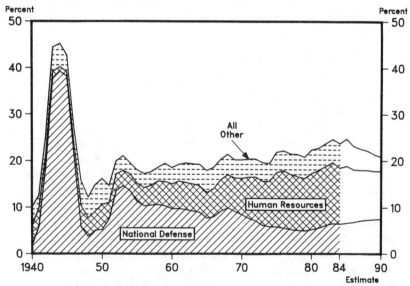

Source: Historical Tables: Budget of the United States Government. Fiscal Year 1986 (Washington, D.C.: OMB, 1985)

government made successive increases in rates of income taxation unavoidable.

In 1935, Congress enacted the Social Security law. At first, this law exacted payments only from selected businesses. Gradually, however, more employees and employers became obliged to participate in the scheme until, finally, it has become nearly universal. Only employees of the federal government, and certain specific institutions, remain exempt from obligatory contributions to social insurance programs.[2] Under amendments introduced practically every other year, the system of contributions has evolved into the second major tax collecting system of the nation. One third of federal revenues are collected in Social Security payments at present.

From the perspective of etatization theory, the two U.S. taxes provide for different kinds of governmental functions. Income tax was enacted to provide financial means for traditional functions. The payroll social security tax was enacted to furnish revenues for new functions, such as care for the elderly and their families who, for reasons beyond their control, cannot support themselves. Social Security was meant to be a self-supporting scheme, based on funds collected from wages and salaries, contributions by employers, and corresponding allocations from the government. This is no longer the case, however. Apart from its traditional functions of defense, maintenance of law and order, and newer functions related to services and transfer payments, the New State is now responsible for protecting the environment, managing the market, and providing civil rights protection. The apparatus involved in these last functions depends on the support of general budgetary allocations. The federal government administers Social Security and bears the principal cost of its administration. Although the initial division of tax roles and the specific intents regarding the Social Security levy are maintained, the division, particularly on the allocating side, is no longer as definite as initially intended.

According to the 1986 U.S. budget, every dollar of government revenue of that year comprised 37¢ collected in income taxes, 30¢ in social insurance receipts, 8¢ in corporate income taxes, 3¢ in excise taxes, 18¢ in borrowed money, and 4¢ in other receipts (see Table 7.1). Of each dollar expended by the federal government, 41¢ went to direct benefit payments to individuals, 29¢ to national defense outlays, and 15¢ to net interest payments on debt; 10¢ were transferred to states and localities, and 5¢ were expended on other operations (see Table 7.2).[3]

Wildavsky draws a distinction between old, "traditional" and new, "program" budgeting. "If the old budgeting," writes Wildavsky (1984, 181), "became anti-analytical because it arrested development at the level of inputs, the new budgeting is dwelling excessively on outputs. A fixation on what is put in has been replaced by a compulsion over what should be taken out." He continues (135–136):

The basic idea behind program budgeting is that instead of presenting budgetary requests in the usual line-item form, which focuses on categories like supplies, maintenance, and personnel, the presentation is made in terms of the end-product of program packages like public health or limited war or strategic retaliatory forces. The virtues of the program budget are said to be its usefulness in relating ends and means in a comprehensive fashion.

Wildavsky further notes that the "traditional procedure increases agreement among the participants whereas the program device decreases it." The new program method burdens participants with calculations and the development of details. In the end, "the specific outcomes in the form of decisions are likely to be different." The difference is not only technical. A qualitative difference has come about in the scope of decisions and the effect of budgeting on the lives of individuals. The new budgeting is distinct, not because authorities adopted a different method of budgeting, but because program budgeting affects a much wider spectrum of functions; it reflects the new structure of conflicts typical of etatized society.

As the state acquires new functions, it requires society to provide funds for them. Table 7.3 portrays the rise of selected federal taxes from 1970 to 1983. Naturally, opinions differ over whether tax increases are in fact commensurate with an increase in benefits provided by the federal state. Downs (1960), in an article titled "Why the Government Budget is Too Small in a Democracy," observes that people resent paying taxes because they do not realize the link between their personal tax contribution and the benefits provided by the government. He implies that the benefits are greater than their cost in taxes. Hansen (1983) agrees. Yet, many people feel they are not getting enough for their taxes, that their money is spent on objectives they disapprove of, or that they could benefit more if they directly expended the money. The tax debate carries on.

In 1985, despite Reagan's efforts to keep taxes down, U.S. taxpayers had to turn over an average of 35–40% of their incomes.[4] Citizens of other Western industrialized societies pay higher taxes. Tax revenues collected per

Table 7.3.   Federal Tax Indexes, by Type of Tax, 1970–1983

Item	1970	1973	1976	1979	1980	1983
All taxes	127.5	172.1	220.7	328.4	359.0	424.2
Personal income taxes	138.1	170.1	220.0	349.4	389.8	448.8
Corporate profit taxes	102.0	144.1	181.8	247.1	234.2	199.2
Indirect business taxes*	119.3	130.8	141.7	170.6	223.2	296.8
Social insurance contribution	134.3	217.7	292.3	439.8	479.5	644.5
Estate and gift taxes	120.1	166.1	182.2	180.9	214.4	192.1

Source: Statistical Abstract of the United States. 1986. Table 507. (1967 = 100; represents tax receipts, net of refunds, as shown in the national income accounts, generally on the accrual basis.)

* Excise taxes and custom duties

capita in 1983 amounted (in U.S. $) to: in the United States, $3,955; Canada, $4,431; Denmark, $5,091; France, $4,228; Federal Republic of Germany, $3,973; Italy, $2,521; Japan, $2,722; Sweden, $5,572; Great Britain, $3,052. Citizens in Western European nations and Canada receive free medical services and other benefits that U.S. citizens are not entitled to; whether they actually get more than U.S. citizens do for their money is, of course, a matter of opinion.

After a plethora of tax reductions, exemptions, and depreciation allowances, corporate income taxes, which in the 1950s constituted 30 percent of federal revenues, have dwindled to less than 10 percent of total revenue.

When the Social Security tax was established in 1937, the maximum annual contribution expected per employee was $30, or 1 percent of the first $3,000 of earnings. When Johnson proclaimed the "war on poverty," the public accepted higher Social Security and income taxes. People believed that, with the money obtained through new taxes, the government would not only eliminate poverty in the United States, but would participate in efforts to reduce poverty elsewhere. Social Security taxes steeply increased in the 1960s and 1970s. Experts fear that, in order to collect sufficient revenues to cover Social Security expenses in the future, Social Security taxes will have to be continuously augmented until, eventually, people begin refusing to pay.[5]

Fiscal Policy

History is replete with conflict, unrest, revolt, rebellion, and revolution caused by fiscal policies, tax demands, and plain tax robberies conducted by monarchs, princes, governments, and the state. Many long-established and even prosperous political systems collapsed through an inability to raise sufficient tax revenues. The three major revolutionary events that initiated our modern era—the English Revolution of 1640, the French Revolution of 1879, and the American Revolution—were catalyzed by attempts to impose new taxes. Tax revolts are common in U.S. history. The current situation does differ however, for a variety of reasons. For the first time in history, taxes are collected to sustain social programs. Although high taxes are not indicative of etatized societies only, collections to maintain social programs and state-run services are. The implications of these qualitative changes are crucial. According to Hansen (1983, 6):

> As nations have grown in terms of revenue, personnel, and function, any actions they take with respect of taxation or spending have a much larger impact on society and the economy than was the case when all governmental activities amounted to 5 percent or less of Gross National Product (GNP). Decisions affecting prices and profits have increasingly come to be made in the halls of Congress and the executive branch rather than by free market operations.

Confrontations over fiscal and budgetary policies have recently proved as divisive and fervent as class conflicts of the past; they may be regarded as class differences revealing themselves through new issues. The budgetary debate is fierce, because never before has the livelihood of such a large percentage of U.S. residents and, correspondingly, other populations been so dependent on budgetary decisions. Transfer payment recipients and government employees are not the only ones affected by budgetary allocations; private corporations, which receive governmental contracts or subsidies, depend on them as well. Ultimately, fiscal policies, taxes, and budgetary allocations touch every citizen. The U.S. federal budget and, correspondingly, budgets of other nations, have become more than just extracting, allocating, and redistributing mechanisms. They now reflect the ideals and social makeup of the society.

The current issues, raised by both liberal and conservative politicians and social scientists, concern who pays how much tax, and with what effect. The debate also focuses on the proportion of taxes to be derived from the middle class and the rich. Liberals assert an ethical standpoint. They argue that moral concerns, compassion, or other considerations of equity oblige contemporary governments to raise sufficient revenues to finance social programs, even at the expense of economic development. Conservatives (Wanniski 1978, 1983; Bartlett & Roth 1983; Roberts 1984) assert the economic aspect; they hold that government's primary obligation is to promote economic growth, not only because it generates prosperity, but also because it solves other problems. If taxes are too high, investment, development, and job creation will diminish. The supply of investment funds will dry up. Excessive taxation, they add, produces tax avoidance, and a growing underground economy, consequently contracting economic growth and reducing the economy's ability to generate revenue.[6] Whether the government professes liberal or conservative objectives, it cannot abnegate either. Both Carter and Reagan have faced this predicament.

Taxation is relevant to the advancement of etatization in several ways:

(*a*) As the state performs more numerous administrative functions, it requires larger revenues to sustain its sophisticated administration

(*b*) The functions of the New State, its services and social programs, must be sustained by collected revenues, by profits from successful state-sector ventures, or by sales of state-owned natural resources, or, failing all these, by loans that acquire interest (see Table 7.4)

(*c*) Contemporary tax structures usually contain exemptions, decrements, deductions, and bonuses that qualify tax requirements as highly effective instruments of social and economic policy; taxes are employed to stimulate investment and consumption and to attain other socioeconomic objectives (*d*) Taxation is part of implementing redistributive policies; the state takes money from those who are better off and spends it, either on collective programs—which are more frequently used by the poor than by the rich—or on direct transfer payments

Fiscal policy is instrumental in attaining more indirect objectives: furthering class and group interests; regulating economic growth; setting limits to financial and economic instability (e.g., employed in reducing inflation); implementing income redistribution; and advancing other equity objectives. Surrey and McDaniel (1985) write that contemporary tax designers are quite conscious of the wide implications of taxation. Governments cannot afford, they say, to disregard the wider economic and social consequences of taxation and budgetary policies. They point out two recently introduced elements in the application of these policies:

1. Current taxes are dually composed. One part contains regular provisions for revenue collections (definition of taxable income and rules of tax assessment, etc.); the second contains special provisions for tax incentives.

2. Taxes are employed as deliberate means in redistribution practices.

They further discern new provisions, often called tax incentives or tax subsidies, as departures from normal tax structure, because they are designed to favor a particular industry, activity, or class of persons, and only indirectly produce revenues. Such incentives take many forms: permanent exclusions from income deductions; deferrals of tax liabilities; credits against tax; or special rates. Whatever their form, these departures from the normative tax structure represent favoritism in government policies, effected through the tax system, rather than through direct grants, loans, or other forms of government assistance. Under such conditions, taxation evolves into fiscal policy; fiscal policies evolve into a part of the complex system of indirect regulatory practices conducted in pursuit of economic and social objectives.

Can a government effectively increase revenue by means other than taxes? Certain nations have made attempts to generate supplementary revenue by directly engaging in business activities. But the United States remains orthodox and relies primarily on tax collection to generate revenue. "In this world nothing can be said to be certain, except death and taxes," wrote Benjamin Franklin. All governments know that a method of generating revenues better than taxation has not yet been discovered. Governments that have attempted to generate revenues by nationalizing more industries have failed miserably. In the 1980s (see table 7.4), governments are trying to maintain the best possible balance of trade, increase production and GNP, and, when these methods fail, raise new revenue by increasing taxes or resorting to borrowing.

Table 7.4.   Revenue Generation by Governments

Domestic

Direct taxes exacted from the population and corporations	Personal and corporate income tax, turnover tax, payroll social security, excise, export and import duties, user fees, charges for services, property and resource taxes, sales and value-adding taxes, property sales and inheritance taxes, emergency taxes imposed for a limited period
Indirect (in some instances hidden) taxes	Charges included in certain fees or licenses, permits, fines, and special taxes included in prices of commodities sold in the market
Sales by government of land, resources, and other state-owned property	Sales of land and land-bearing resources, of gold, and of other minerals, rights of use, government-owned buildings and other state-owned property to domestic or foreign buyers (including arms and other military equipment, used and new), patents, denationalization, and privatisation
Government involvement in profit-making activity	Nationalization of industries, establishment of state-owned enterprises; financing and financial operation through state-owned and privately owned banks, investment corporations, and other financial institutions
International	Conquest of foreign countries; confiscation of foreign property, war reparations
	Promotion of foreign trade, which would produce a positive balance of trade with either total appropriation of profits or of taxes on such trade
	Taxation of citizens who work in foreign countries
Domestic and foreign borrowing	Issuing of bonds and other securities, raising funds domestically or internationally

Deficits

Reagan is not the first U.S. president who promised to balance the budget and failed. Not one president since the 1930s has attained an overall surplus. Since 1969, every year but one has produced a deficit; the exception was the last year of the Nixon administration, which yielded a $3.2 billion surplus. In 1985, the U.S. government spent $945.9 billion and completed the year in red ink with a budgetary deficit of $211.9 billion. According to Treasury reports, in 1985, $178.9 billion was paid in interest on the accumulated $1.8-trillion national debt. It is anticipated (*Historical Tables 1986*, table 7.1) that in 1990 the gross federal debt of the United States will amount to $2,975,163 million. In 1985, the Department of Health and Human Services alone spent $315.6 billion on Social Security and other programs. This figure is close to the entire sum of the federal budget of 1975. The defense department's

Table 7.5. Overall Deficit/Surplus Incurred by Governments of Selected Industrial
Western Nations Under Etatization, 1978–1985
(As Percent of Total Expenditure and Lending Minus Repayments)

	1978	1979	1980	1981	1982	1983	1984	1985
World	-11.79	-9.70	-11.18	-12.59	-14.55	-17.13	-15.28	-16.05
Industrialized Nations	-11.29	-9.34	-10.90	-11.24	-13.14	-17.08	-15.31	-15.28
Canada[g]*	-22.30	-17.96	-15.73	-10.44	-22.13	-24.55	-25.29	-23.94
France[c]	-3.54	-3.81	-.09	-6.37	-6.81	-7.93	-6.73	-6.72
Germany[d]	-6.99	-6.82	-5.94	-7.35	-6.03	-6.28	-5.55[P]	-2.98
Italy[a]	-21.69	-22.36	-25.11	-26.36	-22.52	-23.66	-27.36	-27.98
Sweden[e]	-11.68	-16.63	-18.73	-19.42	-17.89	-20.21	-15.38	-14.25
Great Britain[c]	-13.06	-14.44	-11.69	-11.72	-7.71	-10.53	-7.64	-8.08
United States[e]	-12.39	-6.85	-12.24	-10.96	-16.00	-23.66	-19.88	-21.13

Source: Government Finance Statistics Yearbook. Vol. 10, p. 38 and 11, p. 38 (Washington, DC:
1986 and 1987).
Note: Percentage of data available as follows: a, 95 and over; b, 90–94; c, 80–89.9; d, 70–79.9;
e, 60–69; f, 50–59.9; and g, 20–49.9. p: provisional; *: ending June 30 or other than calendar
year.

gargantuan outlays for 1985 amounted to $244.1 billion. Nearly a quarter of
1985 government expenditures were paid with borrowed money.

The United States is not exceptional in this regard. None of the nations
listed in Table 7.5—none, as a matter of fact, in Western Europe, with the
exception of Norway in 1983—reported any surplus in the last eight years.
Of all the countries of the world, only Kuwait, the United Arab Emirates, and
Bahrain report surpluses.

According to Anderson (1987, 13), U.S. federal deficit figures, as
percentage of total outlays, were as follows (given in negative percentages):
12.85% in 1978; 7.97% in 1979; 12.49% in 1980; 11.63% in 1981; 17.15%
in 1982; 25.70% in 1983; and 21.75% in 1984. To bring these figures up to
date, let me add that, on the basis of press reports, in 1987 U.S. spending
totaled $1.002 trillion, up 1.2% from 1986. The government managed to
increase collected revenues to $854.1 billion. The deficit was $148 billion,
less than the highest in U.S. history—$221.1 billion in 1987, but still big
enough to be a subject of concern. At present, Reagan and Congress are
involved in negotiations attempting to cut budget spending and the deficit
further.

In *The Trillion Dollar Budget*, Pascall (1985, xvii) extensively discusses
the American predicament. His "brutally simple arithmetic" runs as follows:

Revenues are stuck at about 19 percent of Gross National Product (GNP)
and spending is stuck at about 24 percent of GNP. Over time, both are
projected to rise gradually. But the gap between the two will remain and in
fact will increase. Each year the government runs a deficit equal to 5
percent of GNP, this amount (currently $200 billion) is added to the
national debt. To borrow this extra money requires paying at least $20

billion more each year in interest costs.

Continuing his calculations, Pascall observes that should this trend continue, by the year 2472 the economy would produce barely enough wealth to cover the debt-service cost. Generating higher revenues or cutting expenditures are two ways of combating the deficit. Raising taxes, according to conservative economists, produces adverse and destabilizing economic consequences. Hence, Reagan has objected to increasing taxes. Yet, expenditures cannot be reduced. High defense spending, according to the administration, must be maintained to enhance the defense capability of the United States and achieve foreign-policy objectives. The government, as declared in the *Federal Budget* is also obliged to "preserve and maintain the social safety net programs that represent the accrued permanent consensus of the American people over the past five decades."

There appears no remedy for the predicament, except tax increases, which have not been acceptable to the Reagan administration. In the *Budget Message of the President (Budget of the United States Government*, 1987, M-4), Reagan repeated what he said on other such occasions:[7] "This budget shows, moreover, that eliminating the deficit is possible *without* raising taxes, *without* sacrificing our defense preparedness, and *without* cutting onto legitimate programs for the poor and the elderly." The Gramm-Rudman-Hollings act, which established deficit ceilings for the next six years and required that Congress balance the budget by 1991 is, in the opinion of many experts, a Band-Aid approach to a condition requiring major surgery. Economists of the Austrian school, Buchanan, Rowley, and Tollison (1987, 4) write, "Gramm-Rudman-Hollings is the only finger in the congressional dyke, attempting to restrain a US federal deficit flood." Anderson (Buchanan et al. 1977, 34) argues that since he did not recommend massive transfers of wealth *per se*, Keynes cannot be blamed in "any direct sense" for "the rapid acceleration in transfers to individuals via the federal budget after 1967." These economists blame Keynes (39) for "introducing confusion in the public mind and in the minds of politicians," which eventually produced the accepting deficits lightly; they call for a balanced budget amendment to the U.S. Constitution. They are not considering the social change that has occurred, and they are not writing about the contemporary United States, in which Jessie Jackson was a presidential candidate. Some liberals blame the deficit on defense spending. Surely, with serious defense-spending reductions, which cannot be introduced at present for security reasons, the deficit could be abated, but for a short period only. The fact is that other industrialized nations, which spend a lesser percent of their budget on defense than does the United States, are not exempt from budgetary deficits. In a democratic etatized society, citizens expect the state to provide them with basic necessities. Over time, their expectations naturally increase. From year to year, more and more individuals raise more and more claims to both old and new entitlements. Politicians wishing to win votes promise new entitlements. Governments unable to raise revenues at a pace commensurate with the rise of these expectations are caught between their obligation to fulfil numerous state functions, their desire to win the next election, and the necessity to reduce deficits. 43% of budget outlays in 1986 was spent on entitlements under mandatory programs. The deficit is the price (close to $500 billion in 1988 or 1989) the state "family" must pay in order to provide for the basic needs of its members—corporations, defense forces, social security recipients, bureaucrats, and so on.

The Credit Budget

In 1979, for the first time, Congress officially enacted a credit budget separate from its cash budget. The *Special Analysis 1983* (1982) document outlines the objectives of credit programs as follows:

> Federal and federally assisted credit programs play a significant role in the functioning of the Nation's economy and financial markets. This credit assistance is primarily in four forms: direct loans from the Federal Government, Federal guarantees of private lending, lending by privately owned Government-sponsored enterprises, and access to tax exempt credit. Much like Federal expenditures on goods and services or transfer payments, credit programs change the allocation of resources and the distribution of income.

Ippolito (1984, 5), on whose thorough analyses this discussion often relies, writes that the government uses the credit budget "to extend financial assistance while minimizing or even eliminating budgetary costs." Because programs in this realm include mostly returnable loans and, especially, loan guarantees, they appear to cost little or nothing and do not provoke major congressional opposition. To recipients of loans or loan guarantees under credit budget programs—corporations, agencies, foreign governments, farmers, or students—the benefits received are twofold: First, they obtain loans, directly from the government or from private banks under U.S. government guarantee, that they would not be able to obtain in the open market; second, they receive such loans at lower-than-market costs, while the government bears the difference.[8] Over the last fifteen years (Furlong 1982, 60; Leonard & Rhyne 1981; Ippolito 1984, 6), the amount of direct loans and loan guarantees disbursed under credit budget programs has grown from roughly $176.2 billion ($51.1 billion in direct loans and $125.1 billion in loan guarantees) in 1970 to $462.4 billion ($163.9 billion in direct loans and $298.5 billion in loan guarantees) in 1980. At the end of 1985 (*Special Analyses 1987* 1986, F-3), the Federal Financing Bank held in its portfolio $667 billion ($257 billion in direct loans and $410 billion in loan guarantees), which the *Analyses* proudly declared was "about 30% larger than the loan assets of the two largest U.S. commercial banks combined." By 1981, direct and guaranteed borrowing absorbed 35 percent of the total credit raised in U.S. domestic markets. The vast scale of financial activity incited in the market by the federal government, and affecting the social condition of the nation, becomes clear when the list of recipients is considered.

Direct loans are disbursed through a system of government-sponsored enterprises (GSEs): (*a*) in emergencies, for example, crop prices and development assistance to farmers through the Farmers Home Administration (FmHA) and the Rural Electrification Administration (REA); (*b*) in assistance to business corporations, in entrepreneurial undertakings, and toward urban and rural housing development, through the Small Business Administration, and Housing and Urban Development; and (*c*) in promotion of foreign trade, through economic assistance and financing military sales to foreign nations through the Export-Import Bank (Eximbank) and the Commodity Credit Corporation (CCC). Ippolito (37) remarks, in connection with the last class of activities: "Off-budget financing greatly reduces the visible budget outlays required to support direct lending. Of the nearly $56 billion in new direct loans issued during fiscal 1981, only $5 billion surfaced as outlays for on-budget agencies, compared to $21 billion for off-budget agencies. (The remaining $30 billion was accounted for by repayments and other adjustments of previous loans.)"

Loan guarantees, according to *Federal Credit Programs*, "occur when a Government agency enters into a firm commitment to use Government funds as necessary to repay a lender upon default by the borrower." All of the agencies listed above also grant federal loan guarantees. Other major recipients of loan guarantees are the Veterans Administration and the Federal National Mortgage Association. A significant portion of loan guarantees, about $2 billion or more annually—$1.8 billion in 1986—has been expended on student loans. In contrast to other loans granted under these programs, student loans are considered entitlements.

Tax expenditures on GSEs, such as the Federal National Mortgage Association, the Federal Home Loan Association, and the Student Loan Marketing Association for industrial development bonds constitute the third category of programs under the credit budget.

Federal credit, according to the *Special Analysis 1986*, (1985, F-22) and *Special Analysis 1987* (1986, F-21) operates through five GSEs, which, as financial intermediaries, disburse funds to particular economic sectors. The GSEs include: Federal Home Loan Banks; Federal Home Loan Mortgage Corporation; Federal National Mortgage Association (FNMA); Student Loan Marketing Association; and the Farm Credit System and its subsidiaries. Most of the GSEs and their subsidiaries, created as government institutions, were privatized by 1969. According to the special analyses, in contrast to the past when housing accounted for about 30 percent of direct loans of these organizations, at present, they predominately finance business activities.

Among the well-publicized loan-guarantee operations undertaken under the auspices of the credit budget were "rescue missions" or "bailouts" (Melton 1985, 157) of the Penn Central Transportation Company and other railroads; Lockheed; the First Pennsylvania Bank; Chrysler; New York City; the recent rescue of the Continental Bank of Illinois through a takeover by the FDIC , and the Texas City Corp Bank. Ippolito (1984, 77–88) and Greider (1987) also include an impressive number of less-publicized operations of this kind.

The credit budget document admits that federal credit, in some instances, has had "an inhibiting effect on productivity and economic growth" and "distorts the market's assessment of true risk and return." However, by extending credit to farmers, the government saved some of them (mostly those running large farm businesses) from bankruptcy, and maintained the conditions under which agricultural commodities are relatively cheap, to the advantage of consumers and of the government, for which food sales and food assistance are an important element of foreign policy. By granting the loan guarantee to Lockheed, the government prevented monopolization in the aerospace and defense industry. By extending the loan guarantee to Chrysler, the government saved workers from unemployment, protected numerous small businesses that supplied Chrysler, and, perhaps, prevented an even wider disaster that could have affected the economy at large. By saving the Continental Bank of Illinois, "Uncle Sam" reassured bank users that banks are safe, and that a repetition of events that led to the Great Depression is now impossible. The credit budget not only grants favors and manipulates the budget; it is also employed to preserve relative stability in the market economy. Western European governments nationalize industries in crises. The credit budget serves parallel purposes in the United States.

Writers on this area of government activity express concern that defaults on loans from the U.S. government have, recently, increased. They mention defaults on student loans, which are considerably higher than anticipated. Moreover, these loans are unsecured. They are also concerned about the Small Business Administration and FmHA recipients' loan defaults, and guarantees on loans to certain foreign governments. For instance, the federal government has guaranteed loans by U.S. banks to Poland. In January 1982, the Reagan administration was obliged to pay over $70 million to forestall the imminent default of the Polish authorities.[9] Some Latin American governments, with loans guaranteed by the U.S government, have experienced difficulties making payments on their debts.

The credit budget provides a protective umbrella to vital industries facing rainy days or the danger of extinction. Along with the welfare system, credit programs constitute an important component of the New State, yet another system for saving those in trouble and providing benefits to those in need. In the credit budget's family, the needy are not welfare or Social

Security recipients, but large corporations, small businesses, farmers, and students; each receives assistance through the respective administration. These recipients still participate in the capitalist market but, in the meantime, become financially dependent on the state.[10]

Monetary Regulation

In an opinion poll conducted during the summer of 1982, Paul Volcker, then chair of the Federal Reserve, was rated as the second most powerful man in the United States, after Reagan. "The Chairman of the Federal Reserve" wrote *The Economist* (September 22, 1984), "seldom goes on television, does not feel obliged to kiss babies or wear cowboy hats, and his finger is nowhere near the nuclear button. No matter: many Americans thought that Mr Volcker held sway over their mortgages, jobs and shopping baskets." Greider calls the United States "A Car With Two Drivers": the president and the chair of the Federal Reserve. The problem of the United States is how to make the two go in the same direction. Twice each year, the head of the Federal Reserve appears before the Senate Banking Committee to report on the Federal Reserve's assessment of the economic and monetary situation and to outline its current policies in open-market operations. The importance of the Federal Reserve has grown enormously over the last ten years. The fate of everyone, and not only in the United States, is affected by its course of action. A full army of "Fed watchers" keeps a steady surveillance for any signs that might suggest its current orientation.

The Federal Reserve System (the Fed, as it is usually called), was established on December 23, 1913. It was meant to be a bankers' bank, not only because it held reserves and provided loans to banks, but also because it was expected to represent banking interests. The Fed evolved into an semi-autonomous structure, operating on authority delegated by Congress but maintaining a fairly autonomous status and making decisions independently. To secure this independence, the president of the United States nominates the seven members of the Board of Governors, who are then approved by the Senate for a part of or a full 14-year term. The chair of the Federal Reserve is one of the seven members of the board, appointed by the president with Senate approval. The chair of the board acts also as chair of the Federal Open Market Committee (FOMC). The FOMC includes the seven members of the Federal Reserve's Board of Governors and five of twelve bankers chairing Federal Reserve banks. The individual in charge of the New York Federal Reserve Bank, who on behalf of the Fed conducts its international operations, is always a member of the FOMC. The committee meets periodically to set policy on open-market operations. Although the Fed acts independently of the Treasury and other governmental bodies, the head of the reserve consults the secretary of the Treasury and, occasionally, the president of the United States.

The Federal Reserve's principal function is to maintain economic stability. In order to implement this function, the Fed conducts the monetary policy of the nation. The Humphrey-Hawkins act (formally, the Full Employment and Balanced Growth Act of 1978) declares "inflation is a major national problem." The act obliges the Fed to deal with inflation; also to report on the money-supply growth targets it sets. These are now perceived as important parameters of economic policy affecting conditions in the market. The Fed regulates the supply of money in circulation by purchasing and selling government securities in the open market. When it purchases securities, it releases more money into circulation, enabling banks in the open market to increase the availability of loans and correspondingly adjust the credit rate. When the Fed wants to reduce the monetary supply, it does the opposite—sells securities and, therefore, reduces the reserves of other banks and the availability of loans in the market. The Fed is the United States' central bank: the banks' bank, providing other banks with liquidity loans whenever an exceptional need arises. In its reserve function, the Fed regulates the volume of funds that member and nonmember banks, and other depository institutions, are obliged to hold in their reserves; this is another instrument through which the Fed can regulate the supply of money in circulation. Endowed with new powers since 1979, and even more since 1981, this super-banking authority is not only the chief monetary authority; it also strongly affects other aspects of economic conditions in the market. The Fed now also supervises the operation of its own branches, operations of member banks; and, more remotely, the nation's general banking policies. If a major bank meets trouble, or if a problem arises concerning lending operations between banking institutions of the United States and other nations, the Fed, together with other central institutions, organizes rescue operations. In the past, the Fed used to set the funds rate in accordance with the prevailing market rate. This is no longer the case (Melton 1985, 4–16). The Federal Reserve currently sets both the central bank's lending rate and the volume of credit to be extended for purchases of securities in accordance with policies aimed at maintaining stability. Thus, it strongly affects, if not determines, the lending rate of other banks in the market.

The Fed also acts on behalf of the government. It handles the government's debt and the U.S. Treasury's financial operations. While the FDIC audits the government's balance sheets to guarantee that loans and statements reflect their true value, the Fed runs the government's check-processing operations. Melton reports that during 1983, the Fed cleared almost 17 billion checks, together valuing more than $11 trillion. In this, and many other ways, this nominally autonomous body has become a core institution, without which the government and its bureaucracy could not operate.

For years, the Federal Reserve's board and the FOMC were primarily concerned with keeping interest rates relatively stable. It was in 1979, during mounting stagflation, that Carter activated the Fed to its new regulatory role. At that time, GNP growth vacillated near and below the zero point. Prices rose at double-digit rates. Inflation kept rising, because of the oil crisis, because of increases in taxation, because industries were obliged to observe newly introduced environmental protection rules, and because everyone was demanding more: higher prices for commodities, higher salaries, increases in COLA (cost-of-living adjustments). Interest rates reached 20–25 percent. Conservative politicians blamed Carter and the Democrats for excessive spending and taxes, excessive state intervention, and mismanagement of the nation's economic affairs. Economists generally felt that too much money was in circulation. They claimed that the post-World War II economic equilibrium had collapsed because the different variables, previously held together, had gone astray in an economy operating under no authority and only through the market. Some advocated increased government involvement to stabilize conditions. Some recommended putting the economy under more exacting market regulation. Others felt that, instead of relying on direct regulation of businesses and individuals, the government should develop more powerful, sophisticated controls that, though nominally independent of the government, would more efficiently and effectively regulate the growth of variables and secure general market conditions. It is likely that Carter did not perceive the situation through either of these perspectives. But he must have seen that some of this criticism was valid, that the flow of money in circulation needed more control. Choosing a middle road, in 1980 he introduced the Deregulation and Monetary Control Act which, when approved by Congress, accorded new powers to the Federal Reserve to impose more effective control over the money supply and to undertake resolute action against inflation.[11] Carter also initiated the deregulation of some industries. This was one of the few Carter administration policies that Reagan continued and expanded.

Although subsequent developments cannot be analyzed fully in this book, the essence of the changes that followed from implementing this new act may be outlined.

The new act delegated greater authority to the Federal Reserve. It transformed the Fed into a *de facto* supreme regulating authority over factors affecting economic stability. In the past, the Federal Reserve had been expected to stabilize the monetary situation by exerting influence on monetary conditions in the market. In the 1950s and 1960s, it had accomplished this by determining the price of gold; later it focused on interest rates. The new act centralized and extended the power and control of the system over wider monetary aggregates, member and nonmember banks, as well as other depositories; all are required to maintain reserves as determined by the Fed. The Federal Reserve acquired a number of control instruments allowing it to intervene not only in the monetary but, albeit indirectly, in the broader economic condition as well. Previously, the Fed acted as a valve mechanism, releasing excess economic steam. The new act transformed the system of monetary regulation into a steering mechanism of the economy. The Fed's immediate objective was to combat inflation. Later, it was to maintain monetary stability to facilitate general prosperity in the market economy.

The new act complemented deregulation policy. Stricter and more uniform supervision by the Federal Reserve was expected to encourage more competitive conditions in the money market. With this goal in mind, federal savings and loan associations were allowed to maintain NOW accounts and issue mortgages on more flexible terms; this allowed them to compete with banks. The act, while ameliorating the position of savings and loan associations, insured credit unions and other small depositories, simultaneously subjecting them to banking requirements. All such institutions became *de facto* members of the Federal Reserve. They were able to borrow at the established discount rate but were also required to report to the Fed. Interest rates dropped, not on orders from above, but as a result of new competition. Cargill and Garcia (1982, 44–45) and some other authors believe the 1980 act represents a drastic shift from neokeynesian to monetarist policy.

The role of the Fed can be better appreciated by considering the October 19, 1987, world stock-market crash. On the New York Stock Exchange, the Dow Jones industrial average declined 508 points. According to some counts, losses totaled $385 billion; according to others, up to $950 billion. Similar collapses occurred on other stock markets in Tokyo, Hong Kong, Paris and elsewhere. Experts still debate the causes. Analysts have considered the following factors: worries about the continuing U.S. budget deficit (which was reduced in 1988); the U.S. trade deficit; lack of assertive leadership in the White House; signs that the United States is losing world economic leadership; failure of a computer-designed "portfolio insurance" scheme, which was expected to protect big investors from big losses "by trading stocks and stock-index futures simultaneously" and automatically, in the event of a certain programmed situation. To some, it was a self-fulfilling prophecy: Doomsday prophets in the media and a growing body of new books had been predicting a crash for several months, if not years. It was bound to happen, once so many experts believed it would happen. Not surprisingly, as soon as stocks began to decline, investors got panicky and went on selling. Most Japanese investors—now counted among the world's principal stockholders—waited out the crisis; they neither sold their holdings, nor withdrew foreign investment.

Eventually, the stock market recovered, to an extent. The effect of the crash on the economy's performance, and on the life of everyone who directly or indirectly depends on the value of stock investments—both rich and poor, investors, and those dependent on the value of pension-fund assets—is beyond the scope of this book. Some preliminary observations on the ability, under contemporary conditions, of the U.S. Federal Reserve and other central state agencies to cope with the crisis and stabilize the situation is in order, however.

The stock market represents not only the national but the international market. It cannot be controlled and stabilized by a single government, even one as powerful as the United States. In response to this particular crisis, most governments of Western nations cooperated, each trying to act as it deemed necessary. The action in the Tokyo market was most essential. The government there mobilized insurance companies, trust banks, and other financial institutions to bid up the market.

Although it was not able to prevent the crash or fully block the unwarranted decline, the Federal Reserve was able to handle the situation. The Fed's reaction was: (1) to announce, immediately, that it was "ready to serve as a source of liquidity to support the economic and financial system"; (2) to triple its daily acquisition of Treasury securities (from an average of $2 billion to $ 6 billion); (3) immediately to announce the lowering of its prime rate, which, in turn, caused other banks to lower interest rates. In short, the Fed reacted by increasing the available liquidity in the financial market.

The drop in interest rates helped the bond market recover; some recovery in the stock market followed. The crash caused no known major corporation bankruptcy. Individuals, however, lost a great deal. Some companies are now worth substantially less than before the crash; thus, they can be more easily taken over by larger corporations. The crash postponed privatization undertakings by some governments (e.g., in France). A major, uncontrollable economic catastrophe, like that in 1929, did not occur. It is quite possible, however, that the credit budget in United States, and corresponding agencies in other capitalist nations, will still have to cope with some latent consequences of the crash.

Was there anything more the government could have done to stabilize economic conditions? Hypothetically, states rich in gold and other reserves—which the U.S., Japanese and other deficit governments presently are not—could have done more to stabilize the situation; for instance, they could have given more support to currencies and bond markets or even could have purchased stocks to bid up their value. The German and some other European governments used this practice to a limited extent in the 1970s. Of course, such operations would be very risky; the consequences are difficult to predict. But it is one more example of the possible security that a state can provide to reduce the mishaps of a volatile market.

Over the last ten years, certain writers have questioned whether the U.S. Constitution should have four, instead of three, completely separate branches of authority. In the 1970s, this question stemmed from the development of regulatory agencies. Later, it concerned the growing role of the OMB. More recently, it has been asked whether the Federal Reserve could evolve into such a fourth branch of authority. It is doubtful that any such initiative will ever be undertaken. At the same time, however, it is quite evident that, together, these regulatory institutions appear to be growing into a new structure of the authority framework of U.S. society. Regulatory agencies have not become part of the check-and-balance structures constituted by the three branches of authority; it is difficult to imagine how they could become part of this system. They operate on authority delegated by Congress, not independent of it. Yet, the question does not seem completely empty. Agencies implementing direct regulatory functions in daily practice—the OMB developing both the cash and credit budgets and the Federal Reserve acting more indirectly—evidently perform important functions that are entirely new to the U.S. economy and society. And the importance of their functions is growing. The Federal Reserve exercises enough autonomy and power to be deemed a new principal authority. There is a danger to the Fed, however, in formally becoming such a fourth authority; it would then be subject to democratic rules, as the three other authorities are.

Each of the institutions and activities discussed in this chapter was established with a quite narrow objective. Yet the implementation of their functions bears complex macrosocioeconomic consequences, which are only now becoming manifest, and which cause them to play an unanticipated role. Today, a new "super system" grows out of the interpenetrating offices of these organizations. This growth is a part of etatization. Some may say: You are talking about growing bureaucracy. Yes, the New State engenders a growing bureaucracy, which engulfs and interpenetrates society, all its structures and units, including the market.

CHAPTER EIGHT

Two-Sector Economies and Etatization

Development of Two-Sector Economies

In several principal regards, the Type *B* variety (see Chapter 5) of etatized societies, such as Western Europe and Canada, differs significantly from its Type *A* (United States) and Type *C* (Japan) counterparts.

In contrast to the United States, where etatization advanced as a consequence of establishing direct and indirect regulatory practices and related politics, Western European nations became etatized through multifarious initiatives and changes, undertaken by different institutions within the national economy, social groups, and, to a great extent, in consequence of developing two-sector economies.

Immediately after World War II, Western European states became involved in economic reconstruction. It was a novel activity, understood at the time as a limited, temporary involvement on the part of the state. Never before had any state engaged in economic activity on such a large scale. Although initiated by the state, reconstruction and economic development went on to involve private initiatives more and more. Eventually, the market strengthened, regaining its traditionally dominant role, yet a strong role for the state in the economy was established. In certain nations, Italy in particular, where the private sector was weak and did not have sufficient funds to undertake major industrial projects and development programs, the government became involved in areas of economic activity in which the private sector was not sufficiently involved. In France and Great Britain, the state nationalized the coal, transportation, electrical, and certain other industries, which were not profitable but were essential to economic recovery. Another area of principal European state involvement was the economic infrastructure.

Many European states inherited nationalized industries. During the 1950s and early 1960s, the state- or public-owned sector, as it is more often called in Europe, did not significantly affect the private sector or the market. Later, however, the state sector grew bigger and began to absorb more industries, by nationalizing or building new state-owned industries; more and more state regulation and control was required. At this point, the character of the entire economic and social structures of Western European societies began changing rapidly. The economy was transformed from a one- into a two-sector structure; the two sectors cooperated, coexisted, but also collided.

While this was happening in Europe and later in Canada, the United States continued to have a predominantly one-sector, capitalist economy and "publicly" maintained services. Many of its corporation grew into giant multinationals operating under protective umbrella of the U.S. government.

Although both the United States and Western Europe developed public services, they developed them with different emphases. The welfare state and programs to assist the poor were instituted in all Western European nations. Yet, European nations invested much greater effort to prevent widespread unemployment than did the United States. To this end, they established more comprehensive insurance schemes; they engaged also in larger-scale job creation. In many instances, the main objective of nationalization policies was to reduce unemployment by saving unprofitable industries that employ many workers. The concern was well founded: Even now, poverty in Western Europe is more often engendered by structural unemployment and recessions (old poverty), than by personal adversity (new poverty), predominant in the United States.

An incisive analysis of the history and particularities of the welfare system in diverse European nations is presented by Flora and Heidenheimer (1984). They write (22; see also Flora & Alber 1984): "National differences within Europe in the creation of absolutist states with strong bureaucracies and paternalistic traditions may explain the earlier or later beginnings of the welfare state (for example, Germany versus Great Britain or Sweden versus Switzerland)." They point out (50) that the real development of welfare systems was linked with the advance of mass democracy in the last third of the nineteenth century. Social insurance against industrial accidents came first. Disability insurance and old-age insurance appeared next. Eventually, unemployment insurance was introduced. Flora and Heidenheimer trace these developments and discuss the achievements and consequences in various European nations.

One may add, a great deal of these activities was initiated by unions. European unions differed significantly from those in the United States. Unions in Europe tried not only to win gains but to modify the structure of society more permanently. The less ideologically oriented unions in the United States tried mainly to develop insurance schemes that would provide workers with more pay, fringe benefits, and work security, and protect them in time of adversity.

Providing services, social programs, and a welfare system is a chief function of the state in all etatized societies. Consider government expenditures, compared in Table 8.1. Between 35% and 50% of state budgetary allocations in Western Europe is currently expended on social security and welfare. Expenditures on health services consume another 10–18% of budgetary funds; 10–19% is spent on economic services; 5–9% on defense; and 5–7% on general public services. In contrast, more than one-quarter of the U.S. budget is expended on defense, about one-third on social security, and close to 12% on health. Although the government finances a substantial part of Japan's research and development (R&D) expenditures, 30% of Japanese outlays, significantly more than in the 1960s and 1970s, are currently spent on social security and welfare. Also indicative of differences in state policies and the importance attributed to social programs are the much higher taxes paid by citizens of OECD nations, compared with the United States and Japan.

Immediately after the war, socialism was popular among intellectual and certain working-class circles in Europe. Some felt that only through socialism could their societies overcome the threat of massive unemployment, poverty, and war. Socialist and some Social Democratic parties expected that increased involvement by the state in administering economic and social affairs, nationalization of selected private industries, development of welfare systems and other services, partial redistribution of incomes, and initiation of central planning would evolve and, at some point, transform into a wholesome socialist environment. Naturally, when in power, Socialist parties initiated more nationalization programs and developed socialist elements of the structure. Conservative governments usually undertook to reverse the changes instituted by Socialists; their efforts often managed to arrest what programs their Liberal or Socialist party predecessors had started, but only until the Left again won power and a new wave of reforms was introduced.

One additional concern caused European states to develop large, modern, state-owned, and mixed corporations, and, in some instances, to subsidize and support by other means large private corporations where state corporations were absent. During the aftermath of World War II, European nations lost their colonies and were reduced to secondary powers; the United States and Soviet Union emerged as principal powers; China, India, and other Asian nations with large populations began to count as powers, too. Europeans felt threatened, on the East, by Soviet expansionist ideologies and policies and, on the West, by U.S. economic and cultural expansion. Under these conditions, Europeans aspired to restore their position by developing their economic might. Yet, even the largest European and Canadian private corporations, in most instances, could not match emerging U.S. multinationals (see Chapter 12). Individual European nations could not withstand external pressures. Therefore, the states of Western Europe cooperated, organizing economic defenses and developments to help their industries face foreign competition and win markets elsewhere. They wanted to establish a new Europe and transform it into another major world power. Many obstacles impeded this endeavor. There was a long tradition of hostilities between European nations; economic interests collided frequently. Each nation tried to defend its distinctive interests within the emerging coalition. Within, they were divided; without, they tried to stand united.

Cameron (1978, 1255–1260), analyzing the evolution of sixteen Western European nations, Canada, and the United States, raises the question whether certain "structural characteristics in advanced capitalist economies" produce a condition "conducive to an expansion of the public economy." He answers affirmatively: In his opinion, high levels of industrial concentration facilitate the formation, on one side, of powerful employers' associations, and of powerful labor organizations on the other. Employers, management, and unions are then involved in continuing collective bargaining on many complex issues, wages, salaries, employment security, fringe benefits, working conditions, workers' participation in decisionmaking, etc. He points out, correctly, that as a result, large increases in spending of income supplements occur, which cause the rapid expansion of the public sector. Other consequences are also obvious: The state, sometimes acting as a third force, is frequently involved in intermediation. In some instances, certain state agencies intercede in conflicts of employees' unions (e.g., teachers, public workers) with private corporations or other state agencies and state-owned industries. Corporatist development advances. One needs to remember a still different aspect of this development related to the international scene. Cameron does not regard Western European and Canadian development of state-owned industries as a response to U.S. capitalist development. In part this was the case, however.

Out of these strivings and concerns emerged the new Western Europe, a collection of societies with mixed economies. Some nations established incipient central planning; others relied more on the market. All states developed social-security programs, welfare systems, and redistributive fiscal mechanisms. Some attempted to build toward a socialist framework; others instituted similar institutions but preserved the capitalist status quo. Whether under the aegis of the market or the state, after a certain period, whatever was established obtained the concordance of legitimacy and became integrated into the establishment. Capitalist development in the United States, perceived by other nations as threatening their well-being, provoked the introduction of state ownership, state subsidies, and state regulation in Western Europe and Canada.

Two-Sector Economies and Privatization

For three decades, Western Europe and Canada have become increasingly

Table 8.1.   Central Governments of Western Societies: Expenditure by Functions

	Year	Total expenditure	Percent of total expenditure											
			General public services	Defense	Education	Health	Social security and welfare	Housing and community	Other community and social services	Economic services	Agriculture, forestry, fishing, hunting	Roads	Other, transport and communications	Other purposes
			1	2	3	4	5	6	7	8	8.2	8.5	8.7	9
TYPE A														
United States	1984	100.00	5.19	24.72	1.85	11.04	32.07	2.58	.30	7.56	1.72	1.21	1.23	14.57
TYPE B														
Canada	1983	100.00	8.33	7.98	3.61	6.27	35.58	2.07	.76	16.69	2.03	.19	4.53	20.11[1]
France[2]	1978	100.00	6.69	7.25	8.98	15.00	43.92	3.07	.54	7.06	1.17	.86	1.47	7.48
Germany	1983	100.00	4.14	9.32	.83	18.64	49.97	.31	.10	7.00	.31	1.38	3.13	9.68
Great Britain	1979	100.00	7.14	14.49	2.64	12.77	26.15	4.25	.32	7.98				24.26
Italy	1983	100.00	7.10	3.51	8.58	11.52	33.07	1.22	.09	6.11	1.07	1.09	1.65	26.05
Netherlands	1984	100.00	6.45	5.24	10.68	10.97	37.42	3.63	.92	10.06	.81	1.12	2.11	14.63
Norway	1983	100.00	6.36	8.61	8.80	10.55	35.05	1.16	1.35	20.50	7.28	4.57	1.40	9.63
Spain	1984	100.00	4.22	4.42	5.95	.60	62.89	1.27	.60	10.08	3.62	1.07		9.98
Sweden	1984	100.00	6.75	6.69	8.96	1.35	46.67	3.38	.74	7.40	1.41	2.08	2.74	20.43
Switzerland	1983	100.00	4.78	10.36	3.13	13.44	48.95	.71	.30	12.57	4.28	3.49	4.02	6.11
TYPE C														
Japan[3]	1984	100.00		5.80	9.6		22.01		2.80	1.50			12.90	20.70

Sources: *Government Finance Statistics Yearbook*, Vol. 6, 1982; Vol. 7, 1983; Vol. 8, 1984 (Washington, DC: International Monetary Fund), *The Budget in Brief: Japan 1984* (Tokyo: Budget Bureau, Ministry of Finance).

Notes:

1. Includes transfer payments to Canadian provinces.

2. Vol.7/1983 and Vol. 8/1984 of *Government Finance Statistics Yearbook* do not contain data on disbursement of certain nations' budgetary funds after 1980. Data included in Table 8.1 are of the last available year of this publication.

3. Budgetary data for Japan in recent years are not included in the *Yearbook*. To remedy this lack of data, corresponding figures of *The Budget in Brief: Japan 1984* are included here. The Japanese employ a different division in their budgetary expenditure allocations than in the IMF comparisons. In Table 8.1 figures extracted from *The Budget in Brief: Japan 1984* are rearranged for our comparative purposes. A large part of the Japanese expenditures—18.1%—is designated for "national debt" repayment. Social Security (18.4%) and "pensions and others" (3.7%) are here combined. Under the general rubric, "economic services," appear data on economic cooperation (1.1%) and small businesses (0.4%) of the Japanese budget. Under the general rubric, "other purposes" appear figures for local finance (17.9%) and miscellaneous (8.6%). Under Other: transportation & communication are included data on "public works" (12.9—erosion and flood control, road improvement, harbors and airports, housing, improvement of agriculture, forest roads, disaster reconstruction, etc.). Public health service is regarded as part of social security in Japanese budgetary allocation.

The total Japanese budget for 1984 was ¥50,839,442 million. In the allocations by agency, the largest sum: ¥10,383,802, was allocated for the Ministry of Finance; ¥9,155.717 million for the Ministry of Home Affairs; ¥9,249.141 million for the Ministry of Health and Welfare; ¥6,469,711 million for the Prime Minister's Office; ¥4,572,041 million for the Ministry of Education. Only ¥801,503 millions was allocated for the highly important Ministry of International Trade and Industry. Actual spending is somewhat higher.

All figures in the presentation of the Japanese expenditures are for initial budgetary allocations.

etatized through developments in the state-owned sectors of production and financial industries. Toward the late 1970s, the pace of nationalization in these countries accelerated to such an extent that it appeared as if the rapidly developing state sector might swallow most of the private sector. As Table 8.2 demonstrates, at the end of the 1970s, governments of these nations owned railways, electrical utilities, coal, oil, steel, and gas industries, most airlines and telecommunication networks, and a large part of the auto-building industry. Banks and large parts of the insurance and investment industries were also state-owned. Monsen and Walters, who compare state-sector growth in a number of studies (1979; 1983), estimate that in some European nations, around 1980, the state owned nearly half of the industrial sector, and that public-sector investment, as a percentage of the national total, was (1983, 17) 65% in Austria; 55% in France; 45% in Italy; 40% in Norway; 30% in Sweden; 25% in Great Britain; and 20% in West Germany. They report (1983, 1):

> Today state-owned firms can be found in virtually all industries in Europe. New state firms in the 1970s were created or nationalized in pharmaceuticals, electronics, computers, office equipment, oil, microelectronics, chemicals, petrochemicals, pulp and paper, and telecommunications. . . . In addition many state-owned firms have embarked on a strategy for international expansion and diversification. Now many of the top foreign multinationals are owned and controlled by their governments.[1]

During the 1980s, however, this trend has suddenly changed. Attempting to reduce state deficits, and the scope of state ownership regarded as its cause, Western European governments turned to privatization. They were motivated by various fiascos suffered by governments experimenting with state-owned industries. From Great Britain under the Conservative government, to France under the Socialists, to China under Communist government, to various Latin American governments under assorted dictatorships—everywhere governments have transferred industries to the private sector and returned, at least to a greater extent, to market-economy practices. Still, in Western Europe and Canada, the state continues to own many key industries. They are maintained, in part, to regulate unemployment.

The cost of management and labor in state-owned industries is much higher than that in the private sector. Hence, many Western European industries, even large ones, survive only because they are relieved from paying taxes, are subsidized, or receive other state support. For example, Western European industries, on average, invest much more in R&D than do comparable industries in the United States and Japan, but the latter two countries obtain much higher profits from R&D investments. Japan's objective is to conquer and hold markets. The Japanese plan all stages of

Table 8.2 Scope of State-Ownership in Principal Countries Under Non-Communist Governments

	posts	telecom	electric	gas	oil prod	coal	railway	airline	motor industry	steel	ship-building
Australia	●	●	●	●	○	○	●	◕	○	○	na
Austria	●	●	●	●	●	●	●	●	●	●	na
Belgium	●	●	◔	◕	na	○	●	●	○	◑	○
Brazil	●	●	●	●	●	●	●	◔	○	◑	○
Britain	●	◑	●	◕	◑	●	●	◕	◑	◕	◕
Canada	●	◕	●	◑	◑	○	◑	◑	○	○	○
France	●	●	●	●	na	●	●	◕	◑	◕	○
West Germany	●	●	◔	◑	◕	◑	●	●	◕	○	◕
Holland	●	●	◕	◕	na	na	●	◕	◑	◕	○
India	●	●	●	●	●	●	●	●	○	◕	●
Italy	●	●	◕	●	na	na	●	●	◑	◕	◕
Japan	●	●	○	○	na	○	◕	◕	○	○	○
Mexico	●	●	●	●	●	●	●	◑	◕	●	●
South Korea	●	●	◔	○	na	◕	●	○	◔	◕	○
Spain	●	◑	○	◑	na	◑	●	●	○	◑	◕
Sweden	●	◑	○	●	na	na	●	◑	○	◕	◕
Switzerland	●	●	●	●	na	na	●	◕	○	○	na
United States	●	○	◕	○	○	○	◕	○	○	○	○

○ 100% privately owned   ● 100% state owned   ◕ 75% state owned   ◑ 50% state owned   ◔ 25% state owned

Source: *The Economist* (London), December 30, 1979. Reprinted with permission of the journal, and with alterations reflecting change before 1986 (Great Britain, Canada, Italy, France). State ownership in mostly state-owned nuclear industry, petrochemicals, banking, insurance, and other financial businesses is not depicted. Some of the state-owned industries in 1985 are now privately owned (for British privatization see Table 8.3).

R&D and future expansion. Moreover, they invest in fields where they are already ahead, continually perfecting products and reducing prices until they are able not only to win carefully selected markets but can thwart any potential competitors. Examples abound: cameras, cars, steel, TV, appliances, and, more recently, computer chips. The U.S. objective is to obtain the highest possible profit. Industries focus efforts and shift investments accordingly. U.S. investments are concentrated in oil, defense-related industries, medical technology, and chemicals. Western Europeans and Canadians select targets and investment schemes according to social concerns. Their R&D investments are more random, involving considerably less market research. Industries rely on state subsidies to develop and export products, on tariffs and barriers to protect their domain of trade. Europeans invest in R&D to encourage economic development, but, in some instances, such investment is intended more to reduce unemployment than to develop new marketable products. Administrative costs of European R&D are higher than those in the United States or Japan.

Borcherding et al. (1982) published a study of analyses and documents discussing "the putative differential in efficiency between public and private sectors in the United States" and a number of other Western nations.[2] Government inefficiencies (waste) were among principal concerns of the research. Findings are presented in tables with extensive commentaries (134). Borcherding and his associates report their findings to be consistent with the notion that public firms have higher unit costs. They report that of the more than fifty studies considered, only three (Pier, Vernon & Wics [1974] on garbage collection; Meyer [1975] on electrical utilities; and Lindsay [1975; 1976] on veterans' hospitals) indicate public firms to be less costly than private. The Lindsay study also clearly indicates that quality drops in the public firm. Borcherding et al. list five other studies for North America, Canada and Germany on the subject and conclude (135–136) that:

> public firms adopt cost-saving devices and innovation more slowly, if at all; give managers longer periods of tenure; realize lower and more variable rates of return; price less closely to imputable costs and with less regard to peak-capacity problems; favor voters to non-voters, business to residential users and organized to non-organized political groups; and systematically . . . overcapitalize even more than private-but-regulated firms.

In this connection, they also point out that "public managers divert higher shares of their principals' wealth to their own ends than their private colleagues." One can say that Borcherding expresses in scholarly language with documented evidence what numerous politicians, administrators, and regular citizens have expressed in a more simple statement: The state-owned sector is a great disappointment.

One can argue that without state-owned industries employing substantial numbers, unemployment and poverty would be more widespread. This is correct. Yet, Western nations cannot afford indefinitely to maintain large state-owned industries that produce deficits. This is, at least, the feeling of the majority, not only conservative politicians and economic analysts.

Industrial societies are changing into postindustrial ones. To compete with the Japanese and U.S. industries, Europeans are forced to adopt more advanced technologies and reduce numbers of workers. They must become efficient and win markets. Causes of the new unemployment are structural. It is to be hoped that services will absorb most of the job-seekers. Many state-owned industries, maintained in the past to secure jobs, have become redundant and uneconomical; their operations are prolonged at huge expense to taxpayers. Some of these industries in Great Britain and France are being put out of operation, some are privatized. It is a struggle for survival. Thatcher, particularly, considers privatization a matter of great urgency.

Between 1979 and 1985, the British government sold to the private sector: British Aerospace, Cable and Wireless, Amersham International, National Freight, Britoil, Associated British Ports, British Rail Hotels, British Gas, Onshore Oil, Enterprise Oil, Sealink, Jaguar, British Telecom, British Technology Group, and other industries (see Table 8.3).[3] More than 600,000 workers have been shifted to the private sector. Large portions of the shares put up for sale by the government were bought by individuals. The sale of a majority stake in British Telecom yielded close to £5 billion. The biggest privatization sale, of 31.5 percent of British Petroleum for £7.2 billion (U.S. $12.2 billion) started in 1987 and is still in progress. Because of the October 1987 stock market crash, which occurred during the sale, shares lost some value; they are popular nevertheless and are selling well. According to early 1987 estimates, the government has raised more than £12 billion from sales under the privatization program. With new sales in 1987 and 1988, the proceeds come close to between £18 and £20 billion. The government also reaped close to £13 billion through sales of publicly owned lands. By privatizing, the state has not only increased cash inflow but is relieved from the obligation of new public-sector borrowing requirements (PSBR). The *OECD Economic Surveys 1986–1987: United Kingdom* (1987, 19) reports "both the public sector and general government financial deficits (which exclude financial transactions) have fallen rather less as a share of GDP to a little below 3 per cent." Many formerly deficit-producing state-owned industries turned profitable under private ownership. Now, instead of incurring debts, these industries contribute to tax revenues. Of no lesser importance are the social consequences of this shift in ownership. At present, 9–12 million Britons own shares of various corporations. They and new home owners constitute the core of the Conservative electorate.

At present, the drive for denationalization (see *The Economist*, December 21, 1985) is widespread across the world. It is natural that Conservative parties advocate privatization and denationalization. But currently, not only Conservative, but centrist, some Liberal, and even some

Socialist parties, albeit reluctantly, have given up on the idea of profitable state-owned industries. A new distinction is made between industries that are maintained as services and must be state-owned and industries that are profit-oriented and operate more efficaciously under private ownership, without burdening the state with public sector borrowing requirements.

In Canada, the conservative Mulroney government proclaimed denationalization as one of its principal policies. By 1986–1987 it had privatized, however, considerably fewer industries than projected; primarily those both unprofitable and costly to preserve: De Haviland and Canadair in the aerospace industry, and Teleglobe in telecommunications. Eldorado Nuclear, a large state-owned conglomerate, and Air Canada are being put up for sale at present. Part of the Canada Development Corporation, the largest Canadian state-owned conglomerate, was privatized, too. Altogether, forty state-owned enterprises or portions of them, valued at Canadian $4.6 billion have been sold since 1984. Of the provinces in Canada, British Columbia put up for sale assets and government services valued at Canadian $3 billion. Quebec and Ontario (Sheppard 1988) "are resigned to holding expensive oil or iron ore and asbestos investments—with book values of more than $2 billion—that no one seems to want at today's prices," but would like to privatize them. There is a difference, however, between Great Britain and Canada. Many Canadian holdings are being purchased by U.S. interests, whereas British shares tend to end up in British portfolios. Unions in Canada are strongly opposing denationalization policies.

The Conservative Chirac government in France, under the Socialist presidency of Mitterrand, declared that it plans to denationalize not only all industries nationalized by the preceding Socialist government early in the 1980s, but also Renault, state-owned since 1946. According to the program developed by the Ministry of Economy, Finance and Privatization, sixty-five state-owned enterprises were to be privatized by 1991. Only some were privatized by the Chirac government, however; the biggest among them Paribas, St. Gobain, CGCT, and Société Générale. In 1987, France procured the equivalent of U.S. $11.5 billion from selling state-owned companies to private shareholders, $914 million more than expected by the economy and finance ministry. Fifty banks and financial institutions and several major manufacturing industries were prepared for privatization. Because of the recent stock market crash, the decline in value of some of these industries, and the drop in the U.S. dollar's value, and now the change of government, plans may change. Prime Minister Chirac was less resolute in implementing privatization policies than was Thatcher. Now, Socialist Prime Minister Rocard may not privatize all the industries earmarked for privatization by Chirac. Yet, other Socialist leaders are pursuing policies of privatization like those of Liberals and Conservatives. The Socialist prime minister of Italy, Craxi, for instance, in an attempt to reduce the L. 80–90 trillion (over U.S. $55 billion) state deficit that has popped up year after year and has grown

Table 8.3. British Privatization Sales 1979–1980 to 1986–1987[1]

		£ million	
			Total
1979–1980	British Petroleum	276	
	Others	94	370
1980–1981	British Aerospace	43	
	North Sea Oil Licenses	195	
	Others	167	405
1981–1982	British Sugar Corporation (24 percent)	44	
	Cable & Wireless (49 percent)	181	
	Amersham International (100 percent)	64	
	Others	204	493
1982–1983	Britoil (51 percent)	334	
	Associated British Ports (51 percent)	46	
	International Aeradio (100 percent)	60	
	British Rail Hotels (67 percent)	30	
	North Sea Oil Licenses	33	
	Others	75	578
1983–1984	British Petroleum (7 percent)	543	
	Cable & Wireless (31 percent)	263	
	Britoil (41 percent)	293	
	Others	38	1,157
1984–1985	Associated British Ports (49 percent)	31	
	British Gas (Wytch Farm Oil) (100 percent)	82	
	Enterprise Oil (100 percent)	382	
	Sealink (61 percent)	40	
	Jaguar (100 percent)	297	
	National Enterprise Board Holdings	142	
	North Sea Licenses	121	
	British Telecom (34 percent)	1,396	
	Others	40	2,551
1985–1986	British Aerospace	346	
	Cable & Wireless (68 percent)	576	
	Britoil (59 percent)	426	
	British Telecom	1,307	
	Warship yards	54	
	Others	78	2,787
1986–1987[2]	British Airways (51 percent)	431	
	British Gas (35 percent)	1,796	
	British Gas debt	750	
	British Telecom (34 percent)	1,387	
	Others	125	4,489

Source: HM Tresury; here, after *OECD Economic Surveys 1986–1987: United Kingdom* (July 1987, Paris: OECD).

1. Including proceeds from sales of subsidiaries from 1982–1983 onwards.
2. Partly estimated.

even bigger under his administration, finally refused to cover new deficits of state-owned corporations with government revenues. His advice to state corporations was: Sell some holdings to the private sector. The Istituto per la Reconstruzione Industriale (IRI) did and netted L. 2.8 trillion ($1.60 billion) between 1983 and 1985. Now, it plans to sell more. Ente Nazionale Indrocarburi (ENI), the second large state-owned Italian corporation sold some of its industries for L. 120 billion. It, too, plans to sell a much larger package of shares in the near future. (Hemming and Mansoor [1988, 9] give different figures.) Fiat is currently negotiating the purchase of Alfa Romeo, owned by IRI.

The West German government sold to the private sector its holding in VEBA (energy, chemicals), VIAG (aluminum) IVG (transportation) and is now planning to sell its 6 percent share of Volkswagen and half of its Prakla-Seismos (oil and gas) company. Japan is partly privatizing the Nippon Telegraph and Telephone company and rail roads. In Spain, the Socialist prime minister, Gonzales voiced the opinion that in an economy that must dwell strongly on high technology, individual initiative is more appropriate than state ownership of industries. As a test, in 1987, his government sold 39.3% of Ence (pulp and paper) shares to the private sector. In 1988, 39% of Repsol (oil and gas), and 20% of Endesa (coal and electricity) are set for sale on the stock market. Portugal's new, right-of-center, Social Democratic prime minister, Silva, immediately after taking power declared his intention to privatize, gradually and over several years, the entire Portuguese economy.

Many Latin American countries have turned to privatization as well. In a rapid move "to democratize credit," Peru recently nationalized all banks; but President Garcia has declared that he intends to sell 30 percent of these banks back to the private sector. Peru also plans to sell forty of its 140 state-owned firms. President Sarney of Brazil and President de la Madrid of Mexico undertook to sell their state-owned industries. But Brazil is simultaneously nationalizing foreign-owned mineral resources. In Argentina, where the national, provincial, and municipal governments own a total of 305 business enterprises, public expenditures totalled more than 50 percent of GNP. Between 1974 and 1984, thirteen of Argentina's state holding companies accumulated a deficit of more than $23 billion. President Alfonsin is undertaking major economic reform, which involves privatizing many state-owned industries.

Hemming and Mansoor (1988) report that Niger has denationalized all state-owned industries. In Guinea, ninety-three out of 104 state enterprises were either closed or sold to the public sector.

In the United States, *Fortune* magazine reports (May 27, 1985, 92): "Government is starting to reach far beyond contracting for services by looking to private industry to finance, design, build, and run public facilities from waste-water treatment plants to prisons."

Although no other European government is as determined as Thatcher's to privatize all state-owned industries, the worldwide character of the trend is undeniable. (Even the Chinese government has reinstated the importance of the market.) Von Beyme writes (1985, 28): "The growth of the role of the state in the economy has certainly not been brought about by public ownership. Today, there is much less euphoria for direct intervention in the economy through economic planning than there was in many countries in the early 1970s." The 1980s appear as the decade of denationalization of the economy.

Is this widespread trend of privatization a reversal of etatization and a return to more classical capitalism? Certainly not. The state continues to perform the numerous new functions it has acquired. Despite a diminished state-owned sector, the state still manages the national economies of nations that adopted privatization. Not even in Great Britain can the privatization of many industries "unmix" the mixed economy. Privatized industries are not simply thrown into the stormy seas of capitalist markets, amidst multinational sharks, and left to sink or swim. The state still supports privatized industries but expects them to make it on their own. The state continues to run services and remains the biggest employer in the nation. It cannot be significantly replaced in these roles by the private sector. In the cases of Great Britain, France, and Canada, the state cannot easily dispose of certain nationalized industries without accepting substantial losses. Particular industries, such as railroads and electricity-generating plants, are kept under government ownership because they are firmly embedded in the infrastructure of services that the state is expected to maintain.

Even the most market-oriented governments resort to nationalization under certain circumstances. They may not call it nationalization; but often, in order to prevent major economic disasters—e.g., bankruptcy of a major corporation or bank—the state has no choice but to nationalize a collapsing industry. I have mentioned nationalizing the Continental Bank of Illinois at a cost of $4.5 billion, despite Reagan's anti–state-intervention administration, as one such instance.

In Type *B* etatized societies such as Western Europe and Canada, the state encompasses institutions organized as extensions of the central government. There is a difference, however. In two-sector economy (Type *B*) societies the state has transformed itself into the largest conglomerate of the nation, often treating private-sector corporations as subcontractors or clients. By denationalizing some or even many state-owned corporations, by literally subcontracting private corporations, the state does not relinquish its new multifunctional and conglomerate position; it reorganizes itself into a more efficient corporation. Thatcher's Great Britain, where millions of middle class citizens hold stocks, where corporations operate within market conditions while remaining under state tutelage, where the state maintains the authority to manage economic affairs, is still a form of etatized society, however different from how Kinnock, the leader of the opposition and

Scargill, the miners union leader would have it, with unions owning industries and generally running the show.

One could single out a number of strategies employed by parties in power in pursuit of different ends, such as winning elections, reducing budgetary deficits, securing revenues for increasing expenditures, etc. Some of these strategies include:

1. Reducing the cost of government by cutting administrative expenditures, introducing austerity controls on outlays, and reducing personnel (e.g., Thatcher's and Mitterrand's policies)
2. Reducing investments in the state sector and, whenever possible, service and public-program expenditures (e.g., Thatcher's policies)
3. Selling costly state-owned industries, thereby reducing state expenses and covering certain pending expenditures with the money from sales (e.g., Thatcher's, Craxi's, Kohl's, and many Latin American governments' policies in the 1980s)
4. Nationalizing particular industries to create new employment and increase benefits enjoyed by citizens; and turning a blind eye to accumulated debt (e.g., Attlee's, Wilson's, Callaghan's Labour governments' policies in Great Britain; first period of Mitterrand's policies; and, to a lesser extent policies employed by other Socialist governments in the 1970s; to an extent, Reagan's policies)
5. Disregarding promises and certain financial obligations or resorting to practices that decrease the value and buying power of national currency, thereby paying less in transfer payments, salaries, and other obligations even when nominal payments are preserved or increased (e.g., policies of most Western governments in the 1970s and 1980s)
6. Maintaining social security and welfare safety nets but broadening the meshes, thus inevitably providing less support to dependents (e.g., policies of most Western governments at the end of the 1970s)
7. Attempting to improve the national trade balance by developing industries with prospects of winning international markets (e.g., Japanese industrial policy; de Gaulle's, Pompidou's, Giscard's, and Mitterrand's policies in France; Schmidt's in West Germany; Thatcher's in Great Britain; Mulroney's in Canada)

CHAPTER NINE

Decline and Recovery: Great Britain

Decline

In the early 1980s, Great Britain was diagnosed "the sick man of Europe." The symptoms of its malady were identified in a large body of literature. Cranston (1985) enumerated the elements of the British condition as follows: a mismanaged economy, with the lowest growth rate in Western Europe over the last twenty years, experiencing a prolonged recession for the last five to ten years; unproductive coal mines, outdated steel mills and manufacturing industries, which the state can no longer maintain; inefficient private industries, which require rescues from bankruptcy by the state or by foreign takeovers, partly because they are unable to compete in international markets, partly because of an unruly and unproductive labor force wasting a lot of time on strikes; a high rate of unemployment; widespread poverty and crime; "child abuse of one kind or another reaching alarming proportions;" a deteriorating educational system, which "serves only to enlarge the fissures—racial, social, ideological, temperamental;" deteriorating health services and a welfare state, "once considered a model of achievement," now starved of funds—a system of torturing the poor, a massive, expensive, faceless bureaucracy, unconcerned with real human beings; and political parties not only disputing each other, but each bitterly divided from within.

Cranston called this *Britain in Squalor*. Others called it *Britain in Decline* (Gamble 1985); *Britain's Economy: The Roots of Stagnation*; (A. Jones 1985); *The English Sickness* (Tomison 1972); *The Economic Decline of Modern Britain* (Coates & Hillard 1986), *Englanditis* (Jay 1986), *The British Economy in Crisis* (K. Smith 1984); *Deindustrialization* (Harris 1986), and so on. At the end of the 1970s and during the 1980s, bookstore shelves were full of books with such titles. New titles, reflecting recent change, are beginning to appear now: *The Economic Revival of Modern Britain* (Coates & Hillard 1988); *The Uncommon Kingdom: Britain in the*

1980s (Handelman 1988). They are still few, however.

The Left and the Right agreed on the symptoms of Great Britain's deterioration but differed on the principal causes and whom to blame. The decline must be considered first, then the recovery.

Sir Nicholas Henderson (1979), the former British ambassador to Bonn and Paris, in a "confidential report," published by *The Economist* (June 2, 1979) under the title "Britain's Decline," sketched a gloomy picture of the situation in the most objurgatory terms a diplomat could chose in analyzing the condition of his own country. According to Henderson, in the aftermath of the war and the rise of the United States and the Soviet Union, it was only natural that Great Britain lose its leading position in the world. Yet, in spite of this, Great Britain was still a mighty industrial and political power at the time. Henderson's concern was with what happened later and what effect these adverse changes had on both the condition inside Great Britain and the nation's ability to conduct a foreign policy commensurate with its international economic and political interest. He writes:

> We are not only no longer a world power, but we are not in the first rank even as a European one. Income per head in Britain is now for the first time for over 300 years below that in France. We are scarcely in the same economic league as the Germans or the French. We talk of ourselves without shame as being one of the less prosperous countries of Europe. The prognosis for the foreseeable future is discouraging. If present trends continue we shall be overtaken in gdp per head by Italy and Spain well before the end of the century.

In 1954, he points out, French GDP was 22% and West German 9% lower than that in Great Britain. Yet, in 1977, thirteen years later, French GDP was 34% and the German 61% higher than the British. Productivity (i.e., output per person employed) was about the same in Great Britain, France, and West Germany in 1954, with Great Britain marginally highest. But in 1977 (based on figures in U.S. dollars at 1970 prices and 1970 exchange rates), Germany's productivity was 2.77 times, France's 2.66 times higher, while Great Britain's was only 1.68 times higher than in 1977. Great Britain, Henderson fears, is falling behind in this competition and failing miserably. To take another set of figures: in 1977, he writes, the output per man-hour in the manufacturing industry (measured in pounds per hour) was 2.70 for Great Britain; 4.50 for France; and 7.10 for West Germany. That, he implies, means that the British worker produces in an hour half of what the French and one third of what the German worker produces in an hour. Henderson cites other facts and figures, demonstrating the deterioration of the British pound compared with other currencies, and Great Britain's decreasing involvement in world trade. In his words (30): "The average salary of a middle-grade manager, adjusted for taxes and discrepancies in the cost of living, is nearly twice as big in France and Germany, what it is in

Great Britain." In whatever regard we compare the economic condition, he concludes, the British in the last ten to fifteen years have achieved less than others in comparable industrially developed nations. The British not only manufacture less, they earn less, own fewer private vehicles, and generally have a lower standard of living than their neighbors.

> You cannot get away from the fact that a low gdp means a smaller national cake and that there is less wealth to go round. . . . You only have to move about western Europe nowadays to realise how poor and unproud the British have become in relation to their neighbours. It shows in the look of our towns, in our airports, in our hospitals and local amenities; it is painfully apparent in much of our railway system, which until a generation ago was superior to the continental one.

Thus, he writes, unless acted upon these conditions will deteriorate further. For improvements to occur, Great Britain must win a better position in the international market. There is nothing "confidential" in this report. Every traveler to Great Britain, including myself, was returning in those years with the same impression: This country is "going to the dogs." Any Briton approached on the subject expressed this feeling; some of the workers I talked to in Manchester expressed the opinion that it must be terrible in Germany, if it is that bad in Great Britain. And each of them blamed someone else for the disaster.

Margaret Thatcher determined to halt the economic "decline of Britain" by closing unproductive enterprises and denationalizing others, regardless of the increased unemployment it might cause. The consequences were dire, indeed. As industries were closed and put under private management, unemployment rose, from 5.6 percent when Thatcher came to power, to 13–14 percent in the early 1980s. Between 3 and 3.5 million Britons were unemployed then. Eventually, at the end of 1987, the figure subsided to 11.5 percent. Yet, a large section of the jobless became permanently unemployed; the industries in which they used to work no longer exist. The Manchester-Birmingham-Leeds area, heartland of British manufacturing industries, Southern Scotland, and Northern Ireland were most affected by these closures. True, the structure of pay in Great Britain is such that what a menial worker gets on the dole is not significantly different from what he would be paid for work; yet, being unemployed is traumatic even if transfer payments from the state are sufficient for survival. According to Miller and Wood (1982, 49), a family head earning £105 per week would earn only £10 per week more than he would on supplementary benefit pay; and the family with £35 per week would gain £4 per week by not working. Conservatives argued that the unemployed had no incentive to search for work. They claimed benefits were too high. They also blamed unions for demoralizing the labor force, rendering workers unproductive and unwilling to work. The Left argued that wages were too low, causing workers to care little whether they had a job or were on the dole. Unemployment begets poverty. One-third of the British population depends on partial government assistance.

According to some British analysts, the economic decline in the early 1980s, unemployment, and poverty are consequences of high taxes and excessive labor costs, which reduced capital investments in the 1970s. Patrick Minford (1987, 265) posits that "it is a widespread opinion among economists, and one which we fully endorse—that the proximate cause of unemployment is excessively high wage costs, produced either by high wages or by low productivity. We have identified this as a strong mechanism in the U.K." Other economists write that mismanagement, over-bureaucratization, overregulation, and excessive union demands have made the British economy appear no longer safe or profitable for investment. The elements of the vicious cycle spawned by this situation, they say, are obvious: Because private investors were reluctant to accept the risks of modernizing, and because unions opposed most innovations that would reduce the labor force, large sectors of British industry became outmoded. Because industry was becoming more and more outdated, both technologically and organizationally, over the last twenty years, British manufacturers failed to win new markets and lost many of the internal and external markets they had controlled previously. Once in decline, the British economy shrank in other aspects, causing unemployment and poverty to spread. Poverty reduced consumption; and so the spiral descent continued.

Other evaluations blame capitalism for producing poverty and the continuously deteriorating conditions under which the poor must live. They associate the Thatcher government's "piecemeal assault on the British welfare state" with the current situation of the poor in Great Britain.

Keith Smith (1984) expressed the opinion that several factors caused the economic crisis in Great Britain but agreed with others that foremost among them was inadequate investment, both in R&D and in manufacturing activities. Some experts, he writes, have argued that the British have invested more or less equally with other OECD nations in manufacturing machinery and equipment, the nation's most important trading sector. This, Smith states, is correct; but, he points out (195–199), "we have invested less in total, and also less in net terms (which means that our capacity to produce has expanded more slowly than competitors')." Smith's findings reveal that the main criterion of business success is not the size of investment, but the yield investment brings. Not only was the capital-per-worker ratio lower in Great Britain than in other OECD nations, but investments in Great Britain frequently produced lower returns on investment than those in industrialized economies elsewhere. Naturally, investors were affected by the meager prospects of returns. Investment shrank. Discussing this aspect of British decline, J. H. Coates (1985, 85) includes figures on the deteriorating profitability of industrial investment in Great Britain, quoted from *Bank of England Quarterly Bulletin*, June 1981, statistics. According to these data, the pretax real return on trading assets of industrial and commercial companies was lower in Great Britain than elsewhere. The trend of this aspect of decline was as follows: 1963, 11.4%; 1970, 8.6%; 1972, 9.3%; 1974, 5.2%; 1976, 5.4%; 1978, 6.2%; 1979, 4.3%; 1980, 2.9%. Coates writes that "unless the returns to industry improve markedly, there will be little incentive for business in general to invest in new capacity and create new jobs."

The *OECD Economic Surveys: United Kingdom* (February 1980, 5, 7, 9, 47) presented a similar picture of decline and deterioration:

> Economic performance in 1979 was characterized by little growth, accelerating inflation and a sizeable current external deficit. These developments were strongly influenced by large increases in earnings and real personal disposal income. . . . Conditions changed considerably in 1979, partly due to strikes and loss of competitiveness. Profit rates began to decline again, and because of the acceleration in the rate of growth of labour costs and the rise of oil prices coupled with weakening demand outlook both home and abroad led to significant downward revisions in investment plans. . . . Despite the sizeable rise in real disposable income, private residential investment has fallen sharply since mid-1978 and its level in the third quarter of 1979 was the lowest for over twenty years and more than one-third below the 1972 peak. . . . Economic performance over the last few years has remained disappointing. Inflationary pressures have not abated: in fact there was a considerable acceleration in the course of 1979. And while North Sea oil and gas production has risen to an estimated $10–15 billion in 1979, the underlying balance of payments in the non-oil sector has remained in substantial deficit.

The report tries to cheer up the reader by implying: it is bad, but could have been worse.

Year after year, Britons continued to invest less of their GDP, work less productively, make less money, consume fewer personal goods and services, spend less than their European neighbors on housing and improvements. Even so, they lived beyond their means.

Although London was heavily bombed during World War II, British industries were not seriously affected. Immediately after the war, unlike other European nations, Great Britain had no need to rebuild plants, workshops, and mines. This seeming advantage turned into a liability twenty years later, when British industry, equipped with prewar technology and running under old-fashioned management organization, was faced with U.S., German, French, and Japanese companies, equipped with the most up-to-date technologies, employing advanced marketing methods, and operating under information-age, modern systems of management. The new criteria for national ascendancy depend, to a growing extent, on economic performance in global markets. These new, emerging rules, and the type of competition they entail, came as a surprise to the British, who were unprepared to meet the challenge.

Through her colonial territories, Great Britain previously had access to cheap raw materials and large markets. After World War II, however, unlike the French, the British were unable to retain close economic links with their former colonies. The independent states previously ruled by the British found it more attractive to develop close trade links with the United States, other European nations, the Soviet Union, Eastern European nations, and, eventually, Japan. At the same time, much against the interests of the extreme Right and certain sections of the working class, who feared competition with newcomers (see *The Empire Strikes Back*, 1982), Great Britain had to absorb millions of immigrants from her former colonies.

No other Western European nation nationalized as many industries in such a short time as did Great Britain under the Labour government in the 1970s. In a book packed with figures, extracted from official sources, Rees (1973, 231) writes:

> Public expenditure, by the three parts of the defined public sector [involving the central, county, and local government, public services and the state-owned industries], and excluding debt interest, was estimated in 1970–1 to be of the order of £20,000 m or some 45 percent of the GNP. . . . The public sector owns about 45 percent of the nation's capital assets and of the annual fixed investment.

According to Rees' documentation (231, 124), in 1970 the total number of workers employed in the public sector was 6,300,000 or 25.1 percent of the labor force. The total employed by state-owned (public) corporations was 1,920,000 or 7.7 percent. Other estimates have ranked the size of the public-sector work force, including workers employed by state-owned industries and by the state itself, differently. According to the Labour Party estimates (Coates & Hillard 1987, 99), "Twenty seven per cent of the labour force work in the public sector, producing 27 per cent of national income".[1] Regardless of whether public corporations were nationalized in rescue operations or in order to maintain employment, all these industries were modernized at great expense to the government. Despite this and despite receiving sizable investments, subsidies, and write-offs (estimated at between $60 and $80 billion in 1970s), instead of rendering profits, state-owned industries have produced deficits and growing PSBR. As depicted in Table 9.1, PSBR increased from £4,351 million in 1973/74 to £12,686 million in 1980/81. Under Thatcher's administration and privatization, PSBR were eventually reduced to £3,412 million in 1986/87. But at first, year after year, the central and local governments and the state-owned industries incurred new deficits. Great Britain lived on borrowed money. Certainly, most contemporary governments incur deficits. In Great Britain, however, the deficit grew not only because of increased expenses on social services and defense, but particularly because of the deficits produced by state-owned

Table 9.1.   Public-Sector Borrowing and Contributions to the Public-Sector Borrowing Requirement

£ million

	1973/74	1974/75	1975/76	1976/77	1977/78	1978/79	1979/1980	1980/1981	1981/1982	1982/83	1983/84	1984/85	1985/86	1986/87
Central government borrowing requirement	2,106	5,108	8,723	5,856	4,522	7,910	8,262	12,732	7,597	12,734	12,177	10,164	10,962	10,508
General government borrowing requirement	3,634	7,307	9,926	7,225	4,879	8,884	10,414	3,551	8,544	10,064	9,962	9,220	6,892	4,900
Public-sector borrowing requirement	4,351	7,976	10,253	8,304	5,373	9,236	10,020	12,686	8,632	8,859	9,753	10,172	5,815	3,412

Source: *Annual Abstract of Statistics*. No. 119/((1983); No. 124/((1988) (London: HMSO). Table 16.2.

Note: "The PSBR represents the net requirement for finance from the private sector and overseas. But the central government borrowing requirement is counted as covering direct on-lending by central government to local authorities and public corporations. Their additional 'contributions' to the PSBR are therefore equal to their borrowing requirement *less* their direct borrowing from central government.

"General government borrowing requirement is the sum of the borrowing requirements of the central government and local authorities *less* direct borrowing by local authorities from central government. The public sector borrowing requirement is the general government borrowing requirement *plus* public corporations borrowing requirement *less* public corporations direct borrowing from central government" (*Annual Abstract* 1988, 258).

industries. Money was spent on modernization; but in state-owned industries, modernization can mean many things, in many instances only remotely related to subsequent increases in productivity and profits. In spite of new investments, British state-owned industries became less productive than comparable industries in France and West Germany, not to speak of private U.S. and Japanese multinationals. According to a number of analysts, British public-sector industries were not only less productive than comparable industries in other Western industrialized nations, they were also less productive than private-sector British industries. Abraham (1974) compared private and public (state-owned) big business in the early 1970s. He brings out the similarities appearing within enterprises of the two sectors more than the differences. The differences are nevertheless discussed. According to Abraham, private corporations are "to some degree financially accountable to shareholders," while the government is the "sole shareholder" of state-owned corporations. Growth (45) remains the principal objective of both. Neither the private nor the public corporation can concern itself only with profit and external competition anymore. Both (282) "have a social responsibility." Public-sector enterprises tend "to reflect the political climate at the time," which means that they change strategies as different parties are elected to power. At the end of his book, Abraham (315–316) includes tables in which he compares ten biggest private with ten biggest public corporations. According to these data, nationalized industries use higher capital inputs and employ more workers than comparable privately owned industries with an investment turnover twice or three times as high as that of state-owned industries. Table 9.2 contains a similar comparison of nine private-sector and nine public-sector biggest industries in Great Britain. At present, only nine public-sector industries are included among the biggest 500 (considering the value of sales as the criterium).

Nationalized industries have never proved profitable over time. The analysis of the 500 largest British corporations in *Business* (October 1986) reveals that in 1985, British Coal alone incurred a deficit of £2,222,000 thousand, more than twice the total accumulated deficit among all other, both private- and state-sector businesses listed in the report. Of the list of state-owned industries, the British Railway Board incurred the second largest deficit of £288,157 thousand. British Shipbuilding incurred a deficit of £181,736 thousand and was third on the list of state-owned industries incurring deficits. These are not regular business industries, however; they are part industries, part services (in the sense that they are maintained to preserve jobs). Of strict services, the publicly owned Electricity Council produced a £944,200 thousand profit; the Post Office generated £167,000 thousand profit; in most other nations, postal services and electrical-supply services operate at a loss.

From a corporatist theory perspective, contemporary society comprises at minimum three dynamically interacting structures: business, labor, and the

Table 9.2.   Big Business in Great Britain, 1985: Comparison of the Nine Biggest Companies of the Private and Public Sectors

Company	Sales (thousands of £s)	Capital employed (thousands of £s)	Number of employees	Pre-tax profits (thousands of £s)	Pre-tax profit as percentage of sales	Pre-tax profit per employee (£s)	Rank among the 500
Private sector							
1. British Petroleum	40,986,000	20,556,000	129,450	3,613,000	8.8	27,910	1
2. Shell Transportation and Trading	25,237,600	15,495,300	na	3,208,000	12.7	—	2
3. Unilever	16,693,000	5,580,000	312,000	978,000	5.9	3,135	3
4. ICI	10,725,000	5,683,000	118,600	904,000	8.4	7,622	5
5. BAT Industries	8,797,000	6,260,000	185,503	1,168,000	13.3	6,296	6
6. Esso UK	8,580,700	3,684,000	6,097	1,272,000	14.8	208,660	7
7. British Telecom	8,387,000	10,982,000	233,711	1,810,000	21.5	7,744	8
8. British Gas	7,687,200	17,954,900	91,876	687,800	8.9	7,486	9
9. S&W Berisford	7,291,827	551,711	10,871	52,951	0.7	4,871	10
Public sector							
1. Electricity Council	10,742,600	38,933,500	132,858	944,200	8.8	7,107	4
2. British Steel	3,735,000	3,017,000	67,100	42,000	1.1	626	21
3. British Railways	3,557,500	1,322,700	190,046	(288,157)	-8.1	(1,515)	23
4. Post Office	3,247,500	4,037,200	185,293	167,000	5.1	901	30
5. British Airways	3,149,000	1,215,000	37,500	183,000	5.8	4,880	32
6. British Coal	2,018,000	5,881,000	221,298	(2,222,000)	-110.0	(10,041)	49
7. British Nuclear Fuels	545,100	1,744,400	15,678	68,400	0.1	4,363	175
8. British Airports Authority	396,000	1,215,000	7,196	76,000	19.2	10,561	218
9. British Shipbuilders	173,300	61,800	10,160	(181,736)	-104.5	(17,887)	367

Data taken from: *Business*, "The Business 500. Ranking Biggest Companies" (October 1986), pp. 77–147.

state. Depending on ideological proclivity, analysts of the British situation blamed either business, unions and the working class, or the political establishment for British economic failures. A review of these charges is pertinent.

Wiener (1981) blames the upper classes. He maintains that, even though they invented it, the British have never felt comfortable with industrialization, capitalism, modernization, and the idea of "progress." The British, writes Wiener, suffer a conflict of values (6–7): "progress versus nostalgia, material growth versus moral stability—were expressed in the two widespread and contrasting cultural symbols of Workshop and Garden (or Shire). Was England to be the Workshop of the World or a Green and Pleasant Land?" Children of the business class became members of the upper class not only by acquiring money and status, but also the ethos and lifestyle of the gentle class. The bourgeoisie was gentrified and tamed. Gentrified industrialists became psychological, if not actual, *rentiers*. Politicians, civil servants, professionals, and intellectuals developed "a striking fondness for gentry tastes," and influenced society likewise. Thus, he writes (144), "the British businessmen in the twentieth century came to accept a dual orientation . . . combine business with humanity."

Dahrendorf expands on this analysis (1982, 44): "Britain is that strange paradox, a non-industrial industrial society." The riddle of British society, Dahrendorf writes (47–48), concerns the enduring weakness of the class that gains its position through self-acquired property, professional qualifications, or political power. The British middle class, he continues, fails to generate "a core of values which radiates throughout society." Life was difficult for farmers and small-business operators in Great Britain. "For many years, small has not been beautiful in Britain. There is a connection here between the stunting of economic growth at the turn of the century and the loss of dynamism by the middle class. Britain's middle class, too, became stunted compared to that of other countries" (48). In short, the British middle class is less achievement-oriented than the U.S. or the German. The British middle and managerial classes are highly conservative, not necessarily in a political sense, but in their fierce adherence to tradition. Valuing more things in life than strict money-making, they are slow to accept modernity. They are not known for their dynamism, foresight, expertise, inventiveness, management skills, or initiatives. Most of all, they are too civilized. They have left behind the rapacious spirit of the past; such attitudes, however, are even more necessary today, given the level of contemporary economic competition. Whatever the reasons, since World War II, Great Britain has lost a great deal of its market to foreigners; the British were not successful enough in winning new markets, introducing innovative ideas, and aggressively promoting their commodities. In sum, these writers argue, Great Britain, which used to be a nation of conquerors, entrepreneurs, and producers of excellent technology, has now acquired a new characteristic: the lion transmogrified into a pussycat. "I cannot say that I have much sympathy for those who seek to justify our present state of affairs by a pastoral apologia," commented Henderson (1979, 30), in an earlier analysis. Indeed, the new middle class did not appreciate those assessments either.

In his book, *Britain in Decline* (1985), Gamble presents a less explicit, yet similar analysis. Gamble begins with a larger perspective on the issue: He speaks of Great Britain as being in decline for a hundred years now. Yet, he notes, the nation still survives. Gamble points out that while losing all its colonies and dependent territories, Great Britain changed from an empire into a welfare state. He seems to attribute the causes of its sickness more to this than to any other factor. This is difficult to bear for many Britons, he writes. However, Gamble presents ample figures demonstrating that, though Great Britain's decline is real in economic terms, it appears dramatic only when compared to other industrial nations. He elegantly posits that, for the most part, economic decline followed "a gradual descent." Only recently has British performance become intolerably worse than that of other capitalist economies, concludes Gamble. This, he recognizes, is a problem. Still, he holds that Great Britain's decline in competitiveness follows from its decline in political power. The decline is only relative (14). In certain regards, there was not decline at all. The general character of British institutions (102) has not changed much; we are still the same, he says. What was and is real is the sphere of liberty within the society, which has not shrunk (13). This is important to us. "The decline in Britain's world status and world power has been accompanied not by falling but by rising material wealth." We are okay, he says, even if others are much better off. With classic British pride, Gamble verges on exclaiming: We actually love our decline; it is ours. Let me quote Henderson again. He in a sense anticipates such assessments and writes (1979, 30), "Others will argue that the British way, with ingenuity and application devoted to leisure rather than to work, is superior to that elsewhere and is in any case what people want. I do not doubt of this." But, he continues, Great Britain has a large population, accustomed to and skilled in industrial life. And this population deserves to have at least as a good economic condition as the French, Germans, and North Americans have.

Wiener and other such authors have proved to be wrong, however. It is now quite evident that they failed to recognize the potential of the new middle class. The more recently published literature (see Jamieson 1980; Hutber 1976; Elliot & McCrone 1987; Useem 1984, 183–192: Handelman 1988; Hartley 1988) presents an entirely different portrait of the new British middle class. It is this class that is changing Great Britain now.

According to Conservative critics, Labour politics and union blackmail were at the root of the contemporary British disease. Motivated by "collective selfishness and greed," and the desire to protect obsolete jobs and excessive pay, with complete disregard for economically detrimental consequences for the nation, unions inhibited technological modernization and forced industries to accept low productivity standards. The British worker, these writers claim, is strike-happy: The annual average of official strikes over the period 1974–1985 was 1,830, one of the highest among Western societies. In their opinion, unions have resorted to strikes and other direct-action practices too easily, too frequently, and for ridiculously long periods, causing enormous losses in labor hours, adversely affecting business, and producing an atmosphere of class war instead of national cooperation.

> Our unions [writes Joseph (1986, 99)] have been uniquely privileged for several decades. . . . The predictable result has been the growing use of strikes and the strike threat. In a trade dispute most things seem permitted for the union side: breaking contracts, inducing others to break contracts, picketing of non-involved companies, secondary boycotts.

It is because of unions, claim these critics, that British industry, overmanned, underachieving, and beset with poor workmanship, produced overpriced commodities. Needless to say, unions and the Left do not share this view. They argue that workers are paid less in Great Britain than in any other industrialized Western society and that workers must defend their source of livelihood.

Critics who blame the government for deteriorating conditions are divided into two camps: one holding Labour, the other holding the Tories responsible. Keith Smith blames the government for not having developed an industrial policy.[2] He states (1984, 236): "Resolving the long-term crisis means restoring the UK manufacturing sector, in terms of its levels of output and employment, and in terms of its ability to compete against foreign manufacturers both in international markets and within Britain." He recommends establishing an industrial policy; "Let's have an industrial policy" is a fashionable solution. But, an industrial policy can mean many things. As Japanese examples demonstrate, industrial policies require sacrifices. Different parties and different interest groups in Great Britain would probably agree on the objectives of an industrial policy or planning, as outlined by K. Smith, or as advocated in other literature (J. Smith 1987, 46–51) and by the media. They would disagree, however, on questions of priority, strategy, tactics, and, most of all, at whose expense such policies should be advanced.

Since the beginning of industrialization in the eighteenth century, Great Britain's society has been deeply divided along class lines. The different and quite separate cultures of upper and working classes both strongly reinforced this cleavage. Elsewhere in Europe, revolutions erased some of the major class differences. Great Britain went through a civil war in the seventeenth century, but British society never experienced a revolution as the French and Germans did, nor a major reform such as that to which Japan was subjected by the emperor Meiji. Everywhere in Europe, new conflicts emerged that counterbalanced traditional class conflicts; not in Great Britain, however, until the late 1980s. First the aristocracy, later the upper bourgeoisie with what was left of the aristocracy as part of it, then (in the 1940s and the 1970s), the union-dominated Labour governments tried to employ the state to advance their own class interests; always against other classes.

The British state was the model of the classic traditional state, performing the two principal functions of defense and maintenance of law and order, along with several other less important functions. *The Growth of Government* (Fry 1979, 117–121) is a very interesting study of the state's role and functions in the past. Although Fry never specifies it, he clearly portrays, in accordance with the rules of classical theory, the growth of state apparatus, discussing the development of law and order, imperial management, defense organization, foreign policy, and the tax-collecting apparatus of the state. Fry ends by discussing these apparatus in the twentieth century, but does not notice that model democracy and the model state became inadequate in the face of certain contemporary needs. He also fails to recognize that, during the 1970s and early 1980s, not only did industries and the managerial and administrative practice of corporations lose ground, but the techniques employed in running the British leviathan became less and less adequate. The democratic political system, operating under the guise of monarchy, maintained the model of a political system serving the public, but failed to initiate certain new institutions acquired and developed by other nations to conduct the business of government under etatization. Again, as in the past, the British missed out on a revolution; this time, they missed the managerial revolution.

The British state was not equipped to develop and manage a contemporary economy. "The state's role in the economy has not involved the construction of a strong interventionist system for the direction and guidance of industry," write Fine and Harris (1985, 19). They point out that the establishment of the National Economic Development Office (NEDO) was no more than a very pale imitation of French planning; the state failed to develop a base for the new strategic, information-technology industries. Fine and Harris repeat the argument concerning the low productivity of British industries. They blame the "city" (financial capital) for all wrong that happened to Great Britain. The unions, they write, were not sufficiently aggressive; they concentrated on defensive actions, whereas union pressure for high wages, if it succeeded, would have helped induce industry to modernization. They also argue that one of the principal adverse factors in the situation was the dependence of British industries on U.S. TNC—a view opposite to that held by the Tories. In their opinion (15):

> While the state has taken an important role in the economy it is one which has, in important respects, encouraged the preservation of old structures of economic relations instead of guiding the modernisation of capital, or stimulating a type of accumulation that would enable capitalist production

in Britain to be founded on a high wage–high productivity basis.

It is ironic, that this is in fact what Thatcher is doing by supporting new industries and closing old ones. Fine and Harris represent the neomarxist position, away from the (330) "functionalism of Marxist writings on the state that followed Poulantzas and Miliband." No, they are not Thatcherites; they posit (331): "In our view, the issue is whether it is possible to develop an economic strategy to move forward from the crisis *without an extensive economic role for the central state* [emphasis added]."

During the 1960s and 1970s, though for different reasons, the Conservative and Labour party governments failed to develop adequate regulatory management of the national economy. The Tories of those days learned to be less hostile to Keynesian designs. Yet, they continued to believe more in the self-regulatory ability of the market. They were reluctant to involve the state in economic management. The 1974–1979 Labour Party government undertook to implement new social contract policies, tried to involve the unions in national decisionmaking, and tried to nationalize as many industries as it could. This government expanded the welfare system, but ended in having a major conflict with the unions. The party outlined the principal objectives for Great Britain in a definite order: (*a*) full employment; (*b*) "transfer of economic wealth and power from a small economic oligarchy to the people"—that meant nationalization; (*c*) "public ownership of more industries"; and finally, (*d*) NEB—the New Economic Board—called by critics the New Economic Bureaucracy—was to manage this new economic wealth on behalf of the people.

New legislation (e.g., the Industry Act; bills to implement what was called the regeneration of British industry; the Trade Union and Labour Relations Act; the Employment Protection Act; Health and Safety at Work Act; the Equal Pay and the Race Relations acts) was enacted with one principal objective: to shift control and power from one class to the other, reducing the wealth of the aristocracy and bourgeoisie.

Austin Mitchell (1983, 19) writes:

> The public had not been enthusiastic about labour but had given it high marks for getting and keeping the cooperation of the trade unions in contrast to the Tories. That cooperation was shattered and the 1978-79 winter of discontent ruined the government. For the public it was a simple practical test. Labour has failed. For the left in the Labour Party it was a vindication: government failed because it had denied conference decisions against incomes policy. The unions were alienated, less ready to back a leadership that they no longer trusted, against a left which, on that issue at least, had been on their side.

Mitchell thinks (167) that: "Labour's mistake has been not to move up with its people." He wants the Labour, not the Tory party to be the party of the new class. The problem is, however, that what he thinks Labour should but does not do, the Tories are already doing. So he concludes (175), "Mrs Thatcher's time is running out."

In West Germany, Social Democrats under Brandt and Schmidt encouraged a new policy: to rely on the cooperation of unions with the banking and business sectors. The outcome was *Mitbestimmung*— participatory democracy, concertation at different levels of the political and corporate structure involving representations from politics, business, and unions. In Great Britain, neither the aristocracy-bourgeoisie nor the working class were open to such cooperation; the class struggle pursued its course. The Labour Party planned to legislate an industrial democracy act; it was never introduced. In fact, the party did not wish to share industrial democracy with capitalists. They concentrated on providing more rights to unions and improving the conditions of the working class by allocating a larger share of the national wealth to the poorer sections of society. Yet, the redistributive mechanisms they developed acquired many features of an oppressive bureaucracy. Very little was done to increase the production of wealth, to increase the pie divided among classes and groups, to increase Great Britain's ability to win international markets. Elected in the 1970s, the Labour Party conducted government with a class perspective of the 1930s. It failed to produce a vision for society as a whole. It was unable to propose even what the Social Democrats quite successfully advanced in West Germany and Sweden, or what the Socialists later tried to achieve in France.

Berrington (1983, 1) explores why Labour had to pursue this policy, but to explain is another matter. He writes that "corporatism requires, not merely agreement between government and the national leadership of business and labour, but the ability of those two estates to deliver the support of their followers." He refers to Hague (1983, 130–162), who writes that the official union leadership could never be sure of "the support of informal" networks of shop stewards, officers of the particular unions, and the wide membership in the work place divided by sectional jealousies and traditional animosities. The fact is that Labour and the unions have not been able to overcome these problems to date.

In short, Great Britain in the 1970s, whether under Tory or Labour government, was unable to accomplish what the Japanese and the Germans accomplished.

Recovery

Conditions in Great Britain are rapidly changing, however. In fact, while the economy was declining, regeneration began, unrecognized by analysts. As in the rest of Western Europe, though recognized by neither the tradition-oriented Tories nor by Labour in those years, the new British middle class was growing, maturing, and readying itself for a greater role. The ongoing class war and the decline of British economic conditions delayed its coming of age, but as conditions went on changing everywhere in the world, the new class became more visible and began to assert itself in Great Britain as well. Handelman (1988, 100; 143) notes:

> A study commissioned by the National Economic Development Office (NEDO) in 1986 claimed that the industrial crisis had produced a "new" British type, particularly suited to the postindustrial era. Such people were nondogmatic, creative, and, unlike their more reserved compatriots, willing to risk the embarrassment of trying something new. The study . . . actually named the emerging group "New People" and suggested that they, more than any other group in British society, possessed the inventiveness and resourcefulness Britain was going to need to survive in the twenty first century. . . . In the first six years of the Thatcher government, more than 140,000 new businesses came into operation. It was a remarkable rate of business formation at a time when so many other companies in more traditional fields of British industry were failing. According to Her Majesty's Treasury, Britain accounted for two-thirds of all inventory capital raised in the European Community during 1985.

During the early 1980s, no importance was attributed to that phenomenon. Now, it is regarded a remarkable development:

> After a period of hesitation towards the end of 1985, overall economic activity accelerated sharply through 1986 and into 1987 [reports *OECD Economic Surveys 1986/87: United Kingdom* 1987, 9]. Real GDP (average measure) is estimated to have grown at an annual rate of 5 per cent in the first quarter of this year, exceeding its cyclical trough in 1981 by some 18 per cent. Taking 1986 as a whole, real GDP growth may have been almost 3 per cent (or 2.5 per cent if allowance is made for the direct effects of the 1984–85 coal dispute).

Initially, Thatcher conducted the Conservative Party's policy along traditional Tory lines. She tried to dismantle the institutions and structures previously installed by her Labour predecessor. She went on attempting to reduce the power of the bureaucracy and of unions. This, the Conservatives had promised to do before their first election. Then the Falklands/Malvinas War erupted. By taking back the islands, she restored British pride and won the hearts of her people. She simultaneously commenced the long overdue restructuring of the industrial economy. At this point, she introduced a new policy. The undertaking required the closing of unproductive industries. Twenty-five percent of all manufacturing jobs were to disappear, as a result of closing these industries. This was not a popular policy. To those who reminded Thatcher of this, she responded, "The lady's not for turning." Thatcher was determined to reduce the role and size of the state, and to reestablish control by the market economy, at any price. When it became evident that under new conditions, the market economy can only be maintained by state supervision and protection, she changed her policy. Thatcher kept the bureaucracy alive and well but put it on a leash.

"She worships at the feet of entrepreneurs," wrote the *Guardian*. She does indeed; but it is at the feet of the new-style, managerial entrepreneurs that she kneels. While continuing along established Tory patterns, Thatcher gradually began to employ new strategies and set new objectives. Eventually, she came increasingly to reflect the interest of new forces, the new industrial sector in the economy, and the new middle-managerial and entrepreneurial classes.

As a representative of the Conservative establishment, but also of these new forces, Thatcher waged war against unions and succeeded in enacting laws restricting their power in many ways: their use of closed-shop pressure; their ability to organize solidarity actions at plants other than those at which wrongdoing by managers or owners is claimed. She inflicted a crushing defeat on the traditionally most-powerful miners' and printers' unions, forcing these militant labor organizations to capitulate. By closing smokestack industries, she not only reduced expenses borne by the government in maintaining them but diminished the ranks of the class she waged war against.

Thatcher quelled several rebellions within the ranks of her own party. Most of the traditionally minded, patrician Conservatives, who had dominated party politics for a century, were gradually pushed out of leadership positions. New, mostly managerial-oriented men took over in their stead. To again quote Handelman (1988, 142–143): "Thatcher turned private enterprise into a national ideology. She made the entrepreneur a model for the rest of Britain and, by peeling away the layers of protective regulations around business, she doused Britain in a cold shower of self-interest." The Tory party underwent several radical transformations and came out as a party of new social and economic forces, with novel managerial ideas. The Conservative Party was "revolutionized" into a modern organization of corporatist intermediation. At the same time, the Labour Party went in the other direction. Even more than in the 1970s, it changed into a party waging class struggle. In fact, this policy produced the split within its ranks and the emergence of the new, centrist Alliance.

Thatcher is often characterized as having little imagination, as a tyrant running a centralist government. She may not have great vision, as her critics possess, but she evidently has a strong leadership instinct. She has led her party and her country in the direction where money could be made. She backs down rarely but does when it is politically expedient, as in April 1988, when, after welfare revamping, her government agreed to restore £200 million in housing allowances for pensioners, the disabled, and the poorest people.

Nigel Lawson (Coates & Hillard 1988, 8–17) discusses the government's objectives under Thatcher's leadership: "Our first priority was the reduction of inflation." Labour's first priority was reduction of unemployment. Next, Lawson lists "firm control of monetary condition"; reduction of the public sector's burden on the economy; stimulation of economic investment through tax reduction. At the end, he lists reduction of unemployment, which he hopes to achieve as a result of successes in other policies. In *Employment: The Challenge for the Nation* (1985), representing the Conservative government's position, the same point is stressed:

> First and most important is a sound and stable framework of economic and industrial policy. Sustained employment growth needs an economic setting in which enterprise can flourish and industry and commerce can compete successfully and raise output. The first priority has to be control of inflation.

Three instruments have been employed by the Conservatives to secure the economy on the new track: privatization (see Chapter 8, Table 8.4), fiscal policy, and monetary policy. Although there is no evidence it was set up deliberately this way, it turned out to be a clever strategy, rendering not only the desired economic results, but also a social change reinforcing the political position of the Conservatives. By privatizing British Telecom, British Petroleum, British Gas, British Airways, and dozens of other companies, Thatcher obtained funds with which she could reduce the state deficit, particularly the volume of the PSBR, which eventually was brought down to almost zero. Britons are now allowed to invest annually £2,400 tax free in equities. They are also encouraged to save through tax-exempted life-insurance and pension schemes. At present, between 9 and 12 million own shares. "The new capitalists, like the new council-home owners are disproportionally Tory voters," reports *The Economist* (December 19, 1987). During the recession of 1981, against the advice of leading economists, the Tories adopted a policy of deflation. Inflation was reduced from a 22% peak in 1980, to 5% in 1983, and 4% subsequently. It is maintained at this low level. Marginal tax rates were cut from 98% on unearned profit and from 83% on high salaries, to 60%. Incentives for small and medium private businesses were enhanced. Taxes on equity investment in new industries were reduced over a 3-year period. The government also undertook other efforts to attract new investments. The 1988 budget went further. This was a surplus budget and introduced certain new fiscal principles. Great Britain installed a new two-bracket tax-rate system, instead of the six brackets as before. The basic income tax rate was reduced from 27% to 25% (the United States maintains a 29% level). The other, higher rate, instead of rates varying between 27% and 60%, is currently 40%. All these policies obviously were in the interests of Great Britain's new middle class. According to *Money Magazine* (February 25, 1988), only thirty of the top 200 fortunes in Great

Britain are now descendants of aristocratic families; the rest are newcomers.

The new middle class acquired a large volume of shares in the privatized state-owned industries. With this, they also acquired a concern for a Conservative victory. In this sense, Thatcherism entailed a revolution. According to research published in *British Public Opinion* (June 1987) and other analyses (see, e.g., Hartley 1987, 4), "Since 1979 there has been an increase of six percentage points in the upper and middle-class section of the population (from 33% to 39%). Those who own their own houses now number 66% (52% in 1979)." The percentage of population owning shares of industries increased from 12% in 1983 to 19% in 1987. At the same time, membership of trade unions has declined by eight points, from 30% in 1979 to 22% in 1987. The population of those living in a rented council house has decreased from 35% in 1979 to 27% in 1987.[3]

Social change affected the economy. Productivity has increased. Even the public sector's and nationalized industries' productivity is now on the rise. In 1983, Great Britain attained a 2 percent growth of GNP. According to recent calculations, over the last five years, Great Britain's economy grew at a healthy rate of 3.5 percent. It is expected to continue to grow at this rate at least for the next few years. Certain companies, particularly new, high-technology electronic industries, the General Electric Company, Oxford Instruments, and computer software companies, began to produce relatively high returns on investment. A good example is Cable and Wireless. *Fortune* (October 29, 1984) notes:

> A once fading relic of the British Empire, London-based Cable & Wireless has turned aggressive in an effort to keep the sun shining on its worldwide communications business. . . . Revenues have more than doubled in three years to the equivalent of $813 million for the fiscal year that ended in March 1984. Pretax profits have tripled to $238 million. Earnings per share rose 140% and return on shareholders' equity at the end of the last [1987] fiscal year was a splendid 24%.

The list of top British exporters includes, foremost, the major oil companies, but also ICI, British Aerospace, IBM UK Holdings, General Electric Company, and several car manufacturers. With these changes (see Handelman 1988, Ch. 9) came new prosperity. The British economy recovered. It was now rapidly moving ahead of the rest of the European pack. According to the Bank of England's 1987 report, the non–North Sea companies' real pretax return on capital rose to about 8 percent in 1986—up from minus 3 percent (in debts) in 1981. The British economy has recovered, but the unemployed are still jobless.

In contrast to the Conservatives' objective of combating inflation as first priority, the 1985 Labour Party proclaimed "Planning for Full Employment" their chief priority. The party took a rather defensive position on the public sector's role in the economy. The report proclaims (after Coates & Hillard

1987, 100): "We need to rethink the role of the public sector. . . . This may require us to consider other forms of social ownership, including co-operatives." Labour advocated industrial planning and planning public expenditure, stood for fair wage policy, and called for repealing anti–trade-union legislation introduced by the Conservative government.

The Alliance came forward with a ten-point liberal program strongly emphasizing the expansion of education and R&D, encouragement of investment, "a new partnership between public and private finance," profit-sharing, etc.

Thatcher's reelection success in 1983 was explained as a consequence of several factors: enthusiasm over Britain's victory in the Falklands/Malvinas Islands; the split in the ranks of the opposition; and the lunacy of Labour programs. The Conservatives' reelection in 1987 by an almost identical number of votes could not be explained in such a way. According to *British Public Opinion* (May 1987), just before election (during the last week of April), 40% of Britons expressed satisfaction with the way the government was running the country (51% were dissatisfied); 47% were satisfied with how Thatcher was doing her job as prime minister (46% were dissatisfied); 27% expressed satisfaction with how Kinnock was doing his job as leader of the Labour Party (57% were dissatisfied). This determined the results of the election. The Conservatives' chancellor of the exchequer, Lawson, introduced a new budget just before the election in June 1987. It came over as a triumph and strengthened the voting intention of the 44 percent who already declared that they would vote Conservative. In the budget presentation, the government announced plans to spend an additional £5.5 billion instead of the expected £4 billion. Taxes were cut, public borrowing was reduced. Press reports claimed that Great Britain's recovery boosted tax revenues so much that, by 1988 or 1989, there may be no public-sector borrowing requirement at all. According to preliminary calculations, the rise in 1986/87 GNP had been an unprecedented 5–6%; according to critics only half of that, but even half was a great success. The raise was expected to go even higher, to 7% in 1987/88 (up 4% in prices and 3% in real output).

Just before the election (see *British Public Opinion*, June 1987), the Harris, Gallup, MORI, and other polls predicted that Thatcher's Tories would receive 42–44% of the vote; Labour 32–35%; and the Alliance 21–23.5%. The press predicted that Thatcher would lose. She won again, with a nearly identical majority as in 1983.[4]

Yet the 1987/88 year was called both the "winter of triumph" and another "winter of discontent." The triumph has been discussed; the discontent was expressed by the *New Statesman* and related press, the opposition parties, and the leadership of the unions. While a great many average families were "enjoying the vulgar business of becoming richer," as *The Economist* put it, others joined those on strike. Strikes erupted abundantly; those involving Ford and Vauxhall auto manufacturing, teachers, and nurses were principal ones. Many are unhappy with the new income-support scheme that is replacing the supplementary benefit schemes of the past. Fewer people with medium incomes will get benefits now. The big losers, the press reports, are the poorest, young and old. Close to 2.5 million Britons remain unemployed.[5] There is still a lot of catching up to be done. In response to a MORI public opinion poll (*British Public Opinion*, August 1987), 65 percent expressed the opinion that unemployment is the most important issue facing Great Britain today.

This discussion of British recovery must end with a cautionary remark. The October 1987 stockmarket jolt seems to have had a stronger impact on the sizable number of new, small stockholders in Great Britain than in other nations. The 1988 privatization yields turned out to be much lower than expected. On November 25, 1988, Chancellor Lawson had to announce the record monthly deficit in the balance of payments of £2,943 billion. Interest rates, which in May were 7.5%, subsequently rose several times, and stood at 13% in October. Mortgage costs went up accordingly. In view of these trends, the prospects of the British steel, electricity, and water utilities privatizations, undertaken in 1988, did not look as promising as previous operations. Critics immediately proclaimed that the miracle recovery had come to an end. As one would expect, the chancellor's analysis of the situation was different. He declared that the greater than anticipated consumer spending produced some inflationary tendencies that needed to be curtailed. The tightening of the money supply undertaken by the exchequer was to let out the excess steam of the market engine. He expected the economy's growth of 5% to slow to a rate of 3–3.5%, which he proclaimed to be required in order to maintain a lower inflation rate and the continuity of economic stability.

Privatization and other Thatcherite reforms do not take Great Britain back to the Victorian era. The nation is going to remain under state control and regulation, subjected to advancing processes of etatization. At least to the new middle-class majority, the symbiosis between the state—providing general economic management and protection for their interests—and the private sector—running specific corporations—seems the most efficacious solution to the diverse problems of contemporary etatized society.

CHAPTER TEN

From *Étatisme* to *Étatisme:* France

No other nation possesses such a rich history of etatization and diverse experimentation with state intervention as does France. Shonfield (1965, 71–87) reflects on this *étatisme* tradition in his *Modern Capitalism*. He first recalls Colbert's deeds and the work of Friedrich List, the inventor of "national economics." List, he says, in true colbertist spirit—and in contrast to British economic doctrine, which focused on cost and price factors—developed, in 1848, the French idea of state-directed industrialization, wherein objectives were set according to national, not private, interests. He discusses diverse French initiatives to build state regulatory and planning institutions in the nineteenth century and concludes (81):

> Their administrative methods had to be improved if they were to take advantage of the opportunities offered. This was done outstandingly after the Second World War; and the intricate system of economic control, incentives, and subtle moral pressures, operating under the guidance of the Commissariat du Plan, is its most sophisticated expression.

Ironically, Shonfield has nothing but praise for these initiatives, classified by many French writers as a "fatal blindfold," "exemplary failures," "French illness," and so on. According to Peyrefitte (1986, 84), who occupied ministerial positions in eight governments under de Gaulle, Pompidou, and Giscard d'Estaing, and participated in building the first postwar *étatisme* so venerated by Shonfield: "Colbert was chasing a chimera comparable to that the planned societies are pursuing in the twentieth century: to make the kingdom prosper by making every individual the docile executant of economic decisions reached rationally at the top." We still suffer under leaders believing that this chimera can be made reality.

None of the many *étatisme* experiments, costly in both monetary terms and human sacrifices, which make up French history, can be regarded as successful. Each, after a short period of initial success, ended in lasting economic crisis, often revolution, which changed the régime and swept the *étatisme* governments out to the "dumping grounds of history." Yet, new leaders tried again and again to solve the nation's problems by setting up still newer systems of *étatisme*. Colbert and his successors never produced enough revenues, through state control and regulation, to attain their objective. The 1789 revolution instituted its own state *dirigisme*, complete with the proclamation that the object of worship would no longer be God but the holy fatherland, holy revolution, and even the holy guillotine. It also provided a new impetus for the development of the state. This concern is discussed by Skocpol. She (1979, 175) writes:

> Revolution may lie primarily in sociopolitical and juridical transformations—that is, bureaucratization, democratization, and the emergence of a politico-legal framework favorable to capitalism—wrought through a confluence of political struggles for state power and peasant struggles against seigneurial rights, rather than in a basic transformation of the socioeconomic structure effected by the class action of a capitalist bourgeoisie.

As the state grew, the quest for a model superstate continued. *Étatisme*, under highly efficient state management, was considered a universal panacea for all ills befalling society; it was to provide security, justice, prosperity, and equality for citizens, and high revenues for government. After World War II, two similar experiments ended in failure: one attempted by de Gaulle and the other by his archopponent, Mitterrand.

Most of the literature on French political culture points to a seeming paradox: The French have two traditions. One is linked to, first, the old regime and the Church, then to Bonapartism, and, eventually, to love and respect for hierarchy and central authority. The other represents liberal anticlericalism, republicanism, and the revolutionary ideals of equality and liberty. Whenever the French experience a crisis under a regime operating in one tradition, they simply invoke the other tradition. The first tradition appeals to the desire for security, but the French do not enjoy living under the hierarchical and regimented systems set up to pursue this objective. Thus, they revolt and establish the republic of equality. But such regimes do not produce wealth fast enough; the French loath the *bourse* but love the money it generates. Eventually, they institute a new hierarchical order so they can once again compete for wealth. Hating capitalism, they turn to the protection of the state; hating etatization, they turn back to the market. The French oscillate between the state and the market.

Étatisme à la de Gaulle

After World War II, France entered a new stage of etatization. The resistance movement had been divided along party lines. Most of the parties acting in the underground set up special committees to address the task of developing programs for an independent France. Kuisel (1981, 157–187) discusses these programs at length. One manifesto, he reports, came from the Organisation Civille et Militaire (OCM) acting in the occupied territories. Other documents were developed in exile. René Courtin and other experts of the Comité Général d'Études (CGE), which performed official functions for de Gaulle's National Committee, published the "Report on Postwar Economic Policy." It reflected the neoliberal and Keynesian viewpoint popular among economic experts at the time. André Philip and a number of prominent personalities in the Socialist Party developed their program in a different document. The Communists came up with still another. According to Kuisel (179), it "identified the mistakes and omissions of the socialists and the experts without advancing much in its own right." Our present, limited discussion of these various programs focuses, not on the differences of opinion expressed but more on the matters on which these groups shared similar views. All parties expected independent France to have some kind of *dirigiste* régime and a state-managed economy. They were, however, divided over nationalization. Kuisel reports that the OCM experts wanted socialism but were against nationalizing industries. Nationalization, they argued, was no answer because it bred "non-socialist statism." They advocated self-management of enterprises. Other groups favored wide nationalization. Courtin, a typical Keynesian, recommended gradual nationalization and, specifically, nationalizing monopolistic industries. He also recommended "returning to the market as soon as conditions permitted." Courtin expressed the opinion that economic policies must aim at helping the poor rather than supporting the rich. The Socialist Party favored broad nationalization; its representatives stressed, however, the importance of keeping nationalized industries under the control of all those "affected" (Kuisel 1981, 174), i.e., workers, industrialists, and consumers. The Communists called for the most widespread nationalization. They especially stressed the importance of nationalizing financial institutions.[1] While the Socialists linked nationalization with planning, the Communists explicitly advocated central planning for the entire economy.

"Among the ministers" of the postwar government, Kuisel continues (189), "there was general agreement on the desirability of *dirigisme*, planning, nationalization, and renovation." Representatives of the principal parties disagreed, however, on interpretations of these ideas, specifically on how to implement policy. De Gaulle, who believed in the appropriateness of *dirigisme*, was rather reserved and cautious at first. He could not decide which of the suggested programs to adopt. He felt *dirigisme* was needed, but for different reasons than those offered by his ministers and other leading politicians.

Two conceptions of the state coexisted in nineteenth- and early twentieth-century European thought. The first concept, rooted in Hobbes' Leviathan, in Locke's (among others) contractarian theories, and, foremost, in English economic thought, asserts that members of society possess a natural right to pursue personal objectives and choose the lives they will lead. Each individual is an end to itself. The market is the forum where individuals can pursue their endeavors. Under these conditions, the state's functions are limited. It only guards law and order, under which the inalienable rights of individuals to their own choices in the market are exercised. Individuals may pursue their objectives through the state, but no one shall be expected to live for the state.

The second conception is well exemplified by German philosophical literature. Kant's ideas on form and substance apply, but Hegel's ideas are more relevant to our present discussion. According to Hegel (1957, 443–447):

> The State is the realization of the ethical idea. . . . It is the will which thinks and knows itself, and carries out what it knows, and in so far as it knows. The individual . . . has his substantial freedom in the State, as the essence, purpose, and product of his activity. . . . The State is the march of God through the world, its ground is the power of reason realizing itself as will. . . . The union of duty and right has the twofold aspect that what the State demands as duty should directly be the right of the individual, since the State is nothing but the organization of the concept of freedom. . . . The State is an organism or the development of the idea into its differences.

The first school of thought asserts the primacy of the individual's interest, the second advocates the primacy of the state's interest. It was to this second understanding of the individual's position vis-à-vis the state that de Gaulle subscribed. Hegel philosophized that the state expresses itself through the "great man of history." As a leader, de Gaulle considered himself a mouthpiece of France. I do not know whether de Gaulle was familiar with Hegel's ideas. Regardless, the idea that the state is the prime purpose giving meaning to life not only appears dominant in the four volumes of *Discours et messages* and de Gaulle's *Memoires*, in Malraux's (1972) interviews of de Gaulle after he retired, but even in the speeches of his associates. The state is unity; all divisions into classes, parties, or groups are irrelevant. De Gaulle wrote that his personal interests were tantamount to those of France. Authors writing about de Gaulle confirm that de Gaulle's sole objective was to restore France to greatness, without which, according to him (this he repeated many times), there is no France. "All my life," he wrote in his *Memoires* (1954, I: 5) "I have nurtured a precise image of France, inspired by both feeling and reason. . . . As I see it France cannot be without grandeur." It was not enough that de Gaulle was an ardent patriot, that he had a mission; he believed his compatriots obliged to share this mission. The mission was France; the mission was the state. The state represented the general interest of all, standing above sectional interests. The state embodied freedom, democracy, and civilization. De Gaulle identified France with the Madonna. He practiced *dirigisme* as one practices religion, because he considered it instrumental in his mission to restore France's grandeur. *Dirigisme* provided the arch under which de Gaulle strove to unify all his compatriots, to the fulfilment of their high patriotic obligation to the destiny of France. He was a charismatic leader with a large following. But he also headed a bureaucracy within which, contrary to his expectations, functionaries, even his close associates, were primarily devoted to their own individual pursuits. He was not prepared to accept this.

In 1945, as chief of the Provisional Government, de Gaulle declared (quoted in Einaudi et al. 1955, 75):

> The state must hold the levers of command. Yes, tomorrow it will be the task for the State itself to ensure the development of the great sources of energy, coal, electricity and petroleum, as well as the principal means of rail, maritime and air transport and the means of communication on which all the rest depends. It will be its role to bring the major branches of metallurgical production to the necessary level. It will be its role to control credit and to direct the nation's savings.

Immediately after the war, however, de Gaulle did not rush to implement this vision. The economy was in ruins; it urgently needed rebuilding. To advance industrial reconstruction, the First National Constituent Assembly enacted a number of laws. By adopting the Monnet Plan of reconstruction, the assembly instituted selective central planning for the first time. Certain industries were to be nationalized. To an extent, this continued prewar policies. Postal, telecommunication, and most of the railroad services had been nationalized before World War II. Because France lacked oil deposits, the prewar government had initiated the state-owned Régie Autonome des Petroles. After the war, certain firms, such as the Renault auto company, were nationalized in retribution for their cooperation with the occupational forces, against warnings of the resistance. The first postwar constituent assembly also nationalized the coal, gas, and electricity-producing industries. These industries, strategically important to other economic developments, had to be rebuilt despite the fact that their owners did not consider it worthwhile to rebuild them. The Bank of France and a number of commercial and credit banks and insurance companies were nationalized to establish an effective financial base for state-directed economic reconstruction. In the natural course of change, the scope of the state-owned sector expanded. No attempts were made, however, to conform to programs developed during the war. The state became involved in reconstructing and managing the economy because only the state could effectively undertake such an enormous task and mobilize the necessary material and human resources. Thus, without the explicit intention of becoming an etatized or mixed-economy society, France acquired a new economic structure, involving new government functions. Not long after, a more pervasive process of etatization evolved. Einaudi (1955, 81) notes that the Shuman *Inventaire*, published at the end of 1946, listed 103 "publicly owned industrial or commercial companies and mixed corporations of which the state owned a majority of stock"; an increase of ninety-three over prewar figures. According to this document, state-owned industries produced 20 percent of the national output in 1955.

Although *étatisme* was not on the immediate agenda, *étatisme* was accepted as the natural course of development; all groups represented in the first postwar government expected it to take shape soon. As time went by, more reasons for state management began to appear, in addition to those voiced in wartime programs. According to the Keynesian concept, which was then gaining popularity in France (as elsewhere in Western Europe), the state was to engage in economic management and development, not only to reconstruct the economy but in order to reduce and eliminate unemployment, poverty, and other social problems. Only the state could undertake the grand organizational and financial effort necessary to ensure that principal national corporations could compete in foreign markets with U.S. firms and the expanding corporations of other European nations.

The classical work on de Gaulle is, of course, *Decline or Renewal* by Hoffmann (1974). The central part of it, by Stanley and Inge Hoffmann, is dedicated to de Gaulle, the "Political Artist." Mitterrand, characterized him differently. In his diary for September 15, 1971, Mitterrand wrote (1982, 8):

> It was August 27, 1944. I can still hear the monologue he delivered that day. I listened, I observed, I admired. . . . De Gaulle unquestionably had more style, perhaps fewer original ideas, but no one could speak the language of State as he could. . . . He existed. His act created him, and his conviction that he *was* France, that he was the manifest expression of her truth, that he incarnated a moment in some eternal destiny, moved me more than it annoyed me. I have never found this conviction laughable or ridiculous.

In 1958, de Gaulle took the reigns of power for the second time. Contemptuous of political parties and parliamentary maneuvers, this time the general instituted a new type of presidential government (see Charlot 1971; Williams & Harrisson 1971; Andrews 1982). He did not dissolve the parties. He did not abolish the parliamentary system; he reorganized it. Party and parliamentary systems were rendered irrelevant. Williams and Harrisson write (21): "Under de Gaulle even the Gaullist party had for years only a marginal and episodic role." De Gaulle claimed differently. The regime retained its parliamentary character because (Andrews 1982, 24): "Parliament deliberates and passes the laws, controls the government, and has the right to overthrow it." Yet in practice, this was not the case. De Gaulle also argued (1970, 3: 166) that the regime is both parliamentary and, "as in the U.S.," presidential. Under the guise of referenda, de Gaulle reintroduced the tradition of national plebiscites. Through these, he sought both to conduct an ongoing dialog with the people of France and to legitimize his important decisions. De Gaulle saw no real need for intermediary bodies between the head of state and the citizen. Referenda and elections were held frequently. Citizens were called on to vote in support of de Gaulle's intentions. However, if the majority opposed him, de Gaulle was prepared to resign; negotiations or compromises were not acceptable to him. In the *Discours*, de Gaulle repeatedly refers to himself as *Chef de l'État* (head of state); occasionally (1970, 3: 21) as "the guide of France." Certain of his pronouncements reveal that he sincerely considered himself head of the state organism. During a press conference, he asserted (1970, 3: 169):

> We have a good Constitution. Under this Constitution, the president, as chief of the state, exercises an indivisible authority vested in him by the people. No other higher authority, be it civil, military, or judicial, could restrain his authority to govern. Only the will of the people could reinforce or limit his power.

Peyrefitte (1986, 81) writes that de Gaulle occasionally expressed himself as though he believed himself to be the reincarnation of Louis XIV. Like Napoleon, de Gaulle aspired to be the first and foremost representative of his nation. Like Louis Napoleon, he declared that it was his mission to reconstruct and enhance the economic power of France, to be a new national mission. To achieve this objective, he commanded the state bureaucracy to undertake intensive development of selected strategic industries. Social programs were expanded, but to these his ministers attributed only secondary importance. De Gaulle was determined that France become a modern, industrially and economically advanced, politically and militarily strong state; powerful enough to negotiate with the United States and the Soviet Union on equal terms.

Under the new industrial policy, certain large, innovative, privately owned major corporations were chosen as champions of national and international economic development. Little importance was attributed to other economic activities; not to the tourist industry, which was generating a great deal of income to citizens and revenue to the state. Mergers of smaller firms into larger corporations were supported. Government sustained research and developed the economic infrastructure and supplementary production that facilitated the operations of state-supported, privately owned, or state-owned giants; as long as they were French and big, they were good in de Gaulle's eyes. Other industries were heavily taxed to produce investment capital for these initiatives. France's industrial policy was to develop a large-scale, state-directed and bureaucratically managed, system of industries, engaging both state- and privately owned enterprises in objectives set by the government. The declared intention was that France would advance beyond capitalism and socialism. At first skeptical about cooperating with other European nations, de Gaulle later changed his attitude. The state of France was to become the core of a new Western European unity; Great Britain was excluded from this new Europe.

During the first years of de Gaulle's presidency, France enjoyed record economic prosperity. "Results came fast," writes P. Johnson (1983, 596):

> GNP rose by 3 per cent in the second half of 1959, by 7.9 per cent in 1960, 4.6 in 1961, 6.8 in 1962; living standards began to improve at the rate of 4 per cent a year. For the first time since the Industrial Revolution, France became an economic pace-setter. . . . Exports doubled. . . . The number of college and university students, only 78,691 in 1939, had risen to 563,000 by 1968.

Andrews (1982, 205) reports that productivity rose by 177.2 percent during the period 1949–1962. As a result, purchasing power increased 200 percent. Andrews gives a long list of data demonstrating the rapid rise in consumption.

The above figures are quite misleading, however; they are averages. Not all of France developed at an equal pace. De Gaulle accorded privileges to selected industries while burdening other industries with heavy taxes. France had the highest inflation rate in Europe and more than half a million unemployed. Stagflation set in. Workers were unhappy with slow improvements in living conditions. While the student population expanded rapidly, schools and universities suffered from insufficient funding and experienced great difficulties absorbing growing enrolments. Standards of education and services deteriorated. The gigantic, privileged bureaucracy, set up to harness vast masses of people to achieve government objectives, and to administer the society, was widely detested. The multitude of individual and group interests collided within the bureaucracy and the state. Instead of engendering growing satisfaction, the apparent prosperity brought on a crisis of expectation. De Gaulle, concerned to restore the grandeur of France, failed to handle some of its most burning social problems. "In May 1968," writes Peyrefitte (1986, 57), "everyone—beginning with those on the inside during the wild month—was struck by the vacuum that had been hollowed out in the state. Disappointment was scaled to expectations. The state, emptied of its substance, shrank to the size of a government lost in the storm." Everyone was discontented: intellectuals and students, members of parliament, workers, shopkeepers, and craftsman. After ten years under de Gaulle, France's development was stalemated. Suleiman (1974, 384), discussing this situation, posits that by the end of the 1960s, everybody in France felt society was stagnating, even the prime minister. The stalemate is still continuing.

The development program set up to achieve de Gaulle's grand objectives produced a highly privileged, well-educated, managerial, caste-like class. This class was primarily recruited among alumni of the Polytechnique, the École Nationale d'Administration, and other elite business-management schools. These people fostered their own individual and class interests and blocked the ladders of mobility to other aspirants. They impeded members of wider societal circles from participating in the decisionmaking of the nation. Career openings disappeared. As described by many writers, suspense, idleness, languor, and dejection descended on the nation. Under *dirigisme*, France was deactivated. Instead of integrating the nation around grand objectives, de Gaulle had provoked a growing apathy toward the state and greater involvement with personal and group interests.

He eventually recognized the need to involve larger sections of the population in running the country. De Gaulle promised, if he won the referendum, to restructure management and to invite a wider scope of citizens to participate in the nation's leadership. It was too late (see Hoffmann 1974, 177–184, 248). During the 1968 revolt, students and workers in Paris proclaimed de Gaulle's *étatisme* a total failure (Geismar, et al. 1969, 102-110, 120). This verdict was endorsed, through the referendum on regional reform, by people of all social classes. De Gaulle resigned immediately. Peyrefitte (1986, vii) writes that in 1966, de Gaulle lamented: "The French suffer from a deep-seated sickness. They will not understand that the times demand of them a gigantic effort of adaptation. . . . They cannot do without the State and yet they detest it, except when there is danger. . . . They do not behave like adults."

Etatization à la Mitterrand

I must remind the reader that this book is concerned only with selected aspects of etatization processes. France is unique in that it underwent two cycles of etatization. The first cycle involved etatization under the nationalistic de Gaulle government and then under Pompidou and Giscard, his successors on the Right, at a less intense pace. The objective of these governments was twofold: to restore the grandeur of France and to intensify industrial modernization.

The second cycle of etatization, under Mitterrand, entailed a massive nationalization and various social experiments, aiming to engender a socialist society. France is unique in still another respect: the importance its governments attribute to central planning, including industrial policy. These programs, critics write, produced "the Roman Sickness." Yet the French malady was characterized differently by different doctors. De Gaulle believed that France was sick because her citizens were concerned with their individual petty affairs, instead of being totally dedicated to furthering the great designs of the state.

If one believes these declarations, then in the 1970s, Mitterrand and the Socialists represented a position diametrically opposed to that of de Gaulle. They promised to reverse the relationship: Instead of people serving the state, under their rule, the state would serve the people. How was that to be done? By providing people with more entitlements. But first, they had to reduce the profits of the rich and to develop the economy more, to win more markets, in order to generate the funds needed in the implementation of their principal objective. They sincerely believed in these ideals and in the methods they advocated. As it turned out, however, the methods did not work; the objectives could not be attained.

Peyrefitte (1986, 137), who represents the position of those who reject both forms of *étatisme*, affirms:

> That France has been mined by an administrative cancer for the past three and a half centuries is the truth the French know least about. On this point, they are doggedly illogical. . . . The French know too well what they owe the state to resist its logic. It has given them their *grandeurs*; they can't refuse it its weaknesses. So, under a strange illusion, the French have slowly declined while thinking that they were ascending.

During more than twenty years of centrist-conservative-Gaullist etatization, French Socialists had awaited their chance to save France properly. They proclaimed that conditions under which income earners in the top 5 percent possess 26 percent of the total assets of the nation—about as much as that earned by 69 percent of the population at the bottom of the social structure—were outrageous. This discrepancy, they argued, widened, as growing shares of wealth were amassed by executives of big corporations and by high government officials. The cost of Gaullist modernization, in the Socialists' opinions, was too high. They rejected the ever-rising deficits and inflation caused by grand projects. They reasoned that too much money had been wasted on "megaprojects," while not enough was allocated to services and schools. Nor was enough, they believed, transferred to lower-income groups. Socialists denounced the exploitative and repressive *dirigiste* practices developed by the bureaucracy under the authoritarianism instilled by the *patronat* and state hierarchy. They condemned the practice of advocating modernity while generating rigidity, routine, inefficiency, and waste. They promised to change everything and institute a society of social justice, in which government would act out "of respect of man," not in the interests of a minority seeking to increase profits.

The Socialist *programme electoral* comprised 110 propositions. France was to move from a capitalist *société bloque* to socialism. Socialists promised equality; and everyone wanted to be equal with the well-paid bureaucrats and the wealthy. In the end, this ideal proved far beyond Mitterrand's power. After two years of presidency, he began to realize it. But in 1980, the electoral call of the Socialists was, "Big Capital Will Pay."

Once elected, they were eager to put their promise into practice. They made capital pay but failed to achieve the social justice they had promised. After a landslide victory in 1981, Mitterrand proclaimed that, though he stood for neither communism nor social democracy, he would go "much further than the Swedish and West German Social Democrats." The euphoria following the Socialist victory, among party members and in the streets, was as overwhelming as only the French could sustain. The Bastille of capitalism had been overthrown. Immediately, the Socialists engaged in a number of parallel revolutionary reforms; each minister implemented his own pet project. The principal of the reform activities are discussed below.

Improving social conditions.   Faced with chronic inflation—expected to rise to 18 percent—and unemployment of close to 2 million, Mitterrand, unlike Reagan, chose to fight unemployment first. A significant number of the unemployed were given jobs in the public sector and state-owned industries. It was expected that as soon as the newly nationalized industries were reorganized under new management, exports would increase and unemployment would drop further. All this happened, but to a much lesser extent than was expected. Exports and production did not increase sufficiently or fast enough to relieve the government of rapidly growing deficits. Unemployment (see Hayward 1986, 193), in fact, increased when the government had to shut down a number of unproductive mines and steel mills and introduce newer technologies and austerity policies. But this happened later. In the meantime, other significant social reforms took place. The minimum wage was raised by 10 percent. The statutory work week was reduced to thirty-nine hours and, later in certain institutions and workplaces, to thirty-five. Paid vacation increased by a week; pensions were raised by 40 percent; and the retirement age lowered to sixty. In 1982, a system of "solidarity contracts," allowing earlier retirement in order to produce openings for younger workers and youth in general, was enacted. A pilot project was launched to evaluate collectivizing agriculture.

Together, these reforms cost a great deal more than expected, affecting productivity badly. The 1981 fiscal deficit increased to FFr 95 billion (U.S. $15.6 billion), 50 percent more than deficits under the Giscard regime. However, the Socialists dismissed productivity concerns. They interpreted the deficit as an investment, a small price to pay to attain social justice. Social equity is more important than a few billion francs, they argued. The situation would improve because, in state-owned enterprises, exploitation was reduced: Workers would work better. Productivity did not improve. At the time, the story circulated that a visitor to a Renault plant asked how many people worked there. The answer was: about 50 percent, usually. In the end, the government had to pay for its reforms.

Nationalizing new industries. In the mid-1970s, Mitterrand wrote (1982, 210): "Capitalism lives only by devouring itself." In some areas of the economy, in his opinion, the free market was in fact nothing but fiction. Industrial capitalism was dependent on banking capitalism. And big corporations had become so big that they had evolved into technological monopolies. Dassault was in such a position in military aeronautics; Péchiney in aluminum and copper processing; Saint-Gobain-Pont-à-Mousson and subsidiaries in the field of thermal insulation and cast iron; Compagnie Générale d'Électricité or the Thomson group in the field of electrical equipment. There was no reason why these industries should remain members of the free-market economy; as monopolies, they ought to be nationalized, argued Mitterrand.

Jean-Pierre Chevenement, the *dirigiste* minister of industry, was put in charge of nationalization reform and the reorganization of newly acquired industries. Until 1981, the state-owned sector comprised the following major national enterprises of the infrastructure: Électricité de France; Gaz de France; Charbonnages de France; Société nationale de chemins de fer français; Régie autonome des transports parisiens; Air France, Air Inter, and PTT. Renault, SNIAS (air space), EMC (chemicals) and others were state owned already.[2]

Under the February 11, 1982 act, the Socialist government proclaimed the nationalization of five major manufacturing groups: Compagnie Générale d'Électricité (electrical construction, electronics, and heavy engineering); St. Gobain (glass, building materials, and pharmaceuticals); Péchiney-Ugine-Kuhlmann (metals and refined chemicals); Rhône-Pulenc (chemicals); and Thomson-Brandt (domestic appliances and electronics); two financing companies—Compagnie financière de Paris et des Pay-Bas, and Compagnie financière de Suez; and thirty-nine banks. Two steel companies—Sacilor and Usinor—already partially owned by the government, were fully nationalized. A state-controlled holding was imposed on Matra (aerospace), and Dassault (aeronautical construction and armaments), and on three predominantly foreign-controlled multinationals: Honeywell Bull (computers); Compagnie générale du constructions téléphoniques (telecommunications); and Hoechst (chemicals and pharmaceuticals).[3] The government agreed to provide lavish compensation to the owners (see *Haut Conseil Rapport* 1984, 273–275). It is still paying this compensation in 1988. The takeovers cost around FFr 45 billion (around U.S. $6 billion). More than one-third of France's economy was now owned by the state. The government modernized the newly acquired industries with the most up-to-date technology, but, being Socialist, it also tried to keep workers on the job even where enterprises could do without them. This, again, was expensive.

New reforms engendered a vast array of new bureaucratic agencies. Machin and Wright report (1985, 11):

> In 1982, there were no fewer than 300 industrial policy mechanisms, 150 different procedures for aid to industry (including sixteen different categories of help for exports, eleven for boosting employment and eight for energy and saving): overlapping jurisdictions, contradictions and incoherence characterized the work of the "jungle of the competing bodies" involved.

Past nationalizations had affected key industries, on which other industries depended. Nationalized industries had employed large numbers of workers. This time, the Socialists nationalized profitable, high-technology, modern, growth industries that were expected to generate even higher profits, thus enabling the state to further expand its industrial, economic, and social programs. The government borrowed about FFr 20 billion (U.S. $2.8 billion.) to pay for the new takeovers and to reorganize and modernize the new state-owned industries. Within two years, most newly nationalized industries began incurring deficits.

Volume 1 of *Haut Conseil du Secteur Public Rapport*, (1984) points out that the objectives of nationalization were both economic and social (141–162). Economic and financial control by the state was expanded. Thirty-two manufacturing companies were singled out as industrial champions, whose task was to win a larger share of the international market. The public sector comprised now 169 "first-rank" enterprises (see *Haut Conseil Rapport* 1984, 1: 13); 36 percent of the nation's capital investments (value FFr. 117 billion) and 23 percent of the export (value FFr 190 billion) were conducted by state-owned enterprises. Of the thirty-six French large industrial companies involved in foreign trade, eighteen were now state-owned; among the rest, major U.S. oil companies were included. Of forty-four French TNCs, eleven were state-owned.[4] According to *OECD Economic Surveys 1982–1983: France* (1983, 50), "The weight of the nationalized sector of industry is now considerable: the public groups control 29.4 per cent of sales, 22.2 per cent of the workforce and 51.9 per cent of total industrial investment, energy included." It was expected that, strengthened by nationalization and under industrial planning, industrial policy, and central management, French industries would expand international trade and improve internal economic conditions in France significantly. State-owned industries were to be modernized according to the most modern requirements. R&D was to be centralized, the cost of unnecessary parallel R&D reduced.

Nationalization, in the opinion of the government, was tantamount to democratization. In 1983, the parliament enacted a number of laws defining workers' participation in management, and other elements of "democratic management" of the *secteur public*. Nationalization was to be instrumental in implementing Socialist social policy objectives.

Tax reforms. At the same time, new taxes were imposed—a wealth tax of 0.5–1.5 percent on citizens' assets, totaling more than FFr 3 million (U.S. $500,000), and an income-tax surcharge on high incomes. New taxes were added to those exacted on tobacco, alcohol, and gas. This sphere of reform was entrusted to Pierre Beregovoy, the finance minister, who was most closely associated with Mitterrand.

New central-planning structure. After initial skepticism, the public had acquired great respect for de Gaulle's program of central planning. Williams and Harrison (1971, 245) write that "no administrative innovation of the Fourth Republic has been more widely admired and emulated than the Plan." With increasing complexity, however, plans became more and more difficult to follow. On one hand, they were regarded as highly instrumental in establishing targets; on the other, they were blamed, at least by certain civil servants and industrial technocrats, for impeding the adoption of real, dynamic opportunities for growth. De Gaulle's plan and the issue of "democratic planning" thus had become a major political controversy. Socialists, in particular, were critical of the Gaullist approach to central planning. They claimed to have a better idea: more comprehensive, democratic, instrumental planning. After their takeover, however, it took the Socialists several years to produce this new plan. In the meantime, the Socialists merely announced new economic priorities in a "stopgap plan" for 1982–1983. The priorities were reduction of unemployment and export expansion.

The Socialists' plan was to serve two objectives. It was especially to enhance industrial development and production for international markets (in this sense it involved an industrial policy). It was also expected to become an instrument for building socialism. It was simultaneously (see Hayward 1986, 184–89; 223–253) to set social targets and explicitly define many aspects of a future socialist society. Socialists were conscious, however, that such a plan could antagonize a large part of the electorate that was not socialist-oriented. So, after long deliberation, Rocard, *le plan* minister, submitted to the parliament, and subsequently enacted, two bills advancing the Ninth Plan. The first bill proclaimed new principles of planning (*OECD Economic Surveys 1982–1983: France* 1983, 48–49). The second, more concerned with targets, outlined legal and financial procedures for the plan's implementation. As was the French tradition (see Guillaume 1986, 123; Hayward 1986, 188), certain actions were declared *programme prioritaire d'execution.* The parliament enacted a special budget to finance planning procedures and implementation. This was an important novelty. It is also important to point out that according to the new principles, planning was to be democratic, decentralized, and to involve not only the ministry and parliament, but regions, each with a plan specified in *contrats de plan*. A continuous concertation of partners was to be maintained throughout the development and implementation of planning.

By the time the Ninth Plan was put in action, however, the government was more concerned with imposing austerity programs, *"rigueur* discipline." Once it became obvious that the state would not fulfil its obligations in regard to planning, the whole exercise became pointless.

Democratizing local authorities. Gaston Defferre, the mayor of Marseilles, now minister of the interior, was delegated to handle redistributing state power, decentralizing, and democratizing local administrations. This reform was to reverse France's long centralist tradition. Under the *loi Defferre*, a new system of *commissaires*, acting in close cooperation with local councils, was to replace the traditional *tutelle administratif* and prefects. *Départements* and *communes* were to become self-governing entities, equipped with their own plans and budgets for transferred and local funds. They would act under the jurisdiction of locally elected authorities; each would have the right to pursue its own economic development. Writers on the topic (see Meny 1985; Kesselman 1985) agree that, though this was an admirable initiative, structures did not change much under the new rules. In practice, old structures persisted under new names. Ashford (1983, 268) notes that

> every administrative experiment in contemporary Europe suggests that bureaucracies have endless guises to see that change does not threaten their established interests and cherished projects, so the administrative struggle may well continue but within a new set of parameters.

McCormick (1983; 1985) has astutely analyzed the consequences of Socialist reforms. She writes (1983, 53–55):

> In this flurry of reforms, little attention was paid to their cost. Expenditure rose rapidly as new revenues were less easy to find. . . . By February–March 1982, the situation had soured. There were signs that the recovery of late 1981 had been ephemeral; the franc was falling again and the government's political and trade union support was being eroded. . . . By March and April even Mitterand discussed "the second phase of change" to deal with the harsh economic realities. "Discipline," "economic rigour" and "national effort for the economy" were the new slogans and stimulating investment the new priority.

In 1981, combined losses of the recently nationalized industries totalled U.S. $900 million. In 1982, after takeovers of new industries, the losses grew, approaching FFr 15 billion (U.S. $2.1 billion). The increase was attributed to worldwide recession. Nevertheless, the government considered the option of selling back certain industries. Investment was down 10 percent and was expected to decline further (see McCormick 1983, 51–56). Wages had risen dramatically. Inflation reached 14 percent in 1981; 17 percent in 1982; and the trade deficit rose from FFr 20 billion in 1980 to FFr 105 billion in 1981. By the end of 1981 sales taxes were increased on gasoline, tobacco, and alcohol. McCormick points out that unemployment had not fallen in spite of massive public-sector job creation. According to other sources, it went up rapidly. New service companies were appearing on a massive scale in France: more than 50,000 between 1976 and 1983. Yet, these companies employed a great many young women, not workers who had lost their jobs in modernizing manufacturing industries, closed mines, and other old-type industries employing traditional workers who had brought the Socialists to power. McCormick writes (1983, 54):

> With a 27.6 percent increase in public expenditure and an 18 percent increase in revenue, the first projected deficit of 76 billion francs for 1982 (compared to 30 billion francs of 1980) by December 1981 was revised upward to about 95.4 billion francs or 2.6 percent of the gross domestic product.

Le Monde (April 8, 1984) reported with alarm, "On December 31, 1983, the debt stood at FFr 451,000 million. . . . Expressed in dollar terms (at the rate of FFr 8.401 to the dollar) the foreign debt can be evaluated at $53,700 million." Another article warned, "The preceding years had accustomed us to growth rates of 2.4 percent at a minimum and about 5 percent in better times." The newspaper recalled, "the old French adage has it that a Frenchman's heart is on the left but his pocketbook is on the right."

In the face of growing budgetary and trade deficits, declining productivity, an inflation rate twice that of West Germany, and unemployment increases, the Socialist government had no choice but to sound the retreat and turn toward austerity measures. By March 1982, they had entered the second stage of their odyssey, this time under the banner of *rigueur*. It was not a popular undertaking. In February 1983, Chevenement, who had planned the grandiose reorganization and argued for stiffer *dirigisme* regardless of costs, was replaced by Laurent Fabius, a known advocate of sound management and austerity measures. In late March 1983, the government introduced a new, even more pungent package of austerity measures. It consisted of a 10-percent "forced loan" on annual taxable incomes, which affected a large segment of taxpayers; new taxes on tobacco, liquor, and gas; restrictions on money spent abroad, in cash or by credit cards, allowing no more than the equivalent of U.S. $250 per adult; and an increase in utility rates of 8 percent. The government deficit was to be held in check—3 percent of GNP for two years. This forced significant reductions in government spending and further increased unemployment. The government closed some of its least productive steel industries; 20,000 workers lost their jobs. Many more were unemployed as a result of other cuts in both state- and private-sector activities. Unemployment stood at 9–10 percent, occasionally reaching 12–13 percent. When questioned about the parallels between the new Socialist policy and Thatcher's, Fabius replied only that France was more humane in its methods of eliminating unproductive jobs and was organizing retraining and reemployment programs. "His political neck is on the line," wrote Shawn Tully in *Fortune* magazine (1984, 163), "but the French Socialist President's third economic policy in three years promises brighter days for business and for the franc . . . . The unions are howling." The unions saw the reform as an imposition of a lower standard of living on the working class. The Conseil National du Patronat expressed the opinion that even though it imposed heavy sacrifices on the French people, the program "would not permit the righting of the economy." Eventually, the franc was devalued for the third time; it continued to decline. In 1982, the U.S. dollar was worth FFr 6.67; by early in 1984, it was worth FFr 8.40. The government cut planned investment and exerted enormous pressure on state-owned companies to reach a breakeven point by reducing the labor force, increasing productivity, and other measures. In Charbonnages de France, 56,000 workers were told they would have to leave the mines.

People from all sections of society, not only industrialists and the bourgeoisie, increasingly expressed disillusion with Socialist rule. Mitterrand was declared the most unpopular French president in twenty-five years; only 33 percent of the electorate were satisfied with his performance. Soon, as they are known to do, French citizens took to the streets. Massive protests against various government policies sprang up all over the country. Different groups demonstrated for different reasons. In Versailles, 800,000 marched to protest plans to bring private education under tighter state control. Ten thousand coal miners marched through Paris, protesting plans to shut down unproductive mines. Steel workers demonstrated against closing steel mills. Public workers, backed by airlines, railway, and subway employees—5 million altogether—proclaimed a one-day strike to protest eroding purchasing power. Truck drivers blocked highways, demanding changes in border controls and lower gas prices. "Let them eat rats!" proclaimed their banners. Eighty thousand demonstrated in Bordeaux, 150,000 in Lyon, 220,000 in Rennes, 200,000 in Lille. The doyen of the Left, A. Touraine, reiterated the sentiments of a large number of intellectuals when he declared, "The basic merit of the left-wing Government is that it has rid us of Socialist ideology." In the summer of 1984, Mitterrand was forced to ask Prime Minister Mauroy to resign; he appointed Fabius in Mauroy's place.

Did austerity measures work? Under new policies in 1985, the situation finally began to improve. According to *OECD Economic Surveys 1983–1984: France* (1984, 53):

At the beginning of 1983 the situation of the French economy was disquieting. The current payments deficits was increasing rapidly and external indebtedness was growing. . . . The tighter policy stance undoubtedly produced results. The foreign balance improved markedly in 1983 with the current deficit narrowing from $ 12 billion a year earlier to $3.8 billion. The rise of prices slowed after accelerating sharply in the first half of 1983, but the government's target was not achieved.

A 2.4 percent growth of GNP was achieved in the last quarter of 1985. Unemployment, though still high, had stabilized at 10.5 percent. Inflation for 1985 was 4.7 percent, the lowest level in fifteen years. The trade deficit came down from FFr 93 billion (U.S. $14 billion) in 1982, to FFr 24.7 billion in 1984. In 1985, for the first time since 1978, a FFr 5-billion trade surplus was achieved. Yet, by that time it was too late for the Socialists to regain popularity before the 1986 election. The figures pointed to success, but a success achieved through austerity, not redistributive policies. The Socialists were never credited for improvements because the policies they resorted to had been advocated by the opposition. They got the economy back on track just before the Conservatives won power. Mitterrand regained some of his popularity; he turned out, however, to lead a far more social democratic than orthodox Socialist Party.

The Socialists lost the 1986 election. Yet, Chirac's neogaullist Rassemblement pour la Republique and the centrist Union pour la Democratic Française, along with smaller allied parties, won only 289 seats; just a bare minimum to control the 577-seat Assembly. The Socialists, with 210 seats, remained the largest party.

Mitterrand believed that by nationalizing major industries and banks, putting a larger part of the economy under direct state management, introducing more state intervention, and giving more benefits to the poor, he could improve France's economic situation. A stalled society, he believed, could be unblocked by intensifying etatization processes. Mitterrand failed in these policies; he succeeded only under a regime of austerity. In the face of Prime Minister Chirac's plans to denationalize across the board, Mitterrand declared that he would specifically veto decrees to sell any companies nationalized prior to 1981. Effectively, this meant that Mitterand was now defending the 1981 Gaullist status quo ante. Prime Minister Chirac and Edouard Balladur, his minister of the economy, finance, and privatization wanted to erase Mitterrand's early reforms and even go beyond that. They began by denationalizing banks, insurance companies, and television. They planned to privatize much more. They introduced tax cuts and abolished price, wealth, and exchange controls, among other cherished Socialist programs. They tried to eliminate restrictions on firing workers. However, there are certain reforms that it is doubtful they could abrogate: the 39-hour work week, the fifth week of paid vacation, retirement at sixty, and other social benefits.

In 1984, and even at the beginning of 1985, the press regarded the "cohabitation" of a Socialist president with a Conservative prime minister and parliament as effectively impossible. But in our times, cohabitation seems to be the rule. In France, the Socialist president co-exercises power with Conservatives. In the United States, a conservative president administers the affairs of the nation with a Congress dominated by Democrats. In Italy, Prime Minister Craxi governed with a coalition involving his own, allied, and opposition parties. Israel is run by an "odd couple." As time went on, Mitterrand's popularity as president under a Conservative government grew (see Hoffmann, 1988). He chose to continue in this role, with some centrist forces if necessary, for another term. During the 1988 election campaign, Mitterrand hardly ever mentioned "socialism." He stuck to the middle of the road and won. Eventually, he changed his mind and decided to put France under Socialist management again.

The 1789 Revolution ushered France into a new, bourgeois era. According to some historians, it ended with a restoration period. Yet, though attempts to revive the *ancien régime* were successful in certain regards, they failed in most. The restoration attempts of the nineteenth century did bring back certain elements of the *ancien régime*, but they were usually accommodated to the new social and political framework. By failing to cancel previous reforms, restoration attempts only legitimized the newly established structure, institutions, and norms of the revolution. History teaches that the past cannot be restored. Between 1981 and 1986, French Socialists made a great effort to transform France into a socialist society, though without a political revolution. In 1986, Chirac, wanting to revive the past, initiated a new period of restoration. It is evident that he succeeded only partially. So far, these events still await comprehensive interpretation.

Central Planning

Plans are economic instruments of the state; through plans, the state establishes the objectives of its economic pursuit, its foreign-trade targets, what kind of material and human resources it intends to utilize in its economic endeavor and to which ends. The market, on the other hand, is the economic instrument of free enterprise. Any enterprise or person seeking work or business indicates its intentions through market actions. A capitalist, free-enterprise society is unimaginable without a market economy; a model socialist society could not be without a plan. Strictly speaking, full employment, pure capitalism, or pure socialism are models; they cannot be produced in practice. Real societies may, at most, approximate these models. Etatized societies combine both the market and plan models, each to a different degree. In some societies, e.g., the United States, the market retains primacy. The state does only what the market cannot do. If any plan exists in such a society, it is not a document or an institution; it is but an idea, expressed through government policies, budget designs, and fiscal and monetary policies. In other nations, such as France, the state has tried to reduce the sphere of the market economy and increasingly subordinate it to a plan. Etatized societies need a market and a plan. But to have a plan or to proclaim a plan is not the same thing as a plan metamorphosing into a controlling agency of the entire economy.

The Soviet command-system economy operates under comprehensive central planning. Planning aims to determine the entire economic, social, and even cultural life of the nation. In reality, however, no plan has ever been fully implemented in the Soviet Union. As soon as it proclaims the plan and begins to monitor implementation, the party-state starts correcting it. Things always go as they were not planned: the weather is not right, so the harvest is smaller; money must be spent on something else; the army needs newly developed missiles, so other production must be curtailed; workers are not productive enough; a plant costing hundreds of millions is built 200 kilometers from where it was planned and, since it is not ready as planned, other plants cannot achieve their production levels. The plan involves too many conditional factors. Nevertheless, they strive to follow it as strictly as possible. People are punished for not completing their targets. But in the end, the government is forced to improvise. At present, Gorbachev is trying to bring some flexibility to the makeup of the Soviet economy.

Japan is another nation that uses central planning. The Japanese, however, do not closely follow details in their plan; they keep to general objectives. Their industrial policy is like a military operation: They set targets but are highly innovative in implementation.

The French concept of planning differs from both the Soviet and the Japanese. The French can never agree on what role the plan is to perform. However, planning is the backbone of *étatisme* and state socialism; so, once agreed that the state should exercise a dominant role in society, the French had to accept the plan, as its important institution. Kuisel (1981, 170–179) discusses the debate over planning during World War II. When the state engaged in reconstruction, it was only reasonable to accomplish it under a plan. The first, 4-year Monnet Plan, introduced in 1946, aimed to fulfil this end. The plan helped reestablish the 1929 output of production and, later, to surpass it by 25 percent. The plan set out to modernize and reorganize state-owned industries and to set in motion processes involving the private sector. In short, this plan served the specific objective of development. The Monnet Plan (see Baum 1958, 22–26; Cohen 1977, 81–103) was simple, with no specifications for particular industries. It pledged public funding in certain areas and attempted to produce favorable conditions that might attract private investment in specific authorized ventures. Cohen writes (101): "They concentrated all their efforts on their long-term investment and modernisation programmes." He avers that "Monnet's planners were proselytizers." They tried to make conversions among their enemies, the *hauts fonctionnaires*, business class, and politicians. He reports that they sought to change and succeeded to a great extent in changing attitudes as well as styles of management and business. They tried to overcome the "extraordinary rigidity of attitudes and structures," and encourage new developments.

Subsequent, more complex and technically sophisticated plans encompassed increasingly diversified objectives, relating to wider ranges of industries. The number of indicators employed to evaluate target achievements continually increased. De Gaulle's and his successors' plans were intended to channel investments, persuade citizens to participate in particular developments and not others, encourage definite consumer patterns and not others. Most writers on this topic emphasize that, in contrast to socialist countries, French planning was indicative, selective, and flexible with regard to targets, and the allocation of financial and man-power means. French plans, they write, put less emphasis on physical output, stressing financial output. Ozenda and Strauss-Kahn (1985, 101–103) identify two fundamental features of French central planning: (1) plans are employed to clarify social and economic objectives, set by the government, and to forecast trends of development; and (2) plans provide a platform for concertation. "This means that the main interest groups present, debate, argue and confront their different objectives and points of view."

Under de Gaulle's indicative plans, the targets were state objectives, rather than general development objectives, which could be sought by the private sector as well. Encouragement and discouragement continued. Certain industries and firms were favored champions in international trade. Participation in implementing plan objectives was propagated as a patriotic venture, as well as worthwhile economic entrepreneurship, an educational process, and a new kind of corporatist participatory democracy; corporations, communities of industrialists, unions, and the administration were to unite to pursue common state objectives. Under the Pompidou and Giscard regimes, attention focused on combating inflation and responding to unanticipated changes in exogenous factors; less importance was attributed to central planning. "The Plan," writes Green (1981, 104), "fixed for its five-year term, has been unable to take account of environmental uncertainty or adapt to unexpected crises." Another point is stressed by Guillaume (1986, 123): "No matter how well it is designed, a plan is unlikely to achieve success on all fronts." According to other observers, in France the Plan had attained its limits: It became more an impediment to than an inducement to economic development. Socialists, nonetheless, attempted to restore the importance of central planning and, in addition to its above-listed functions, make it an instrument of socialist development. They tried to plan not only economic but social targets as well.

There is no question that central planning can yield great results. Under a system of central planning, governments can rapidly mobilize human and material resources to attain definite, strategically important objectives. Management under central planning carries definite risks, however. The state allocates enormous resources to principal selected targets. Benefits accrue only insofar as objectives are chosen correctly and all factors are accurately anticipated. Contemporary conditions are extremely volatile; they are affected by numerous endogenous and exogenous factors, difficult to predict. No amount of expert calculation and opinion can completely ensure that a plan will not be adversely affected by unanticipated factors. Under systems of central planning, errors in target-setting can cause vast, disastrous, and irretrievable losses, affecting millions of people. Plans like those in Japan, involving few, strictly defined targets, implemented flexibly and leaving most to the interplay of the free market, are safer; they bear better results than those that cover large areas of economic activity. Under market conditions, resources shift to more innovative and advantageous opportunities, as they appear. Under central planning, this is much more difficult. Any change can affect the entire plan. In short, while enhancing rapid development in certain regards, central planning impedes innovative development in others.

Diagnosing French Bureaucratic Malignancy

"No writer on postwar France," pronounces Hoffmann (1974, viii), "whether or not he endorses the analysis and prescriptions offered by Crozier . . . can afford to ignore [his writing]. We all must come to terms with a theory that is so powerful it sometimes seems to explain everything." Although he does not employ the concept, Crozier is a theorist of French etatization. His field of interest is organizational theory. It includes a theory of bureaucracy. Crozier develops his analysis in a number of books.[5]

In *The Bureaucratic Phenomenon* (1964) Crozier combines a discussion of empirical research with analytical theorizing. Through this approach, he sketches the reality of contemporary France. In other studies, Crozier expands on these findings. He posits that bureaucracy is instrumental in forming superior structures of organization; and that bureaucratic systems of organization offer a reasonable combination of independence and security to those within them. At quite a price, however! The modern observer, writes Crozier (1964, 208), is especially struck by the dysfunctional role of bureaucracy: "What people gain in security they lose in realism." Bureaucratic systems of organization inevitably rely on the use of a certain amount of compulsion. The extent of compulsion experienced by members of an organization depends not only on objective factors, which can be identified easily by examining the content of laws and regulations, but also on cultural and subjective factors, which cannot be defined easily but which strongly determine the extent to which individuals are willing to submit themselves to minute rules imposed by others. The latter factors are not so obvious and cannot be accurately measured. Thus, bureaucracy can be comprehended only empathetically. Also, the evils of bureaucracy constitute part of the contemporary condition. Bureaucrats tend to be more concerned with exploiting their position to obtain personal objectives, than with serving the objectives of the organization. This is not so much because they are evil, but because such circumvention is the only way they can survive. They develop (Crozier 1964, 208) "the skimpy outlook of the petty power struggles of a tight social system." Furthermore (198), "a bureaucratic system of organization is not only a system that does not correct its behavior in view of errors; it is also too rigid to adjust without crisis to the transformations that the accelerated evolution of industrial society makes more and more imperative."

In *The Fifth Republic at Twenty*, Hoffmann (1981, 472) recalls Crozier calling France the *terre de commandement*. Crozier does not employ this concept in his own works. Nevertheless, this seems to be his main concern. In *The Stalled Society*, Crozier discusses de Gaulle's etatization and the students and workers' 1968 rebellion against the authoritarian *société bloque*, which, they felt, denied them a future and excluded them from the journey to prosperity. Three points are emphasized (Crozier 1973, 106):

1. Despite its apparent flexibility, the bureaucratic administration imposed on France to implement state objectives had proved so excessively onerous as to exclude the private sector, and with it a large part of society, from widespread involvement in generating national economic growth.

2. The educational system, which traditionally determined the character of social stratification in France, had become outdated. Any reform would have had been against the vested interest of certain bureaucracies, which feared an influx of people from new social circles.

3. The centralized political system, hand in hand with the administrative system, had impeded integrative activity at intermediate levels, thereby quelling grassroots initiatives and the development of integrative activity therein.

Bureaucratic systems are the fundamental reason for the stalemate affecting French society. France is in perpetual crisis under bureaucratic rule. The stalemate affects everyone. However, bureaucracy is maintained because it suits the interest of the bureaucrats, who clutch onto the status quo. Despite its obvious inadequacies, the bureaucratic system persists, retaining the nation in a perpetual crisis, only interrupted by periods of more rapid decline. In *Actors and Systems* (Crozier & Friedberg 1980), more empirical evidence and new theoretical arguments are presented. Crozier's concern remains the same. *Actors and Systems* advances certain proposals for a strategy of change. Crozier has proved much better at identifying ills, however, than at finding remedies.

In *On ne change pas la société par décret* (1979), which appeared under the title *Strategies for Change* in English translation in 1982, Crozier further inquires into the causes and symptoms of the French "disease." He attributes the malady to both the universal features of bureaucracy and, specifically, the French cultural personality. Crozier assumes that France's cultural traits and the social condition enhance one another, so that, together, they constitute highly fertile ground for a national bureaucratic mentality. Crozier is particularly preoccupied with two traits. He writes that the French fear and avoid direct, open, face-to-face communication. When such interaction becomes necessary, they resort to artificiality, impersonality, and appeal to mediation by higher authority. They fear insecurity and risk. To escape any situation of real or imagined adversity, as individuals or in groups, the French appeal to the state. All the state can provide, however, are more numerous, more pervasive bureaucracies. Crozier posits (1982, 26):

> Power in itself is not evil; what is evil is its relations and the structure of the system that maintains them. . . . At all levels of society the French, once they gain entry into an influential group, instinctively try to keep other people out. Furthermore, they continue to maintain a pattern of government that is based on social distance, secretiveness, and closed lines of communication. This can be called the monopoly of power: everyone has a private preserve.

He characterizes the French bureaucrat as overwhelmed by routine, stagnation, impersonal relations within organizations, inclined to curtail developmental initiatives, and lacking concern for the effects of adverse bureaucratic action on the lives of subordinates and dependent citizens. Larger bureaucracies affect society to a larger degree. Regardless of size, however, the characteristics of bureaucracy and administration cannot be changed by decree or through reorganization. Elitism is at the root of the French illness. Authority is wielded, secretly, at the top. Those who inhabit the top of the power pyramid isolate themselves from those below. Motivated by their own interests but unable to communicate them to the elite, frustrated individuals and groups in the lower echelons of the bureaucratic structure frequently paralyse or undermine the exercise of power from above. No one can successfully steer such a system. Each pattern repeats itself at all levels of the social order. Each group, by imposing its own regulations and restrictions, jealously guards its status and privileges and tries to institute its own monopoly to combat other group monopolies. The channels most guarded and restricted against outsiders are career ladders. Every individual holding a bureaucratic position fears the unveiling of his own, or his group's, weaknesses. Thus, every individual shields himself behind rules, instructions, and regulations, creating a capsule for his own isolation.

Crozier criticizes the etatization process advanced under de Gaulle, Giscard, and, especially, the Left. The Left, he feels, is even more inept, immobile, and destructive to the causes of development and freedom than is the Right. What solutions does he put forward? The state's concentration of power, says Crozier, must be reduced to an absolute minimum and channels of mobility must be opened. Reforms cannot change the character of bureaucracies, he argues. Only by reducing the size and power of the bureaucratic order can conditions ever be improved. Crozier (1982, 47) also remarks that the French society's paralyses are not evenly distributed. Three orders of the framework around which the rest of society is built are particularly affected by the blockage: (1) the system of education; (2) the civil service, which runs all the affairs of the nation; and (3) the system for the recruitment of leaders.

Although he never explicitly says so, Crozier analyzes the French condition from a neoskeptical perspective. Like Pareto, Mosca, and Michels, he assumes that a healthy political system requires that channels of mobility and circulation remain open to all members of society. Decadence within the elite, and blocked mobility channels, assumes Crozier, have prevented new, energetic, innovative individuals from joining the French elite. The marasmus and malady of France developed as a result of these factors.

France has a long tradition of *étatisme*, but also a long history of intellectual, bourgeois, and working-class opposition to *dirigiste* rule. Conflicts over etatization run across the class structure of French society. There are many brilliant works of French origin rejecting the idea of a state-dominated society. The eighteenth-century *philosophes* were, in a way, precursors of this tradition. De Tocqueville, Proudhon, and Sorel represented it later (see King 1967). The leading contemporary anti-*étatisme* involves intellectuals of the Left and the Right. Crozier, Revel (1977), and contemporary *philosophes* (Glucksmann 1977; Levy 1981; Benoist 1970) are the most expressive spokesmen of this tradition at present. Since they have experienced many different impositions of *étatisme*, the French are, perhaps more than most nations, sensitive to any ominous encroachments on freedom. They remain disillusioned with the state.

Opinions vary over the extent to which France's sickness is French in character, and to what extent it is universal, i.e., typical for all bureaucracies. A widespread mood throughout Western Europe reflects the feeling that all of the West has become afflicted by "the disease." The British, as was discussed, describe the malignancy as a general disorder, a combination of widespread malaise, despondency, disorganization, growing poverty, unemployment, deteriorating productivity, a declining standard of living, and the blackmail of society by unions, the poor, and the rich, in Great Britain and other countries. Hayward (1986, 18), who discusses the economic development of contemporary France, emphasizes in his diagnosis: "*Most of those who are essential to liberal, social and economic democracy are excluded from the economic policy community, whereas most of those included—notably the elite economic bureaucrats and the select business leaders—have no democratic legitimacy.*" The French, and particularly Crozier's, diagnosis of the "plague" is markedly distinct from British analyses. Crozier and others say that the calamity is bureaucracy. The French seek order; societal and political developments in France tend to consolidate and solidify under bureaucratic order, complete with a political and bureaucratic elite on top. Order reigns; but order produces stagnation. Nothing is ever resolved. Conflicts accumulate in succession, until they explode, unexpectedly, bursting asunder the existing order. The people cry out for change; a new regime comes into existence; and bureaucracy takes over once again. France did not suffer a decline as did Great Britain. Yet, many French people believe that they would have been much better off under a state with a much smaller bureaucracy, which interfered less in many spheres of social activity.

CHAPTER ELEVEN

Centralized Management in West Germany, Italy, and Sweden

In discerning Type B etatized societies, it was assumed that these are societies that developed two-sector mixed economies and instituted distinct management organizations to control and administer the economy and the social structures as a whole. This chapter discusses the effectuation of some of these features in West Germany, Italy, and Sweden.

Nationalizing industry

West Germany

The prewar German economy was dominated by cartels, which implemented Nazi objectives and enhanced Germany's military power. After their victory in 1945, the allied occupational forces enacted a law prohibiting cartels in Germany. However, numerous provisions (see Lampert 1976, 171–175) contained in the law allowed cartel-type organizations to operate, under "exceptional circumstances." Under these provisions, many prewar giant corporations were restored. The conservative Christian Democratic government of the newly established Federal Republic of Germany preserved also its extensive patrimony of state-owned industries, inherited from the Third Reich. Some of these previously nationalized or state-developed industries were transformed into public services. The state converted other assets into companies having share holders and mixed ownership. Rather than engage in sweeping nationalization, as did Great Britain and France, the German state chose to pursue a flexible policy involving gradually acquiring and subsidizing strategic industries. Few industries were fully owned by the state. A large sector of industries was, however, held under mixed ownership by the state and large, private-sector, financial corporations. The state developed mechanisms that allowed it, as owner or part-owner, to control such industries from within, as well as from above through state bureaucracies. In certain instances, this was done to preserve jobs in declining sectors of the economy; in others, to cause mergers strengthening the position of German TNCs, to promote state subsidized R&D, and, on occasion, simply because it was good business for the state to become involved with these corporations. Consequently, the German state evolved as a manager of the general economy and as part-owner of the national industrial assets. The mixed-sector economy continually expanded, both to serve the private sector and to tackle social problems. The private sector, favored by the Conservative government, grew while cooperating with the growing mixed sector and benefiting from the state's development of the infrastructure. By 1969, when Brandt's Social Democratic and Liberal coalition ascended to power, 40% of the coal and steel industry, 62% of the electrical production industry, 72% of the aluminum industry, and 60% of credit institutions were owned by the state. Other principal state assets included railroads, postal services, and shifting investments in a variety of industries. A list of principal industrial firms owned by the state is found in Table 11.1.

Under the Schmidt SPD/FDP government, the scope of partial state-ownership increased. The Federal Cartel Office and other central agencies acting on behalf of the state induced mergers of giant heavy-industry corporations. In some instances, the state provided subsidies or other benefits facilitating mergers. In others, it was involved in supervising corporate operations; in still others, it intermediated between forces within these

Table 11.1   State-Owned Industries in the Federal Republic of Germany, 1970

	initial value of assets in millions DM	% owned by the state
Saltzgitter AG (SAG): mines and chemicals	460.0	100.00
Vereinigte Elektrizitäts-Bergwerks AG (VEBA): mining and electricity; petrochemicals*	825.0	40.23
Vereinigte Industrie-Unternehmungen AG (VIAG): manufacturing; steel*	254.0	100.00
Volkswagenwerke AG (VW): automobiles*	750.0	16.00
Saarbergwerke AG (SBW): coal; iron	350.0	74.00
Industrieverwaltungsgesellschaft (IVG): manufacturing*	50.0	100.00
AG für Binnenshiffahrt	2.0	100.00
Howaldswerke Hamburg AG (HWH)	12.5	100.00
Prakla Gesellschaft für praktische Lagerstattenforschung mbH	4.0	100.00
Deutsche Industrieanlagen (DIAG): manufacturing	5.0	90.00

Source: Hans O. Wagener, *Neue staatwirtschafliche Funktionen bundeseigener Industriebeteilungen.* (Meisenheim am Glan: Anton Hain, 1972), 19, 179. Reprinted with permission of the publisher.

* Substantially denationalized and slated for complete privatization under Kohl's government in the 1980s.

gigantic structures, and between these and other corporations, industries, and other forces in society. The cartel law was modified in 1973. Earlier, through legislation such as the Act against Restraints and Competition of 1957, the market was fortified with mechanisms enhancing free-market competition. Under the modifications to the cartel law, (see Lampert 1976, 174–175) the state was allowed to increase its share of ownership and exercise both direct and indirect economic management much more effectively. The modified cartel law specifically empowered the state to initiate, supervise, and manage a variety of cooperative schemes, affiliations, mergers, and amalgamations. It significantly enhanced the state's managerial role.

In 1974, the federal government owned shares in 750 to 900 German firms. Huge investments and subsidies were provided to modernize large, newly merged industries. The Social Democratic–Liberal coalition increased taxes, issued bonds, and indebted the state in order to generate rapidly the financing of these endeavors. Katzenstein (1987, 103) estimates that "West Germany's total subsidies amount to between 80 and 100 billion deutschmarks in 1980–81." Beck (1984, 7) notes that, after this policy began under Schmidt's leadership in 1973, West Germany's debt rose from 18 to 38 percent of the GDP. The conservative coalition of the 1980s continued this policy. Mückl (1982, 160) writes:

> In 1950, the federal government was officially DM 20.6 billion in debt. In 1960, the debt increased to DM 52.2 billion. The first real recession experienced by the Federal Republic in 1966–1967, accelerated the now continually growing indebtedness of the state. At the end of 1967, the debt expanded to DM 107.2 billion. At the end of 1975, the debt bulged more; it was now DM 256.0 billion. At the end of 1980, the state sat on a debt mountain DM 468.6 billion high.

He also discusses parallel, though not as steep, increases in *Lander* and localities indebtedness. Mückl claims that the debt grows at a faster rate than GNP; he perceives it to be dangerous to German stability.[1]

Webber (1983, 79) points out another aspect. Industrial policy did not affect all sectors of business equally: The tax burden imposed by the reforms on the more labor-intensive (small and mid-sized) enterprise was greater. These firms had to bear the greatly increased burden of taxes and social-insurance contributions imposed by both federal and provincial governments, to produce the funds transferred by the state to big corporations. They also had to accept the new tripartite system of management involving owners, managers, and unions in decisionmaking. "At the same time, these firms typically benefitted least from government subsidies to industry, government grants to firms for research and development, for example." Social Democratic policies favored the banking industry and large investors. Webber adds that banking capital was drawn tightly into the web of consultations between Government, labour, and capital. An extremely close relationship exists between the banking community (especially the three biggest banks) and the Bundesbank, which is independent of the Federal government and determines monetary and interest rate policies. In their capacity as the (part-) owners and (effective) controllers of a vast number of industrial enterprises, the big banks were also intimately involved with the Government and unions in the formulation of plans to restructure declining industries and major companies that ran into financial difficulties.

Banks participate at every level of the decisionmaking structure, including the highest "summit level," involving the chancellor and union leaders. Amidst the many types of Western societal structures, German society best represents the corporatist model of economic management and intermediation.[2]

Küster discusses a number of mergers organized with government participation. Although small in pages, this is quite illuminating work, allowing us to appreciate the role of the federal state and central banking institutions in complex intermediation among owners, managements, unions, banks producing the large megacorporations that now form the pillars of contemporary corporate Western German economy. Among these, the most important involved establishing the Ruhrkohle. Küster writes (1974, 74–77) that the Ruhrkohle was formed from twenty-six mining companies, which turned over their mining assets, together with the debts involved, and received an interest-yielding obligation of Ruhrkohle A.G. in compensation. The obligation and interest were guaranteed by the Federal government and by the state government concerned. In effect, the former owners, while retaining some measure of influence and control, traded their uncertain claim to future profits for a government guaranteed stream of income.

Küster also discusses the 1968 merger in the oil industry. In this case, the government granted state aid to the new company, in subsidies and loans equaling DM 575 million (U.S. $144 million), for a period of six years. Similar undertakings affected the aerospace industry (where five companies merged into two corporations), the nuclear industry, the computer industry, and so on. In all cases, the government agreed to support the new enterprises until they became financially self-sufficient. In many deals, in return for guaranteeing to private owners interest returns on their capital, the government subjected industries to strong state-controlled corporate management.

Germany's steel industry sticks out as the one case where the government failed in organizing mergers. In this field, too, the government (see Katzenstein 1987, 162–163) had planned to merge numerous private and state-owned companies into several larger corporations. The Rhine group was to involve the Thyssen and Krupp companies. The Ruhr group would include Hoesch, Klokner, and Saltzgitter. Although the government was prepared to finance these mergers with DM 3 billion, company managers felt DM 10–12 billion were needed. Thus, the government objective was never met. Nevertheless, the state has had to subsidize separate steel-producing companies, essential to auto-making and other heavy industries, in order to preserve some hundreds of thousands of jobs.

Under *Mitbestimmung* or codetermination programs, the state also sold shares of state-owned and state-controlled industries in the market, or offered them to employees in place of wage increases or other benefits. State ownership of the German industrial sector continually fluctuates. In 1985–1986, only a small number of larger companies were officially listed as state-owned (Saltzgittcr, with sales of U.S. $3 billion, assets of $2.9 billion, and 42,000 employees; Saarbergwerke, with sales of $2.5 billion, assets of $1.9 billion, and 30,000 employees; VIAG, with sales of $2 billion, assets of $2.5 billion, and 22,000 employees). However, at the same time, the state owned over 25 percent of shares in almost 500 German companies. Under the new Kohl conservative-liberal administration, the government embarked on a policy of gradual denationalization, which affected VEBA, Volkswagen, VIAG, and other state-owned corporations.[3]

Most management of the economy, and of specific industries, was conducted by the German state through the banking system. In contrast to the British Labour and French Socialist parties, the German socialist-liberal and, particularly, the conservative-liberal coalition governments have been strongly concerned with financial viability when advocating and implementing social objectives. This has paid off in the long run. Germany's budgetary deficits and rate of inflation have been consistently lower than those of other Western European nations. In the late 1980s, the German economy is rated as one of the most stable and most prosperous in the West.

Italy

In Italy, the process of nationalizing industries and instituting state intervention started before the war, with the Fascists. They had planned to undertake major industrialization. This began with major agricultural reform and the nationalization of banks. The Fascists also established several huge, state-owned manufacturing and business organizations. The biggest of these *enti*, after World War II, became Istituto per la Riconstruzione Industriale (IRI). With a significant consumer market, Italy was in most respects ready to modernize. However, after World War II, its private capitalist sector was not potent enough to undertake the major industrialization required. The task was undertaken by the Christian Democrats, who led postwar Italy for more than thirty years. They developed the economy by expanding existing state industries and establishing new petrochemical, energy, shipbuilding, communication, and other industries under state boards. Many parastatal industries subcontracted small private firms to produce technological components and equipment for maintenance and repair, and to provide other services required by the larger, state-owned corporations. These associations typify Italian etatized conditions. Every third employee in Italy works for a level of state-owned industry; many more work for private subcontractors whose only customer is the state. In no other country has the fusion of state and private sectors become so close. A discussion of the three largest state-owned corporations in Italy—IRI, Ente Nazionale Indrocarburi (ENI), and Ente Nazionale di Energia Electrica (ENEL)—exemplifies this statement.[4]

IRI was established in 1933, under the Fascist regime, to spearhead industrial development by attracting capital and providing financial support to both state and privately initiated economic ventures. Today, IRI remains one of the largest state-owned conglomerates in Western Europe. In the 1960s and 1970s it got the reputation as a model of efficient economic entrepreneurship (see Holland 1972): neither capitalist nor state-directed, but run by experts, employing advanced technocratic practices. The Christian Democratic state provided IRI with huge capital. The corporation was then subdivided into several subholding groups: (1) Finsider (iron and steel); (2) Finmecanica (engineering); (3) STET (telephones and communication); (4) Finmare (shipping); (5) SME (food); (6) Sofin; (7) Finsiel; and (8) Italstat (holding companies). IRI controls four commercial and three merchant banks. Finelectrica, originally included in this scheme, eventually disbanded and reorganized into a separate, new corporation: ENEL.

Certain general objectives and rules, developed by the government or enacted at the highest corporate level, oblige all companies. Nevertheless, the corporation remains decentralized. Each large group or subholding company operating under IRI aegis determines autonomously its financing priorities, production objectives, price-setting and marketing practices, and other policies.

During the 1960s, IRI controlled 80 percent of Italian shipbuilding. In 1974, the group's turnover was L 8,168,000 million; 320,000 (63%) of its staff was employed in manufacturing; 121,000 (24%) in service sectors; and the remaining 70,000 (13%) in banks, holding companies, infrastructure, and construction. At the end of the 1970s, IRI owned 48 percent of the Italian merchant fleet, and produced 30 percent of all electrical energy and 48 percent of steel and iron. It also owned one of the largest banks in the nation and 70 percent of the broadcasting system. Eventually, IRI expanded further. Through SME—still another holding company—IRI obtained widespread control over a conglomeration of privately owned companies: large chains of supermarkets, food-processing companies, paper-producing plants, transportation, and part of the aerospace industry. All these companies depend on IRI credits and financial support. Alfa Romeo, the state-owned auto industry, operates as an independent company but depends on IRI's financial scheme. "IRI banks hold 14% of Italy's checking deposits," reports *The Wall Street Journal* (July 10, 1984). "IRI companies produce nearly 4%

of Italy's goods and services. They make 11% of its cement, 90% of its ships, 15% of its cars and 22% of its ice cream." IRI makes steel, aluminum, and Albatross surface-to-air missiles. IRI makes just about everything. Only, the newspaper concedes, "One thing IRI does not make is money." In 1984, IRI's debt was $21.7 billion, a little bigger than Yugoslavia's. Strangely, this is not widely known in Italy. Of the more than 520,000 people employed by IRI, many never heard the name of the colossus. *The Wall Street Journal* continues:

> Once a trailblazer, IRI became a trash collector. It picked up every tattered company that ordinary buyers wouldn't touch—a thousand of them. "The trade unions," Prof. Prodi, who heads IRI, says, "the politicians, the bishops all came and said, 'This is important for our community. IRI must take it.' "
> Thus did the Italian state shoulder the burdens of manufacturing cast-iron radiators and gumballs.

This statement carries sociological significance. IRI relieves owners of defunct companies from the obligation of declaring bankruptcy. IRI reduces unemployment by keeping on the payroll tens, or even hundreds of thousands of individuals whom it does not need. Without IRI, *la dolce vita* would not be *dolce* for many people in Italy. All this costs money. "For every 100 lire of fixed assets the private companies produced on an average twice as much as the public concerns," writes Are (1982, 53).

In contrast to IRI, which operates strictly in areas previously under state control, ENI, the other big Italian conglomerate, operates in new areas of entrepreneurial activity. ENI sprang out of Azienda Generale Italiana Petroli (AGIP) at the end of the 1940s. The Christian Democrats had initially intended to disband this economically unviable corporation, established under Mussolini to promote oil exploration and refinement. After the discovery of oil deposits in the Po Valley, however, this intention was abandoned. AGIP was incorporated into ENI, the new, gigantic state corporation involved in oil explorations, petrochemical production, oil-pipelines, and nuclear-plant construction. Like its sister corporations, and outside its initial mandate, ENI became involved in other money-making activities. It presently owns publishing houses, daily newspapers, motel chains, and a large number of insurance businesses. ENI obtained a large holding package of the huge Montedison corporation, as well as the artificial fiber-producing Snia-Viscosa. In addition, it owns large holdings of stock in private sector corporations.

In the 1985 *Fortune International 500*, IRI listed at third place (fourteenth on the world's largest corporations list including the United States). Its sales for the year approached $27 billion (losses were $664 million). ENI (with sales of $24.5 billion and a profit of $427.1 million, after years of losses) was rated as the fifth biggest international corporation outside the United States and the Communist world (sixteenth in the world).

Partially controlled by ENI, Montedison, was at fifty-sixth place.[5]

ENEL, the third large state corporation, owns energy-producing enterprises. It took over this industry from IRI, which the government compensated, providing it with money to expand into new fields. At the time, the Fanfani government, under the first Italian National Plan, undertook a major program of general economic development. This initiative specifically focused on industrializing the poor, Southern, *Mezzogiorno* area. Implementing its policies required significant volumes of electrical energy. ENEL was expected to provide this cheaply.

In addition to the three giant, state-owned corporations, which each dominate major fields of economic production and trade, a number of smaller state corporations operate in Italy. Lieberman (1977, 262) lists 350 state holding enterprises in the 1970s. According to Lieberman, these enterprises employed 510,000 workers in Italy and 22,000 Italians working abroad. The figure may be misleading, however, because some of these enterprises seem also to be part of the IRI-ENI-ENEL system.

Italy's state-owned sector was developed with the hope that it could provide solutions for major national problems. As a financing industry, it was to engage in capital formation, to invest in the development of the economic infrastructure, and to support industrial programs undertaken by the government. As a structure of holding companies, it was to finance the undertakings of the private sector. While performing these functions, it was to reduce unemployment and provide training for millions of people joining the industrial labor force. As a system of public corporations, it was to provide services to the population and revenues to the government. As an economic force, it was to stimulate the economy of Southern Italy.

Italy consists of a relatively industrialized North and an underdeveloped South. The gap between the North and South widened during the 1950s, when both state and private companies invested in the North. In the 1960s, the government tried to remedy this situation. Limited land reform programs were undertaken to improve agricultural conditions in the South and to provide the landless population with some land to cultivate. Simultaneously, IRI, ENI, and private corporations were encouraged to invest in the South. However, most of these developments were capital intensive; they never produced much-needed, large-scale employment. Although discrepancies in economic development between regions were reduced, the rate of unemployment and poverty in the South remains higher than that in the North.

The Italian state sector not only comprises large industrial enterprises and smaller, parastatal businesses; it also operates on a regional and local basis, under central management provided by several overlapping organizational hierarchies. As in IRI, each level of this structure, while centrally supervised, exercises considerable autonomy. Appointees to managerial positions in public-sector enterprises are generally expected to further government policies. They must report to ministries and to the parliament. They are obliged to obey the general rules and instructions of the central managing authorities. Apart from this, however, they operate like private industries. They compete with one another; and they engage in ventures with other industries—both private and state-owned—under market conditions. State-owned corporations are required to transfer 65 percent of their profits to the central government; they usually have no profits, and when they do have any, they claim to need them urgently to make new investments. Specific managers can be held responsible for mismanagement, faults, and losses. But, as in the case of state industries elsewhere, because the government bails them out, the *enti-statali* cannot go bankrupt. Consequently, state-owned corporations are more interested in investing profits and claiming losses than they are in returning profits—albeit a portion—to the state. Table 11.2, from an article in *L'Espresso* (January 19, 1986, 120) discussing this situation, illustrates that the more money the state grants to the *enti*, the bigger are the deficits they incur.[6]

The state-owned and private sectors of Italy coexist in a highly symbiotic, complementary mesh; the state sector finances and sustains a large part of the private sector and engenders private entrepreneurial ventures. Private-sector enterprises operate as extensions of state sector industries. Whether in the state or private sector, individual incomes are supplemented by additional legal and illegal innovative transactions. No one can comprehensively explain how the Italian economy works, and how, in spite of countless problems, it continues to grow—most often in spurts, but enough to support its population relatively well. The Italians attribute it all to *miracolo*, the major miracle occurring after World War II, the second enjoyed in the 1980s, and others occurring daily.

Sweden

The Swedish social democrats and unions still strongly believe in ideas advocated during the first part of the century by working class socialist thinkers Unden, Karleby, and, particularly, Wigforss (Tilton 1979; Anton 1980, 4–19). They believe that by developing social welfare, industrial democracy, and economic planning, and by extending progressive taxation, capitalism can be transformed into socialism. At the same time, though they do not admit it, they fear that such policies may cause the prosperity that they enjoy to collapse. Thus, in spite of the socialist rhetoric, the proportion of industries nationalized in Sweden is less than that in other industrialized European nations. While this could soon change, in the period 1985–1987, most large Swedish corporations remained in private hands. In 1985, the list comprised Volvo, with sales of $10 billion, assets of $8.4 billion, and 68,000 employees; ASEA with sales of $4.7 billion, assets of $5.5 billion, and 61,000 employees; Electrolux, with sales of $4.6 billion, assets of $3.9

Table 11.2 Funds Received from the State and Deficits Incurred by *Enti*

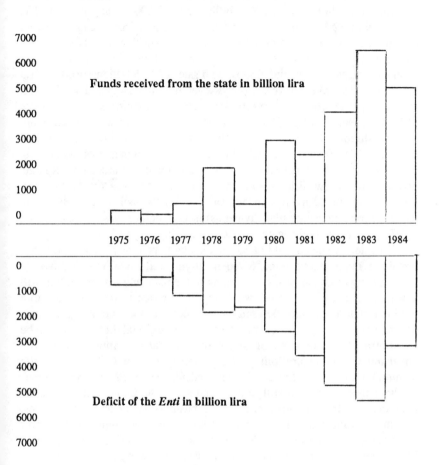

Source: L'Espresso (January 19, 1986), 120

billion, and 93,600 employees; L. M. Ericksson Telephone, with sales of $3.8 billion, assets of $4.9 billion, and 78,000 employees; Saan-Scania, with sales of $3.7 billion, assets of $3.5 billion, and 47,000 employees; and SKF, with sales of $2.3 billion, assets of $2.9 billion, and 46,500 employees; all appear among the largest 500 corporations in the world, as listed by *Fortune*. One should note several smaller, state-owned Swedish corporations, in contrast: The steel-producing SSAB, with sales of $1.5 billion, assets of $1.5 billion, and 15,000 employees, ranked seventh on the Swedish list of largest corporations; Procordia—formerly Statsfloretag—conglomerate, with sales of $1.4 billion, assets of $1.7 billion, and 25,500 employees, ranked tenth; and the shipbuilding Sweyards, with sales of $1.3 billion, assets of $1.3 billion, and 18,000 workers, ranked twenty-sixth. As a matter of fact, during the 1980s, the indicators (volume of sales and volume of assets) of all large, privately owned Swedish corporations have increased considerably. *Fortune* notices: "For the 12 months ended May 31, AGA's total return to investors (stock price appreciation plus dividends) in U.S. dollars was a pocket-filling 471%." Other listed private corporations are doing very well, too.[7]

Whether Sweden should nationalize its large privately owned industries remains a major public issue. Sweden's highly influential unions advocate nationalizing more industries. According to the plan, any nationalization will advance gradually. The proceeds of a special tax are to be funneled into a fund that will, eventually, be used by five regional boards to acquire shares of the principal private corporations. The regional boards are to be predominately composed of union representatives appointed by the government. Demonstrations protested this policy in 1983. In a public opinion poll, four out of every five respondents expressed negative opinions on the subject. Although still in its initial stage, the implementation of the plan, despite strong opposition from the business sector and other circles, continues its incremental advance. The unions are determined to take over the industries sooner or later. Businesses warn, "Do not eat the goose that lays golden eggs." The unions may try to have a piece of it, nevertheless.

Central Management

A two-sector economy, with a large state-owned sector and a developed system of services and welfare institutions must be managed from a center. The systems of management, control, and regulation developed by various Western European nations to this end vary in the degree of centralization, pervasiveness of control, regulation, and autonomy they allow the industries and enterprises within the market economy.

"In the Federal Republic," writes an analyst of contemporary German conditions, "2.3 million officials are regulating the lives of 61.5 million citizens and they are doing it with a Teutonic penchant for perfection that stifles private initiative and frustrates many people." "The omnipresent bureaucracy is profligate and merciless," writes another. West Germany's national economic system operates under centralized bureaucratic control, management, and a balancing corporatist tripartite—government/ management/union—codetermination. The current new centralism represents, however, more a response to coalescing modern contemporary needs than a continuity of cultural tradition. Even during the interwar years, Germany remained divided into traditionally different *lander*. As a divided nation after World War II—first by four occupational zones, later by two states—unity is an issue of great importance for Germany (for documents on the issue see Schweitzer et al. 1984, 138–162). Centralization advanced to cement West German unity. Economic centralization and concentration were considered the most crucial basis for the state. Although the conservative Christian Democratic Party ostensibly opposed increased state ownership and control and advocated the integrity of the free-market economy—drawing from German tradition, Bismarck, and other conservatives—they helped lay the groundwork for centralization; they began the etatization later continued by the Social Democrats. Under Schmidt, Germany evolved into a highly centralized economic power that redistributed social benefits through bureaucratic channels. As socialists, the Social Democrats advocate central planning and centralist, mostly banking management. As democrats, they espouse the idea of *Mitbestimmung* (codetermination of important decisions by government/business/unions' tripartite involvement) as a unique form of German industrial democracy. Central planning reaches only to selected economic and, in some instances, budgetary targets.[8]

Every book discussing the history of postwar West Germany devotes a chapter to how the "phoenix rose from the ashes," how the "economic miracle was accomplished." At the time of the miracle, German opinion was divided over the economy. The Social Democrats, based primarily in the former British zone, were influenced by Labour Party doctrines; they favored planned development under the direction of the state. The Christian Democrats, influenced by U.S. opinion, developed the theory of the "social market economy"; the idea was to generate "prosperity through competition." Both the first chancellor, Adenauer, and Ludwig Erhard, the vice-chancellor and minister for economic affairs at the time, who later became chancellor, were Christian Democrats. Erhard's (1962, 128) position was that

> The law maker must regard it as his task to exclude factors which disturb market trends by (a) preserving, to the greatest possible extent, competition between companies; (b) preventing the abuse of monopoly power in markets where complete competition is impossible; and (c) creating a State organ to supervise and if necessary to influence the market.

Erhard ostensibly opposed state intervention; he advocated limiting state involvement to developing the economic infrastructure and providing adequate training for the labor force, in order to facilitate the growth of free enterprise. Erhard (186) declared himself against any policy that "aims at granting a man complete security from the hour of birth, and protecting him absolutely from all hazards of life." In practice, however, he acted differently. Whether referred to as "pragmatic intervention," as in the early years of Christian Democratic rule, or the "development of participatory democracy," as under Social Democrats, economic *dirigisme*—financial and fiscal regulatory practice—ran Germany in the postwar years. In 1967, the parliament enacted the bundesbank act ("Instruments of Monetary Policy in the Federal Republic of Germany," 1971) and other laws, which transformed the Deutsche Bundesbank and the central fiscal system into principal regulatory agencies and induced corporations to engage in economic activities specified by government objectives. Reuss (1963, 36–40) identifies the essential characteristics of this *dirigisme*:

(a) By offering favorable rebates and providing industries with subsidies and other supports, the state encourages mergers, capital concentration, and other economic policies, according to its evaluation of benefits, at any given time

(b) The taxation system encourages taxpayers to save and, whenever possible, invest in national growth by participating in shareholding

(c) The state, also a mighty financial empire, generates complex financial operations to enhance its established objectives, either directly through the central bank, or indirectly through subsidiary organizations or state-owned corporations

All these developments are balanced through the preservation of the political and economic decisionmaking autonomy of *Lander* (provinces), cities, and communities; and through codetermination.

In France, the state manages the economy through the plan. In West Germany, the state relies strongly on subsidization, taxation, tariff protection, and regulations restricting competition, to manage the economic performance of the nation. Excellent analyses of these management-instrument performances are presented periodically in *OECD Economic Surveys*. For instance: the *OECD Economic Surveys 1985–1986: Germany* (1986: 24) reports that national accounts subsidies continually increase. They were DM 18.7 billion in 1973; DM 31.1 billion in 1979; DM 30.5 billion in 1980; and DM 36.4 billion in 1985. Subsidies and capital transfers increased from DM 30.1 billion in 1973 to DM 70.6 billion in 1985. Financial aid and tax relief increased from DM 43.1 billion in 1973, to DM 65.3 billion in 1980, to DM 76.5 billion in 1985. According to the survey (25), "Subsidisation in Germany is not high compared to many other countries." Still, nearly every citizen is dependent on some kind of subsidy or another, which allows the state to run things smoothly. These data confirm earlier analysis by Reuss: The German state runs a highly effective financial *dirigiste* practice.

Katzenstein (1987) offers a different interpretation. He points out (16–30) that the *Lander* in West Germany have primary powers in important areas—education, culture, law enforcement, regulation of local government; also that "West Germany has a field system of administration with only a very small number of bureaucrats in the federal capital." Although it is not properly a legislative body, the Bundesrat performs an important legislative role. It is composed in part of state (*Lander*) representatives. Katzenstein attributes importance to this fact: "The Basic Law gives clear priority to the chancellor as the head of government rather than the president as the head of state" (169; for a different view, see Hirsch 1980, 121–138; Laufer 1974). "Decentralization characterizes the state's provision of many of its welfare payments and services." The German private sector, he argues, is "thoroughly centralized." It is represented by three major associations: Bundesverband der Deutschen Industrie, Bundesvereinigung der Deutschen Arbeitgeberverbande, and the organization representing small-business interests—Deutscher Industrie und Handelstag. Unions are centralized. Other interest groups, farmers, and professions are also represented by centralized organizations. All these centralized forces operate vis-à-vis federal agencies. It must be noted that while the German state looks quite decentralized to a U.S. citizen, it looks highly centralized to a Canadian, where the provinces have much more power than do the *Lander* in Germany.

Codetermination (see Schweitzer et al. 1984, 273–280) was introduced through several enactments defining the form and scope of activities, first at the shop-floor level in 1951, and later under the 1972 act defining codetermination at both the shop-floor and board levels. All enterprises employing five or more employees are currently required to have "works councils" that have some codetermination rights. Larger companies, having 2,000 or more employees, whether under state administration or privately owned, must include employee representatives on all boards and executive committees, and involve them in the decisionmaking processes affecting their institution.[9]

Conclusion

In Western European nations undergoing etatization, the principal issue of concern is growth: economic versus state growth. There is no question that, under contemporary conditions, the state must do what the market cannot do. The state must satisfy society's collective needs, such as environmental protection and the reduction of social problems to which the market is blind. It must intervene in and regulate corporate growth, which, left uncontrolled by the state, would end in self-destruction. But difficult problems ensue when the state goes beyond these limits: when it undertakes to do what the market does better. Once charged with certain authorities, state institutions develop a dynamic of their own. Systems of social security and social programs are sustained by tax revenues. Problems arise (see Katzenstein 1987, 186–208) because social programs and services, once initiated, continue to expand, irrespective of economic growth, stagflation, recession, and other conditions. In fact, demands on social programs tend to increase at a faster rate when the state raises fewer revenues and is less capable of providing funds than in times of economic improvement. Problems multiply when the state is expected to perform more functions regardless of the realities of economic growth or contraction.

CHAPTER TWELVE

Etatization and Nationalism: Canada

Three concerns determined the course of Canadian history. The first was the relations of the dominion with her mother countries, Great Britain and France. Canadians of British extraction remained loyal and obliged to the British monarchy. The French, abandoned by France, felt no loyalty to the mother country or Europe as a whole, but continued as an outpost of French culture and Catholicism. Save for a few mutinies against local authorities, Canada never experienced any major rebellion or revolution. After the American Revolution, and always concerned to preserve its link with Great Britain, Canada fought a string of wars against U.S. campaigns to make it part of the United States. After World War II, the link with Great Britain became symbolic but remains important nevertheless.

The second concern was and still is over the unity of the nation and the nature of Canadian identity. The French and English sectors were to be integrated. The old and newly established provinces, each with closer economic relations with the United States than with each other, had to be linked into one. Canada aspired to become a unity preserving linguistic and cultural diversity, and the economic and, to a great extent, political autonomy of the provinces. The British North American Act of 1867 proclaimed the federation of all colonies. Only in 1982 did Canada adopt its first constitution. However, the constitution was not signed by Quebec, who claimed a special status within the federation. The process of nation-building is still far from complete. The Meech Lake constitutional accord concluded recently between the federal and provincial governments, but still not ratified by all provinces, was to accomplish this objective.

The third concern is over the economy.

The Economic Issue

Canada's economic condition greatly depends on trade with the United States. This most complex issue can be defined as follows: How to develop a national existence and separate Canadian cultural identity, while expanding vital Canadian–U.S. trade and economic cooperation, which in a sense undermines Canada's cultural and social aspirations and its separateness from the United States.

Canada continually troubles itself over its position vis-à-vis its southern neighbor; this is called the American Problem. The problem is that people in the United States do not have a "Canadian Problem" and are not concerned with any problem "up there" beyond the northern border. Average U.S. residents may express a positive or negative attitude toward the British, Japanese, Chinese, Germans, Russians, toward any nation in the world. Toward Canadians they have only a feeling of "friendly indifference," which many Canadians find rather insulting. Canadians feel that they are taken for granted. Meanwhile, they cannot take the United States for granted. In the words of the *Report of the Royal Commission on the Economic Union and Development Prospects for Canada* (1985, 1: 299–300), "Most Americans live their whole lives only dimly aware of Canada and its people, but Canadians in all provinces have always fretted about our neighbor to the south. It is not easy to live next door to the most powerful, energetic and wealthy nation in the world." And again (59): "We suffer from interdependence without security in a context wherein our dependence on the U.S. market is not reciprocated by an equivalent American dependency on the Canadian market." The issue is not only psychological, it is political, economic, and cultural. A huge body of literature has appeared on this subject in Canada; a few books and articles in the United States. I believe that this situation goes a long way to explain Canadian etatization. Canada can face the United States, U.S. TNCs and financial interests investing in Canada, the U.S. market, and U.S. cultural influence only as a state.

Canada is a unique country in many regards. It runs under a parliamentary democracy, but its system of democracy operates also through checks and balances between federal and provincial authorities. The provinces own most of the natural resources, control education, provide services to the population, and collect an equal or larger share of taxes than does the federal government. Not all provincial prerogatives are strictly defined; federal-provincial conflicts arise frequently. These can be resolved only through negotiations or in the courts. The provinces' consent to any important national decision the federal government makes is vital. Prime Minister Trudeau strove for a unified Canada under a centralist system of government. However, provinces frequently expressed the opinion that this is incongruent with Canadian tradition. Although Canada's political system was modeled on the British pattern of parliamentary democracy, it resembles more the early U.S. system of politics. Canada, to a great extent, is still a federation of quasi-autonomous states under a weak central authority. The previously mentioned Meech Lake Accord among the eleven governments of Canada over the federal and provincial jurisdictions produced a great deal of opposition, particularly among those who advocate a more unified and centralized Canada. It and the free-trade agreement with the United States were central issues in the November 1988 election.

With an area of 9,970,610 square kilometers, Canada controls the second largest national territory in the world. In contrast to the 237.5 millions in the United States in 1986, Canada's population was less than 25.5 million. Canada is the principal mineral exporter to the United States. Crude petroleum, natural gas, and gas byproducts constitute 66 percent of Canada's total exported mineral values. With more than 30,000 lakes greater than three square kilometers, and numerous large rivers, the country has the largest reservoir of fresh water in the world. Canada has one of the most industrialized economies in the world. Yet, it does not have an internal market large enough to keep up its high economic standards without foreign trade. It also must sustain populations in less-developed and poorer Atlantic provinces and can do so only by generating excess revenues in other provinces and a surplus in foreign trade. The prosperity of Canada is strongly dependent on U.S.–Canadian trade and relations.

In the early 1970s, the United States had a positive balance of trade with Canada, but on the whole, the balance vacillated around zero. By the end of the 1970s, however, the situation had changed. Since 1978, Canada has maintained a positive balance of trade with the United States, which contributes to the U.S. trade imbalance and is of great concern to some in the U.S. Congress.[1] This positive balance of trade with the United States is a result of a number of factors: low prices on Canadian crude petroleum and natural gas, and relatively lower prices on Canadian soft wood, pulp, and newsprint paper, which makes these commodities attractive to the U.S. consumer. The value of the Canadian dollar was consistently 20–30 percent lower than the U.S. dollar. It is cheaper to buy and produce in Canada.

More than 70 percent of Canada's trade is with the United States. On the other hand, though Canada is the largest U.S. trading partner, only about 20–25 percent of U.S. trade is with Canada. As Table 12.1 demonstrates, the value of total exports from Canada in 1985, was Canadian $119,474,511 thousand. Of these, $93,059,385 thousand, or about 75 percent, was traded with the United States. The value of total imports to Canada, in 1985, was Canadian $104,355,196 thousand; of these $73,816,736 thousand or around 80 percent came from the United States.

According to the U.S. statistics, the total value of U.S. exports in 1984 was U.S. $217,888 million; of this, exports to Canada totalled $46,524 million; to Japan $23,575 million, and to Western Europe $58,019 million. The total value of 1984 U.S. imports was $325,726 million; of these $66,478

Table 12.1.   **Value in Thousands of Canadian Dollars of Total Imports and Exports by Geographic Regions, 1985**

	Imports	Exports		Balance
Western Europe*	12,552,901	8,190,720	-	4,362,181
Eastern Europe	296,293	1,910,371	+	1,614,078
Middle East**	371,189	1,259,284	+	888,095
Africa	1,033,731	1,079,267	+	45,536
Asia***	11,219,370	10,146,438	-	1,072,932
Oceania	604,801	877,857	+	193,056
South America	2,394,949	1,446,052	-	948,897
Central America	2,061,656	1,470,617	-	591,039
United States	73,816,736	93,059,385	+	19,242,649
Other, North America	3,572	34,522	+	30,950
Total, all countries	104,355,196	119,474,511	+	15,119,315

Source: Canada Year Book 1988 (Ottawa: Statistics Canada, 1988) Ch. 21: 37–41.

Note: 1985 is exemplary; for other years and by nations see the original.
* The principal trading partners are Great Britain, West Germany, and France. ** The principal trading partners are Iran, Israel, Turkey, Libya, and Saudi Arabia. *** The principal trading partners are Japan, China, South Korea, and Taiwan.

million were from Canada, $57,135 million from Japan, and $71,153 million from Western Europe. The total 1984 U.S. trade deficit was $107,858 million. In 1986, the U.S. trade deficit exceeded $175 billion. It subsided somewhat in 1987, but remained high and of concern to Congress. While the United States is concerned about high trade deficits with Japan and other trading partners, Canada is concerned that most of its trade is with one partner, the United States.

Every government in Canada expressed concern with the national economy's high dependence on U.S. trade. Most have tried to increase Canadian trade with other nations in order to attain a more variegated interdependence. Between 1957 and 1963, Diefenbaker's Conservative government set itself the objective of diverting 15 percent of Canadian trade to British markets but failed. During its sixteen years under the Liberal government of Trudeau, Canada again unsuccessfully pursued the "different option" policy. Trudeau also failed in his attempt to forge more current ties with the EEC. The Conservative Mulroney government initially tried to expand trade with Far Eastern nations, but to no avail. With the exception of raw materials, fish, and a few other commodities, broad international markets are closed to Canada, partly because Canada is not a member of the EEC, partly because Canadian commodities are made according to U.S. standards; nations seeking these commodities obtain them in the United States. Canada can trade electrical energy, gas, and other resources to no other nation but the United States.

Trade, however, is only the first of the several complex aspects of U.S.–Canadian relations; another is U.S. ownership in Canada. "In 1982," according to the *Report of the Royal Commission* (1985, 2: 233), "foreign companies held 49 per cent in Canadian manufacturing, 45 per cent in petroleum and natural gas, 43 per cent in mining and smelting, and 26 per cent in all other industries, excluding agriculture and finance." More specifically in 1984, 80 percent of direct foreign investment in Canada was U.S.–based.[2] In 1974, the U.S. portion of ownership was much larger, close to 50 and in some instances exceeding 50 percent.[3] Proportions have changed since the establishment of large state-owned and mixed corporations, purchase of some U.S. holdings by Canadian firms, and wholesale nationalization, as in the cases of the potash and asbestos industries. On the other hand, Canadians own a great deal in the United States. If one is to believe Malcolm (1986), the United States is currently being invaded, if not already dominated and to a large extent owned, by Canadians.[4]

In 1984, 230 of the top 500 Canadian corporations were Canadian-owned, 166 were U.S.-owned, 3 were conjointly Canadian- and U.S.-owned, 34 were British-owned, 19 were owned by corporations of other European nations, 12 were Japanese-owned, 12 were owned by corporations in still other nations, and 24 had diverse share ownership mostly in Canada.[5] The following corporations were listed as the leading ten on the *Canadian 500* list in 1984 by *Canadian Business* (*Special 1984 Annual*): General Motors (U.S.–owned), Canadian Pacific (Canadian–owned), Imperial Oil (U.S.), Bell Canada (Canadian), Canadian Pacific Enterprises (Canadian), Ford Motors (U.S.), G. Weston (Canadian), Alcan Aluminum (Canadian), Loblaw (Canadian), and Texaco (U.S.). Among the top 100 Canadian financial corporations in 1984 (*Financial Post 500*, May 1985) seventeen were U.S.–owned, and twenty were owned by corporations of other nations. According to calculations derived from the special, June 1984 issue of *Canadian Business*, the assets value of the 166 U.S.–owned Canadian 500 was Canadian $70.8 billion. In 1983, these corporations employed 620,000 individuals. If one were to include smaller U.S. companies not listed among the Canadian top 500, and smaller Canadian banks owned by U.S. interests, the total value of U.S. assets in Canada and the number of individuals employed is much higher.[6]

A more recent issue of the *The Financial Post* (Summer 1988) reports that on average foreign ownership in Canada dropped from 37% in 1973 to 29% in 1985. Still, the manufacturing of 98% of tobacco, 88% of transportation equipment, 76% of chemicals, 68% of electrical products, 67% of petroleum and coal products, 52% of textile mills, 52% of machinery, 37% of beverages, 26% of food, paper and metal mining was foreign-owned. During the period 1973–1985 the total foreign investment in Canada rose by 403%. The pattern of investment changed, however, most of it (72%) were investments in Canadian bonds.

The economies of Italy, France, West Germany, and Great Britain are currently between 20 and 30 percent foreign-owned. The Japanese and U.S.

economies are only 5–7 percent foreign-owned. Recently, U.S. mass media began to express serious concern about foreign ownership of U.S. assets, even it is less than 10 percent. Canada's economy, in the 1970s was 40 percent and now is 30 percent foreign-owned. This is a cause of worry, but Canadians have learned to live with it quite well.

Canada needs U.S. dollars, but can get them only by selling to the United States and attracting U.S. investment. The rate of U.S. investment affects Canadian growth rates. Whenever the United States experiences a recession, Canada suffers immediately. Canadian economic conditions do not improve until restabilization in the United States is quite advanced. Canada's manufactures, e.g., the auto and telecommunications industries, largely cater to the interests of U.S. corporations. On a number of occasions, U.S. firms invested in developing Canadian industries—the aviation and electronic industries are examples—only to shut them down later and let their own firms dominate the Canadian and international markets. In the meantime, the Canadian government had take care of the resulting unemployment. From a market perspective, the decisions of U.S. firms in such instances served strictly business concerns. Many Canadians, however, interpreted these events differently: U.S. businessmen, they claimed, were taking advantage of their dominant position.

And yet, Canada is lucky to have the gigantic U.S. market just across a mildly controlled border. It benefits from, among other things, easy access to the extensive R&D undertakings of U.S. universities and corporations. However, standards of living in Canada are, on the average, about 20 percent lower than in the United States. At present, Canada currently has a 8–9 percent unemployment rate, while the U.S. rate is only 5–6 percent. Canada enjoys better economic conditions than many European nations, but at the price of selling off its nonrenewable natural resources. Most critically, Canadians feel they are not masters of their own homes and international destiny. The Canadian government frequently pursues international policies different from those of the United States, particularly in regard to economically underdeveloped nations. However, some Canadian writers believe that, given Canadian dependence on the United States, Canada is a Third World nation itself.

Canadian Culture and the State

Throughout history, Canadians have worked to develop a nation culturally and socially distinct from the United States. To an extent, they have succeeded. Canadian lifestyles are somewhat different from U.S. ones; this must be so, if for no other reason than the presence of the French element in Canada. On the other hand, the Canadian lifestyle is also quite similar; this is due to the proximity of the United States and many connections across the border. Nonetheless, a large part of the Canadian cultural establishment feels threatened by U.S. influence and aspires to maintain a more distinct Canadian culture.

But what is Canadian culture? John Jackson (1985) calls the issue a "dark problem." He points out, nevertheless: "The very notion of Canadian culture insofar as it has been linked to the centralist vision is a consequence of and reinforces political and economic centralization and metropolitan dominance." He refers to Harold A. Innis, who, in *Essays in Canadian Economic History* (1956), repeatedly emphasized that without state intervention, Canada could not have survived as a separate nation. Lipset (1985, 157), discussing a large body of literature in which Canada and the United States are compared, also refers to Innis. He concludes:

> The United States has grown more centralized politically, while Canada has moved in the opposite direction. The same inverse relationship has occurred with respect to nationalization of politics; similar lines of cleavage increasingly cut across all sections south of the border, while in the north, regional diversity has increased. Behavioral indicators of Canadian and American economic cultures, for example, with respect to savings or use of credit, suggest greater, not less, variation across borders. The differences in class organizational behavior in the two countries, as reflected in rates of trade-union membership, has also grown greatly.

Lipset points out that in nation-building, the United States pursued the "melting pot" policy. Canada, on the other hand, advanced the "unity and diversity," "vertical mosaic" policy. He asserts that Canadian political parties, including the Conservatives, are more "welfare state" oriented than are parties in the United States. He acknowledges other differences, such as in size, power, and "awareness of the other," which, in turn, affect cultural variations and attitudes in the two nations. He lists certain similarities—increased concern with equality of opportunity and growing secularism in both nations.

Canadian culture can be characterized by outlining three of its most essential features:

1. Canada is a bilingual and to an extent a bicultural nation, simultaneously stimulating the preservation of other principal ethnic group autonomies. Canadians individually retain much stronger cultural links with Great Britain (e.g., in British Columbia and Nova Scotia) and France (Quebec), and to an extent with other European nations of origin, than do people in the United States.

2. Since its inception, the United States was a nation developed in pursuit of free enterprise. The territories, and particularly the "Wild West," were conquered by settlers pursuing their private business. In contrast, the army and the Royal North-West Mounted Police played an important role in

securing the Canadian West as a national objective. The Canadian Pacific Railway was built by the state with several national objectives: to reinforce the conquest and control of the territories, to bring immigrants to new Canadian lands, and to forge an iron band linking Canada "into a nationality." Canadian National, Trans-Canada Airlines (now Air Canada), and the Canadian Broadcasting Corporation were set up or developed by the state in pursuit of similar objectives. "The role of the state in the Canadian political economy is inextricably entwined with the nature of that political economy and its position within the world economy," write Laux and Molot (1988, 38). And in fact, the state initiated and directed most Canadian economic development processes. The state subsidized cultural ventures. There would not be a Canadian culture without the state providing for it. Preservation of sovereignty (defense) is one of the elementary functions any state is obliged to conduct. Sharing the continent with the United States but not wishing to be overwhelmed by its neighbor, Canada protects her cultural identity and economic separateness by relying on the state.

3. In the present analysis, Canada is listed under Type *B*. Canada has developed a two-sector economy and a welfare and service structure similar to those of Western European nations. Although Canadian economy is tightly meshed with the U.S. economy, and Canadian lifestyles quite resemble U.S. ways, in many regards Canada remains a non-American nation of the Americas. Like Western European nations, Canada belongs to the North Atlantic Treaty Organization (NATO) and has a defense treaty with the United States, but Canada does not belong to any closely cooperating international constellation. Canada is the only American nation that has never joined the Organization of American States (OAS). At the same time, it does not belong to the European community where, as a nation with a two-sector economy and as highly developed a welfare system as in Western Europe, it should belong.

A Nation at the Crossroads

Canada is a case of etatization advanced in response to the international situation and its dependence on the United States. To ensure the survival of Canadian industries in a world dominated by gigantic U.S. corporations, the state in Canada developed its own large state-owned and mixed corporations and engaged in fiscal, monetary, and other macroeconomic policies to support smaller, private corporations.

In 1968, in *The American Challenge*, Servan-Schreiber raised an alarm over U.S. economic penetration of Western Europe. He estimated that the volume of U.S. investments in Western Europe at that time was $14 billion. If not arrested, he warned, the long-term effect of growing U.S. investments in Europe would be similar to the effect European domination had over

Africa and Asia. Servan-Schreiber cautioned (29): "What threatens to crush us today is not a torrent of riches, but a more intelligent use of skills." He called for a "counterattack" against U.S. invasion. The response (153–154), he wrote, was to involve unification of European forces, creation—through mergers and under the auspices of national states—of large industrial units, which "are able both in size and management to compete with the American giants," modernization, broader education, and, "finally as the key to everything else, the liberation of imprisoned energies by a revolution in our methods of organization—a revolution to revitalize the elites and even relations between men."

Servan-Schreiber's fears were widely shared in Western Europe. Here is a part of the November 28, 1972, entry from Mitterrand's (1982, 60) diary:

> While our minds are on other things—wars, crime, elections, famous loves—Zorro is coming. Zorro is already here. Contrary to legend, his manners are so discreet and his step so stealthy that no one even turns his head when Zorro walks down the street. What is he doing? He is buying. Everything. Anything. At the rate he is going, he will soon have bought up the entire collection of enterprises that go by the name of France. But he has other ambitions besides settling in the suburbs. France is small potatoes for the man I'm referring to. One day Zorro will rule the world.
>
> Do you think I'm writing a children's story, or the lyrics of a popular song? The Zorro to whom I'm referring is the arrival on the scene of a phenomenon as important in history as the birth of nations: the advent of the multinationals. Thirteen of them are among the fifty top economic entities of the world. If you extrapolate from the tendency we have seen happening from 1960–1968, some sixty companies, three quarters of which are American-controlled, will by 1985 control all the channels of power. Each of the sixty will have a business volume greater than the gross national product of a country like ours. Taken together, they will dwarf the GNP of the United States itself.

Of course, the irony is that to many Frenchmen a few years later, Mitterrand became the Zorro, who was buying everything and anything and dispossessing French corporations. Mitterrand's analogy is brought up to illustrate a different point—how capitalist development in the United States became a factor in provoking etatization, and, specifically, the establishment of large state-owned corporations in Western Europe and, eventually, Canada. To match U.S. and Japanese developments and to win international markets, governments in Western Europe and Canada nationalized certain industries, instituted mixed enterprises to produce large corporations in other areas, supported mergers and their ventures in international markets. "Small is beautiful" does not apply to corporations.

Canada at first chose a different course of action. In the 1950s and 1960s, it did not have much choice; if it wanted to expand its economy quickly, it had to let foreign corporations invest in Canada. Later, however, it began to develop its own large state-owned corporations. These policies, most of them introduced in the late 1970s and early 1980s, under the Trudeau government, are outlined below: Canada developed its own strong energy base, owned principally by the Canadian state and provinces and in cooperation with Canadian private corporations, in order to reduce its dependence on the Organization of Petroleum Exporting Countries (OPEC) and major U.S. corporations' oil imports. In the 1960s and 1970s, Canada exported oil to the U.S. Western states while, at the same time, importing oil from OPEC nations for Eastern Canada. Clarkson writes (1985, 61–64):

> First, came the priority of *freedom from oil imports*. The goal was called self-sufficiency in the green paper of 1973, rechristened self-reliance in 1976, defined again as self-sufficiency by the Progressive Conservative government in 1979, and then relabelled as energy security by the Liberals in 1980.

It was advanced further under policies of Canadianization of oil resource. High levels of foreign ownership had been of little concern to public, politician, or bureaucrat in the 1960s, Clarkson points out. During the oil crises of the early 1970s and particularly in 1978–1979, however, Exxon and certain other U.S.–owned oil companies raised consumer prices excessively and also diverted to the United States oil shipments originally destined for Canada, causing this oil-exporting nation to experience shortages. To prevent this happening again, the Trudeau Liberal government developed, literally overnight, a new, huge oil industry owned by the federal government, provinces, and Canadian private investors. It began competing with U.S.–owned oil companies in Canada in divergent business ventures, such as explorations of new oil fields, refining, and retail sales. The objective was to establish Canadian ownership in more than 50 percent of oil fields. Substantial tax-revenue funds and loans were invested to purchase Petro-Fina and develop Petro-Canada, Dome Petroleum, and Syncrude tar sands, where oil developments were undertaken with PanArctic, Atlantic Ritchfield, and Pacific Petroleum in the Arctic. The oil industry was developed into the backbone of the state-owned sector.

There was another reason for nationalization. During the 1960s and 1970s, as in Western Europe, Canada developed its social-security and health-care programs. As in other industrially developed nations, the cost of welfare, medicare, old age security, unemployment insurance, and refunds in family allowances increased rapidly from year to year.[7] Social security and welfare expenditures by all levels of governments rose (in thousands of dollars) from $2,384 in 1962, to $7,478 in 1972, to $32,512 in 1982, to $47,732 in 1985. Federal expenditure (as part of it; the other part was borne by provinces) rose from (in thousands) $1,946 in 1962, to $6,062 in 1972, to $23,468 in 1982. Total expenditures on health care of all levels of government grew from $1,159 in 1962, to $4,886 in 1972, to $19,586 in

1982, to $39,168 in 1985. Total (regular, sickness, maternity, retirement, fishing, training, and other) unemployment-insurance compensation rose from (in millions) $2,260.8 in 1970, to $4,008 in 1979, to $8,576 in 1982, to $10,227 in 1985. Each year, the cost of these programs increased, relentlessly.

The percentage of Canadians dependent on transfer payments from the state is particularly high in the Atlantic provinces. Unemployment in Newfoundland during the 1970s and 1980s oscillated between 15 and 20 percent. It was largely the federal government's responsibility to generate necessary funds, to transfer them from richer to poorer provinces, and to create jobs.

The list (see Tupper & Doern 1981) of public Crown corporations—as they are called in Canada—established by the federal and provincial governments is long. According to more recent press reports in 1988, the value of the assets controlled by the currently operating 268 federal and provincial Crown agencies was $220 billion. Even when these corporations are profitable, as are Telesat Canada, under mixed ownership, or provincially owned Hydro-Quebec, they still require capital investments from federal or provincial resources.

After 1978, the federal government, in need of funds to cover its increasing investments, the deficits of state-owned enterprises, the growing cost of social-security programs and services, and interest on debt, imposed higher taxes on oil profits earned by provinces and private, mostly U.S.–owned corporations. Subsequently, in 1980, for the first time, the federal government proclaimed an economic plan: the National Energy Program (NEP). Both private oil companies and certain provincial governments opposed the program. Clarkson writes (1985, 23): "The American oil companies, finding their Canadian possessions under attack, screamed in outrage when they found out that the NEP had changed the rules of the continental game they had been playing profitably for decades." Provinces engaged in nationalization on their own.[8] John Dingell (Michigan), Thomas Luken (Ohio), and other Democratic Party representatives in the U.S. Congress expressed opposition to these and other Canadian policies. Other disputes between Canada and the United States, over acid rain, fishing rights, and Canadian exports of pulp and paper, shingles and shakes, erupted simultaneously. Within Canada, the provinces opposed federal policies that increased federal control and the federal share in the wealth generated by provincial industries. NEP was meant to bear numerous additional benefits for Canadian firms and the population at large. The huge megaprojects initiated by Canadian and foreign-owned corporations were expected to enhance other industrial developments and to generate employment across the country.

The results were different. As elsewhere under state ownership, the benefits failed to materialize. Arctic oil in the Beaufort Sea became too costly to be economical at a time when markets were glutted with Middle East crude. Similarly, after it had consumed billions of taxpayers' dollars, the Syncrude development was abandoned for the time being. Nova and Dome Petroleum, instead of benefiting other developments, evolved into monsters devouring huge state investments and incurring deficits year after year.

NEP produced a need for the Foreign Investment Review Agency (FIRA). Established on the initiative of Trudeau ministers, in 1980, this agency was to review new foreign investment initiatives in Canada, to enhance counteroffers by Canadian firms with government loans, and to bolster Canadianization in new areas. A large part of Canadian business, fearing that after regulating foreign firms, the state would increase its regulation of Canadian firms, perceived FIRA as a dangerous precedent. Both NEP and FIRA produced certain ominous effects. Not only did the inflow of U.S. and other foreign investment decline, but substantially more private Canadian investment began to filter southward, beyond the reaches of Canadian state control. The Conservative government of Mulroney, wanting to attract new capital, abolished both NEP and FIRA, and initiated, frequently against the resistance of unions, the privatization of a number of state-owned businesses, reducing state shareholdings of some and selling others to the private sector.

Three parties compete for power on the federal level in Canada. Each province has its different constellation of separate political parties. The Liberal Party, led for sixteen years by Trudeau, and now by Turner, can be considered the centrist and nationalist party. The Progressive Conservative Party, headed by Mulroney, is like neither the Republican Party in the United States nor the Tory Party in Great Britain. It can be best characterized as another liberal party, yet much more supportive of the private sector than the party that calls itself Liberal. The third is the New Democratic Party (NDP), sometimes called Socialist or Liberal-Socialist, which favors nationalization of principal industries and banks, gradual withdrawal from NATO, expansion of public services, and a more distributive orientation in economic policy.

The governments of Canada and the United States are currently involved in negotiating a free-trade agreement, which would give Canada greater access to U.S. markets, and the United States greater access to Canadian markets and resources. There is opposition to the free-trade agreement in both countries. In the United States, senators and congressmen representing industries fearing Canadian competition opposed the treaty. To many Canadians, however, this was not merely a trade agreement, but a change requiring a closer link with the United States and, they felt, the relinquishing of certain aspects of Canadian sovereignty. In Canada the debate of the treaty evolved into a highly emotional national controversy. The November 21, 1988 election was turned into a *de facto* referendum over the free trade agreement with the United States. The ruling Conservatives; certain provincial governments, particularly of Quebec and Alberta; and the

Canadian corporate establishment favored the treaty and closer association with the United States. The Liberals proclaimed their crusade against the free trade treaty in a continuation of the nationalist defense of the Canadian distinctiveness, culture, and sovereignty, which has been waged against the United States for 150 years. The NDP, unions, and the Left identified the struggle against "the deal" with their pursuit of a more redistributive, socialist oriented society.

The election was important from yet another perspective. Europe is soon to change from a community of twelve nations into a unified market of 320 million people free of internal tariff and custom barriers. Some U.S. and Japanese politicians fear that this new "fortress Europe," as it is called in the press, would be inclined to adopt protectionist policies, and by expanding import quotas, antidumping, and reciprocity requirements might seriously restrict the economic interests of their nations. They express fears that in response to such developments, facing organized European competition, the United States and Japan too would have no choice but to organize similar trade zones. Some Japanese politicians maintain that a free trade treaty between Japan and the United States could solve many problems of both nations. For some time, Reagan was emphasizing the importance of the relationship between the United States and its close neighbors to the north and south. For once, the world press began paying attention to Canada; the results of the Canadian electoral decision turned out to have international importance. The concern of Reagan was serious enough for him to make a short speech on the Canada-U.S. free trade agreement a few days before the election. Thatcher proclaimed in an interview that if the trade deal was to be rejected, it would be "very difficult for any prime minister of Canada to negotiate another international agreement with another country." Spokesmen of Japanese financial interests announced, that if Canada withdrew from the deal, the Japanese would have to reduce investments in Canada. Could Canada stay alone in the global village?

The Conservatives won the election. They captured 169 seats in an expanded, 295-seat House of Commons. It was a victory, but a lesser one than in the preceding election. The Liberals increased their standing to 83 seats from 38, the NDP to 43 seats from 30. The electorate voted 43 percent for the Conservatives, 31.9 percent for the Liberals, 20.4 percent for the NDP, and 4.7 percent for a number of smaller parties. Mulroney interpreted the victory as a clear mandate to implement the historic Canada-U.S. free trade agreement. *Macleans's,* the nation's most-read magazine (101, no. 50. December 5, 1988), summed up the results of the election "The nation audaciously opted for a hazardous trading partnership." Yet not only the 55 percent or so who voted for other parties, but even many of those who voted against the NDP and Liberals for a variety of reasons continue to oppose the new order.

CHAPTER THIRTEEN

Soft Etatization: Japan

Japan is Number One

Writers on economic development view Japan as special because they believe the Japanese are "The Best at the Game" (*The Economist*, July 18, 1981; see also Vogel 1979; Pascale & Athos 1981; Ike 1974). To many businessmen and politicians, Japan is number one because it holds a virtual monopoly on production of the best cameras, TV sets, video devices, and other equipment; no one is capable of wresting this part of the market from them. Japan is also special because its 120 million industrious people, inhabiting a territory somewhat smaller than California, have proved themselves better than most at building cars and ships, at forging steel, and at producing new electronic technologies. Japan is the emerging leader in the development of new computer technology; the Japanese have outclassed both U.S. businesses and the Europeans in producing office machines, computers, and other electronic equipment. When the first 1k RAM memory chips were invented in the early 1970s, no one could compete with U.S. firms in this new technology. By 1975, 12 percent of the new 4k RAM memory chips market had been captured by the Japanese, who subsequently won 40 percent of the market for 16k RAM chips, introduced in 1981, and 70 percent for the 64k RAM chips, introduced soon after. The Japanese are now trying to win the market for 256k RAM chips. Their control of this new field is unsurpassed. Recently, they claimed to be developing knowledge-information processing systems (KIPS) and fifth-generation computers, which they expect will not only react to conversations and pictures but actually "think" intelligently (Feigenbaum & McCorduck 1984). Developed by the Institute for New Generation Computer Technology, the first of these new computers is expected to appear on the market in 1990. Japan also has the largest operating population of industrial robots in the world.[1] The Japanese are advancing into other novel areas of production, such as genetic

226

engineering and fusion reactors.

From another perspective, Japan presents a special case because it boasts one of the leading economic growth rates among industrialized nations, and the lowest unemployment and inflation rates. Experts tackling social problems envy Japan's highly effective health-and-welfare system, which, in comparison with the programs of other nations, costs taxpayers much less.[2]

According to 1985 data, of the 100 largest commercial banking companies (total assets $5,390,027,048,000) outside the United States, thirty were Japanese (total assets $2,246,100,000,000). Of the ten banks among those with the highest assets per employee, nine were Japanese. In contrast to U.S. and West European banks, Japanese banks rarely invest in risky ventures in the Third World and as a rule do not loan money to Eastern European nations. Consequently they enjoy a highly stable position within the international banking business. Japan is now the world's largest creditor nation. During the late 1970s, Japan's annual direct foreign investment was between $3 and $5.5 billion. It climbed to $12–15 billion in the mid-1980s. And now, at the end of the 1980s, the Japanese annually invest between $25 and $30 billion.

How did this nation, defeated in World War II and producing shabby commodities that were a common target for comedians in the 1950s, manage to attain such success by the 1970s and 1980s? A flood of books and articles has appeared, each attempting to answer this question. The authors of these books do not only salute the Japanese for their achievements. Like Ouchi in *Theory Z*, they seek to convince the rest of the world that other nations could achieve similar success by adopting Japanese-style management to bring increased productivity, harmony, and happiness to society.

How have the Japanese achieved their leading position in many fields of technological development and in the international market? Chalmers Johnson (1982, 8–16) examines four schools of thought on this question. The first attributes Japanese success to the making of the state. The second encompasses believers in a "no-miracle" explanation. Experts of this group argue that what happened in Japan was a normal outgrowth of market forces, which were allowed to operate freely. These authors claim that many elements of the Japanese economy—the prominent role of the banking system in capital formation and investment, the absence of national unions, the high saving propensity of the population, and a variety of other factors that are different in Japan than in market-oriented Western societies—produced its success. The third school ascribes Japan's success to the influence of "unusual Japanese institutions," particularly to "lifetime" employment, the seniority wage system, and enterprise unionism. The fourth school of thought argues that Japan benefited from a combination of incidental factors. Because of its postwar alliance with the United States, Japan "has not had to devote much of its national income to armaments." It also obtained information from scientific research performed in the United

States and other Western nations at relatively low cost. It was able to rely on a rapidly growing internal market; and it simply made certain good decisions.

Johnson, the author of *MITI and the Japanese Miracle* and other books on Japanese public policy, considers himself a member of the school "that stresses the role of the developmental state in the economic miracle." He points out that, in contrast to the United States or Western Europe, both oriented toward market rationality and efficiency, and the Soviet system, which operates under ideological rationality, Japanese society operates under a system of "plan rationality." The Ministry of International Trade and Industry (MITI) is the principal institution of "plan rationality." Japan, he writes, owe its success to the state's economic bureaucracy, which implements industrial policy and gives administrative guidance to the nation's businesses. The issue, stresses Johnson (1982, 17–18), is not state intervention alone, but how the government intervenes and for what purposes. The book provides detailed analysis of how MITI is organized, what kind of internal and external conflicts it faces, and how it implements adopted programs. However, many questions remain unanswered. Could other nations follow Japan and adopt the orientation of plan rationality? Many writers answer this question affirmatively. Johnson's opinion differs. He implies that what was good for Japan is not necessarily good for other nations.

The success of Japanese society was orchestrated by the state. From the perspective of the present analysis, however, it must also be stressed that the Japanese state and society is composed of highly disciplined, duty-conscious people, willing to sacrifice much of their own interests and freedom for the collectivity; in some instances this involves "yielding under protest", in others, reacting with a display of "responsive dependence to the decisions of MITI"; and, in still other instances, being motivated by nationalist or familial sentiments. "Japan's government exercised a much greater degree of both intervention and protection than did many of its Western European counterparts; and this brings Japan closer to the experience of another set of countries—the centrally planned economies": Johnson quotes (1982, 31) another expert, with whom he obviously agrees. However, there are limitations to this viewpoint. The fact that Japan never experienced a democratic revolution waged by the masses is of great importance, and this puts this nation in a distinct category. The Japanese respect bureaucracy because it represents to them a continuation of the *samurai* tradition. People in other nations feel differently. Japan's present situation results from an interplay of politics and culture. Japanese bureaucrats (Johnson 1982, 39) "inherited from the samurai something comparable to their code of ethics and their elite consciousness." Japan retained and incorporated into new organizational structures, many elements of traditional, so-called feudal relations. Thus, new vehicles of modernity carried a great deal of the traditional ethos.

Despite the widespread awe for Japanese economic performance, an increasing number of experts write that not all is well. There is the "other Japan," too, they warn; the world should expect to hear more about it in the future. Fukutake (1974) writes of crowded cities in a highly polluted environment; of standardized box-houses inhabited by people forced to live identical lives under the control of computers and automatons that are introduced, whenever possible, into the manufacturing process, into offices, and into services; of life on a transmission belt under state control; of a seemingly harmonious society with volcanic and epidemic outbursts of violence directed against teachers, corporations, or the state; of daily drills, strict discipline, and organizational efficiency in which everyone must take part. He discusses further aspects of this system of unhappy happiness. He does not fail to point out that Japan, which may pride itself on technological and economic achievements, has produced few Nobel prize winners, original philosophers, or leading theoreticians.

Gibney (1979, 354) summarizes the feelings of Japanese youth as reported in the prime minister's 1973 "World Youth Consciousness Survey." He notes that the Japanese have created "a society, where production is given top priority and individual happiness ignored; a national concentration on what is good for the country as a whole, to the exclusion of individual hopes and aspirations; a political system that runs counter to peoples' hopes; a materialistic way of life that thinks money can solve any problem; a society that treats its aged shamefully." In this survey, Gibney points out, 73.5 percent of Japanese youth admitted experiencing deep dissatisfaction with their way of life. Youth in other nations were also dissatisfied, but in the United States, West Germany, and Sweden, only 45 percent expressed dissatisfaction. In the next survey, conducted in 1978, the percentage of "dissatisfied" or "pessimists" was smaller, only 57 percent—but that still was among the highest figures for the world's young (Gibney 1979, 355). A Gallup poll, commissioned by a Catholic research center early in 1982, found that only 30 percent of Japanese were proud to be Japanese as compared with 80 percent of U.S. respondents proud to be American, 60 percent of Britons proud to be British, and an average 40 percent of Europeans proud of their respective countries. Kojima (see *Public Opinion Quarterly*, Summer 1977) and other researchers claim that attitudes are changing in Japan. People are still nationalistic, but they are increasingly concerned with human rights. Researchers witness growing opposition to the practice of leaving everything in the hands of professional politicians.

On October 25, 1986, *The Economist* reported that the average annual income of the Japanese had reached $17,000, compared to the $16,000 average income of the 240 million in the United States, and the $8,800 average income in Great Britain and Italy. (Unreported income of around 5 percent in Great Britain and 25-30 percent in Italy, derived from the black-market economy, must be added to these figures). This does not mean, however, that the Japanese enjoy a higher standard of living than do U.S. residents. Although they may possess electronic gadgets in abundance, many Japanese homes are still not equipped with bathroom facilities; many Japanese live in small apartments in which bedrooms are transformed into living rooms during the day. Homes and food are much more expensive than in the United States (see Haberman 1988). *The Economist*, discussing conditions in Tokyo, does not fail to point out that a piece of land the size of a magazine's page costs ¥1.8 million ($12,000), two to three times as much as a comparable area in Manhattan.

Achievements admired and envied by some writers evoke resentment and worries in others. Year after year since 1970, the United States has suffered a negative balance of trade with Japan. In 1975, the U.S. balance of trade with Japan was minus $1.862 billion; the estimate for 1985 was minus $37,000 billion. Theodore H. White (1985), in an analysis published in the *New York Times Magazine*, claims that "all in all, on the line, in the old shops, where Americans make things, we have lost 1,834,000 jobs" as a result of the Japanese trade invasion. Not only do the Japanese sell better-quality products more cheaply in the United States, but "we cannot sell our exports freely in Japan." The Japanese imposed import restrictions on quite a few commodities. Recently, the Japanese began investing their exports surplus in other nations, including the United States. White quotes Secretary of Commerce Malcolm Baldridge, who said, "Japanese export policy has as its objective not participation in, but dominance of, world markets." This same accusation has previously been leveled against the United States, by Europeans.

Japan faces many difficult problems, among them its trade surplus with many countries in the world, which enrages other governments, and its great dependency on world markets. What would happen to Japanese prosperity if other nations reduced trade with Japan? The Japanese are not happy about it, but the condition of their society rules that Japan cannot afford to be less developed, less disciplined, less successful, or less productive. Considering population growth—from a 1.5% growth rate in the 1930s, to 2.8% in the 1950s, down to 1.4% in 1955, and to 0.7% in 1980—the limiting size of its territory (143,574 square miles), and the lack of natural resources, Japan could have ended up like Bangladesh, had it not adopted its present growth orientation and modified its value system to one that combines Confucian norms, Western standards, and highly potent elements of economic nationalism.

The Legacy of Emperor Meiji

Looking at it from a historical perspective, Japan originated the system of economic management that can be regarded as one preceding the one in the contemporary New State. In Japan, nearly a century ago, the state industrialized the nation and, subsequently, developed the market economy. Only now, thirty years later than Western European nations, is Japan developing a system of welfare institutions and services—the other component of the European and U.S. New State.

Emperor Meiji established the new state in Japan. Nearly overnight, under the rule of a new emperor, Japan was reunited and transformed from many principalities into a nation, smoothly administered under a new central bureaucracy. From there, Meiji and the party of young *samurai* supporting him turned toward even more ambitious objectives. They strove to transform Japan into an industrialized nation, complete with a modern conscripted army, a modern system of education and science, and a modern economy with adequate organization of trade and culture. They built Japan into a nation strong enough to defend itself against colonial powers and aggressive enough to claim a colonial empire for itself. Sweeping reorganizations occurred in every sphere of Japanese life. In transforming Japan into a modern nation, Meiji was able to count on his supporters, who were not only willing to implement thoroughly any orders they received but felt honored to sacrifice personal interests and privileges in order to attain national goals (Lebra 1973).

Meiji introduced four sweeping reforms, which produced the new state in Japan and, subsequently, etatization.

1. Traditional Japanese society comprised several graded orders. *Samurai* (nobility) held the highest status; food-producing peasants were second in rank; craftsmen and merchants comprised the inferior status positions. Meiji and his advisors soon realized that, in order to attain their objectives, they needed to place Japan under the administration of a unified, efficient bureaucracy and foster an entrepreneurial class capable of engaging in industrial undertakings. Without any hesitation, they accorded entrepreneurs a comparable status to that held by the *samurai*. Since this was decreed by the emperor and supported by the new ruling elite, not only did Japanese society as a whole approve it, but even the *samurai*, whose status was downgraded as a result, accepted with dignity this change. In 1889, Meiji proclaimed a Western-style constitution, which did not recognize traditional ranks. The new constitution declared office-holding, entrepreneurial activity, and business undertakings open to any aspiring individual with talent, regardless of ancestry. Analysts of these changes note that, since only sons of *samurai* were adequately prepared to compete for positions in the bureaucratic power structure, societal structure continued to be dominated by the *samurai*. Lebra's expert book on the *samurai* ethic explains the motivations of thse people: (1973, 55):

The Meiji Restoration was an elite revolution, a feature which distinguishes it from other major world revolutions. It has been estimated that while only 5 per cent of the population at the time of the Restoration were *samurai* or *shizoku* class, in 1882 61–2 per cent of the bureaucracy were still *shizoku*.

Distinct from the failed efforts, a century and half earlier, of Peter the Great of Russia, who tried to transform his backward country into a modern nation by decree—without changing the mentality and value orientation of its people—Meiji's reformers attributed enormous importance to value changes. Their principal concern was industrialization; yet they knew that the success of their endeavor hinged on advancing modernization in every area of life, including creating new needs and aspirations. It was not enough simply to declare that entrepreneurs, the merchants, and craftsmen, were equal in status to others in traditionally valued occupations and positions. Their roles had to be widely recognized as honorable, so that the samurai might strive to engage in them. Several authors discussing these innovations (see, e.g., Marshall 1967, 30–50; Clark 1979, 25–29) observe that in contrast to tradition, which praised military virtues, Meiji and his reformers stressed the right of entrepreneurs and merchants to profit. Through their activities, they argued, these people provided society with badly needed industries and raised the general welfare of the population. Clark (1979, 27) notes the similarity between this argument and the one propagated by advocates of the Protestant ethic in Western Europe.

2. What took European nations decades or centuries to achieve, the Japanese tried to accomplish in one generation or less. While stimulating modernization and entrepreneurial activities, the state took it upon itself to engage in certain industrial activities that were perceived as urgently needing support. Norman (1940, 125–133) points out that, in Europe, light industries producing consumer goods emerged first. Only after the expansion of light industries did industrialists begin to concentrate their efforts on producing capital goods requiring higher capital investments. In Japan, the evolution of industries followed a different path. Equipping the army and navy was a top priority. The state first established arsenals, engineering works, and shipbuilding docks. It then engaged in the development of chemical, cement, and similar industries. Only later did the state develop industries producing market commodities. Heavy taxes were imposed on peasants to obtain revenues for development. According to some sources, 80 percent of the revenue during the years 1868–1880 was obtained through land taxes.

By 1880, it became obvious that, rather than developing into "a source of profit for the exchequer" as was earlier expected, most industries under state ownership continued to be "a drain on revenue." To relieve the state from this burden, the emperor proclaimed the Law on the Transfer of Factories to private entrepreneurs. In retrospect, this act can be regarded as the first major case of privatization of state-owned industries. Initially, the government tried to dispose of those enterprises producing nonmilitary commodities, regarded as having small strategic importance. Eventually most mining and shipbuilding enterprises were sold to private entrepreneurs, usually favored financiers. The Japanese soon discovered that many industries that were unprofitable under state management became profitable under private ownership. They therefore decided that, henceforth, the state would involve itself only in initiating new industrial development and facilitating conditions for growth. In short, the state restricted itself to husbandry of the economy. It no longer meddled in production and business, except in essential industrial services like railroads, which are essential for the economy but are not profitable enough to incite private investment. These industries, now public corporations and services (see Tsuji 1984) are still maintained by the Japanese government. But, as in Meiji's time, the contemporary Japanese government wishes to privatize them whenever it might be feasible.

Despite privatization, the Japanese state has retained tight control over many industries. Over the years, different types of control have been practiced. The more stringent were for industries of strategic importance. Banks play a much greater role in Japan than they do in other market-oriented societies. A great deal of state "guidance" and control is exercised through the Bank of Japan and other cooperating banks. Not only do these banks transform savings into capital, they also exercise a heavy influence on investment decisions. Investors desiring to act at their own risk and against the advice of state officials are allowed to do so. The best-known example of this occurred in the automobile industry and was quite successful. Most of the time, however, investors accept state guidance.

3. Both the army and the rapidly appearing new industrial enterprises required a large number of well-educated individuals. The state instituted a new, universal system of education able to produce people prepared to fill these needs.

4. The greatest difficulties were encountered in attempts to instill individualism in private relations and to foster modernity in many aspects of life. Many traditional attitudes were seen as obstructing a new, more conceptually innovative lifestyle. The Japanese government made an effort to change the lifestyle and attitudes of the population from those reflecting traditional dependencies to ones fitting industrial relations. Certain elements of the traditional value system, especially familism, were adjusted to suit more modern needs. A strong dose of Western norms and standards was injected into Japanese culture. The government, however, could not change the culture as simply as it had changed the social structure and many other elements in society. A new kind of collectivistic culture and value orientation evolved out of the clash between these efforts to Westernize and the continuity of tradition.

Western, Soviet, and Japanese Economic Systems

Unlike other nations in the capitalist world, Japan is a more growth- than welfare-oriented state. Black (et al. 1975) felt this and other peculiarities to be so important that Japan and the Soviet Union should be regarded as alternative models of modernization. Most of the differences between these modernizations are quite obvious.

The Soviet system aimed to build a superior socialist society. Japan wanted to adopt Western, essentially capitalist, modernization. Japan's reasons were pragmatic: originally, to develop an economy that would allow Japan to remain independent; after World War II, to develop an economy that would allow the nation to survive and improve its condition through participation in international trade.

In Russia, prior to the revolution, family and community bonds were very strong. Now, Soviets are expected to be dedicated to single-party rule and not to family. Family loyalty has been considerably weakened; familism was condemned as a cause of nepotism.[3] In the West, the individual is primarily dedicated to his own objectives. In mimicking the West, the Japanese government tried to induce contractual relations in many spheres of Japanese life. But familism persisted and still constitutes the basis of the Japanese ethos. Haitani writes (1976, 39):

> The Japanese statism has its roots in familism. In the traditional Japanese view, the whole nation is a family. The state is not merely a part of the system, but the very framework of it. The Japanese feel that in the beginning there was the nation house called Japan and the people were born into it.

The Japanese state is family. *Zaibatsu* combines and conglomerates; business companies, political parties, and all associations constitute other family units. Such institutions are regarded as quasifamilies, not because they are controlled or owned by individual families, but because they operate through family-like interpersonal loyalties and dependencies, because employees and members of these organizations identify themselves totally with the leadership and the group involved, and because, in turn, these groups provide their participants with family-like support. In Western society, personal and business interactions are founded on the understanding that conflicts of interest are inevitable, even among close friends or spouses. Ultimately, everyone is on his own. As a result, relations inevitably take the form of contractual agreements. The Japanese, however, do not expect serious conflicts to appear within groups that are held together by quasi-familial ties. Interpersonal relations, from their point of view, must be based on trust, on the expectation that anyone undertaking a task will be dedicated to it, and on an understanding that what is good for the company, the organization, or the state is also good for its members. Conflict and disagreement, should they occur, should be solved by friendly and amiable discussion. In reality, however, the Japanese tend to avoid expressing dissatisfaction. Thus, when conflict eventually comes out into the open—among employers, management, and unions, or between separate groups in an organization—it frequently results in extreme hostility, typical of people who once were close, but who discover that their relations are actually different than they assumed. In the end, both parties feel betrayed.

Soviet society operates under a system of central planning. All industries are owned by the state. The plan, the basic management instrument of the Central Committee that runs society, is designed to attain ideological objectives. The state controls the allocation of raw materials and finances, and the distribution of human resources and rewards. Targets are set for republics, administrative areas, industries, enterprises, work brigades, and even individuals. The system is rigid. Under Gorbachev's *perestroika* it is changing, but it still has not changed much. To attain different objectives, the Japanese state plans, encourages, and provokes development. It consistently strengthens the position of national industries, regulates their economic performance, and conducts research and development. Its main objective is to conquer international markets. There are other differences from the Soviet system. First, the Japanese state does not own the economy. Second, it can only regulate, exert pressure, and persuade the private sector to act according to its instruction; its power to command and to enforce outright economic coercion is limited. Third, the Japanese state is not engaged in building socialism or any other model society; it makes plans to attain concrete targets that will generate a greater inflow of profits. The state is principally involved in protecting trade, in R&D, and in advising investors, usually to facilitate the attainment of its objectives.

State management of the Japanese economy and society is both highly centralized and decentralized. The state manages the general economy but allows companies to decide how they will operate. State intervention, when necessary, is carried out with as many respectful bows to industry as possible, and with many polite apologies for interfering with affairs in which the state would really prefer not to be involved. The state reminds industries about certain formalities and necessary conditions regretfully. Business circles respond attentively; they know that the state works for them.

An extensive network of "attached organs," independent of state administrative agencies but funded by the state, operating as extensions of the state and as autonomous organs of society, runs the systems of education, medical care, road maintenance, water supplies, space development, certain banks and investment agencies, research institutes, railways, airlines, and telephone and other services. Tsuji (1984, 38–41) discerns several categories of these state-owned corporations. He lists 102 of them altogether. This sector of parastatal services, regarded in Japan as the second-class economy, absorbs a growing part of the labor force of tertiary industries.

Johnson (1978, 22–23), referring to Sadaju, lists seven major means by which the Japanese government provides "guidance" for private corporations:

1. Monetary and fiscal policies conducted through the Ministry of Finance, the Bank of Japan and, partially, MITI
2. Taxation (including tax bonuses for exporting industries and tax relief to industries investing in antipollution devices,)
3. Subsidies (only available when absolutely necessary) are important but rarely awarded by the state
4. Rationing to restrict excessive production
5. Licensing businesses and new lines of production; approving investment plans; similar regulatory practices to exert pressure on business (e.g., firms that respond to guidance are frequently rewarded with better and speedier treatment.)
6. Direct government investment in mixed enterprises and involvement in setting up new industries or in maintaining vital industries that benefit the national economy but are too risky or unprofitable to draw private investment
7. Other mechanisms of state guidance, particularly planning and research development

Japan conducts long-term economic planning. In 1949, Japan introduced the first Draft for Economic Recovery. An Economic Planning Agency was established in 1955. The same year, the agency proclaimed the first Five Year Program for Economic Independence. Its objective was to increase growth and employment in order to create stable economic conditions and to make Japan economically independent of the United States. In 1957, the agency introduced the Long-term Economic Program, designed to maintain the annual growth rate above 6.5 percent. In 1960, it announced the Twenty-Year Development Plan. In 1970, the agency adopted the so-called Tanaka Plan. Subsequently, Japan proclaimed the *Sanzenso*, or Third National Comprehensive Plan. Johnson (1978, 21) points out these plans fulfil primarily decorative and mobilizing purposes. They act as neither directives nor restrictions. More important, in his opinion, is the budgetary planning exercised by the Enterprises Bureau of MITI and certain other ministries. Budgetary planning involves both financing particular projects and allocating funds for research and development.

The Japanese state's initiatives in R&D, particularly in areas of new technology, are of great significance. The state invites all private companies who may be interested in using the results of research efforts to contribute funds. The ministry obtains the necessary patents.[4] The technology is then developed, modified, and perfected until it is ready to be presented as a commodity capable of conquering international markets. Japan developed successful steel, auto, electronic, and a number of other industries in this manner. Until recently, Japan depended on theoretical and innovative research from elsewhere, particularly the United States. Thus, it was able to focus its efforts on applied research. At present, Japanese agencies are facing the need to initiate projects in basic research to ensure support for future technological projects.

Japanese writers like to characterize their political and economic administration as "soft." This term quite accurately describes the Japanese variety of etatization. The Japanese state controls and regulates the economy and society through persuasion, negotiations, consensus, and support in its dealings with companies, instead of emphasizing "hard" approaches, such as outright regulations, rules, commands, and coercion. Rather than employ threats or negative sanctions, the state appeals to familial and patriotic obligations. Decisions are more particular than general: frequently applying to the actual situation of a specific company or group at a certain time, rather than to all companies and groups at any time. The Japanese state fosters conditions that encourage companies to initiate their own programs as identified and desired by the state, rather than directly exerts pressure to push them in a definite direction. The state takes great care to avert frictions among statal agencies and business circles, companies, unions, and intellectuals. On the other side, these groups seek to avoid confrontation with the government. Although they may feel disappointed or frustrated by some particular government policy, only rarely, and when there are occasional disclosures of corruption, do large sections of the population unite against state policies. The state does what a great majority of the Japanese think it ought to do.

Nakagawa and Ota (1981) offer a lucid discussion of the Japanese style of societal management. They employ a distinct metaphor to contrast the Japanese system with Soviet and Western economies. The market, they say, is like an ocean. The government, companies, corporations, and other agencies that exercise economic power represent islands in this ocean. Most of the islands in other parts of the world comprise "hard organizations." In contrast, the islands in the sea of the Japanese market economy are made up of "soft organizations." The Soviet economy, they say, consists of one, huge, solid, rock island of state ownership under planned governmental control, which aspires to determine every aspect of economic activity. It covers most of the territory of its sea and only narrow straits surround it; it is largely inflexible. Islands in the Western economy are made of "hard organizations" also, each pursuing its own interests and disregarding the interests of others. These islands include large and small state and corporate institutions and agencies, the biggest usually being the state. They often operate at each other's expense in a wide, unpredictable, and stormy market sea. More recently, the principal isles of the state in such seas have been growing.

Japan represents the third variety of oceanscape. In contrast to Western and Soviet systems, the Japanese economy comprises numerous floating islands in the sea of the market economy; as flexible entities, the "soft organizations" of statal agencies and business companies rarely collide or encroach upon one another's territory. They coexist within a well-balanced structure compounding centrifugal and centripetal forces under "multi-umbrella mechanisms" provided by tradition and the state.

Nakagawa and Ota (11) list three of these mechanisms. "In Japan companies prefer to procure funds, not through the stock and bond markets, but from banks and trading houses." Money flows from investors to the Ministry of Finance and the capital market, to the Bank of Japan, to commercial banks, to trading houses, and, subsequently, to the producing companies; always in that order. Management control, credit status, supervision, financial expertise, and administrative guidance are attached, and flow parallel to the flow of funds. Financing is centralized; then it is decentralized and diffused, at each level of this financing hierarchy. As a result of the dispersion of each investment through triple or quadruple layers of investment management, before actual investments in industrial and trade activities are made, financial risks are minimized. Potential conflicts and bankruptcies are generally avoided, because they are anticipated before they erupt, and subtle state intervention, including negotiations and additional capital infusions, are provided whenever warranted.[5]

By producing conditions under which cutthroat competition rarely occurs, the system of lifetime employment constitutes the second multi-umbrella mechanism. It generates loyalty on the part of employees, and, on the employer's side, a sense of responsibility for employment conditions. All parties obtain a sense of security. They are each part of the family.

The third multi-umbrella mechanism is secured by decisionmaking procedures stemming from consensus, obtained on the basis of exchanged information and ideas. In the opinion of Nakagawa and Ota (28), competition in Japan is much more intensive than elsewhere, including the United States. In Japan, however, competition affects only a small number of individuals specializing in any particular area. They compete primarily for prestige and recognition, and they do not seek to destroy or completely eliminate the other party.

It should be noted that the Japanese system was not consciously and deliberately developed under any plan or ideology. The Japanese economy evolved toward the present system because Japanese society has always been devoid of social or economic dogma; it grew in pragmatic response to needs.

MITI not only conducts market research and initiates research on new commodities, it also persuades companies to merge whenever this is deemed in the national interest. It advises them on where to find capital, credit, and raw materials, and on how to protect and open avenues for trade and development. The Japanese annually invest about 22–28 percent of their GNP in growth and development. The United States and other Western societies, on average, invest less than 15–18 percent. The Soviet Union, according to various estimates, invests an even larger share of their GNP than does Japan, but primarily invests in heavy industry, in the manufacturing of weaponry, and in products that have no world market. It is important to remember that the Japanese work more hours per week than most Westerners (according to OECD 1984 data, the Japanese worker spends on the average 2,152 hours on the job; the U.S. worker 1,898 hours; the European worker, even less). The Japanese take shorter vacations, have fewer strikes, and are more productive. The main point, however, is that not only do the Japanese invest a large share of their GNP, they invest wisely. They invest in selected fields until they attain a level of perfection that allows them to capture a large share of the world market in that particular field. After the conquest, they continue perfecting the product, and, meanwhile, they single out a new field of conquest.

Table 13.1 presents in condensed form a comparison of the economic systems of the West, the Soviet Union, and Japan.

Japan's Concerns: Today and Tomorrow

Despite all their great successes, the Japanese worry more about the future than do many other nations. They are primarily concerned that their society is rapidly aging. In 1950, the aged—those 60 years old and over—equalled 7.7% of the population. This figure reached 10.7% in 1970 and 12.6% in 1980, exceeding 10 million people. Japanese demographers worry that, by the year 2000, the aged will comprise 14.3% of the population, implying a relative decline in the proportion of working-age individuals who would be required to sustain the population. The Japanese already have the world's longest average life span. Total expenditure on pensions increased from ¥323 billion in 1970, to ¥1,600 billion in 1980. Expenditures on public health increased during the same period from ¥343 billion to ¥2,000 billion; and social insurance expenditures increased from ¥2,848 billion to ¥20,014 billion. Experts are concerned that the cost of maintaining so many old people will be too high for the society to bear. However, the Japanese still have a relatively low percentage of dependents on transfer payments from the state. In all industrialized nations, expenditures on pensions and social security are increasing, but the Japanese take a grimmer view of these changes than do experts in West Germany, France, Great Britain, the United States, and other, younger nations. This is because, in the past, they spent very little of their budget on welfare, health services, and old-age pensions. Japan succeeded as a nation because, among other things, it instituted the New State and managed to maximize the use of human resources; and because it did have a sufficiently large working-age population. As Ibe (1978, 78) writes: "Japan has lost the [demographic] conditions that made its

Table 13.1 Western, Soviet, and Japanese Economic Systems Compared

| | I. Western Systems | | II. The Soviet Systems | III. The Japanese System Type C |
| | Type A | Type B and D | | |
	1		2	3
ECONOMIC ENVIRONMENT	Market economy under increasing state control and management "market rationality"* Orientation: money-making; partial redistribution of GNP		Planned, command system of economy "plan ideological rationality"* Orientation: first, producing goods required by the state; second, producing goods required by the population	"State-guided" economy under "multi-umbrella mechanisms"* "plan rational economy"* Orientation: conquering international markets and producing goods for domestic markets
GENERAL CHARACTERISTICS	One-sector, U.S. capitalist economy private ownership of means of production	Two-sector, mixed economy private and state ownership of means of production	One-sector, state-owned economy	One-sector, "state-guided," privately owned capitalist economy
	state management of the economy by means of direct and indirect monetary and fiscal control	state management of the economy by means of general state administration and establishment of nationalized industries	all principal means of production owned by the state or state-controlled collective farms	all means of production privately owned, with the exception of unprofitable services (e.g., transportation)
	industry and business respond to market expectations; protectionism in some areas of production and international trade; subsidies from the state		central authorities set standards and prices for products; market highly controlled by the state	adjustment to market conditions under state guidance; highly developed state protectionism
	capitalism with elements of redistributive society and welfare system		official socialism	capitalism combined with familism
FLOW OF MONEY IN THE ECONOMIC STRUCTURE	30–50% of population depends on transfer payments from the state; works for the state or state-subsidized institutions		95% of the population depends on jobs and transfer payments provided by the state and state-controlled collective farms	25–30% of population depends on transfer payments and works for the state
	40–60% of individual incomes appropriated in taxes; largest part of revenue expended on entitlements		10–13% of individual incomes appropriated in taxes; all increments produced by industries appropriated by the state	30–35% of individual incomes appropriated in taxes; large part of state revenues spent on R&D
FINANCING	15–18% of GNP reinvested		20–30% of GNP reinvested	25% of GNP reinvested
	industry and business financed by equity obtained from stock- and bond-...		technology, raw materials, labor force allocated by the state; targets set by the state; industries not responsible for their...	funds, credits, and financial services obtained from banks and trading houses; state subsidies ...

...continued	shareholders interested in the company only as a financial investment		shareholders strongly associated with specific companies; interested in their growth, profits, dividends
	10-20% of GNP generated in the underground economy	20-25% of GNP generated in the underground economy	5% of GNP generated in the underground economy
ECONOMIC CONTROL	oligopolistic structures and megacorporations dominate market; business at investor's risk	state monopoly; enterprises subordinated to industries and central party and state authorities do not compete with one another	zaibatsu-type combines, mostly with own banks and association with small companies in various capacity
	large companies frequently self-sufficient; seek to win resources of raw materials, equipped with plants producing parts; networks of distributors; corporations obtain stock holdings in other areas of economic activity to increase profitability	companies dependent on supplies from other companies of the same or other industries; deliveries of raw materials and parts; distribution of produced commodities in accordance with orders from the center and state plans; under *perestroika* this is to be modified	company involved in a dual economy; large companies depend on subcontractors**
OBJECTIVES	*profit* principal measure of success	*implementation of state targets* principal measure of success	*market share* principal measure of success**
ECONOMIC FUNCTIONS OF THE STATE	maintaining the economy in balance and growing; stimulation of exports; protecting major industries in time of adversity; subsidization of weak sectors of the economy—overall regulation and management of the market condition; maintaining services and the welfare system	setting general economic developmental objectives and translating objectives into targets of branches of the economy—industries and enterprises; supervising implementation of central planning	setting objectives of industrial policy; involving major industries in implementation of these objectives; development of the infrastructure and R&D
RELATIONS AT WORK	low emphasis on community ideals in company organization	social relations within company under strict party control	company is ideally a community**
	sharp distinction within the hierarchical structure of organization; managerial positions related to particular functions	sharp distinction in privileges and pay within the hierarchical structure of organization; strong emphasis on hierarchy	distinction between managers and workers less significant than in other nations; strong emphasis on hierarchy in which age and length of service is critical
	success in achieving productive and business targets most relevant in promotion claims	party membership and implementation of state assignments critical in promotion	age and length of service criteria in promotion
	authority and responsibility ostensibly specific**	authority of party control diffuse; authority of managers specific	authority and responsibility ostensibly diffuse**
VALUE ORIENTATION	self-orientation; individualism; relations principally contractual, job security: an ideal	officially collective orientation; in practice, strong self-orientation	collective orientation; consensus; patronage, familism, life-employment norm commonly practiced

*From Chalmers Johnson, *MITI and the Japanese Miracle* (Stanford, CA: Stanford University Press, 1982).
**From Rodney Clark, *The Japanese Company* (New Haven, NJ: Yale University Press, 1979).

high economic growth possible in the past. . . . The only way for the Japanese people to survive hereafter is to use their brain." Will they be able to outsmart the United States and the new, aggressive, "Small Dragon Nations," such as South Korea, Taiwan, Singapore, Hong Kong, and Thailand, who are already challenging Japanese supremacy? Resentment against Japanese success is growing. Japan may soon encounter a world market built of barriers against Japanese trade. The Japanese fear the future more than others because they are less independent than other nations.

Aging is just one of Japan's numerous, troubling concerns. The Japanese are presently experiencing on one hand a labor shortage and on the other, for the first time, unemployment. They need more workers in order to sustain economic expansion. But they are xenophobic and fear the problems with foreign workers that they witness in West Germany and France. To compound this, their country is already overcrowded and highly polluted. The Japanese employ the largest number of robots—14,000—of any nation in their industries. With new robots, Japan may attain even more perfect production and perhaps solve its problems of labor shortage and disproportionate numbers of retired workers. But the Japanese cannot be sure that other nations will accept growing competition from Japanese robots. To retain their current position in the world economy, the Japanese are making great efforts to remain ahead and unbeatable. But what if other economies collapse and can no longer afford Japanese goods?

To reduce the dissatisfaction of other countries over unemployment caused by Japanese economic exports, and to make use of surplus capital, the Japanese have begun exporting capital, developing industries in foreign countries (e.g., the United States, Brazil, Spain, and Canada). In the future, Japan would like to transfer more of its heavy, polluting industries to other countries. Other nations, facing unemployment, currently welcome Japanese investments. But will they continue to accept Japanese terms of trade and investment? The *Maekawa Report*, developed to answer these questions for the Japanese government, recommends pursuing greater international economic interdependence, increasing exports, and even balancing them with increased imports. To accomplish that, they would have to overcome a difficult problem—the Japanese consumer's aversion to foreign-made commodities.

Certain Japanese experts recommend going even further: concluding a free-trade treaty with the United States. The free-trade zone created by such a treaty would encompass an area producing more than a third of the world's GNP. Prime Minister Takeshita favors this policy. Some Western European experts express irritation with such an initiative; they would prefer a Western European treaty with Japan, excluding the United States. They want to get a larger piece of the Japanese market. But are they prepared in return to offer a larger piece of their market to Japanese TNCs? The U.S. government that opted for such a treaty would have to overcome very stiff opposition from unions and a large sector of U.S. business; opposition in Europe would be even stronger. The world is becoming too small for Japanese expansion. The prosperity and, in fact, the very economic existence of Japan depends on foreign supplies of raw materials and, even more, on foreign markets for Japanese commodities—in short, on the well-being of other nations, the United States, Canada, and Western European nations particularly. But Japanese exports are one of the factors that undermine this well-being.

In Japan, as in other industrialized nations, the state is expanding its role as provider, distributor of income, manager of social services, and social planner. As more people are employed in the state services providing benefits to state dependents, the ratio of employment in primary, secondary, and tertiary industry is changing. Japanese analysts are unhappy about the fact that, in contrast to 1956 when 42% of their labor force was involved in primary, 23.9% in secondary, and 34.1% in tertiary industries, in 1980 only 12% of the labor force was involved in primary industries, 28% in secondary, and 60% in tertiary industries. They call themselves "the first postindustrial nation." Japan cannot return to a rural economy; it can succeed only if other nations succeed.

There are still other reasons why the Japanese are exasperated. Large sections of the population are grumbling about many things, perhaps not as much as people in United States or Europe complain, but enough to worry government and business circles. Pessimism among youth has been mentioned. Some groups feel that Japan is overdeveloped. They complain that the country is too materialistic, too obsessed with growth, gadgetry, robots, and information systems; they call for a return to more austere, traditional ways. Others question the meaning of it all. As in the United States and elsewhere, work, duties, and obligations, without noble, spiritual content, are experienced as purposeless. To a growing number of Japanese, contemporary Japan is too collectivistic and too restrictive; to them, familism is anachronistic. There are also those who argue the need for greater freedom, to generate conditions where a new breed of inventors and creators can pursue new scientific approaches and new technologies; they also want more freedom from oppressive work, family, and state control. Still others resent the high cost of housing and commodities, even though incomes are now higher as well. So far, the sun still rises over Japan, and each day it rises higher. But the Japanese worry that one day, it may fail to rise because of too much growth, too much technology, too intense a familism, not enough capitalism or socialism, or too much of both.

PART THREE

THE CONTEMPORARY INDIVIDUAL AND THE HISTORICAL INEVITABILITY OF ETATIZATION

CHAPTER FOURTEEN

The New Morality

From the Protestant Ethic to the Other-Directed Mentality of the 1950s and the New Morality of the 1970s

Changes in value orientation appeared concurrently with the rapid advance of etatization. The processes are interrelated in circular causation. Changes in values caused people to expect more from the state. The fulfilment of these expectations brought etatization and the New State, which advanced the change in values further.

It was observed that, paralleling the development of capitalism, the value orientation of Western societies underwent several major transmutations. The first of these major shifts consisted in the wide adoption of fundamental capitalist norms and values. Although still controversial, Weber's *The Protestant Ethic* interprets most incisively the motivations and behavior of individuals during the early stages of capitalist development. His Protestant ethic is an ideal-type concept. Rather than preoccupy himself with the distinct Puritan, Lutheran, Calvinist, Huguenot, Anglican, Mormon, and other Protestant groups' distinctive ethical codes, Weber focused on norms that these groups shared. Although mostly developed by Protestants, this work ethic was embraced by non-Protestants as well. Protestants observed it as a religious requirement; others adopted elements related to work and business attitudes, because these represented standard norms of the time. The Protestant ethic evolved into an ethic of capitalism.

What Weber called "the spirit of capitalism," others described as the bourgeois mentality of the late Victorian age, of *la belle epoque* in France, and so on. More than ever before, people strove to satisfy their desires, to impose their will on others and on nature in pursuit of money. Conquerors and builders of political and business empires were heroes of this era. Balzac, Zola, Dickens, and other great writers of the time depicted a sinister side of this new capitalist morality. They also noticed a variety of undercurrents that were bound to cause shifts from existing conditions to other values, norms, and lifestyles. Weber noticed this as well. The last pages of *The Protestant Ethic* (1958, 181–182) contain the famous pronouncement on escape from the iron cage of the Protestant ethic into the "world of materialism":

> The Puritan wanted to work in a calling; we are forced to do so. For when asceticism was carried out of monastic cells into everyday life, and began to dominate worldly morality, it did its part in building the tremendous cosmos of the modern economic order. . . . But fate decreed that the cloak should become an iron cage.
>
> Since asceticism undertook to remodel the world and to work out its ideals in the world, material goods have gained an increasing and finally an inexorable power over the lives of men as at no previous period in history. To-day the spirit of religious asceticism—whether finally, who knows?—has escaped from the cage. . . . For of the last stage of this cultural development, it might be truly said: "Specialists without spirit, sensualists without heart; this nullity imagines that it has attained a level of civilization never before achieved."

Marianne Weber writes (1975, 120) that Max "always judged political events on the basis of one thing to which he clung all his life: *intellectual freedom.*" In capitalism he saw a system rewarding no other values but work and market rationality. This, he felt was right. But Weber believed that the ideals of substantive morality (and rationality) derived from a sense of duty toward collectivity and immanent righteousness, more superior to that derived from market calculations. Under no other system has intellectual freedom been practiced as widely as under capitalism. But that meant freedom for anti-intellectual and anticapitalist forces as well. He recognized the inherent dynamism of capitalism. He feared that as a result of its own development and of antifreedom forces' activity, capitalism might evolve into a system of "unfreedom" and caesarist bureaucracy. He saw it happening in his time. As Marianne writes (125), Weber felt that "'the shift of generations' had taken place. The sun of culture had moved on; other problems were illuminated for the young generation than had been exposed to their fathers, and with them they received different impulses for action and investigation." In other words, the values of society have changed.

He was right: The initial conditions of capitalism and of the Protestant ethic did not last long. A second major shift in the value orientation of Western societies began to materialize in the 1920s. This new shift accelerated rapidly during the two post–World War II decades of extraordinary ebullience, prosperity, and massive increases in consumption. General living standards improved; more and more new commodities appeared on the market. Individuals proudly flaunted their newly acquired modern gadgets. *The Lonely Crowd*, by David Riesman, and *The*

Organization Man, by William H. Whyte, scintillatingly portray the value orientation of that time. Riesman writes that the shift was multisided. From one primarily concerned with production, society changed into one preoccupied with consumption, opportunities, and even more material acquisitions. At the same time, it changed from one composed of large families to a society with a smaller number of children and decreasing focus on family life. He writes that, in contrast to "inner-directed" individuals of the past, the new breed of people was highly "sensitized to the expectations and preferences of others." Conformist attitudes prevailed. Instead of the family, church, and community, as in the past, the school, mass media, and peer group determined most people's behavioral patterns, norms, and lifestyles.[1] First in school, and later in the business community, clubs, and higher circles of society, people strove to emulate successful peers and members of the elite: to do what others do. Riesman calls them "other-directed" because of their relentless obsession to "keep up with the Joneses."

Success was measured by wealth and ostentatious consumption. As Riesman points out, the earlier belief that success and respect could be attained only through the pursuit of virtue gave way to a veneration of success regardless of the means used to attain it. Whyte discusses different aspects of this post–World War II mentality and societal structure. He distinguishes another set of institutional factors that engendered new values and lifestyles. For organization men, writes Whyte, corporations are the "citadels of belonging." For most of them (1963, 288–289), "The job . . . is not to keep up with the Joneses. It's to keep *down* with them. . . . *It is the group that determines when a luxury becomes a necessity.*" The organization man lived in suburbia. He was linked with other men of his kind and their spouses by "webs of friendship." Those in the "web of friendship," and those in the neighborhood of suburbia, met at the Valentine's costume party, the picnic, the Saturday night party, the New Year's Eve party, the Eggnog-before-Poinsettia Ball, the Saturday night bridge groups, and countless other parties. The most important characteristic of the organization man was that he was one of the group. He had few ideas of his own; and the ideas he expressed came (129) "from the group, not from the individual." For these men and women, the most important thing was to participate and not to be alone. Whyte interprets them as participants in a "false collectivization," in a fictitious "private socialism." During the 1950s, such people were praised as promethean, possessed by the urge to create, innovate, and acquire. Books such as *The Achieving Society*, by McClelland, and most literature on modernization acclaim this value orientation as the source of prosperity. Achievement-oriented individuals, asserted writers, tended to engage in activities that require energetic, innovative performances, and a high sense of personal responsibility, not so much to attain wealth, but because achievement brought meaning to their lives. "Money to them," wrote McClelland (1961, 237), "was the measure of success. It gave them the concrete knowledge of the outcome of their efforts that their motivation demanded." Wealth was the by-product of success, not the sole purpose of their initiatives. Literature on social problems appealed to this perspective as well. Poverty and the absence of growth in economically underdeveloped areas were attributed to a lack of achievement-orientation. People in such areas were too tradition-oriented. "Get modern!" became the catchword. Anyone who chooses to modernize and achieve, argued experts, can attain living standards equal to those of the prosperous in industrialized societies. "Get up and get rich!"

In the 1950s, people saw the West as a land of affluence and democracy developed by achievement-oriented people. In the mid-1960s, however, a new vision of the United States, and of capitalism as a whole, suddenly came to the forefront. The new perspective strongly reproved capitalism as a "military industrial complex," conducting imperialist policies and promoting uncontrolled technological expansion that threatened to devastate the planet. Discrimination against ethnic minorities, women, and the poor, participation in an unjust war in Vietnam, and an obsession with material things and technological gadgets were prominent elements included in this spiteful image of the United States and the West. Many of these criticisms were not new. Only in the 1960s, however, did they gain a widespread voice, when Western values and lifestyles emerged as the central issue of concern for a large section of the intellectual community. Visions of the future were gloomy: an overcrowded planet of lonely people roaming in a devastated country without animals, birds, flowers, trees; a world without natural resources, plagued by war as everyone struggled to survive. Instead of promising beautiful dreams and the attainment of humanitarian ideals, reality seemed to turn into a nightmare.

For most young people, this future contrasted too starkly with the depiction of society they knew from home and school. They could not accept it; had they been cheated by their parents, teachers, the president, the *chef de l'état*, and all the other authorities they had sincerely trusted? As sincere idealists, these middle class children who trusted in the victory of truth, freedom, justice, equality, and equity, revolted against what they saw as evil: a vainglorious band of Mammon worshippers with materialistic values, parading as honorable do-gooders; a society shamelessly implicated in countless calamities. They did not want to be part of such a world; they determined to change it immediately. Reich (1972, 240) offers a succinct description of the emergence of this movement:

> What happens is simply this: in a brief span of months, a student, seemingly conventional in every way, changes his haircut, his clothes, his habits, his interests, his political attitudes, his way of relating to other people, in short, his whole way of life. He has "converted" to a new consciousness. . . . Over and over again, an individual for whom a conversion seemed impossible, . . . transforms himself into a drug-using, long haired, peace-loving "freak."

Reich calls this change "conversion to Consciousness III"; the traditional outlook of the U.S. farmer, small businessman, and worker typify Consciousness I; the consciousness of the corporate state—the principal target of his and the new Left's repulsion—classifies as Consciousness II.

Roszak, Yankelovich, and other writers focused primarily on changes in the sphere of attitudes, interpersonal behavior, and lifestyles. But similarly rapid transformations occurred in other spheres of life: No area can be singled out as the source of all other revolutions. The 1960s was a time of many overlapping revolutions (see Nelson 1968): The "second industrial revolution" was unfolding, with corporations burgeoning into megamultinationals. The credit card began replacing cash money in circulation; national economies increasingly integrated into the growing international markets and banking systems; university education expanded and was made accessible to the majority of youth; masses of women joined the labor force; the sexual revolution and permissive society erupted. Values, moreover, were in a continual state of flux. In the 1960s, revolt was the rule; while in the 1970s, abandoning desires for materialistic achievement and turning to self-fulfilment was the fashion. The "me-generation" came into prominence.

The cultural revolt of the young against society failed. It rejected the West's heritage and bourgeois norms and values, but failed because it did not offer concrete substitutes to the established order. The revolt did not attract the support of the working class. Western European Communist parties did not support the cultural revolt because, as a genuine grassroots movement, it refused to accept discipline and direction from the party. The movement refused to develop an organization. The young grew disillusioned with the leaders and philosophers of their revolt. Some, in their abhorrence of bourgeois society, turned to various forms of escape: drugs, cults, sects, or simply drifting. Some of the "me-generation" became narcissistic freaks, concerned primarily with discovering the truth of "Who am I?" Some ventured into self-fulfilment of other kinds. Others became yuppies and joined the "new class." Nothing predicted by this movement ever occurred. Most living experiments, such as communes, undertaken to create harmonious and self-fulfilling environments, were unsuccessful. The search for the true, spiritual good life based on real equality and equity failed to developed into a condition appreciated by those who had created it. In the New State, instead of increased harmony, tenser and more competitive conditions emerged.

The rebellion faded; but not without leaving its mark. Originally loose movements, associated by their rejection of the status quo, different groups—feminists, ethnic groups, environmentalists, and others—evolved into single-issue movements attracting wide support. They soon became established as permanent elements of the new political scene. Changes in lifestyles, values, and conditions, provoked by the rebellion of the young, continued because these changes also responded to other, "overlapping revolutions", occurring simultaneously.

It was assumed in the 1970s (see Yankelovich 1974) that "the orientation of the campuses" was becoming a full-fledged ethos embraced by large sections of the population. This ethos spanned all classes, the wealthy and the poor alike.[2] Major political parties, particularly parties of the liberal orientation of each Western nation, have taken up many fringe-group concerns and certain aspects of the "new life" philosophy. Some ideas and norms of the new wave have become acceptable even among conservatives. Analysts (Yankelovich 1981; Inglehart 1977) even predicted that the new, postmaterialist ethic of self-fulfilment would replace the old value orientation, causing a complete restructuring of society. This, it is now evident, occurred only partially. These writers failed to notice that though attitudes were changing, seeds of conservative traditions remained, preserved in the consciousness of many promoters of the new morality.

The process was much more complex than the analyses of these writers suggest. In the 1930s, Schumpeter observed the coming of this rebellion. He also explained some of its causes. He wrote that the bourgeois are born with a developmental mentality. They cherish a nostalgia for the past but are also motivated by a longing for a prosperous (on the Right) or radiant (on the Left) future. One thing is sure, they are never satisfied with the present. During the late 1960s, impatience with the present became unbearable for a large section of the middle class. In addition, social and technological developments preceded and further advanced changes in the value orientation. Although in some sense engendered by changing values, the expansion of universities, large enrollments in social science departments, increases in the number of social science professors, the spreading influence of television, the greater determination of lifestyles by the market (supply) than by tradition (demand), development of the welfare and service systems in connection with the changing roles of the family, and the decline of other traditional institutions were also among causes of changes in values that occurred during this period.

The Academic, Mass Media, and Social Security Revolutions

The rebellion in the 1960s, whether in the United States, France, or elsewhere in Europe, was primarily a student and underclass rebellion. In the past, most young people inherited their parents' occupations and social roles. They lived lives similar to their predecessors. This changed after World War II. Channels of mobility became more open. In the 1960s, college or university degrees become attainable to many. Those who obtained a degree were offered good jobs and had only to wait for the good life to come. New universities mushroomed in all Western societies.[3] Enrollment sky-rocketed (see Table 14.1). In the foreword to *The Academic Revolution*, a fundamental study by Jencks and Riesman (1977), Trow writes:

> In the twenty years between 1948 and 1968, enrollments in American
> colleges and universities had grown from 2.6 million to 7 million. That
> growth was the product of two independent but mutually enforcing factors:
> a tremendous growth in the college age population and a rapid and
> uninterrupted trend among young Americans to continue their formal
> education beyond high school.

The number of university and college teachers during this "great leap
forward" increased in the United States from about 200,000 to 500,000.
Universities lost their prewar elitist character. Instead, they offered mass
education: skills and diplomas that launched individuals on their journey up
the career ladder. Parallel processes occurred in all Western societies. In the
1950s, those with university degrees experienced few difficulties in entering
promising careers. By the end of the 1960s, however, the situation had
changed.

The output of the educational system was too large. The rungs of
mobility ladders became clogged with aspiring candidates. Graduates with
degrees in management, engineering, or medicine did not experience
difficulties in entering promising careers. These graduates could expect
salaries twice as high as those offered in social sciences and arts. Students in
social science departments, sociology in particular, were in a different
situation. They believed themselves to be not only in pursuit of truth, but
catalysts of social justice. The two structures of education were producing
members of different parts of the new middle class. Those in management
and engineering were preparing themselves to join the corporate
establishment and, eventually, the conservative movement. Those in the
social science departments sought careers with the state and in social-
program organizations. Social scientists expected to become social
engineers, transforming the world into a more equitable and happy place for
all. Often, however, their talents, idealism, and commitment were rejected by
the market, by the system that many among them condemned as wrong.

Table 14.1.   Total Higher Education Enrollments

	1950-1951	1960-1961	1965-1966
Canada	88,000	175.800	326,800
France	178,000	274,263	505,278
Great Britain	170,000	286,218	431,132
Italy	240,718	284,341	424,717
Japan	399,900	711,618	1,085,119
Sweden	22,000	39,981	77,623
United States	2,296,592	3,610,007	5,570,271
West Germany	170,070	336,834	423,274

Source: Development of Higher Education 1950–1967 (Paris: OECD, 1971), 250.

Hence, many social science students and some of their faculty turned into militants of the rebellion. Lipset (1981, 1–2) writes: "In line with their voting record, faculty are much more likely than the public to identify their political orientations as left or liberal." Lipset illustrates these findings by a chart demonstrating that, in each of the more recent U.S. presidential elections, the percentage of social science faculty supporting the Democrats and Left, third parties was consistently more than 75 percent; among all faculty members generally, close to or more than 60 percent; and among the general electorate, about 40 percent (in 1964, 61 percent).

In the United States particularly, sociologists and other social scientists formed the vanguard of the rebellion in the 1960s, but the phenomenon was universal. Jencks and Riesman (1977, 37) point out that the "free universities" of Western European nations were breeding grounds of protest. The amassing of large numbers of young people in schools and universities, they note, resulted in an "increasing separatism of teenage culture" and produced conditions and an atmosphere within "which the basic legitimacy of adult authority has been increasingly called into question." In earlier decades of the twentieth century, entrepreneurs and organization men had molded the value patterns of the capitalist ethic. In the 1960s and 1970s, university students and graduates acquired the role of pattern-setter.

Widespread television viewing began in the 1950s. At present, 98 percent of U.S. and more than 80 percent of Western European homes are equipped with one or more TV sets. The "tube" remains on in those homes for an average of 6.5 hours per day. There is no need to prove the massive consequences of television-viewing. TV influences everything: what people eat, buy, believe in; whom they elect to Parliament or Congress; people's manners, lifestyles, and value orientations. Television informs, entertains, and educates. In democratic societies, television, like the press, is also expected to provide a stage for the advocacy of public issues. Some writers assume that television programming represents the interests and views of owners; interests in making money, perhaps; views, obviously not. More frequently, TV provides a forum for reporters and politicians. Television plays a part in the check-and-balance structure of the democratic political system. Thus, TV, with the exception of state-owned channels in France, inevitably takes a critical, if not an adversarial, position on everything that can be criticized: government policies, interest groups, corporate activities, and the economic and political systems. As a forum for any popular perspective in Western societies, television is predestined to disseminate novel ideas, lifestyles, and values, and the opinions of the cultural establishment, which as a rule tend to be liberal. A large percentage of television personnel inevitably comprises social science graduates. Entertainment in the spirit of the Protestant ethic or Catholic morality does not attract a large number of viewers. Considering television's value-shaping role, one inevitably concludes: Television reflected and promoted the new ideals of "the Silent Revolution," of postmaterialist and self-fulfillment values.

As access to a university education and television-viewing spread, so did welfare and social security systems (see Flora & Heidenheimer 1984). These systems should be regarded as the third principal vehicle of the new morality. Established with the ostensible objective of creating more equitable social conditions, and the less proclaimed objective of ameliorating the frustrations and hostilities of the poor and the deprived, these systems actually aroused significant discontent. No social program can ever satisfy the expectations of dependents or those disturbed by the conditions of the poor. The system may redistribute part of the national income to those suffering adversity and need, but it does not eradicate poverty and related social problems.

By the end of the 1960s, conditions had shifted radically. Instead of the Church in the role of supreme moral authority and the family and community in auxiliary roles providing moral guidance and a single value orientation for society, instead of the dominance of achievement-orientation advanced in the 1950s, a number of institutions—including the mass media, universities, political parties, single-issue movements, and the market—promoted differing information, ideas, values, and norms, advocated by a new, Left-oriented liberalism.

Three Realms of Society

Recent observations allege that during the twentieth century the overlapping spheres or realms of economic, cultural, political, and societal activities have become simultaneously progressively more articulated, differentiated, and separated. Some writers argue that politics, economics, "expressive symbolism" or culture, the spheres of public and of private action within primary and secondary groups, and other forms representing different aspects of the social structure, are not simply perceived as separate realms. Such realms now evolve independently, despite the fact that they are more centrally regulated than ever before.

Bell (1978, 10–13) writes that it is useful to think of contemporary society as comprising three, principally distinctive realms: the *technoeconomic*, the *polity*, and the *culture*. Each realm is set up to perform a different set of functions.[4] During the last two decades or so, he argues, the functions of these realms have differentiated to such a degree that they now lead autonomous existences within separate institutional structures. Each functional sphere promotes different demands on society as a whole, and on the individuals under its control. Some groups identify strongly with one realm, rejecting the others. As a result, society is torn apart by new kinds of conflicts and cultural contradictions. Currently, the normative and value structure promulgated by each realm conflicts with the objectives, normative patterns, and ethical rationales of the other two. Bell (12) writes:

> One can see thus that there are different "rhythms" of social change and that
> there are no simple, determinate relations among the three realms. The
> nature of change in the techno-economic order is linear in that the
> principles of utility and efficiency provide clear rules for innovation,
> displacement, and substitution. A machine or process that is more efficient
> or more productive replaces one that is less efficient. . . . But in culture
> there is always a *ricorso*, a return to the concerns and questions that are the
> existential agonies of human beings.

Thus, Bell observes, in culture, the new does not replace the old.
Rather, it adds to or enhances the eternally cherished and valued treasure of
civilization, in which both new and old coexist. Discussing the relevance of
these ideas to current developments, Bell states (15): "The principles of the
economic realm and those of the culture lead people in contrary directions."
He posits that the multiplication of contradictions and conflicts in Western
society is a direct result of growing discrepancies between economic needs,
the processes of political decisionmaking—which has its own autonomous
objectives sometimes more linked with the economic, sometimes with the
cultural establishment—and the proliferation of ethical and aesthetic
concerns and norms that usually reject the values of the economic and
political establishment, regardless of its position. Historically, the three
spheres of activity developed together, each performing different functions in
society. Today, the different interests developed within each realm divide
society and generate conflicts along vertical lines. Representatives of each
realm disagree over principles of ethics, income distribution, taxation, and
budgetary allocations; almost everything.

If Bell is correct, the outcome of these assumptions is even more
consequential. Contemporary U.S. and other Western societies must now
operate under the guidance of, at minimum, three dominant elites, each
representing different forces and advocating different values. Furthermore, it
follows that there is a culture of economics and a politics of economics,
which do not constitute the culture of culture and the politics of politics, and
so on. If that is true, it must be also true that, while each of the discerned
spheres generates its own value orientation and certain groups espouse norms
and standards from only one of the three realms, all three realms affect the
mentality and behavior of the majority. As a result, in different situations,
most people display a combination of elements representing different,
sometimes contradictory ideals, principles, and moral norms. People in
leading positions in the market (technoeconomic) realm tend to give priority
to economic objectives and frequently espouse conservative views; yet only
a minority are conservative in all regards. Many of those involved in the
corporate system adopt a liberal lifestyle, express liberal opinions on such
matters as abortion, smoking marijuana, or race relations, but remain

conservative on issues pertaining to social programs and the economy; the effect is that seemingly liberal publics in the United States, Great Britain, France, and West Germany elect conservative governments; and seemingly conservative publics elect a Democratic Congress or Socialist Parliament. People who operate primarily in the cultural realm tend to espouse liberal ethical principles; they believe welfare and other public services to be inadequate and they continually support increased social-justice efforts. They profess liberal ideals but, again, in certain activities or judgments they may remain quite conservative or libertarian. In the realm of politics, authorities too appear either vacillating or divided. Some politicians ally themselves with the cultural and liberal forces; others, with the economic and conservative forces. With the exception of a small minority of thoroughly convinced and dedicated conservatives and left-liberals, most individuals in contemporary society are more consistently pragmatic; in one situation, they lean toward liberalism, in another, they will choose a conservative approach. The personality of candidates and advocates of issues is very important; it frequently affects choices more than does the issue itself. The Western value orientation today is divided in a variety of ways, and over a multitude of issues; it never stops fluctuating. Principal divisions are between liberals and conservatives; in some nations, between liberals, conservatives, the new Left, the communist extreme, and the conservative extreme. A divided morality pervades contemporary society.

This interpretation reflects on only one of a number of aspects of the changing structure of conflict in contemporary society. Chapter 2 and 3 pointed out some other changes. Precapitalist societies stressed the importance of harmony and complementarity. More classical capitalist societies were divided primarily by the principal class conflict. The etatized, New State society is fractured by new conflicts of interest, by single-issue movements and processes of corporate intermediation, and in many other ways. Yet, the old cleavages have not disappeared. Thus, one should not perceive contemporary society from one perspective only. A complementary approach combining many interpretations better explains the current condition.

Value-Change in the 1970s

The value-orientation changes of the 1960s and 1970s are discussed in a large body of literature. Some books analyze survey and public-opinion-poll results on changing norms and opinions in the United States and Western Europe. Among this literature, the following works seem particularly important: *The New Rules* (1981) by Yankelovich; *The Silent Revolution* (1977) by Inglehart; *The Nine American Lifestyles* (1983) by Mitchell; and *The American Ethos* (1984) by McCloskey and Zaller. Books by Keniston

(1971; 1977), and *America's Quest for the Ideal Self* (1983) by Clecak represent a different kind of literature on the same theme. The latter express opinions, personal observations, and convictions developed during the writers' own participation in the "movement."

Yankelovich, Inglehart, and Mitchell employ diverging concepts, rely on different sources, and choose variant methods of analysis. Yet, they convey a similar message: The preoccupation in contemporary society is shifting from a tone focused on material well-being and the physical security of the family toward an engrossment with one's self, personal well-being, quality of life, and self-fulfilment. The contemporary individual wants to escape obligations and duties; wants to live, primarily, alone—but within a community of equal, like-minded others. The contemporary person is at the same time conscientious and concerned about social issues, but only as a volunteer. These people object to having obligations. They expect the state to be obliged. In this sense, these writers agree, the value orientation of Western societies is becoming increasingly liberal. This liberalism, however, differs from any liberalism of the past.

New Rules. In the late 1960s and early 1970s, Yankelovich focused on changes in students' attitudes. At the time, he referred to the phenomenon described earlier by Keniston as the formation of the "I–thou mystique," the "post-modern style," among other things. Keniston (1968, 275) writes that "post-modern youth is open, flexible, in motion," and in search of new forms. These youth consciously identify themselves as members of a generation, not of any group, class, institution, or other structure that might entail exploitative relationships with authority. The value orientation of this generation glorifies "nature" and the "natural" and instigates a quest for the "real" and the "sacred." "All values, roles, and organizations that impede or subvert person-to-person relationships are anathema" (279). This is confirmed in Yankelovich's earlier books, also.

Yankelovich probes public opinion on the subject and, in each of his new books (1972; 1974; 1981), reports on the advance of the process. In *The Changing Values on Campus*, Yankelovich (1972, 169–170) cites issues reflecting the changing values of the younger generation in the late 1960s and early 1970s.[5] In *The New Morality* (1974) he acknowledges that, while the central theme on campuses in the late 1960s was the search for self-fulfilment, in place of a conventional career, by the early 1970s, students had begun searching for self-fulfilment *within* a career. He observes that, though youth had become less interested and involved in radical political movements, rejecting society and its norms to a much lesser degree than before, they had nevertheless adopted the new kind of morality and sense of fairness. They espoused modified versions of the ideals and norms avowed by the counterculture. The new values had diffused widely throughout the college population, and their effects had spread beyond campuses. "In some categories (e.g. sexual morality) the spread continues unabated. In other categories (e.g. attitudes toward work) there has been a moderate reversal of earlier trends. The overall picture is one of a steady process of dispersion and assimilation of the New Values" (1974, 12).

In *New Rules*, the portrayal changes: The focus shifts from the proclaimed morality on campuses to the new ethical "rules" at large. Although Yankelovich does not state this explicitly, evidently he assumes that concerns have changed as well: Instead of demonstrating actively against the evil power structures of society, the carriers of the new morality worry about the deteriorating environment and social conditions, but are primarily concerned with their selves. Instead of advocating social change, they "experiment" with changing personal lifestyles. The equality of minorities, women, and homosexuals is now regarded as a moral norm. In *New Rules*, Yankelovich classifies the new morality as an ethic of self-fulfilment; in some ways, as an "ethic of commitment." Numerous surveys and interviews conducted across the United States reveal, he reports, a tremendous increase in preoccupation with self. In his own words (1981, 4–5): "By the late seventies, my firm's studies showed more than seven out of ten Americans (72 percent) spending a great deal of time thinking about themselves and their inner lives—this in a nation once notorious for its impatience with inwardness." Instead of asking, "Will I be able to make a good living?" "Will I be successful?" "Will I raise happy, healthy, successful children?" these individuals ask themselves, "How can I find self-fulfilment?" "How can I best realize the commitment I have to develop myself?" Most of these people, remarks Yankelovich, want some elements of familial success—marriage, family, material well-being, and respectability—but, at present, they are genuinely struggling to make room for greater personal freedom against institutional encroachments. Getting "more out of life" is their primary objective. He claims that the concern for personal growth that supplants the previously dominant ethic of self-denial will become even more dominant with the coming stages of the cultural revolution.[6]

Yankelovich feels that changes in lifestyles reflect the increasing tendency of the cultural revolution to establish patterns that secure greater personal freedom. Other researchers (Inglehart 1971; Marsch 1975; Mitchell 1983) isolate similar trends in Great Britain, West Germany, the Netherlands, and other Western societies, and compare these with trends in the United States. Their findings corroborate Yankelovich's observations.

The Silent Revolution. Inglehart (1977) analyzes the changing values of the Western public and the spread of what he calls "Post-Materialist values" in ten Western European nations and the United States. Like other writers, Inglehart (181–182) discerns three stages in the development of the value orientation of the West. Each stage involves the succession of a new set of "variables," which affect and dominate previous conditions: (1) religion, language group, and race are classified as "pre-industrial" variables, characterizing the ascriptive value orientation transmitted from generation to generation; (2) income, occupation, education, and labor-union membership are classified as "industrial" variables, engendering "a tendency for sons' occupations to resemble their fathers' but educational level and occupation aspirations reflect an achieved rather than ascribed status"; and (3) individual values—generated particularly by "post-economic needs," which are likely to take an institutional form but, when deeply internalized, cause a "long-term political cleavage"—constitute "post-industrial values"; they are (38) espoused most widely by middle class individuals. In eleven Western European nations surveyed by Inglehart, "the Materialist preponderance ranges from a ratio of about two to one to better than five to one. Western society remains predominantly Materialist. It is only among the youngest age-cohorts that the Post-Materialists are almost as numerous as the Materialists."[7] The postmaterialists, he notes (183) "are recruited mainly from the more affluent strata of society." Inglehart (290) expresses the belief that "with continued economic expansion one would expect the base of recruitment for Post-Materialist radicalism to expand." He relates the shift from old to new attitudes to the transition from industrial to postindustrial society. He discusses economic development, the expansion of secondary and higher education, the discontinuities in the life experiences of different age cohorts, and the inadequacy of existing institutions to meet new political needs; the spread of protest activity, the formation of new political movements, and the decline of nationalist sentiments as the "sources of change" in value orientation. Inglehart singles out two factors as particularly important: unprecedented prosperity and the absence of total war. According to Inglehart, economic and technological development, rising levels of education, and expanding mass communications, when combined with the absence of total war, are bound to cause changes in values, as manifested in the quest for self-realization, new lifestyles, the decline of social-class conflict, the "declining legitimacy of the nation-state," and the "rise of elite-challenging issue-oriented groups." Neither he nor Yankelovich connect these processes with changes in the structure of ownership in society, the emergence of mixed economies under bureaucratic management, or the establishment of state institutions that relieve individuals and families from certain traditional obligations, while rendering them dependent on state patronage and protection, under which the new rules and values can be pursued.

The Nine American Lifestyles. Mitchell (1983) distinguishes four principal groups in U.S. society. He subdivides them into nine lifestyles. He draws parallels between similar lifestyles of groups in the United States, France, Italy, Sweden, and West Germany (180). Income, education, age, and social standing, he concludes, determine the character of values and the lifestyles of different groups under contemporary conditions. He also maintains that the "value groups" and lifestyles reflect different stages of a developmental process. People change values and lifestyles as they advance in life, he writes. Those unable to advance in time beyond certain levels and lifestyles (survivors, sustainers, belongers) continue to live at lower stages of lifestyle development, while others move on and acquire more sophisticated value orientations. Some (the corporate-oriented in our terms) attain the lifestyles of emulators and achievers, others (liberal and culture-oriented) join the progressive I-Am-Me, experientals, or societally conscious lifestyle groups. Only a minority attains the highest-level, fully mature value orientation and lifestyle of the integrates, who fuse the other- and inner-directed value orientations into one. One third of the population, reports Mitchell—the largest group in U.S. society—still belongs to other-directed groups. But generally he affirms that: "we are turning inward." The "inward turned," "inner-directed" group, he writes, is not only growing among the middle classes but has now made its way to the upper strata and the power elite; it is quickly becoming the dominant group in U.S. society. In the meantime, 20 percent are classified as "inner-directed," 67 percent as "outer-directed," and 11 percent "need-driven," "survivors" and "sustainers." Those individuals who have completely embraced the new values are clearly the younger, better-educated elements. Mitchell anticipates an even greater percentage will turn inward and adopt what he calls "the lifestyle of societally conscious people" in the future.[8]

The American Ethos. It is interesting to compare *The American Ethos* (1984), by McCloskey and Zaller, with other studies, because this work offers an analysis of change in value orientation from a political science perspective; the other works were by sociologists. Also, McCloskey and Zaller discuss public attitudes toward the state and the market, which are relevant in the view of etatization theory. According to McCloskey and Zaller, the value orientation of Western societies has evolved around two conflicting traditions: the values and practices associated with the capitalist market economy and the theory and practice of democracy. They take particular interest in the contradictions emerging from the evolution of these traditions in the United States.[9] They discuss this theme by considering both public opinion and the opinion of those whom they call "opinion leaders" and "influentials"—i.e., individuals exerting wide influence in society—expressed in response to McCloskey and Zaller's questionnaires and found in a number of other sources, chiefly *Opinion and Values of Americans Survey, 1975–77* and Gallup polls.

McCloskey and Zaller write that the incompatibility between capitalist and democratic values in the bourgeois ethos, which has existed since this tradition emerged during the French and American revolutions, has recently become more evident and divisive (7): "Capitalism is primarily concerned with maximizing private profit, while democracy aims at maximizing freedom, equality, and the public good. From this difference, others flow." For some sections of the population, the values of capitalism are more dear; others attribute greater importance to democracy. Most people, however, combine the orientations, thus expressing conflicting opinions and desires. People in the United States, these writers posit, want capitalism but also want the welfare state and more democracy. It may be added that Europeans express similar conflicting desires.

According to the data assembled by McCloskey and Zaller: 17% of U.S. respondents considered themselves deeply religious; between 48% and 56% felt themselves fairly religious; 69% of the less sophisticated and 39% of the highly sophisticated believed that the best hope for the future of humanity lies in faith in God (26). Seventy-nine percent believed that prayers in schools should be permitted (31). Yet, more than 50% supported the freedom of atheists to make fun of God and religion, except in places of worship (28); between 89% and 97% claimed to believe in free speech for all, with no exceptions (37). Despite these figures, McCloskey and Zaller observe (42): "Intense feelings of religiosity . . . are associated with the desire for orthodoxy in political and social as well as religious affairs." While the general public has a low tolerance for left-wing or right-wing group ideologies, 77% of the opinion leaders are highly tolerant of left-wing radicals, and 55% of right-wing group ideologies (49). The U.S. population is still intolerant, write McCloskey and Zaller (55), of moral perspectives that differ from their own; half of the population still "hold conventional beliefs" on issues such as homosexual marriages, pornography, and the censorship of "obscene books." Still, people in the United States are portrayed generally (70–73) as champions of "equality." McCloskey and Zaller point out that 74% believe that teaching that certain people are better than others goes against the national idea of equality; 64% believe that, regardless of endowment or social rank, all individuals should be treated the same, and 98% say that everyone should have an equal opportunity to get ahead. Yet, "most Americans have tended to regard differences in wealth and status as evidence not of inequality per se, but of individual distinction, character and achievement." Thus (84), 78% affirm that, under a fair system, people with more ability should be rewarded with higher pay; 77% to 87% express the opinion that "our freedom depends on the free enterprise system" (110); and 84% agree that ownership of private property is crucial to economic progress (140). Twenty two percent consider public ownership of large industry a good idea, while 44% believe it is a bad one (102). "They worry about monopolies, excessive power and profits, misleading advertising, ruthless competitive practices, depression and unemployment." Thus, 82% express the opinion that "big business" has too much power. Seventy percent (91% of influentials) report that "we can do everything needed to get prosperity without changing the private enterprise system very much"; but many favor specific regulations, "to keep industry from becoming too powerful" and for a variety of other reasons.

McCloskey and Zaller compare responses from forty-four items on their democratic and twenty-eight items on their capitalism scale. They report (163) that "among those scoring high on the index of democratic values, 22 percent are high on the capitalist index; but among those scoring low on the democratic index, 84 percent score high on capitalist values—a difference of 62 percent points." Several chapters discuss and compare liberal and conservative ideologies. They report that 61% of "strong democrats" think government has not done enough, while 69% of "strong capitalism advocates" believe government has done more than enough, to help needy people improve their lives (283).

A Return to Traditional Values?

The ascendancy to power of Conservative leaders, Thatcher in 1979, Reagan in 1980, and Kohl in 1982, was perceived as a revolt against excessive regulation, bureaucratization, and, in Great Britain particularly, against excessive union power. Throughout Western nations, these events were interpreted also as a protest against the spread of permissiveness and liberal excesses, and as a return to traditional, conservative values.

The press reported that the pendulum of public opinion had swung back to the Right. Monetarist and supply-side theories were gaining influence in academic, government, and corporate circles. The credibility of neokeynesian and Marxist theories was waning. Militant religious fundamentalism, orthodox pro-family and anti-abortion movements, on the defensive for some time, began taking the offensive; their supporters grew in numbers. Traditions and traditionalism, which not long ago had been written off as outdated and absurd in a technologically advanced and permissive age, suddenly regained respect and became fashionable again.

In April and May 1981, the French paper *Le Monde* published a series of articles on work opportunities for young people in France, based on interviews obtained in *lycées, écoles de commerce, écoles nationales de perfectionnement*, and other schools and student residences. Among the responses of the young, one theme prevailed. As expressed by one young woman: "The thing is, you can't have everything. If I find a job, I'll ignore what I don't like, that's for sure. Working, having a job, that is the main thing." This view is quite representative of large numbers of young people in France, Great Britain, Canada, and the United States. "Young people put security before job satisfaction," concludes one of the authors in *Le Monde's* series. "Most French young people," writes another, "are forced to spend months, sometimes years, submitting to the humiliation of part-time employment." In 1981, forty-two percent of the young, aged sixteen to twenty-five, in France were unable to find their first job. These people look for work—any work. Few expect it to provide anything like self-fulfilment.

The new generation of students is mainly concerned about marks and career prospects; it is being seen as more conservative than in the past. A survey of freshman attitudes of 204,491 students entering college in 1986, compared with those who entered college in 1975 and 1985—undertaken by the University of California at Los Angeles and the American Council of Education and reported in the January 18, 1987 *New York Times*—indicates similar shifts of attitude among students in the United States. According to this survey, 55.7% of students entering universities in 1976 and 58.6% entering in 1986 expressed the opinion that "abortion should be legalized"; 48.8% in 1976 and 51.1% in 1986 felt that "a couple should live together for some time before deciding to get married"; 82.4% in 1976 and 78.0% in 1986 felt strongly that "the Government is not doing enough to control pollution"; 48.9% in 1976 and 21.3% in 1986 felt that "marijuana should be legalized"; 47.0% in 1976 and 52.2% in 1986 agreed strongly that "it is important to have laws prohibiting homosexual relationships"; 32.6% in 1976 and 25.4% in 1986 agreed strongly that "the death penalty should be abolished."

It is too early to conclude from this and other recent surveys that the new morality is now changing into a *new* new morality or that the ethic of commitment is metamorphosing into a morality of no-commitment. Certain trends, however, definitely differ from those anticipated by Yankelovich and other researchers a decade ago.

The sexual revolution is over, announced *Time* magazine in 1982. Weddings and births are on the increase, divorce is down. "Thesis, antithesis, synthesis, as Karl Marx said . . ."—exclaims Betty Friedan (1983, 35). "As our revolution converges on larger economic upheavals, I said, we must come to new terms with family and with work. Some didn't like my saying that."

A revitalized patriotism and nationalism have sprung up and spread throughout the United States, Great Britain, West Germany, and France. In 1983, the press carried many articles with such titles as "Patriotism is Back

Table 14.2.   Freshman Attitudes, 1987

Think it essential or very important	1976	1985	1986
To promote racial understanding	35.8%*	32.0	27.2
To be very well off financially	53.1	70.9	73.2
To help others in difficulty	63.1	63.4	57.2
To be involved in environmental clean-up	27.7	20.3	15.9
To develop a philosophy of life	60.8	43.3	40.6

* 1977

Source: New York Times, January 18, 1987. Reprinted with the permission of the *New York Times*

in Style." On TV, the world watched U.S. students kissing their home soil on returning from Grenada. Flags were raised on many occasions. Bumper stickers proclaiming "Proud to be American," appeared across the continent. In a telephone poll conducted by *The New York Times Magazine* ("Patriotism Pulse," December 11, 1983), involving 1,145 adults across the United States, 53% declared themselves very patriotic; 55% (62% of men) said they would rather risk the destruction of the United States than accept any risk of Russian invasion. In November 1983, 44% (in June 51%) thought, "you can trust the Government in Washington to do what is right"—compared with only 25% in a survey made by the University of Michigan in 1980. In an article interpreting these trends and the new mood in the United States, as he noticed it after a prolonged stay in Great Britain, Apple (1983) reflected on this "new stirring." Although there was not much agreement as to exactly what constituted patriotic or unpatriotic conduct, he wrote, people in the United States are nevertheless rapidly returning to patriotism: 36% of those who said they were patriotic explained it as appreciation of American freedom in general; 29% as appreciation of certain specific freedoms or of democracy; and 9%, as appreciation of other features of U.S. life, e.g. living standards.[10]

The Economist called 1984 "The Year of the Patriot," because of the patriotic outpourings during the 1984 Olympic games, the Republican and Democratic conventions in the United States, and manifestations of patriotism in other nations. It was everywhere. On the wave of patriotism bolstered by the British victory over Argentina in the Falkland/Malvinas Islands, Thatcher won a landslide victory in 1982, despite growing unemployment and mounting economic problems (Clemens 1983: 178, 182). Patriotism was a principal issue in the 1988 U.S. presidential election.

Today's youth have different values than the youth of a generation ago, writes Ladd (1984, 21). A larger percentage of college students believes that extramarital sex is generally wrong; a larger percentage (67% in comparison with 35% a decade ago) support the death penalty. A smaller percentage of today's young in the United States believes the nation spends too much on defense. Ladd concludes (21) that "*today's college population is at once more liberal and much more conservative than the college generation of the early 1980's*" (emphasis added). It is more mature and less idealistic. Ladd's article refers to Yankelovich's new, 1983 theory, which states that after the initial, widespread, and impulsive call for changes—primarily by the young, especially college students—some "sorting out" occurs. Eventually, "a new 'package' results, different from that obtained before the change began, but different, too, from the 'reaction' stage.

In this connection, it is worth mentioning Clecak's book, *America's Quest for the Ideal Self* (1983). Clecak explains what Yankelovich and others initially failed to notice. During all those years, he writes (327), when it seemed to shift toward the liberal-left stance, despite the persistence of

Democratic majorities in the Congress, society retained an underlying conservatism. Clecak further implies that the liberal-left innovations of that period reflected only impulses. Society changed only on the surface. This is not an entirely correct appraisal. Society has changed, perhaps not as much as Clecak would like it to have changed, but significantly nevertheless.

By the end of the 1970s, Clecak points out, the highly publicized quest for social equity and the restructuring of income distribution began to run into "transcending limits of all sorts": limits to economic growth; limits to institutions; limits to the state; limits to the generosity of individuals; limits to power at home and abroad. Partially as a result of its own dynamic and partially under pressure from a persisting conservative mood, the liberal-left quest evolved into a more authentic articulation, combining new liberal-left attitudes with society's conservative tradition. According to Clecak (328), "the conservative mood . . . did not subvert the search for fulfillment but rather allowed people to explore other factors implicit in the ideology of the quest."

Consensus and Discord

A new ethos is in the making in Western societies. No supreme authority, neither Church nor State, has fostered this new orientation; it emerged from societal practices, out of confrontations and conflicts, out of processes of etatization. The patterns of behavior and values comprising this orientation have sprung from new ideals of equity, reinterpreted traditions, and most of all from an emerging consensus over certain fundamental issues. The consensus, in turn, has influenced the selection of representatives to the U.S. Congress and to parliaments elsewhere and the advocacy of public issues in the media, thus advancing the new ideals in practice. Elements of this new consensus have already materialized in legal enactments; for example, in laws defining conditions of the welfare system and services maintained by the state, and the appropriation of budgeted funds for activities under these programs; laws protecting minorities, women, and homosexuals from discrimination. While certain elements of this new sense of equity have been widely accepted in all Western nations, other aspects of new programs are still regarded as controversial. The new consensus is molded by continuous intermediation involving the state and the multitude of interest groups in society.

One must be very circumspect in describing the makeup of this new consensus. Let us distinguish between the sphere of principles, in which a degree, frequently a high degree, of consensus exists, and the sphere of issues not regulated by any authority or degree of consensus. The first sphere is one of macrorelations; in other words, of creeds and rules determining the actions of governments and their representatives. The second is the sphere of the individual's private behavior. Few widely recognized and enforceable rules have been established for this sphere.

The basic elements of the new consensus can be formulated as follows:

1. Contemporary society shall function under both market requirements and under state control and regulation. The market or the state alone cannot provide adequate conditions. To what extent society should be ruled by the market and to what by the state shall be determined through intermediation and ongoing negotiations. No fixed formula is acceptable.

2. The state shall be headed by individuals elected in a democratic process. The rules of the democratic process shall be subjected to negotiation and intermediation.

3. The state shall maintain services expedient to the economy and the well-being of citizens. Civilized, democratic, and economically developed contemporary society is obliged to maintain a safety net of social and economic security and provide citizens unable to take care of themselves with certain basic life necessities. As discussed in Chapter 3, the scope of such services and welfare institutions, and the share of GNP expended on their maintenance, remains an issue of ongoing controversy.

4. People in contemporary society shall not be discriminated against because of their race, religion, ethnic origin, language, gender, or sexual orientation. The state shall maintain institutions that equalize the life chances of citizens through education and other equal-opportunity mechanisms. The actual dimensions of equality and equity shall remain open for intermediation and negotiation in each instance.

5. The state shall protect the natural environment on which the life and condition of all on the planet depend. The concrete aspects of this activity, as for instance reducing the effect of acid rain and closing nuclear-energy generating plants, shall be left open for continuing intermediation, negotiation, and electoral decisions.

A lengthy list of issues, moral norms, and values on which there is no consensus could be developed. I am limiting my discussion to a brief comment on consensus and continuing discords.

Through recognizing the market process as a fair procedure for the allocation of wealth and income, Western societies under etatization retain the consensus of the past. However, a new consensus, as outlined in the above points, has developed alongside the previous one. According to this new consensus, a portion of wealth, income, status, authority, and prestige is to be allocated by the state on behalf of society to different groups, regardless of market processes. While liberals believe that the new consensus has come to predominate over the old, conservatives argue that the earlier consensus must be respected as more obligatory. Since public attitudes shift from conservative to liberal, election results confirm ephemeral preferences.

Private Behavior

In a democratic society, the strength of an authority structure depends on the degree of its acceptance by the population and quality of the consensus it is able to generate to support its objectives. Yet, many writers have described contemporary Western society as normless; operating under the paternalistic authority of the seemingly omnipresent state that actually generates only tenuous consensus. The consensus outlined above reflects the condition in etatized societies maintained by the New State. Yet, many norms and values of the contemporary condition are not determined by any consensus.

Yankelovich, Inglehart, and other writers focused on self-fulfilment, self-realization, rejection of achievement, or postmaterialism as a principal norm of the emerging new morality. At last, they write, individuals are liberating themselves from the shackles of tradition.

What some perceived as a quest for self-fulfilment, the appearance of an ethic of self-commitment, postmaterialist morality, and liberation, others interpreted as hedonism, the spread of narcissism, decadence, and a resurgence of nihilism. Bloom (1987, 174–176) compares concern over the self with the ancient concern about the soul. He explains, "millennia of philosophizing about the soul had resulted in no certitude about it." Hobbes, he writes, first incited individuals, "Be yourself. . . . Feel!" Bloom writes that "throughout the whole tradition, religious and philosophic, man had two concerns, the care of his body, and the care of his soul, expressed in opposition between desire and virtue." He continues by discussing Machiavelli's, Hobbes', Locke's, and Rousseau's views on the matter. Things have changed: "The true self is not only good for individuals but provides a basis for consensus not provided by religion or philosophies." Bloom concludes (178):

> The ambiguity of human life always requires that there be distinctions between good and bad, in one form or another. The great change is that a good man used to be the one who cares for others, as opposed to the man who cares exclusively for himself. Now the good man is the one who knows how to care for himself, as opposed to the man who does not.

The shift in appreciation over concerns with the self has produced the great divide within contemporary culture. Lasch (1979, 31; 1975), scoffing at Tom Wolfe's interpretation of the new narcissism as a "third great awakening," agrees with Sennett (1978, 72) that contemporary "narcissism has more in common with self-hatred than with self admiration." Furthermore, Lasch points out that

> having surrendered most of his technical skills to the corporation, he [the contemporary individual] can no longer provide for his material needs. As the family loses not only its productive functions but many of its

reproductive functions as well, men and women no longer manage even to raise their children without the help of certified experts.

It is true that millennia of philosophizing about the soul failed to produce any certitude about its existence; but at least in the past, the soul was the property of individuals who were part of a religion, community, and family. Concern over the soul was thus a shared concern. With advancing capitalism, concern over the soul turned into a preoccupation with the ego. The quest for achievement, wealth, and power brought new meaning to life. In contemporary society, however, the individual can exist without the soul, family, or friends. He is left with the self vis-à-vis the state. The pundits cannot agree whether this is to be considered progress or degradation. As for individuals, they have to make their own decisions whether they are going to have a personal life geared only to self-fulfilment or to duties and obligations.

In the past, European societies were governed by the twin authorities of the monarchy and the Church. Although secular authority enacted laws and privileges, the Church reigned supreme in matters pertaining to standards of morality, values, and incumbent norms. The French, American, and other revolutions abolished this condition, separating the Church from the state. The state established itself as a secular authority, seeking approval for its legitimacy and legality through elections, not through the Church's recognition. The Church retained its traditional function as moral authority, but in a restricted manner and in an ever-declining role. Capitalism never stands still. In the market, expectations of gain—and not much else—determine the content of ideals, principles, norms, and formal and informal relationships, while fixed religious rules do not apply. Changes in the economic sphere and structure cause the normative and ethical structure to modify in step.

The state has taken it upon itself to legitimize secular ethics, including normative patterns not sanctioned by religious authorities, but the state still does not claim the function of supreme moral authority. Under etatization, the state not only maintains law and order within boundaries delineated by its sovereignty but also institutes and maintains the legal structure that regulates normative conduct in many aspects of life. Yet, legality and morality are separated: The first is the state's concern; the second is an individual's choice. Through tax bonuses, the state rewards those who donate money to public causes. Otherwise, it does not concern itself with the morality of its citizens. The mass media, especially television, performs an important normative role. But the media can hardly be regarded as a singular normative authority. Since in practice no authority regulates these affairs, morality has been subdivided into a public morality, for show, and private morality, which is nobody else's business.

Under these conditions, contemporary Western ethics are awash with every possible variety of philosophical belief and moral principle. "Anything goes" refers not only to the way people dress, but to personal relations on the job and in private, to sexual life, ideals, and value-striving. Like other commodities, certain ethical principles come and go, as fashion dictates. In accordance with need, style, mood, and taste, individuals are free to wear and profess any combination of ethical choices. Within the West's ethical agglomeration, certain values change drastically and fast, while others remain the same for a long period of time. What values people profess at any time is determined by many factors: technological trends, the individuals' dependence on the state, changing conditions at work, fashion, and, in certain instances, religion. Values change not only because individuals opt for new ones, but often because working and living conditions demand them.

There is a Russian saying: "In contemporary society, a man without a document is an insect. But an insect with a proper document is a big, big man." Of all factors affecting the contemporary mentality, bureaucratization seems one of the most consequential. Presently, at minimum half of the labor force holds jobs in bureaucratic structures, or positions which can be characterized as clerical. Virtually everyone plays a bureaucratic role to some extent. In his astute analysis of contemporary bureaucracies, Hummel (1977, 133–135) posits: "There is a distinct 'bureaucratic personality' that cuts across the various 'role identities' associated with different tasks and different office levels in different bureaucracies." He exaggerates when he states (45) that "bureaucracy replaces society." Yet, though this is an exaggeration, he at the same time conveys well what is widely felt about the direction of societal development. Work affects the family condition in any historical time. At present, both men and women spend most of their working time outside the family, much more than in the past. For some people, work is the only context of social interaction. For most people, work means a job in some type of bureaucracy or quasibureaucracy. The attitudes developed at work are brought home. The Protestant and similar inner-directed ethics that evolved into other-directed ethics are now changing not only into the postmaterialist ethic of self-fulfilment as characterized by Yankelovich and others, but into the bureaucratic mentality as described by Hummel.

Like a geological structure, the current ethos comprises a number of metaphoric value-strata, partially melded into a new amalgam of values and partially preserved in their original content as they were developed in the past. In this sense, the contemporary ethos of Western societies retains residual elements of previously dominant value orientations: the Protestant and other Judeo-Christian ethics, nationalistic and parochial loyalties and animosities, market and corporate morality, concerns advocated in the 1960s, elements of the new postmaterialist morality, and a selection of foreign additions promulgated by groups attracted to foreign cultures and religions.

On the whole, society is becoming more liberal. In matters of moral or ideological principles, some people remain conservative, more strictly traditional, while others take a liberal stand. But because the public takes a more conservative stand on some issues and is more liberal regarding other issues, public opinion swings back and forth. In matters pertaining to work and family, economic and social conditions determine individual practices and lifestyles more than do any grand value-orientation ideals propagated by institutions of the Left, liberal, or Right establishments. In daily life, people employ a combination of normative pronouncements, on a practical basis, to rationalize their actions. At the level of practicing values, the lines of division are frequently blurred. Consequently, lifestyles range from the strictly traditional to capitalist to postmaterialistic. Such a society must have, and does exhibit, a fragmented, oscillating morality. Such a society necessarily encompasses several ideological camps. Rather than be regarded as transient, this situation must be recognized as reflecting normal and typical conditions under etatization.

CHAPTER FIFTEEN

Is Etatization Inevitable?

Historical Inevitability: The Concept

Must capitalist society *inevitably* change into a state-controlled and state-regulated, that is, an etatized society?

St. Augustine, Vico, Kant, Herder, and Hegel attempted to discover if there is any pattern or meaning to history as a whole. They claimed that there is and designed speculative schemes that attempted to discover the order in which history developed in the past and in which, in their opinion, it would develop in the future. Nash, in his Introduction to *Ideas of History* (1969, xiv–xv), discusses these ideas. He begins by discerning two types of this philosophy—speculative and critical—as distinguished by Broad. He then discusses Vico's concept of divine providence; Hegel's vision of history as the spirit's self-realization; Toynbee's formula of challenge and response; Spengler's hypothesis that each culture follows a determined biological course of birth, growth, and decay; and foremost, Marx's theory of economic determinism; concepts that have significantly influenced our contemporary understanding of history. One cannot imagine contemporary philosophy or a historical analysis of economic, societal, and cultural development of modern societies devoid of an analytical frame derived from the works of these thinkers. Furthermore, concepts and concerns developed in these works can now be regarded as constituting an important element of the Western value orientation. The very same ideas and theories—especially of historical determinism—have, however, been strongly repudiated by many scholars claiming to defend the values of Western civilization. Berlin (1954, 13–15) is one who has argued against historical inevitability, in a trenchant rebuttal of the determinist philosophy of history:

> The notion that history obeys laws, whether natural or super-natural, that every event of human life is an element in a necessary pattern has deep

metaphysical origins: infatuation with the natural sciences feeds this stream, but is not its sole nor, indeed, its principal source. In the first place, there is the teleological outlook whose roots reach back to the beginning of human thought. It occurs in many versions, but what is common to them all is the belief that men, and all living creatures and perhaps inanimate things as well, not merely are as they are, but have functions and pursue purposes. . . . To understand is to perceive patterns. To offer historical explanations is not merely to describe a succession of events, but to make it intelligible; to make intelligible is to reveal the basic pattern; not one of several possible patterns, but the one unique pattern which by being as it is, fulfills only one particular purpose, and consequently is revealed as fitting in a specifiable fashion within the single "cosmic" overall schema which is the goal of the universe, the goal in virtue of which alone it is a universe at all, and not a chaos of unrelated bits and pieces. . . . The attitude is profoundly anti-empirical. . . . We are plainly dealing not with an empirical theory but with a metaphysical attitude which takes for granted that to explain a thing—to describe it as it "truly"' is—even to define it more than verbally, that is, superficially—is to discover its purpose.

In Berlin's opinion this attitude, as any other form of genuine determinism, entails eliminating individual responsibility. Norling (1970, 99) agrees, but claims also that this attitude contains devastating implications for the future of democracy. Other critics have opined that theories of historical inevitability are based on ill-founded generalizations, and that the thinkers advocating historical inevitability are more concerned with ideological objectives than with discovering the meaning of history. Revolutionaries perceive revolution as inevitable; conservatives promote approbation of the status quo as brought about by providence—the world spirit (*Weltgeist*)—that makes use of heroes of history and of the universal state, said to be the only reality.

The view represented here is less extreme. Neither the idea of historical inevitability nor all criticism of it is completely acceptable. It seems that understanding history as a manifestation of historical inevitability, and other related theories assuming that history represents the materialization of certain general laws directed toward definite objectives, can be compared to the way certain religious concepts are perceived. People believe or do not believe in religious concepts regardless of evidence or logic. These are not concepts that can be proved or disproved by empirical evidence or logical argument. They are important not for what they declare, but for the inspiring influences they exert.

Many philosophers of history not only claim to have discovered the laws of history, but also to have distinguished stages and trends of historical development that support their visions. This is most important for the analytical interpretation of history and of processes of societal development. Such philosophers teach us to view historical development not just as a chain of events, but as structured processes that can be meaningfully interpreted.

History should not be regarded as an organismic development, however. Even if we were to believe in repetitive patterns in the past, how could we be sure the past would inevitably recur in the future? Such theorizing is speculative and must remain hypothetical. On the other hand, however, it is quite obvious that to a degree our behavior is determined by past and present situations, by the environment and economic conditions, by our beliefs and the beliefs of other people whom we imitate or who imitate us, by our culture, and by our objectives. We cannot predict what actually will happen, but we can study these factors of our condition and assume that if known factors continue their interplay, the consequences will in all probability be the same as those previously experienced or logically flowing from known development processes. At the same time, we must remember that in certain regards, each event is unique, as it is repetitive in others.

In other words, at each juncture of historical events, people have many options. Their actions can be explained by reference to traditions, culture, economic conditions, aspirations, and current ideological and ethical trends. Their course of action has certain causes, and can be explained—though not as a result of a priori historical inevitability. One can envision only the probability of events should given trends continue in a condition comprising the same factors. We can influence development, but we cannot produce or even discover historical inevitability. This book expresses some opinions as to what could happen. Principally, however, it is a study of what is happening and why. It is on the grounds of such an analysis, not on the assumption that an existing stage of development must inevitably lead into a specified other, that we can distinguish a new stage in societal development. It is on the basis of the study of continuity and acceleration of current trends of development that this book argues that a new, postcapitalist condition has begun to appear in Western societies. Of course, I do not know whether this development shall continue. In this sense, this study does not postulate historical inevitability.

Classical Marxist theory asserted that societal development begins in the sphere of economic organization—the base—and then continues in all other spheres of societal organization—the superstructure. Lenin, Trotsky, Stalin, and other Russian Marxists amended this theoretical and ideological maxim after the revolution. They claimed that in certain circumstances, such as Russia's, development may begin with changes in the superstructure, with, for example, the institution of a new political regime and a new value system introduced by the party, and then cause growth in the economic base. In spite of the fact that they recommended applying the theory "upside down," they still argued that the general rule as established by Marx is correct.

A different view is represented in this book. First, I follow Schumpeter, Perroux, and certain other theorists in reserving "growth" for processes engendered by evolution. I use "development" primarily to characterize processes organized by authorities in their effort to attain certain objectives.[1]

Second, I assume that societal development could be initiated in any sphere of societal activity, not necessarily only in the economic sphere. In certain circumstances, technological development or economic change is more visible and seems more to determine the course of events; in others, changes in value orientation or political organization seem to be the determinants. The beginning and the end of such development—the causes—can never be pinpointed with great accuracy. All that is certain is that rapid changes in one sphere cause changes in other spheres.

Developmental processes within societies tend to be uneven; they can be gradual, less or more rapid, disruptive and violent, or uneventful.[2] At a certain point, changes, not causing significant consequences, begin to cumulate rapidly. Societal development turns into societal transmutation when a new kind of society begins to emerge within the old, still-existing condition. Usually, such shifts coincide not only with the appearance of many technological and economic innovations, but also with new modes of thought, worldviews, appreciation of world relations, and interpretations of moral standards; such novelties within existing old structures become, in some instances, causes for political upheavals, rebellions, and revolutions. Subsequently, a fresh concept of social justice and a novel normative standard begin to prevail. New forms and themes of artistic expression appear. Eventually, it is realized that an era has ended, and that a new kind of society has emerged. This was the case for the emergence of capitalism and its eventual transformation to a more mature, late form. This is also the case for the current transformation of capitalist societies into etatized societies. While societal transmutations are themselves inevitable, their eventual outcome cannot be predicted.

The societal transmutation that eventually produced capitalism began in medieval Europe, finally exploding into the English, French, and other political revolutions. The *ancien régime*, with its system of privileges for the aristocracy and nobility, was abolished by revolutionary acts. The new society, which granted citizenship to all, was instituted. Subsequently, the socioeconomic structure of capitalist society and various systems of democracy were established and developed. Marx attributed a great deal of importance to this transition. He studied it thoroughly, but principally with one idea in mind: to transform the explication of this evolution into an element of his general historiosophical theory of societal development and to demonstrate the inevitability of revolution and transition to socialism. In Marx's words, repeated by Lenin (1960, 27: 89) and numerous other writers:

> For the bourgeois revolution, which arises out of feudalism, the new economic organizations are gradually created *in the womb* of the old order, gradually changing all the aspects of feudal society. The bourgeois revolution faced only one task—to sweep away, to cast aside, to destroy all the fetters of the preceding social order [emphasis added].[3]

The whole argument of the *inevitability* of the forthcoming socialist revolution hinged on this. Marx reasoned that if revolutions, and particularly bourgeois revolutions, were indeed inevitable, then a new revolution is also inevitable. Then, "the contradiction between socialized production [as it occurs in big, corporate-owned enterprises] and capitalist appropriation manifested . . . as the antagonism of proletariat and bourgeoisie" is certain to produce the revolution that will transform capitalism into socialism.[4]

I see contemporary Western societies in the midst of a process of growth and, more recently, a process of societal transmutation and development that is bringing about the new, etatized society. I feel that the change now occurring is so consequential and transformative that the society it is generating, though retaining some elements of the capitalist structure out of which it developed, is no longer strictly capitalist. More precisely, it is becoming less and less capitalist and more and more a new type, not anticipated in the past. Most theorists have become so accustomed to the idea that capitalism leads to socialism that they have difficulty accepting the idea that capitalism is metamorphosing in another direction. They assume, therefore, that if it is not socialism, it must still be capitalism, though of a different kind. We are analyzing changes, the full significance of which it will only be possible to understand in the future, retrospectively. I think, nevertheless, that changes that have occurred in the last two decades have attained a magnitude significant enough to make it worthwhile to consider that they have produced a societal system different not only from that of the nineteenth century, but also from that which is called modern capitalism.

The emerging society may retain some institutions and socioeconomic relations of the past. More important, it has a different economic structure than that which existed forty years ago. It has a different system of ownership rights and many new institutions that play more important roles than do those old institutions that persist. It retains the market, but it has also a redistributive system maintained by the state. It still is divided into classes, but it is also a society in which, as Schmitter, Lehmbruch, Offe, and others affirm, interest groups engage in intermediation instead of becoming more involved in class wars. It is a society fragmented by multiple, overlapping antagonisms, which also produce linkages, cohesion, and, increasingly, a growing web of intercessions and negotiations determining the status and life station of everyone vis-à-vis everyone else, every group vis-à-vis every other group and vis-à-vis society as a whole. In addition, it has a new value orientation, normative structure, and a new type of social stratification. Etatization is *not* a result of historical inevitability. It occurs because governments develop certain institutions and relationships, which we chose to call the New State. The process differs from country to country. Nevertheless, the tendency is similar, and everywhere we see a new kind of power elite incorporating the old one, dominating the society, and developing its new identity and interests.

It has been observed that societal and civilizational transmutations result from numerous overlapping "revolutions"—economic, technological, cultural, scientific, ethical, religious, or sociopolitical. These overlapping "revolutions," wrote Nelson (1968, 162–163; see also 1972), tend to generate "new rationales, systems, structures of reasons, explanations, procedures establishing requirements in respect to truth, virtue, legality, fittingness." During transmutation periods, new legitimacies and legalities appear in rapid succession. The socioeconomic order changes quickly.

The Quest for Social and Economic Security

At the end of World War II, Europe was in ruins. Forty to sixty million had died on the battlefields, in bombardments, gas chambers, concentration and deportation camps, or from starvation and sickness. Industries were destroyed; the economic framework was shattered. Many cities in Central and Eastern Europe, and other battle areas were reduced to vast heaps of rubble. Agriculture was devastated; Western Europe could barely produce one-third of its prewar output. Without the aid provided by the United Nations Relief and Rehabilitation Administration, Europe would most probably have suffered massive food shortages, and perhaps, widespread starvation. Coal mines, which had been prewar Europe's main source of fuel, stood inundated by the withdrawing German troops. Most bridges and utility installations had been blown up. Millions of homeless and jobless Europeans wandered across the continent, some eastward, others westward, in search of shelter and a new life. Among them were numerous former concentration camp prisoners, people deported by the Germans from their homeland, and many who could not return to their native countries because of new boundaries or new political regimes. The entire population of what had been eastern Germany and became part of Poland, and from areas incorporated into the Soviet Union, moved westward. Great Britain, the only European nation that had succeeded in defending itself against German invasion, faced, as a result of enormous war expenses, bankruptcy. It lost its empire and, amid the rubble, in a sense lost itself; it did not know how to continue as one postwar European nation, equal to others.

Governments of Western Europe had an immense task: to rebuild destroyed roads and bridges; to restore and build new industries; to help labor camp survivors and army veterans start a new life; to resurrect the market. For the first time in the history of capitalist nations, the state undertook a massive and concerted effort of reconstruction and modernization. In postwar conditions, only governments could undertake these new functions; no one else in Europe had the means or the authority required. Such a role had been anticipated by neither nineteenth- nor early twentieth-century philosophers of history. At the time, the state's new role was a necessity, but it was not a historical inevitability, predetermined by any historical law.

In many instances, the first act of Western European governments was to nationalize particular industries. The reasons, as was discussed, differed. The French government nationalized Renault and certain other industries in retribution for their owners' cooperation with the Nazis. In other instances, industries were nationalized because owners refused to reconstruct. In still others, as in Great Britain, nationalization aimed to prevent widespread unemployment. In Austria, Karl Renner, the popular Social Democratic prime minister of the postwar government, embarked on a wide nationalization program (banks, heavy industry, the Danube Steamship Company, etc.), in order to prevent the Soviet Union, then occupying parts of Austria, from confiscating enterprises on the ground that they were former Nazi property. Later, (Toch, nd) nationalization (*Vergesellschaftung*) was advanced by unions and social democrats as a way of introducing elements of socialism. In Italy, the Christian Democratic government, wanting to raise its nation's development to a level equal to that of other nations of Europe and in the absence of major private corporations, assigned this task to five state-owned companies. In addition to postwar nationalization schemes, some Western European governments inherited, from before the war, some state-owned industries, mostly in the service sector—railroads and utilities, for example.

Some politicians saw nationalization as a move toward socialism; others felt it to be merely necessary to induce faster reconstruction and other development. People realized that national prosperity, and, in some instances, economic survival, depended on foreign trade. Only large, multinational corporations can play an important role in international markets in our times. Thus, all European governments began to recognize their obligation to support and develop state-, mixed-, and privately owned megacorporations capable of winning international markets. New ministries, departments, and administrations were established to run the newly developed state-owned sector of the economy, to encourage international trade, and to manage the national economy in general. People hoped there would be no more wars. Some saw the military as redundant, while others argued for a better-armed military to protect peace. And everyone feared the return of the prewar depression more than any threat of a new war.

In spite of massive destruction, economic reconstruction advanced quickly. Five years after the process began, around 1950, instead of the predicted return to prewar depression, the economies of Western Europe were not only restored but raised to an unprecedented level of prosperity. By the end of the 1950s, Western Europe's economic output was one-third higher than prewar levels. As a whole, the twelve leading Western industrialized nations (the United States, Great Britain, West Germany, France, Italy, Sweden, Norway, Denmark, Belgium, the Netherlands,

Switzerland, and Canada) achieved, during the 1950s, a 3.5–4-percent annual increase in productivity. This was twice the growth rate as the average for the whole of the period from 1913, just before World War I, to 1950.

The extraordinarily rapid increases in output per worker were accompanied by mounting labor demands. Unemployment was practically nonexistent. Toward the end of the 1950s, many Western European nations began to experience labor shortages; they eventually brought in workers from North Africa, the Middle East, less-developed areas of Sicily, and Spain. A combination of factors—the large flow of funds under the Marshall Plan, private U.S. investments, credit made available by Western European governments to the private sector, full employment, and developing international trade—helped to create conditions under which the demand for new consumer goods, new industries, and new investments kept growing, and kept generating newer demand for development. Pachter (1975, 277–278) writes:

> Every problem was turned into a new start, every drawback into an asset. .
> . . Demand was likely to exceed supply for some time to come. . . . By
> 1960, many countries produced twice as much as before the war, and
> consumers had 50 per cent more goods and services at their disposal than
> on the best prewar days.

It was called *Wirtschaftwunder* in Germany, *miracolo economica* in Italy. In Great Britain, with a relatively lower growth rate than elsewhere in the West, Harold Macmillan announced the 1957 election with the call, "We have never had it so good". Most people expected things to become even better. Not only was income per capita climbing, but every wage earner felt that year by year, month by month, he or she could afford more. European and U.S. lifestyles changed drastically. Western nations were labeled consumer, affluent, achievement-oriented societies. Was this historically inevitable? No, but it happened; and it happened while, in all nations, government increasingly involved itself in new economic activities. The tremendous economic recovery and success can be attributed to the achievement orientation, to the then-prevalent spirit of modernization, to the advantages of Western democracy, to "the American challenge," to various other causes. Nearly every working family had a car, a television set, a telephone, a washing machine, a refrigerator, and other appliances that had been luxuries in the prewar era.[5] People took vacations, enjoyed only by the rich in the recent past. "It has now," writes Shonfield (1965, 66), "come to be taken for granted, both by governments and by the capitalist countries, that each year should bring a noticeable increase in the real income per head of the population."

This, however, was not enough. People in Western Europe wanted to make sure their jobs would last, no matter what. They wanted to assure themselves a steady income, despite temporary unemployment; they wanted pensions after retirement. They wanted access to the best available health care, while ensuring that its costs would not deplete their savings. They felt obliged to help the less fortunate. They wanted a new security system that would reduce and eventually eliminate poverty, since poverty was a plausible cause for the social unrest feared by a large part of the middle class. The idea of a public educational system, which would make education accessible to all, was also popular; such a system could provide equal opportunity for even the underprivileged and improve the skills of workers. The middle class was ready to pay an affordable price for all these programs.

The idea of a welfare system had appeared in various European nations during the second part of the nineteenth century. In 1883, Bismarck had announced a series of enactments introducing compulsory sickness insurance and an old-age-pension scheme for workers. This program was intended to win over supporters of socialist programs. During the Victorian era in Great Britain, initiatives had been launched promoting public assistance programs for the poor. At first, such programs were not very different from those of early charity institutions, but eventually such endeavors evolved into new forms. In 1911, the Liberal government in Great Britain passed the National Insurance Act, providing workers with assistance in times of sickness, accidental injury, and, to a limited extent, unemployment. Both employees and employers were obliged to contribute to the system, which was also partially financed by the state. In 1925, the U.S. government adopted a compulsory old-age-and-survivors-insurance scheme. Later, during the Great Depression, it created programs to assist the unemployed, the poor, and the starving. During the late 1930s, full employment became a popular objective. But initiatives to enact full-employment legislation were undertaken in Great Britain, the United States, and other nations only after World War II. Franklin Roosevelt set a double task for his government: to save the capitalist system and to assist those most affected by the disasters of the depression. The U.S. Congress passed the Social Security Act in 1935. Agencies were established to implement its objectives: the Federal Emergency Relief Administration, whose task was to transfer funds for unemployment relief and other assistance to the states; the Civilian Conservation Corps, which involved the young unemployed; the Tennessee Valley Authority, which helped develop rural areas along the Tennessee River and built electricity plants, dams, and channels; and the Home Owner's Loan Association, which loaned money to home owners unable to pay their mortgages. New old-age, survivors, health-insurance, unemployment, welfare, educational, and family-assistance programs appeared and expanded in the 1960s in all Western nations.

Lord Keynes, who in the late 1930s published his highly acclaimed work, *General Theory of Employment, Interests and Money*, became involved in setting up prototype systems of economic management to control unemployment and poverty. He believed that the government should create conditions facilitating the growth of consumption and the expansion of business activities in the private sector and, if necessary, create work in public enterprises. To implement this, he recommended day-to-day state regulation of the economy. Keynes was not popular with governments, but he was respected by a large circle of fellow economists who, in turn, influenced those in decisionmaking positions in government. Among politicians, many who did not fancy the man liked what was then called Keynesian economics. "The economic collapse of the early 1930s undoubtedly made possible the second World War," writes Paul Johnson (1983, 659). "In the aftermath, Western statesmen earnestly sought guidance to prevent this pattern recurring. The result was the Keynesian age." Johnson explains that, in a letter to the *New York Times* in 1933, Keynes recommended increasing national expenditure, financed by loans, to fight such social disasters as massive unemployment. Among other postulates, Keynesian economics recommended large spending even at a cost of deficits, as good politics, in instances when such spending would increase consumption, enhance economic stability and growth, and produce low—close to zero—unemployment.

Early in the 1950s, conditions were ripe for a major restructuring of the social and the economic conditions of Western European nations. Some experts perceived this restructuring as implementing elements of socialism; others, as a natural extension of developing democracy and equal opportunities; still others, as implementing sound Keynesian programs. Eventually, during the 1950s and 1960s, all Western governments adopted what then were believed to be Keynesian principles of regulating unemployment and inflation. The idea of the Philips curve was developed; economic stability and development were guarded and developed accordingly. Tongue's (1974, 3) view represents the opinions of the majority of economists at that time. He wrote that though the science of economic forecasting had not progressed to the point where it would be possible to employ it in "fine tuning" the economy in every detail—to make it grow just enough to absorb the growing labor force and to produce just enough to satisfy market demand—economists had, finally, nevertheless mastered the mechanisms of economic regulation and control to the extent that they could declare, "our economic future is, in fact, in our hands and need not be ruled by the unseen hand of destiny which forces us this way or that whether we will or no." Keynes argued that conditions must be molded by the state. He urged government intervention and increased government spending to combat social problems. Keynesianism was adopted also at the international level. Keynes initiated institution of the World Bank and the International Monetary Fund to start solving worldwide problems. And neokeynesian economists later widened expectations of the state in economic affairs. The government was also to maintain equilibrated economic growth by ensuring that all the variables of the economic condition develop at the same pace.

The extension of services, education, and various social welfare programs in all European nations was initially seen as a mere expansion of social schemes enacted earlier in the century. Under conditions of increasing economic prosperity, it seemed only fair to widen existing programs and to introduce many new ones. The issue of affordability did not arise until the late 1970s.

In the meantime, the Cold War erupted. It is shortsighted to view the Cold War as simply an exercise in ideological warfare, a competition for influence over the world. It was also a competition in which governments of capitalist and communist nations competed to prove whose system could produce the best way of life; the market or the planned economy. Kennedy, in his inaugural address, proclaimed: "I believe that Americans are ready to be called to greatness." Greatness meant having more freedom, opportunity, achievement, modernity, and prosperity than any other nation, and that each citizen could share in these virtues. The United States had achieved the highest standard of affluence in the world, the greatest military might, and advanced space programs. It prided itself on being a nation within which every individual had a chance "to make it." It was ready to lead the rest of the world in attaining the same prosperity, freedom, and equality. Khrushchev challenged the United States and announced that, within fifteen years, the people of the Soviet Union would enjoy a higher standard of living than that of U.S. citizens. He was one of the last Russian leaders who sincerely believed in the ideals of the revolution. He told his advisers that socialism was pointless, unless it produced for the Soviet worker better conditions than those that U.S. workers enjoyed under capitalism. The United States was prosperous, but 15–20 percent of its people still lived in poverty. After World War II, to escape poverty in the South, poor Blacks moved in large numbers to the Northeastern states to look for work. However, this was a time of rapid technological modernization. The availability of jobs for unskilled laborers was declining. Theirs was a new kind of emigration; they missed out on the famed and prosperous United States. Instead, they met with "New Poverty," as it was later to be called.

Kennedy's and Johnson's governments developed economic policies based on Keynesian precepts. Taxes were cut to stimulate consumption and increase investment. Nevertheless, millions of U.S. households still depended on welfare. The United States could not become the "Great Society" it aspired to unless it became great for the poor, the deprived, and the victims of discrimination, as well for the middle class. The United States was already spending billions on the war in Vietnam. Now, Johnson declared another war on "poverty and racial injustice." This war proved to be even more costly. Carroll and Noble (1979, 395) observe:

> While federal expenditures increased at the rate of 8 percent a year, rising from $37 billion in 1943 to $246 billion in 1972, state and local expenditures increased at a rate of 10 percent a year, leaping from $18

billion in 1948 to $180 billion in 1972. In the four years between 1967 and 1971, state taxes increased on the average of 67 percent and local taxes by 50 percent. [In Canada and West European nations, they are close to double that.] Laboring under the burden of increasing inflation, the federal government ran deficit budgets every year after 1964 with the exception of one.

The recognition of the new poverty in the United States was the first major symptom that all of the West had begun to face big problems. Discrimination against minorities in the United States, Great Britain, and France was discovered next. Poverty, discrimination against minorities, crime, and other ills existed before; now they have been recognized as social problems to be dealt with by the state. After years of developing various "throwaway" habits, the prosperous Western societies discovered, in the late 1960s and early 1970s, the many evils of pollution and destruction of the natural environment. For twenty years or so, the GNP of the United States and nations belonging to the Organization for Economic Cooperation and Development had grown at an average annual rate of 2.5–4 percent; Great Britain's at an average 2–3 percent. This steady growth had engendered the prosperity of the 1950s and early 1960s. In the mid-1970s, however, annual growth rates dropped to between 0 and 2.5 percent and, occasionally, below. Demands for funds from social, health, educational, and defense programs, and for expanding government services, tended to grow independently and, frequently, at a faster pace than national GNP and GDP and the state's ability to procure revenues. Economists still did not know how to correlate these factors or how to run an economy in trouble.

Faced with continually increasing demands for entitlements, governments of most Western nations were inclined to impose higher taxes. Such actions, however, were the exact opposite of what Keynesian principles prescribed. As businesses were forced to pay higher taxes, they, in turn, tried to raise prices; thus, the stagflation spiral of the 1970s and early 1980s was set in motion. The quadrupling of oil prices in 1973, and the increase in oil prices in 1979, also contributed to rapid inflation. Under conditions of high inflation, workers demanded raises, at the same time, they consumed less. Middle-class entrepreneurs were forced to give up and lay off employees. In often-desperate attempts to increase revenues and prevent sudden eruptions of widespread unemployment, many states nationalized more and more industries and began more actively to regulate the economy.

The story is well known. What was originally intended as merely an improvement of established capitalist conditions and a commitment to greater equity evolved into a complex system of etatization—the most recent stage of Western societal growth and development. The prosperity of the 1960s metamorphosed into the stagflation of the 1970s. Simultaneously, the euphoria over modernity, growing prosperity, and rising standards of living, prevalent in the 1950s and 1960s turned into widespread dissatisfaction with materialistic aspects of life; disillusion with a seemingly pointless rat race, a deteriorating environment, and a host of other problems; and frustration over the insufficiency of material conditions. Two extreme positions can be argued in view of these events: One can claim that this metamorphosis occurred as a consequence of etatization and corporatization; or that etatization in fact diminished or softened the deleterious character of certain inevitable social and economic transformations.

The 1970s and early 1980s differed from the 1950s and 1960s in many regards. The earlier two decades were years of growing prosperity; the later two brought stalemates and stagflation. The 1950s involved reconstruction and recovery; the 1960s and 1970s expanding ctatization. To these observations, one may add that the style and content of political life changed over those decades. During the 1950s and 1960s, electoral races tended to shape up as a competition between two or more not fundamentally different teams. Each offered to conduct the business of governance with a somewhat different style, but not in the interest of different classes or as representatives of distinct values. Ideological differences between parties became blurred rather than exacerbated. They also became less significant to the electorate. This was the time when Bell published his famous and controversial *The End of Ideology*. Many writers advanced also the concept of convergence between the West and the Soviet Union.

At the end of the 1960s, ideological differences began to accumulate and concentrate around one central issue, which has continued to divide societies ever since: state control and regulation, and redistribution of wealth. During the 1970s and 1980s, ideological divisions over this issue among parties widened. At present, they often seem unbridgeable. In the 1950s and 1960s, after the war, people wanted more stability and more security. In the 1970s, the very same sense of stability came to be regarded as unfair, uncomfortable, petrifying, in need of change. In the 1980s, the desire for stability reappeared. Is history "advancing in cycles"? Or have people simply become dissatisfied with their dreams and accomplishments, and turned to embrace new aspirations?

Rather than attribute the processes of change and conflict since World War II to the manifestations of historical inevitability, it may be more appropriate to consider them as consequences of discrepant interests expressed in political systems that need to be changed but cannot be changed because of conflicts of interest.

Technological Development as a Vehicle of Historical Inevitability

In 1954, Ellul published *La technique: L'enjeu du siècle*. Ellul's book is not merely about technological development, as the English title, *The Technological Society* (1964), implies. Rather, it addresses principally the decline of Western civilization and the spread of "technological barbarism." In Ellul's eyes, Western civilization is being overwhelmed by destructive forces from both without and within; from without by foreign values, from within by the spread of "technique." Although anti-Marxist, Ellul, like Marx, believes in technological determinism and inevitability. He is at variance with Marx because he believes that technological development engenders a condition that makes a totalitarian state indispensible. In both *The Technological Society* and in *The Technological System* (1984), Ellul discusses society's current pursuit of technical efficiency, which, in his opinion, rarely serves ethical and higher civilizational aims. Technique, in his interpretation, is more than just technology; it is, in fact, the entire lifestyle that is determined by the uses of contemporary technology at work and home. Technique, writes Ellul, advances economic standards of living; however, it also abets an oppressive uniformity, vulgar simplifications, and a growing disregard for individuality and other essential and unique values of the West. Technique integrates everything, avers Ellul: machines into gigantic plants; plants into industrial systems; specific techniques into higher-level techniques and increasingly universal technological systems. The technological system, Ellul (1980) explains, is a qualitatively different phenomenon than civilizations or societies employing technologies have experienced in the past. Under the new condition, technology not only determines the lifestyle, but the totality of relations and norms, including ethical standards. Technical elements, he claims, (1964, 93) "combine among themselves, and they do so more and more spontaneously." He calls that "technological self-augmentation." He writes (1964, 89):

Self-augmentation can be formulated in two laws:
1. *In a given civilization, technical progress is irreversible.*
2. *Technological progress tends to act, not according to an arithmetic, but according to a geometric progression.*

No power in the world can arrest this march unless it destroys the civilization that begot it. Relieved from the limitations of ethical concerns, technique not only develops independently from economics and politics, and (1964, 133) "elicits and conditions social, political, and economic change. It is the prime mover of all the rest." It sets its own standards and requirements. It forces society, the economy, and civilization to adjust to its needs and developments; it relinquishes specific cultural standards and qualities. Dependence on the technological environment steadily increases. Thus (1964, 265), the nation is no longer a primarily human, geographic, civilizational entity; it transforms into the object of the technological state and becomes a machine, an economic power, whose resources, men, money, raw materials, and technology, must be put to work, and to which a "yield" must be returned.

In the extensive literature discussing current technological growth, three principal concerns have been voiced: (1) that modernization involving new technologies—computers, robots, automated factories—will produce massive unemployment; (2) that pollution generated by proliferating technologies has already destroyed the natural habitat of large areas of the planet, continues to deplete natural resources, and will destroy and deplete the planet even more should technological development continue to advance at even its current pace; and (3) that certain individuals or states will exploit sophisticated technologies to develop inimical, inhumane systems within which individuality and intellect will be totally suppressed.[6] Ellul, Orwell, Westin, Rule, David Burnham, and Walter Cronkite have each expressed this last concern.

While Orwell and others warned that such regimes *could* appear, Ellul writes that highly oppressive totalitarian systems will *inevitably* appear, as a natural outgrowth of technological development. Conditions are ripe for elements of such structures, already inherent in Western democracies, to grow into full-scale systems, Ellul believes; and their development cannot be restrained or arrested. Thus he writes (1964, 284), "technique causes the state to become totalitarian, to absorb the citizens completely. . . . Even when the state is resolutely liberal and democratic, it cannot do otherwise than become totalitarian."

Ian Will takes a similar view. According to him (1983, 19), as it advances, technology becomes "largely self-sustaining." Subsequently, social stratification will adapt to its needs. Will envisages a future society divided into three functional and one nonfunctional class: those who control technology; those who service technology; and those who service those who control and service technology. The working class, in his opinion (see also Jenkins & Sherman 1977), transformed into a "non-working" class, "will serve no functional purpose other than to exist."

As a prominent member of the French resistance and a champion of various cultural causes, Ellul, a propagandist of several *causes célèbres*, is reputed to represent the conscience of France. Ellul's observations are astute, but sometimes his conclusions seem exaggerated. Certainly, the technology imagined by Orwell in the sinister Big Brother society is crude compared with the technology presently available, which could be exploited to control masses of people under a Big Brother–type society. However, the idea that such a society is inevitable and, in fact, is presently emerging, as Ellul claims, needs at least further investigation. Technologies are available to conduct such societies, as they are available to carry out nuclear annihilation, but the potential does not have to be realized. It might happen, but it is not inevitable. One cannot be certain whether either the recently started missile disarmament of the United States and the Soviet Union, or *glasnost* and democratization in the Soviet Union, will advance, but these recent developments are quite demonstrative that tendencies opposite to those anticipated by Ellul and like theorists are quite possible; freedom and peace could expand regardless of technological advancement.

The approach of the year 1984 was seen by many writers as a good opportunity to discuss the fears Orwell expressed in his book. Some compiled long lists of recently developed technological devices that could be used by governments, corporations, and organizations in systems employing pervasive control and compulsion, many of them more tortuous and macabre than those portrayed in distopian literature. The list included: computers that secretly monitor how fast and accurately employees are working, which could also be employed by a government wishing to observe the behavior of citizens at any time; remote sensors; mind-manipulating drugs; data banks specializing in "paper trails"; satellites and microwave antennas that can place virtually anyone under constant surveillance; lie-detector tests; handwriting and voice analyses; genetic-screening techniques; directional microphones for listening to conversations from long distances; techniques of subliminal propaganda messages on television or on movie screens; low frequency microwave bombardments of the mind; biological engineering; and a wide assortment of drugs that "tinker with genetics" or can alter the personality of individuals, which can be employed in designing and producing desired servants of the state. Most writers believed such means to be available but stressed that, for the most part, they are used only in rare instances. Most writers noted that, on the whole, technological developments had produced positive achievements: improvement in general health conditions and longer life spans; expanded personal freedoms; higher education levels; broader suffrage; greater opportunities; and an increased participation in public spheres of life. Of course, there is no guarantee that, in the future, surveillance and manipulative technologies will not be massively employed to create a new kind of inhumane system; but the argument that such a society will *inevitably* appear remains groundless. Besides, the type of totalitarian society that Ellul calls technological, and others call by other names, was established in the past, without today's advanced technologies: the Stalinist regime; Nazi Germany's "Super Society"; the Khmer Rouge regime in Cambodia; China under the Cultural Revolution; Khomeini's Iran, etc. Society can be effectively controlled by technological means, but people can also be controlled quite pervasively by traditional, non-technological methods.

According to Ellul, technological development is the carrier of historical inevitability. At present, he writes, it carries the transition from a classic industrial society to a technological and totalitarian society. Ferkiss (1974); Miller (1971); Westin (1967); Severn (1973); Rule et al. (1980); Donner (1980); and Wicklein (1981) do not write about the inevitability of totalitarian societies. They are all concerned, however, with the decline of privacy. They discuss the threat of databanks, government and private agencies' intelligence gathering, and the abuse of constitutional rights by different information-gathering and "snooping" agencies. To support their arguments, they refer to many official U.S. Senate and congressional reports on the decline of privacy, illegal databanks, computer controls, and their contribution to eroding the rights of citizens, as well as, indirectly, to emerging societal conditions described by Ellul. Directed by human will, technology can determine important societal elements. Any technology can be and is employed to different ends, with different results, depending on certain cultural and social factors. The same technology (e.g., computers) can be employed to impose coercive controls or to expand and advance liberties, education, and cultural achievement. The dangers envisioned by Ellul, Ian Will, and David Burnham are real. But in Western societies, such dangers are balanced by rights and liberties. People have the means to fight back. They can use the electoral process, the mass media, the courts, and/or demonstrations to express their will. Some argue that people's will is easily manipulated or disregarded; that current rights and liberties cannot adequately counterbalance advancing technological controls. Perhaps; this could be true. Over the last twenty years, both control by the state, equipped with modern technology, and rights and participation in the democratic process have expanded. The struggle itself, between these two forces, is all that is certain.

Masuda (1981), who calls the new society "computopia," holds an opposite view to that of Ellul and other distopian theorists. According to his analysis (159), the future promises an "ideal global society in which multi-centered, multi-layered voluntary communities of citizens participate voluntarily in shared goals and ideas flourish simultaneously throughout the world." In computopia, information will become the principal means of production. An abundance of information, and equal access to it, will ultimately engender a society of equality and equity. Masuda recognizes the possibility that, instead of computopia, an "automated state" will emerge from this development. But he expresses hope and predicts (153) "that the catastrophic course to an 'Automated State' will be avoided." Naisbitt's (1983) book on the information society, apparently designed for top executives, contains similar ideas. These writers are not concerned about ethics, erosion of privacy, or many other new realities. The new source of power, writes Naisbitt, is not money in the hands of a few but information in the hands of many. Naisbitt claims that most current social problems will diminish, since goods and information will be distributed more rationally under a computer-controlled system. This victory of progress, he claims, will happen not only within national boundaries, but globally. The information society will be simultaneously global and decentralized. Representative democracy will become participatory democracy. Hierarchies will be restructured as networks. Thanks to computers, alternatives of today will flourish as multiple choices in the future. Both Naisbitt's and Masuda's books represent a multitude of publications advancing similar perspectives.

According to this viewpoint, under the new conditions, information will become the principal means of production and consumption. It will be available to all, in unlimited quantities. Furthermore, its production will not damage the environment. In certain presentations, these ideas are crude; however, they cannot be ignored. Not only do an increasing number of people believe in them, the information society—albeit still lacking most of the promised elements of utopia—is actually emerging. It already has its problems as well: computer "viruses"; computer hackers; structural unemployment caused by the inability of some to adjust to technological innovations; restricted accesses to some information.

Although always in demand, information now "runs the world." Hence, any information that can be marketed or stored by government agencies has value. Different information serves different clienteles. The media perpetually seek sensational information that, at least briefly, will focus the attention of the world on whatever revelations may be at hand. Business corporations need information pertaining directly to production processes, secret formulae, innovations giving a competitive edge, market conditions, current and future trends in regulatory activities, their particular clientele, and changing patterns in lifestyles. In order to perform its own incessantly multiplying functions, the state requires expanding volumes of information concerning every aspect of the activities of its citizens; both in their public and private affairs. The state requires this information not only to alleviate social problems, prevent disruptions, and thwart undesired activities, but also to determine the need for new regulations and future courses of action. In order to know what it needs to know, or at least what some zealous functionaries think it ought to know about society as a whole, and the groups and individuals comprising it, the state must invade the privacy of individuals to obtain information. The rationality of this intrusion into private affairs, and the real and unnecessary collection of information, can always be justified, as it can always be questioned.[7]

Information-collecting by state agencies and corporations is not merely epidemic "data-mania." These organizations feed on information: big organizations more than smaller ones, and the biggest of them all—the state—more than any other.

The emerging information society is evidently not a society of equality. Some have the knowledge and the means to tap valuable information; others do not. Some have access to expensive information; others do not. Like other materials, information can be stolen, acquired, made available to friends and associates, and made exclusively available to a privileged few. Neither technology nor computerization generates etatization. The opposite occurs: The state's organizational growth creates a demand for computerization and an information society. Ellul and others maintain that technological growth not only causes social and cultural change, but produces conditions for the emergence of state-controlled and state-regulated societies. Technological development, however, is not the sole factor in these societal changes. It combines with other factors and processes. The contemporary condition, including the increased involvement of the state in solving social problems and managing the economy, results from a conglomeration of causes. The New State is more technological than was any state before. Technological development is, however, a factor in many different processes, producing diverse societal systems.

CHAPTER SIXTEEN

The New State:
Neither Capitalist nor Socialist

In writing this book I was motivated by concerns raised by Schumpeter, in his *Capitalism, Socialism and Democracy*, published first in 1943, and in the address, "The March into Socialism," delivered before the American Economic Association in New York on December 30, 1949, and included in the later (1966) edition of his book.

During the 1930s and 1940s, Schumpeter lived first in Great Britain, then in the United States. *Capitalism, Socialism and Democracy* is the product of his observations of developments in these nations, as well as the rest of Europe at this time. Like Marx, Schumpeter envisions socialism emerging from capitalist development. Unlike Marx, he expects capitalism to transform into socialism without revolution, not as a result of collapse and demise, but as a result of capitalism's inherent drive to perfection. Schumpeter deprecates Marx's scholarly work. He writes, however, that Marx was correct in predicting that capitalism would evolve "under its own steam," into the new society of socialism.

In Schumpeter's opinion, capitalism never stops developing; it advances in a continual and repetitive process of creative self-destruction and renewal. In his analysis of the history of capitalism, he points out that at first, capitalist development erased the monarchy and aristocracy, reduced the authority of the Church, and abolished or weakened other institutions of the preceding feudal structure. Later, in its pursuit of renewal, capitalism turned at an accelerating pace against institutions of its own creation. This process continues. Schumpeter's principal interest is focused on this development. He writes that capitalism cannot stop changing, because it strives for higher and higher yields. In this pursuit, old, but still productive, enterprises are abandoned and replaced by newer ones, operating on a larger scale and generating improved products at a faster pace. Small and mid-size businesses are pushed into bankruptcy or are swallowed by larger and larger corporations. Once shares substitute for ownership and industries submit to management by hired personnel, the original concept of property loses its significance. With the evaporation of what Schumpeter calls "the material substance of property," allegiance to property also declines. The whole attitude of holders, managers, and workers changes. Larger and larger conglomerations become involved in processes of competitive interactions generating monopolistic tendencies. A natural conclusion follows from this logical analysis: Would it not be rational for the state, the biggest of them all, to absorb the whole? Schumpeter concludes: Capitalism naturally transsubstantiates into centralization.[1]

He considers other aspects of the situation. The standards of living and leisure of the masses improved tremendously under capitalism. But, people with capitalist values are never satisfied with what they posses; they demand more. The strongest voice of dissatisfaction with current conditions and capitalism comes from intellectuals; from some because they are unemployed and unemployable; from others because they feel insecure in the positions they occupy in political bureaus, newspapers, and other institutions; from still others because they consider it their function to criticize any existing order. Under current capitalist conditions, the bourgeois family disintegrates. The vestiges of "Victorian standards of morality," the only morality that flourished under capitalism, are withering away. The new men and women, following hedonistic desires, are less willing to fulfil traditional roles in capitalist society: the essential functions of earning, saving, and investing. They, too, writes Schumpeter, absorb and reflect the current radicalism and hostility to bourgeois lifestyles.

Eventually, Schumpeter continues (1966, 131):

> A more or less stationary state would ensue. Capitalism being essentially an evolutionary process, would become atrophic. There would be nothing left for entrepreneurs to do. . . . Profits and along with profits the rate of interest would converge toward zero. The bourgeois strata that live on profits and trade would disappear. The management of industry and trade would become a matter of current administration, and the personnel which runs it will unavoidably acquire the characteristics of a bureaucracy. Socialism of a very sober type will almost automatically come into being.

Socialism, he asserts again and again, is a logical and natural continuation of capitalism. It comes into being as an extension of growth and development processes originating in the pursuit of profit and the self-perfection of the economy under capitalism, not as a result of its failure and collapse, as Marx and others assumed. This development attains its destiny and fulfilment under socialism. "I define (centralist) socialism," states Schumpeter (415–416), "as that organization of society in which the means of production are controlled, and the decisions on how and what to produce and on who is to get what, are made by public authority instead of by privately owned and privately managed firms."

This sounds like a paragraph of the Soviet constitution. Yet, Schumpeter's feasible socialism is as removed from the Marxist variety of socialism, or that of other nineteenth-century socialists, as it is from the utopian schemes of a Thomas Moore. It is not a society of complete justice, freedom, or equality. It does not bring the cessation of the "exploitation of man by man," as promised by most socialists. Schumpeter's socialism involves the social operation of a more efficient, more goal-oriented, less wasteful economy. Schumpeter stresses: "I do not advocate socialism. I do not 'prophesy' or predict it. I merely recognize the facts and point out the tendencies which those facts indicate."

An admirer of British democracy, Schumpeter dedicates pages to advocating democracy as the most suitable way to run public affairs in both capitalist and socialist societies. Under democratic socialism, which Schumpeter prizes, the economy is centrally planned and managed. The bureaucracy implements distributive policies, which become essential for certain sectors of the population. In politics, declares Schumpeter, as in anything else, the electorate depends on the services of others; in this field, too, the public should rely on the best experts. Democracy, in his interpretation, is a marketplace in which the electorate secures essential services and authorizes a chosen party to conduct the political and administrative business of a given group, area, or nation. Democracy is the best system, Schumpeter believes, because it allows market participants to decide for themselves which services and programs offered by the various parties or companies in the marketplace best suit their needs.

In "The March into Socialism," Schumpeter again proclaims that capitalist civilization is rapidly passing away and will be supplanted by socialism. This time, however, he admits to the possibility that trends toward socialism "may fail to work themselves out completely." The socialist tendency, he concedes, could lose momentum. A social reorganization, difficult to predict, could divert development away from socialist tendencies (416). In such an instance, the development toward socialism "may eventually 'stick' at some halfway house." Such is the case, Schumpeter states, with "laborist capitalism." Should this development continue, he indicates, such societies may actually never become socialist and may evolve in new directions, still difficult to predict. This new point is not sufficiently developed to change the general perspective advanced by his book. Still, Schumpeter was the first theorist to envision the possibility of a new turn in development. His address, therefore, can be considered to anticipate etatization and the New State.

Schumpeter's speculations, barely apparent in 1949, began to materialize a decade later. Western societies, instead of "marching to socialism," turned at what he called the "halfway house" and began marching in a new direction. It must be emphasized: This is not a convergence. These societies remain capitalist. Under the New State, they have adopted some elements of socialism. The New State protects the capitalist system and also redistributes some of the wealth produced by it. More distinctly, however, it performs many new functions not anticipated by Schumpeter or other theorists in the past.

In 1981, the importance of Schumpeter's *Capitalism, Socialism and Democracy* was recognized in a unique way. Eleven eminent social scientists and financial economists, differing in ideological orientations—Paul A. Samuelson, Tom Bottomore, William Fellner, Gottfried Haberler, Robert L. Heilbroner, Hendrik Wilm Lambers, Arthur Smithies, Peter J. D. Wiles, Herbert K. Zassenhaus, and Jelle Zijlstra—published a special volume, *Schumpeter's Vision: Socialism and Democracy after 40 Years*, to pay tribute to this great scholar and to appraise the actual evolution of Western societies in view of Schumpeter's vision. The book appeared under the editorship of Arnold Heertje. Some of the same authors who participated in this book had contributed to *Schumpeter: Social Scientist*, a similar publication edited by Seymour E. Harris, which appeared in 1951.

Although a conservative, Schumpeter did not represent any typical conservative perspective. His ideas were equally seminal to socialist, liberal, and conservative academics. Among contributors to the new volume, only a few recognize Schumpeter's discussion of the "halfway house," and the new directions that could develop from it, as an important new idea. Apart from providing an inspiration for developmental analyses, the collective work fulfils a special niche, as a sort of probing gyrocompass, a gauge, assessing recent developments in Western societies: How far has society moved in the direction envisioned by this great economist?

It seems that at present, fifty years after Schumpeter's analysis, fewer people are attracted by the prospect of "marching into socialism," be it of the Schumpeterian or Soviet variety; more precisely, fewer people believe that any kind of real socialism is attainable. Paradoxically, anti-Marxists and critics of socialism can claim less credit for this change in public opinion than can leaders of the socialist nations. Attitudes toward socialism changed primarily as a result of criticism, voiced by Khrushchev, of the Stalinist period, the current criticism by Gorbachev, of both Brezhnev's and Stalin's eras, and as a result of other initiatives taken by socialist leaders to alter the conditions of socialist societies. These include initiatives to liberate part, only a very small part, of the Soviet economy from the strict controls of central planning and the command-system economy, both regarded by Schumpeter as superior to the free-market economy. A large part of the economy in China was liberated from direct state control by Deng Xiaoping; new policies were undertaken in other socialist countries to better conditions, in some regards, by adopting elements of free-market enterprise. There have been citizen rebellions in socialist nations, particularly the Solidarity movement in Poland, against Soviet control and centrally controlled economic planning in Eastern Europe. The failures of socialist experiments in Great Britain, France, and other nations must be regarded as factors in this change in attitudes. Finally, the New State, though far from perfect, has emerged as a relatively better solution than classical capitalism and socialism. It is not so much that people love profit and find ways to gain it under socialism, as under capitalism; it is more that neither capitalism nor socialism works without an element of the other. Over the last fifty years, it has become increasingly more evident that command systems work well in the army, but only with great difficulty, producing meager results, in the sphere of the organization of production, trade, and consumption, or in any sphere where results depend more on grassroots initiatives than on command from the center. The Chernobyl disaster, though merely an accident, has nevertheless revealed itself to be as much a bureaucratic as a technical disaster, proving again that, despite the enormous potential of centrally structured command systems, they are overwhelmed by inefficiency, inefficacy, corruption, and impotence more often than are competitive market structures.[2] This is recognized by Gorbachev and his associates. As I am completing this book, the press reports that Gorbachev is proclaiming a "new concept of socialism." Under this new system, the party intends to borrow political and economic ideas not only from other socialist countries, but even from the capitalist West. Keller, (*New York Times*, October 5, 1988) reports from Moscow that the party is now siding with those who call themselves new thinkers. Members of the Politbureau Yakovlev and Medvedev, the new ideologists of the party, proclaimed: "Present-day realities" mean that "universal values" such as avoiding war and ecological catastrophe must outweigh the idea of a struggle between the classes. . . . The market is an indespensible means of gearing production to fast-changing demand, and a major instrument of public control over quality and cost. . . . Our previous concepts of public property; our attitudes to this problem, have proven to be untenable."

Soviet socialism includes not only what economists call (see Katsenelinboigen 1978, 165–202) the "red market," operating under state-decreed price systems, but also a "pink market," with lower prices for privileged functionaries, a "white" flea market, for new and used items, a "grey" market for items of personal consumption and services sold at higher-than-state prices, a "brown market," for goods scarce at the red market, and a large black market. In addition, farmers are allowed to sell products from private lots outside the state system; fresh vegetables and fruits are frequently available at higher-than-state prices only at such farmers' markets. The Soviets now recognize more the need for markets outside state control.[3] They recognize the need for *glasnost* (publicity, openness) in their system, to ensure a public check on bureaucratic control and greater freedom of expression. They acknowledge the need for wider public access to information, to prevent disasters and instigate innovations. *Perestroika*—the major reorganization of the economy—is being undertaken in recognition that neither economic command systems nor utopian societal models can work in practice unless people have more freedom of initiative. The Soviets are not becoming capitalist. However, by introducing changes and lessening controls, they are admitting to the world that centralist socialist systems are far from perfect; and that, to ameliorate the problems engendered by excessive control, the system must be changed into one less centralized, allowing for more private initiative and recognition for the human factor in the economy and society.

This is not to say that attraction to socialism has vanished. Many people believe that there must be a better way than capitalism. Many call themselves socialist, or advocate reforms that they hope will contribute to changing capitalism into socialism. There is one cardinal difference in this regard between Schumpeter's time and the present, however; today, most of those who believe that there must be a system better than capitalism also believe that there must be a better way of doing things than as they are done under systems currently operating in countries that call themselves socialist.

The West, for its part, has fewer reasons to march toward the direction from which the Soviet Union and China are currently withdrawing. A new, more popular model has arisen on the horizon. This model includes a system of democratic and semisocialist institutions dwelling within a capitalist economic structure. This new ideal is distinct from both the Marxist Atlantis, and any rigid conservative dream of a free-market economy as was supposed to exist in the past but never materialized. It respects the right to own private property but sustains a redistributive welfare system. The new redistributive system depends largely on inputs provided by a well-functioning economy. It can be alternately managed by socialists, social democrats, liberals, or conservatives. In the United States, Great Britain, West Germany, and Canada, it is currently governed by conservatives. In Italy, France, Sweden, and Spain, it is currently governed by socialists. However, it cannot be run by one category of people: extremists, whether of the communist, socialist, or conservative persuasion. It cannot be administered by a party that would abolish the market or reduce the state to a minimal existence, as was postulated by Herbert Spencer and other nineteenth-century liberals. Increasingly, elections prove that the majority believes that only an economy comprising profitable, entrepreneurial, privately owned or mixed businesses can generate sufficient GNP for new investments to face international competition, to maintain social services, to support systems of entitlements, to invest in defense, to protect the environment, to preserve living standards, and to keep smaller, job-producing enterprises in business. These people do not trust the market wholly. They want the state to perform more functions, preserving the market among others. Parties that do not follow this instruction lose elections to parties that promise to correct their mistakes.

In other words, under present conditions, capitalism is feasible only under the patronage and regulation of the New State. Attempts to develop economies organized exclusively around nationalized industries failed equally under the Meiji regime in nineteenth-century Japan, and in contemporary Great Britain, France, and other Western European nations in our time. For far too long, critical and academic theorizing has confined itself to the schematized dichotomy: capitalism versus socialism. New conditions, under the New State, are taking shape regardless of theoretical recognition. It is now evident that the route of contemporary evolution lies perpendicular to the capitalism—socialism axis, envisaged in classical literature. Rather than converge, new developments in capitalist and socialist societies advance coextensively. These evolutions are schematically depicted in Table 16.1.

The New State, resulting from etatization, has not been recognized in the principal constitutional enactment of any nation. It appeared and developed under its own impetus. Its functions were legalized by enactments based on reinterpretations of older legislation. As has been pointed out, patterns that persist long enough are usually recognized as principles and eventually metamorphose into consensus. The New State appeared in response to the public's desire for greater social and economic security. However, in the process of its evolution, new perils have arisen to threaten the attained social security. The dangers are: deficits; excessive regulation of business and the private affairs of citizens; overbureaucratization petrifying society; and the appearance of groups endowed with too many privileges. New legislation

Table 16.1 The Direction of Etatization vis-a-vis the Axis, Capitalism-Socialism

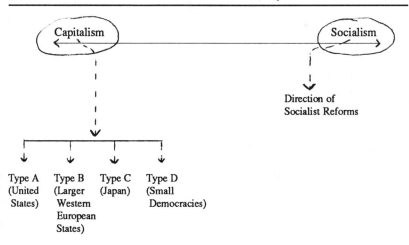

explicitly defining the role of the New State is needed, not only to define the new functions of the state and appropriately recognize its regulatory institutions, but also more strictly to delineate those areas the state is prohibited to invade, such as personal privacy and the autonomy of the market. Such laws should proclaim broader human and civil rights and insure their protection by the state and against state encroachment. It is easy to foresee the many difficulties that a legislative body wishing explicitly to recognize the functions of the New State in a constitution or constitutional amendment would encounter, but such enactments sooner or later will be necessary.

Today's etatized society took shape only recently. The evolution of etatization has not yet reached the stage from which further developments can be predicted. Because postindustrial societies will come to encompass even more differentiated and more interdependent structures, every element of the new organization will become more specific and unique, but at the same time, will necessarily become more interdependent and will operate on a much wider scale. The only development feasible is that even under a preserved status quo, etatization will increase.

Notes

INTRODUCTION

1. The Introduction, Chapter 1, and Chapter 2 contain certain ideas earlier discussed in Chodak (1983).

2. This quotation represents Dahrendorf's statement in an interview conducted at Russell Sage Foundation in May 1987 (Dahrendorf 1987).

3. See Chodak (1973) and Chodak (1983).

4. The concept obtained some currency in Eastern Europe. Etatization was also adopted in some Western literature discussing developments in the USSR and Eastern Europe (see, e.g., Lewin, 1974). Etatization seems, certainly, less confusing than similarly unwieldy and lumpy words, such as "statization," "statism," "governmentalization," or "state engrandizement," suggested by some readers of this book in manuscript. Etatization may sound elephantine to some English-speaking persons. However, no other word better denotes the idea on which this book hinges.

5. Thomson (1969, 33, 60, 126, 167), for instance, states: "Bonapartism represented the tradition of *étatisme* as strongly as the Liberals." In his opinion, in contemporary France, "the whole body of *functionnaires* as a class" professes *étatisme*. He regards de Gaulle and other presidents as representative of this tradition. Peyrefitte (1981, 84) and some other writers employ colbertism synonymously with *étatisme*. Still others (e.g., Stevens, 1980, 81) write about the "tradition of state intervention," also calling it *dirigiste* and Colbertist tradition.

CHAPTER 1. STATE FUNCTIONS

1. These eight processes are discussed throughout this volume and are not here given in the order of discussion.

2. In some instances, "state" is employed synonymously with "nation," while in others it denotes "government" or, more generally, "political authority." In this last sense the state has existed throughout known human history. Certain writers employ a different interpretation, however, defining or tacitly assuming "state" as a structure of sovereign authority, propelled from a social realm of citizenry, exercised over an internationally recognized territory and in contrast to structures encompassing subjects, tribal members, or dependents in traditional social structures. In this

understanding, the state (or rather modern state) is a product of postrevolutionary England, France, and the United States. D'Entreves (1967), suggests that though the word was used by medieval scholars in reference to the Greek *polis* and medieval principalities, it actually is a neologism, a derivative from "the Latin word *status*, a neutral word meaning condition or way of existence." He points out (3-32), that Machiavelli first employed "state" in this contemporary connotation. In Machiavelli's writing, in fact, "state" denotes, variously, government, people, and territory. In the United States, of course, the state is a semi-autonomous administrative unit (a province in Canadian terms) of the larger entity, which is a union of states.

In Hegel's philosophical system "the State" is an ideal. The concept represents the ultimate embodiment of the divine will; it is regarded as the end-result of the development of history, rationality, and civilization. He theorized that the "civil society" was no more than an agglomeration of social classes, institutions and conflicting interests. The state, in contrast, was seen as a purpose-providing, integrating supreme spirit, will (*Geist*), and reason (*Vernunft*), which appeared out of the dialectical process elevating the conflict-ridden civil society to a higher entity. Marx and other nineteenth-century writers adopted this understanding from Hegel, yet took a different approach. Marx, specifically, criticized Hegel for writing on the state only as an idea, instead of discussing the actual state as it serves the ruling class.

3. On Marxist theory of the state see Avineri (1970, particularly Ch. 8); Miliband (1969); Poulantzas (1974); Jessop (1982, 1–31); Bottomore (1985), and Giddens (1983, 182–252).

4. Stepan (1978, xii–xiii) also writes that the state should be "viewed as a mechanism of domination and control, but in some regards it can be "procedurally neutral," and that "the state is not necessarily unitary and monolithic"; different forces within it represent different interests.

5. This division is, in a sense, arbitrary. A. W. Lewis (1965, 377–418), discussing economic functions performed by governments in advancing economic development, lists the following functions: (*a*) maintains public services; (*b*) influences attitudes; (*c*) shapes economic institutions; (*d*) influences the use of resources; (*e*) influences the distribution of income; (*f*) controls the quantity of money; (*g*) controls economic fluctuations; (*h*) ensures full employment; (*i*) influences the level of investment. He also lists alternative results of these functions causing stagnation.

CHAPTER 2. PRINCIPAL FEATURES OF ETATIZATION

1. Many secondary associations—for instance, unions, consumer protection associations, feminist organizations, and single-issue movements—exert a strong influence on politics. Most of these mass movements do not require supporters to be involved in the movement's activity on a daily basis.

2. Many writers refer to the introductory chapter of Schmitter and Lehmbruch (1979) for an umbrella concept embracing the variety of contemporary corporatist phenomena.

Schmitter's position can be summarized in three points. First, he recognizes (11) that "there is simply too much normative variety and behavioral hypocrisy in the use of the corporatist *ideological* label to make it a useful operational instrument for comparative analysis." He wants to overcome this condition by transforming the concept into a useful, operational, heuristic, ideal type, logicoanalytic construct. With this objective in mind he writes (13):

Corporatism can be defined as a system of interest representation in which the constituent units are organized into a limited number of singular, compulsory, non-competitive, hierarchical ordered and functionally differentiated categories, recognized or licensed (if not created) by the state and granted a deliberate representational monopoly within their respective categories in exchange for observing certain controls on their selection of leaders and articulation of demands and supports.

Schmitter's second objective is to offer an "alternative to the paradigm of interest politics" as employed by "pluralist" theorists. He posits (16):

The former suggest spontaneous formation, numerical proliferation, horizontal extension and competitive interaction; the latter advocate controlled emergence, quantitative limitation, vertical stratification and complementary interdependence. Pluralists place their faith in the shifting balance of mechanically intersecting forces; corporatists appeal to the functional adjustment of an organically interdependent whole.

In his third point, Schmitter discerns two kinds of contemporary corporatist structures: state corporatism, which appears under the authoritarian, centrally controlled, bureaucratic, antiliberal, "delayed capitalist," neomercantilist state; and societal corporatism, which is a structural element of "the post-liberal, advanced capitalist, organized democratic welfare state." Schmitter definitely shows more interest in the latter. He points out (23) that "the origins of societal corporatism lie in the slow, almost imperceptible decay of advanced pluralism; the origins of state corporatism lie in the rapid, highly visible demise of nascent pluralism."

3. Marx writes that the worker is dehumanized and experiences alienation because he does not own the means of production and the product of his labor but still is forced to work, in order to obtain a minimal reward—the basic necessities for living. Durkheim, who does not employ the word "alienation," links the phenomenon with periods of anomie. He points out that societal development, the growing complexity that emerges from advanced division of labor and results in "higher" and more "organic" integration, also produces periodic discontinuities and conditions involving disintegration and deterioration of morals, periods when old values suddenly appear redundant and new ones are not available or not widely accepted. During such periods, which arise frequently in times of economic ruptures and other crises, a significant increase occurs in the number of "anomic suicides." Seeman's (1959) theory reflects on the subjective, psychological experience of an individual lost vis-à-vis incomprehensible forces in society. He writes that the alienated individual feels powerless, meaningless, isolated, and self-estranged in a normless condition.

4. The *Statistical Abstract of the United States 1986* (1985), records that in 1960, 39.9 million persons (22.2% of the U.S. population) lived below the poverty level. The figures (in millions) for subsequent periods are: in 1966, 28.5 (14.7%); 1971, 25.5 (12.5%); 1976, 25.0 (11.8%); 1980, 29.3 (13.0%); 1984, 33.7 (14.4%). Wattenberg (1984, 147–148), using different figures, argues that the benefits that the poor receive in kind, i.e., food stamps, medicare, housing, etc., should also be counted at their cash value in estimates of assistance to the poor. According to his figures (source OMB, calculated in constant 1983 dollars), federal spending on social safety was, in 1970, $155 billion; in 1981, $367 billion; in 1985, $403 billion. The poverty line is set at different "minimal" levels of income by different nations. For

instance, in Canada, it is set at a higher level than in the United States. A larger percentage of the population in Canada is, therefore, entitled to welfare assistance. Not all entitled are accorded assistance, however. According to the Canadian *Poverty Profile* (April 1988, 7) 1,002,000 (20.8%) of Canadian families lived below the poverty level in 1969. The special report of a special Canadian senate committee on poverty, published in 1971, estimated the rate of poverty to be around 30% (among families headed by single women even higher). In 1979, this figure declined to 788,000 or 13.1%; it was 869,000 (13.2%) in 1982; 908,000 (13.3%) in 1985, and in 1986, 851,000 (12.3%). These statistics report that conditions have improved recently, but that poverty particularly afflicts the unattached individual: in 1986 982,000 single persons were poor (34.3% of all unattached individuals).

5. An illustration of this new phenomenon is the letter to *Izvestia*, April 19, 1988, reprinted in the *New York Times*, April 24, in English translation:

> I am tired of being ashamed of myself, I believe that now many people feel the same way. I'm not ashamed about my past life (to wit my orders and medals), but about the fact that, like about many, *nobody cares about me.* You write that average (monthly) earnings in the country far exceed 200 rubles, but I receive a pension of only 50 rubles a months. I have read about the charity agency that is now being set up. But it can't take care of everyone in need. A state program for the poor is needed. It is time to admit that they exist even in our country. The reasons vary, but as a result people end up being helpless to face the present day, let alone tomorrow, should prices rise. We don't need to be pitied, but helped. This should become one of the points of perestroika, for moral accountability is needed in addition to economic accountability.
>
> N. Ivanova, Moscow [emphasis added]

6. On development of unemployment insurance in Western Europe, see Garraty (1979), Flora and Heidenheimer (1984), Malinvaud and Fitoussi (1980), Creedy (1981), Hughes and Perlman (1984), and Jahoda (1982).

7. Coleman and Rainwater (1978, 49), discussing current changes in "social standing in America," write that respondents to their surveys "constantly coupled an occupational characterization with either an amount of money or qualifier like 'successful,' 'average,' or 'successful business people,' 'college graduates in management doing fairly well,' and 'doctors and lawyers making lots of dough.'" They point out that the concept of class has many faces in practice. It is interesting to note that, according to their analysis, schooling accounted for 50 percent of the variance, the effect of job-holding for 19 percent, and income for the remaining 23 percent of the variance in social standing (283). They report that family background has to be regarded as having a considerable influence on standard deviation of their scheme. They also refer (52) to the importance of "connections" in attaining a desirable "social standing."

8. The term "new class" was first employed by Djilas (1979). Djilas discussed the power elite of the Soviet Union and other East European societies under Communist rule as comprising individuals of "the new class." In Bruce-Briggs' (1979) edited volume, "the new class" is defined differently by different writers. All authors agree that the new class does exist and is assuming greater importance in contemporary society. Some define the new class as a new component of the power elite.

9. For different opinions see Stauffer (1985) .

CHAPTER 3. CONFLICT OVER SOCIOECONOMIC ISSUES

1. Coser (1969, 126–127), who reinterpreted Simmel's idea into an operational concept of contemporary sociology, writes that conflicts may be regarded to be "productive" in two related ways: (1) they lead to modifying and creating law; (2) applying new rules and laws leads to the growth of new institutional structures centering on their enforcement. Simmel's propositions suggest a third unifying function of conflict as well: that conflict brings into the conscious awareness of the contenders and of the community at large, norms and rules that were hitherto dormant.

2. See, particularly, paragraphs 2178–2200, Pareto (1963), in which he analyzes different uses of force: violence, threats and blackmail, diplomacy and negotiation, business competition, economic warfare, and enmity, between the elite and the counter-elite, and within the elites.

3. Functionalists define class not only in relation to the means of production, but as is suitable in relation to other factors, such as income, education, lifestyle, and residence. From this perspective, class is both an objective and subjective construct. They assert that classes complement each other regardless of conflict.

4. The evolution of this contrariety, since the eighteenth century, under capitalism was recently discussed by Sennett (1978).

5. The quintile is a statistical unit of measure used most often for income distribution surveys. The method consists of dividing a nation's households into five equal groups and then ranking each according to its share of the nation's wealth.

6. The use of data on income distribution to individuals, as a rule, demonstrates that the higher quintiles receive a larger share of national income than is demonstrated when income distributed to families is accounted for.

7. For other comparisons see Ross (1980, Table 2).

8. The lines between quintiles are drawn differently in different nations. What are considered to be high incomes in some nations might be considered relatively modest in the United States or other rich nations. Correspondingly, a low income earner in the United States would be included in one of the middle quintiles in a poorer nation.

9. This is noticeable in the press. Articles with titles like "A Taxing Problem" (D. Alexander, *San Francisco Chronicle*, February 16, 1986); "Bring Fair Play to Taxing of 'Perks'" (F. H. Stark, *New York Times*, September 18, 1983); and "Who's to Say What They Are Worth?" (M. J. Roming, *New York Times*, September 18, 1983) have become frequent. Roming writes: "The fracas arises not so much over which fringes ought to be taxable but rather over *how* these fringes should be taxed. How are benefits to be valued and how are costs to be allocated among employees?" He points out that these are not issues that can be adequately resolved by legislative acts and tax rules, whatever those acts and rules would impose. Some fringe benefits can be taxed, but how to estimate and tax the value of various benefits in kind or favors, which are frequently more valuable than monetary receipts? The nature of entitlements is not clearly defined either. Is the right and even the obligation to send children to school an entitlement? How much is it worth in pecuniary terms? Can a government-paid hospital stay be considered income?

10. The article, "How Aid to Elderly Hurts Young Workers" (*San Francisco Chronicle*, April 10, 1986), by the syndicated economics writer Warren T. Brookes, illustrates this point well. Brookes writes: "Since 1969, poverty among America's young adults has risen more than 130 percent, from 7.3 percent to nearly 17 percent, a stunning number that has been largely obscured by the rapid 57 percent *drop* in poverty among the elderly from 16.8 percent to 7.3." He quotes a number of writers, who have developed similar statistics.

According to U.S. and Western European (German, particularly) press reports, since 1980, benefits for the elderly rose between 15 and 20 percent (U.S. = 21 percent). Germans, Swedes, and others take early retirement, some claiming to be unfit to work at age fifty and even earlier. At the same time, the real value of wages earned by young workers, measured in constant currencies, has declined by 2 and 5 percent. The rate of unemployment and poverty among the young (18–25 years) is higher than in any other group, except ethnic minorities.

11. Before adoption of European concepts, in other parts of the world rights differing from private ownership had been recognized. For instance: most African tribal societies operated under some variety of land-tenure system. In some instances, under such a system, different sections of the population were entitled to different rights to the same land. In others, land was periodically reallotted to users in accordance with changing needs of families. In the Middle East, many societies operated under systems of ownership characterized by M. Weber as "prebendal domain." Although members of society possessed use rights, which they could sell to other individuals, the monarch retained superior owner's rights to all property under his domination.

CHAPTER 4. CONFLICTING PHILOSOPHIES

1. The conservative camp comprises several movements: the traditionalists, neo-conservatives, economic monetarists, libertarians, religious fundamentalist, the radical right.

2. Carnoy and Shearer (1983), who published several books in which they literally call for a new social contract, and are considered in some circles new contractarians, do not refer to Rawls' work.

3. Thus, Wolff (1977, 17) notes:

The constraint Rawls hit upon was so minimal, so natural, so manifestly a constraint under which any person would consent to operate insofar as he made any pretensions at all to having a morality, that Rawls would, if he could prove his theorem, be in a position to say to a reader:
If you are a rationally self-interested agent, and if you are to have a morality at all, then you must acknowledge as binding upon you the moral principle I shall enunciate.

4. Daniels (1974, xiv) notes that:

the dominant moral and political ideology of our time reflected in these principles is, of course, a form of liberalism. Perhaps it is more egalitarian liberalism than dominated the eighteenth and nineteenth centuries, but it is liberalism nonetheless. Rawls' goal, then is to produce a persuasive, coherent framework for this liberalism.

Wolff, who repeatedly praises the elegance of Rawls' allocution, ends his book by asking (1977, 195, 210), "Is Rawls right?" He answers:

I find it extraordinarily difficult to get a grip on this question, despite the care with which Rawls develops subsidiary themes in his theory. The problem, in part, stems from the fact that Rawls says little or nothing about the concrete facts of social, economic, and political reality. . . . One could characterize it briefly, even brusquely, as a philosophical *apologia* for an egalitarian brand of liberal welfare-state capitalism."

And, further (210): "by focusing exclusively on distribution rather than on production, Rawls obscures the real roots of that distribution." Wolff refers to Nozick (1974, 198), who makes a similar point and writes that Rawls describes things as though they fell from heaven like manna, as though no one has any special claim to any portion of anything; the only thing to do is to distribute everything equally. Wolff raises what seems to me the most important question (202). Of the redistributors, "be they econometricians, elected representatives, or philosopher-kings," he asks, "How are they to acquire this power? How will they protect it and enlarge it once they have it? Whose interests will they serve?" In other words, he suspects that they would become just another power elite. Barry (1975, 166) is even more critical:

> The significance of *A Theory of Justice* is as a statement of liberalism which isolates its crucial features by making private property in the means of production, distribution and exchange a contingent matter rather than an essential part of the doctrine and introduces a principle of distribution which could, suitably interpreted and with certain factual assumptions, have egalitarian implications. If socialism is identified with public ownership or with equality, then this form of liberalism is compatible with socialism; though, by the same token, socialism defined by either of these criteria is also compatible with the anti-thesis of liberalism.

Schaefer (1979, 106), the author of *Justice or Tyranny?*, who is highly critical not only of Rawls' but of the liberals' mode of philosophy and ethics in general, states that:

> the widespread acclaim that *A Theory of Justice* has received from the intellectual community seems explicable only in the light of something extrinsic to the author's reasoning: the fact that Rawls' sense of justice is widely shared by other members of the contemporary intellectual class in America.

He calls this work an example of "redemptive egalitarianism," a term coined by Charles Frankel. And he points out (107) that

> the real root of the movement for redemptive egalitarianism is in the phenomenon of liberal guilt—the feeling on the part of relatively wealthy and well educated people that they must atone for their superior privileges by demonstrating their commitment to promote 'social justice' for the less advantaged.

For other criticism, see Barber (1975); Van Dyke (1975); Chapman (1975); Harsanyi (1975); Fishkin (1975); Rae (1975); and Bloom (1975). Some of these critics propose modifications, which in their opinion would make Rawls's theory "rational."

5. *Statecraft as Soulcraft* has so far been favorably received by most of the press; patently, with some exceptions in certain conservative publications. The conservative *The American Spectator* (October 1983) published a lengthy review by Joseph Sobran, the editor of *National Review*, in which he accused Will of being not conservative enough. Certain journals carried articles in response to the criticism of George Will by "more conservative conservatives": "George Will and American Conservatism," by James Nuechterlein in *Commentary* (October 1983); "A Special Kind of Conservative," by Nelson W. Polsby in *Fortune* (July 26, 1983). See also R. Emmett Tyrrell, Jr., "Why Will?" *The American Spectator* (September 1986). For a sample of Will's articles on contemporary issues, see Will (1986).

6. For a different argument see Zetterbaum (1977).

CHAPTER 5. ECONOMIC AND POLITICAL SYSTEMS OF WESTERN NATIONS: TYPOLOGY

1. This is not to deny that democracy in some conditions can be ineffectual in certain circumstances or that democracy cannot be manipulated.

2. The book, *Les Règles de la méthode sociologique*, was first published in Paris by Alcan in 1895. For rules relevant to this book, see the English edition (Durkheim 1966, 133–140). For a discussion of Durkheim's covariations, see also Marsh (1967, 6–9, 21-26). He points out that Durkheim

> distinguishes three applications of the comparative method or the method of co-variations: (1) the analysis of variations within one society at a single point in time, (2) the comparison of societies generally alike but differing in certain aspects, . . . and (3) the comparison of societies generally dissimilar yet sharing some feature, or different periods in life of the society showing radical change.

The New State can be classified under the second method.

3. Vallier's (1973, 203-204) characterization of comparative analysis is applicable to this book. In his words:

> *1*. Macro-structuralists, whatever their particular inclination or position, are preoccupied with problems of structure and change in large-scale, complex units, e.g. societies, international systems, institutions, bureaucracies, or wide-ranging organizations.
> *2*. Their styles of thinking and modes of addressing problems are characteristically guided by classical theories, abstract classificatory schemes, ideal types, and systemic models which serve to reduce or order complex ranges of empirical phenomena into manageable units or clusters.
> *3*. Macro-structuralists evidence a deep and pervasive interest in structural variations and socio-cultural universals, both of which stimulate them to make explicit and often bold applications of the "comparative method."
> *4*. Discourse and analysis are typically holistic and contextual, bringing attention to multiple levels of socio-cultural reality, part-part and part-whole relationships, and patterns of interdependence among major structural entities.

4. A quantitative analysis would seek to discuss the growing functions of

the state and produce a typology of etatized societies based on the analysis of data as tentatively outlined:

(*a*) Percentage of GNP appropriated annually by the government through taxation and other levies imposed on the population by the state or extracted in the form of profits from state-owned industries of the economy and distributed through budgetary allocations; (*b*) comparative assessment of the total value of assets owned by the nation as a whole, including the private sector (the total to be subdivided into ownership of productive means, consumptive property, infrastructure, and administrative means or other categories); (*c*) governmental budgetary data and analyses, particularly government expenditure, subdivided into external, domestic, and other budgetary categories (e.g., allocations for defense, transfer payments, administration, repayment of debt, protection of environment, maintenance of the infrastructure, etc.) related to national income. Nutter's (1978) comparative analysis of trends in OECD countries and the United States exemplifies this type of work. Rose's studies of mixed economies, the welfare system, and budgetary allocations are strongly based on quantitative analyses. Rose, however, also develops qualifying conclusions. Data would include also: (*d*) figures on the percentage of labor force directly employed by different levels of government and in state-owned industries (as compared to those employed in the private sector), and figures on the percentage of the population dependent on transfer payments, receipt of goods, and other benefits from the government; (*e*) figures on services provided by the state to the population; (*f*) figures reflecting the size and role of state-owned industries vis-à-vis the private sector, and the ratio of state-owned industries to mixed and privately owned corporations (considering the volume of assets and outputs involved, net income, size of the labor force involved, the growth rate, and other data).

   5. Lindblom (1977, 133) lists the following rights and prerogatives accorded to citizens in polyarchic systems: freedom to form and join organizations; freedom of expression; right to vote; eligibility for public office; right of political leaders to compete for support; right of political leaders to compete for votes; alternative sources of information; free and fair elections (open, honestly conducted, one man–one vote), which decide who is to hold top authority. Institutions in polyarchic systems depend on votes and other expressions of preference. He concludes by stating "All polyarchal authority systems include by rule each of these guarantees, though all imperfectly." He, in fact, equates political democracy with polyarchy—the rule of representatives of many, involving a wide gamut of freedoms: expression, association, initiative, and the protection of individual and group interests (on polyarchy, see Dahl 1971). Such a system must inevitably include freedom of entrepreneurial initiative. As I write elsewhere in this book, contemporary understanding of democracy includes also maintenance of the safety net, the structure of social services maintained by the state.

   6. One can think of a method of summation, estimating, and applying credit points for characteristics displayed by the institutions and correspondingly marked in relation to both the polyarchy-authoritarian and etatization scales, which would be more quantitative than the scales applied in this book. In such a depiction of nations, positions on the table would be more exact. Yet, the political situation in contemporary societies is volatile, and such estimates would have to be constantly amended. For a different analysis of politicoeconomic aspects of the state see Nell (1983).

   7. Although small nations are distinguished in our classification under a separate (*D*) type, the small democracies under etatization included in this category can also be regarded as a subvariation of type (*B*).

   The characteristics discerned in this group can be outlined (Katzenstein 1984) as

follows:
- (a) The political and national management processes in these countries are advanced through consensus before the issues are officially debated in parliaments and other decisionmaking bodies.
- (b) Austria, and, to an extent, Switzerland are democracies "with a strong flavor of oligarchy, where almost all the decisions are taken by hard-headed men talking together in smoke-filled rooms behind closed doors " (Katzenstein 1984, 66).
- (c) In the small democracies, bureaucracies are weak. The state, cooperative, and private sectors are fused under consultation between leaders of principal interest groups. In each of these nations, a single interest group particularly influences the decisionmaking processes. In Austria (Katzenstein 1984, 77), "the consensual system of governance" is particularly influenced by the Trade Union Federation (*Österreichischer Gewerkschaftsbund*; ÖGB). This is also the opinion of other observers. Hughes (1962, 34), for example, remarks:

Swiss democracy is geared to pressure groups; it is a form of government calculated to call such groups into existence and give them power. The system could conceivably continue for a time without parties, but without pressure groups it would not work at all.

In Switzerland (see Katzenstein 1984, 113–116), changing from a "voting democracy" into a "bargaining democracy," the unions are decentralized, but big business is strongly integrated under an umbrella organization—the Vorort (116): "The Vorort in Zurich sets the switches for the government in Bern." We are informed by Katzenstein that once consensus is reached, the parliament makes no changes, or only minor changes, in 80 percent of the bills that it considers.

One could notice that some of these characteristics apply to other small nation democracies, e.g., to Israel or Denmark as well. In Israel (Ben-Porath 1986), the Histadrut—acting as a trade union, maintaining a developed system of social and health insurance, and as an owner of a large economic sector (transportation and construction businesses), and representative of rural settlements (*kibbutzim, moshavim*), cooperatives, and a variety of other enterprises—determines to a large extent the character of the national consensus. The Israeli economy can be characterized as a mixed economy, in which roughly three-fifths of the product originates in the private sector, one-fifth in the state-owned sector, and the other fifth in the Histadrut sector. Histadrut is also the most important force behind the Labour Party. Ben-Porath points out further that in the 1980s, the "etatist bias" has somewhat shifted from the socialist and Histadrut ideology to the greater determination of the economy by the state.

CHAPTER 6. DIRECT REGULATION

1. Some writers interpret "indirect regulation" as self-restraint and self-regulation to avoid negative sanctions; others define it still differently.

2. For an analysis of European systems of regulatory practice see Peacock (1984).

3. Mitnick (1980, 4–20 analyzes a wide variety of definitions and theories concerning the structure of the U.S. regulations and introduces four of his own definitions:

(1) Regulation is the intentional restriction of a subject's choice of activity, by an entity not directly party to or involved in the activity. (2) Regulation is the policing, with respect to a goal, of a subject's choice of activity, by an entity not directly party to or involved in that activity. (3) Regulation is the policing, according to a rule, of a subject's choice of activity, by an entity not directly party to or involved in that activity. (4) Regulation is the public administrative policing of a private activity with respect to a rule prescribed in the public interest.

He considers the first definition to be most general, and discusses other definitions, relating them to different concepts of "public interest." Mitnick also introduces his own typology of public interests. It is interesting to compare these and other authors' definitions of regulations to the one developed by OMB and included in the *Budget of the U.S. Government, 1987* (6a–15):

Federal regulations provide a large variety of goods and services to the public, including the protection of the environment, the creation of incentives for the development of useful innovations, and the fair and efficient disbursement of Federal entitlements. These three types of regulatory activities are examples of the major categories of regulation: social, economic, and managerial.

The document explains that social regulations establish standards "for the characteristics of product or for the methods of producing products." They are usually aimed at curbing unintended harmful effects of such activities (e.g., pollution, accidents). Economic regulation directly controls prices and market competition, and "curbs monopolistic behavior." Managerial regulation "sets the conditions for the efficient and proper use of Government funds and property."

4. The press reports that a new regulation, affecting the banking industry and the stock market, is currently in preparation. According to these reports, the Glass-Steagall regime is to be abolished. The Federal Reserve and the SEC is either to merge or to become more closely linked. The new body would control mergers and keep a more watchful eye on insider trading.

5. According to other estimates, figures were actually higher.

6. Subsequently, both the trucking and aviation industries became deregulated.

7. For more examples, see MacAvoy (1970); Weidenbaum (1979); Jacobs (1979); and Gatti (1981).

8. In other terms, as Bernstein (1955, 74) put it:

The life cycle of an independent commission can be divided into four periods: gestation, youth, maturity, and old age. . . . Some commissions maintain their youthfulness for a fairly long time, while others seem to age rapidly and apparently never pass through the period of optimistic adolescence.

Some may resist the debilitating pressures of old age for a longer time, but eventually, in his opinion, all become debilitated, turgid with routine, and wastefulness. I may add that even when regulatory agencies outlive their purpose, as the case was, for instance, with the Appalachian Regional Commission, they are often maintained for a long time under different pretenses, because they provide sinecures for friends of influential people or fulfil other, like needs of the administration.

9. The regulation advocates (Tolchin & Tolchin 1983, 4) frequently claimed that "complaints of executive regulation had become management's all purpose cop-out."

10. Five years later, the Roper organization conducted another survey on public attitude toward government regulation (*Roper et al. Report 84–8.* August 11–18, 1985; here after *Public Opinion* August–September 1985, 14). Questions asked and answers obtained were as follows: Taking everything into account, in general, would you say that government regulations . . . improved the safety of products that are sold? *Have 75%, Have not 17%*; Resulted in higher prices, or lower prices, for regulated products? *Higher prices 73%, Lower prices 6%*; Reduced the use of unsafe products and ingredients? *Have 65%, Have not 23%*; Burdened companies with unnecessary red tape and paper work? *Have 60%, Have not 22%*; Reduced pollution? *Have 57%, Have not 33%*; Have been enforced too strictly, or not strictly enough? *Too strictly 10%, Not strictly enough 56%, About right 22%*.

The researchers conclude: "On balance the public believes government regulation to be beneficial. While people acknowledge that regulations in general raise prices and burden companies with unnecessary paperwork, they also feel that the rules serve a larger interest."

11. The task force disbanded in September 1983, before the new election campaign. In its final report, the task force claimed to have saved consumers more than $150 billion over the next ten years.

12. The exception is Eads and Fix (1984). The book contains papers presented to a conference on the practice of regulatory activities under the Reagan administration. Of course, one can list articles in the daily press and magazines on the subject. However, under the Reagan administration, regulation ceased to be a burning issue. For a balanced analysis of direct regulatory activities in the United States from the perspective of the 1980s see Leone 1986.

CHAPTER 7. INDIRECT REGULATION

1. According to the *Budget of the United States Government, 1987* (6e–41), the total percentage of GNP appropriated by the federal government during the last twenty years was: 1968, 17.9; 1969, 20.1; 1970, 19.5; 1971, 17.7; 1972, 18.0; 1973, 18.0; 1974, 18.6; 1975, 18.3; 1976, 17.5; 1977, 18.4; 1978, 18.4; 1979, 18.9; 1980, 19.4; 1981, 20.1; 1982, 19.7; 1983, 18.1; 1984, 18.0; 1985, 18.6; 1986 (estimate), 18.5. Final government consumption as percentage of GDP in 1984 was, for: Canada, 21.0; France, 16.4; Federal Republic of Germany, 20.1; Great Britain, 21.9; Italy, 19.4; Japan, 10.0; Sweden, 27.8.

2. Private employees of federal and state governments are currently required to pay social security taxes. The annual maximum taxable earnings and contribution rate of employees (and employers) in 1984 was $37,800; the maximum annual contribution in 1983 was $ 2,391.90 (*Background Material* 1984, 58–59). At the time this book will appear in print, one would expect the allowable contribution to be around $2,800–3,000.

3. This book first used the 1986 U.S. budget's analysis. Later, the 1987 budget was considered. Because I decided, regardless of exceptions, to consider this research as taking into consideration developments until the end of 1985, the discussion is more focused on 1986 data (the budget released in 1985). Let me point out some differences, nevertheless: In 1987 every dollar of government revenue comprised 39¢ collected in income taxes, 30¢ in social insurance receipts, 9¢ in corporate income taxes, 4¢ in excise taxes, 14¢ in borrowed money, and 4¢ in other receipts. The 1986 general proportions were retained on the expenditure side, with the exception of spending on defense 28¢ instead of 29¢, but spending on other federal operations 6¢

instead of 5¢ as in the previous year.

4. Reagan's tax-cutting reform, the Economic Recovery Act of 1981, was enacted with the declared objective of reducing taxes by 25 percent. A number of other changes in tax laws were introduced simultaneously. Individuals and corporations under the new reform were expected to pay about $750 billion less in taxes in the coming six years than they would have had to under previous legislation. The administration expected that the savings would produce additional investments, a significant upturn in economic growth, and, eventually, higher revenues. Yet, the immediate effect of increases in social security and defense spending produced the larger deficit. New tax reform was introduced in 1982, with the objective of raising $98.3 billion over the next three years. Rather than imposing higher taxes directly, the government resorted to hidden taxes; 15 cents was added to the price of cigarettes, a tax was included in the price of telephone and certain other services. Loopholes on tax payments were closed, exemptions reduced, and existing tax rules more strictly applied to collect higher revenues. A minimum 20-percent tax on incomes higher than $100,000, after certain allowable exemptions, was also imposed.

5. Social security funds in the United States are held in three trusts. At the end of the 1970s, the Old Age and Survivors' Fund experienced a shortage. In order to escape "bankruptcy," the fund borrowed $600 million from the fund for the disabled. Although the three funds are now in a more stable condition, all three, according to some experts, face the prospect of substantial deficits in the future. On the coming crash of social security, see Peterson 1982; Ehrbar 1980; 1982. On the current social security surplus, see the *New York Times*, November 27, 1988, sec. E5.

6. According to Gutmann (1979) $176 billion in 1976, and $220 billion in 1978, was generated in the U.S. "subterranean economy." Feige (1979) expresses the opinion that two or three times as much money was involved. Feige (1979) claims that the "'irregular economy' in the U.S. was in 1978 equal to 27% of the measured U.S. GNP, and may be growing at around 40% a year in nominal terms." According to other estimates (see *U.S. News & World Report*, September 26, 1983), $298.9 billion of income in 1981 was not reported for taxes ($15.0 billion by corporations; $34.2 billion in illegal activities in drug trafficking, gambling, and prostitution; and $249.7 billion by tax-evading individuals). It has also been estimated that almost half of the capital gains received from the sale of securities and real estate have been unreported. For another report on the "shadow economy" in different nations, see *The Economist*, September 19, 1987. Blades (1982, 29), in a review of the literature on the "hidden economy" in OECD nations and the United States, reports: "Several writers have recently suggested that 'hidden' or 'underground' economic activities are a large and growing proportion of total economic activity in many OECD countries." Blades refers to Charreyron, who cites estimates that hidden activities may amount to nearly 8 percent of GDP in Great Britain and 10 percent in Sweden. He also writes that Forte has calculated that the hidden economy in Italy has generated value equal to 20 percent of GDP in 1978 (see also: Stuart 1981; Ray 1981; Bawly 1982 ; Smith and Wied-Nebbeling 1986) Bawly's analysis of "how inept government and inflation feed the subterranean economy" is particularly interesting in view of the perspective developed in this book.

7. In his message introducing the 1987 budget, Reagan expresses the opinion of how the deficit could be reduced as a result of "restructuring and returning the federal government to its proper role." He posits: High priority programs should be adequately funded, but unnecessary programs are no longer affordable. Many other programs should be reduced to a more appropriate scale. The government should not compete with the private sector. Many services can be provided better by state and local governments. Remaining federal activities should be better managed. Finally, user fees should be charged for services where appropriate. [Each of these sentences

is the title of a longer discussion by the president.]

8. For a more detailed explanation of these functions, see *Special Analysis* of the *Budget of the U.S. Government, 1986* and *Budget of the U.S. Government, 1987.*

9. In January 1982, when this became a big issue, the principal debtors of the Third World, mostly to U.S. banks, were Brazil, $38.3 billion; Mexico, $33.5 billion; India, $17.3 billion; South Korea, $16.3 billion; of the Soviet bloc, Poland (mostly to West German banks) $27.0 billion ($16 billion to banks and $10.5 billion to governments); Soviet Union, $19.00 billion (according to other sources $65.4 billion); East Germany, $13 billion; Rumania, $10 billion.

10. In Western Europe, rescue operations of corporations induced or undertaken by government are regarded as part of the crisis-management function of the state. For an analysis of a number of such operations in West Germany, see Dyson (1984). Dyson discusses two modes of crisis management induced by the state: "bank-led rescue operations" and "the crisis cartel resolution". Cases discussed involve some of the largest German corporations: AEG, Grunding, Ruhr and the Saar, shipbuilding, and Krupp.

11. According to Cargill and Garcia (1982, 40; for documentation see Mortimer 1982):

> Four factors created the environment for successful passage of the Deregulation and Monetary Control Act: (1) the accelerating inflation rate in late 1979 and early 1980; (2) the increased ease with which binding constraints on competitive behavior were circumvented; (3) the reinterpretation of the banking collapse of the 1930s; and (4) the reevaluation of the Great Depression as part of the monetarist Keynesian debate.

CHAPTER 8. TWO-SECTOR ECONOMIES

1. Monsen and Walters (1983, 16) note that the state sector employs a much larger part of the labor force than cited in official statistical reports, which continue to regard many predominantly state-owned industries as belonging to the private sector.

2. Borcherding reports that two approaches were employed in his analyses: (*a*) "The Property Rights Approach," results of which are presented in a table, and (*b*) "The Public Choice Approach." Analysis of government waste is discussed as part of this concern. Borins (1986) is also instructive in this regard. Hemming and Mansoor (1988) of the IMF, weight out the social benefits of having "public enterprises" against the economic benefits of letting the private sector run industries, in a circumspect analysis.

3. The government intends, however, to keep some of the shareholding of these and other industries, which are believed to be revenue-producing, and of the National Coal Board and some others that cannot be privatized for various reasons. To demonstrate to the public that privatization is just a measure to enhance productivity and stimulate efficiency, the government is also planning to institute a system of pervasive regulation of monopolies and "natural monopolies," which would apply to privatized industries. In the mid-1980s, the Labour Party announced that when they are in government again, they will renationalize most of what has been privatized. That they did once before. The steel industry was nationalized, denationalized, and then nationalized again under changing Labour–Tory–Labour governments. Now,

they rather stress that privatization produced massive unemployment.

CHAPTER 9. GREAT BRITAIN

1. The size of the public sector in Great Britain, also called nationalized or state-owned, was estimated differently, depending on employed criteria and definitions. In government documents published in the late 1970s, narrow definitions were employed. According to such criteria (*The Economist*, November 27, 1976) those industries are nationalized whose assets are in public ownership vested in a corporation, engaged in industrial or other trading activities under boards, composed not of civil servants but appointees of a secretary of state. Such industries were differentiated from other public corporations maintained to produce income in trade of goods and services. Thus, the Bank of England, the British Broadcasting Corporation, the Housing Corporation, the British National Oil Corporation, Hawker Siddley Aviation, and numerous other industries nationalized at some date by the state were not listed as nationalized industries. *A Study of U.K. Nationalised Industries* (1976) and the background paper to it, "Financial Analysis" (1976), published by the National Economic Development Office, employing these criteria, list only nine nationalized industries in 1976: British Airways, British Gas, British Rail, British Steel Corporation, Electricity Industry England and Wales, National Coal Board, Post Office, National Bus Company, National Freight Corporation. The combined figures for the nine were: 9.3% of the value added revenue (£8,662 million); 6.7% of the labor force employment; and 13.5% of fixed domestic investment. The list recognizes the existence of other nationalized and other public-sector corporations (11.1% of the national value-added revenues, 8% of employment, 19% of national fixed investment). Other official documents listed British Telecom, BL, British Shipbuilders, British Airports Authority, Civil Aviation Authority, and the British Waterways Board as nationalized or publicly owned.

Some authors (Rees 1973; Abraham 1974, 315–316, citing *Times 1,000*, 1972–1973), listed up to thirty-five large nationalized industries in 1975. Pryke (1981, 2), in a list titled "Public Enterprise in Perspective, 1977," includes eleven industries: British Electricity Boards, Telecommunications, British Gas, British Rail, NCB collieries, Postal Services, BSC: Iron and Steel, BL: Vehicles UK, British Airways, National and Scottish Bus Groups, National Freight Corporation, and a number of other public enterprises. According to this count, in 1981 nationalized industries employed 2,345,000 individuals (9.4% of the labor force) and produced 12.7% of GDP, before stock appreciation. The *Government Finance Statistics Yearbook* (1983) lists in the section "United Kingdom" forty-five nonfinancial public enterprises and five public financial institutions.

State ownership in the economy extends beyond the formally nationalized industries. The British government acquired shares of a number of companies in "rescue operations." Although such companies were administered by government appointed directors, supervisors, and members of boards determining financial and productive targets of such corporations, these companies continued to be listed as belonging to the private sector (e.g., Rolls Royce Ltd., British Sugar Corporation, International Computers Ltd., British Petroleum, Beagle Aircraft Ltd.). Under Thatcher's privatization policies, these and other companies listed in some records as private enterprises, were privatized. Analogies of this situation exist in other nations.

2. K. Smith (1984, 189–191) argues that there is no evidence that the British middle class is less dynamic and less entrepreneurial than comparable classes in other Western societies.

3. For a discussion of the new middle classes in Great Britain see: Hutber

(1976); Useem (1984); Jamieson (1980); Elliot and McCrone (1987); Abercrombie and Urry (1983).

4. Summing up the election results, *British Public Opinion* (June 1987) reports, "The 1987 general election saw the most professional and well presented Labour campaign in the party's history. Despite that, it also saw, for the first time in the century, the third successive election of a Conservative Prime Minister."

5. At 8 percent in October 1988, unemployment was lower than 10.2 percent a year ago, and lower than in West Germany and France, but it is still considered high.

CHAPTER 10. FROM ÉTATISME TO ÉTATISME

1. One may recall that one of the main points of Marx's criticism of the Paris Commune was its failure to nationalize banks.

2. As of March 1981, 16% of employees earned salaries in the central administration; 9% in the local administration; 1% in the social security administration; 6% in public and nationalized industries; and 68% in the private sector. *Annuaire statistique de la France* (1986) reports that in 1985, 2,155,545 individuals were employed by various levels of government. One cannot find in this or other statistics data on comparative employment in the state-owned sector as contrasted with the private sector.

3. The *Haut Conseil du Secteur Public Rapport*, Vol. 1, 1984, contains the most extensive analysis of the nationalization policy and management of state-owned industries in France. The report does not include services, educational and medicare systems, or welfare and pension schemes in the public sector. Key industries, which can be regarded as part of the infrastructure, tend to be classified in the literature as *Grandes Enterprises Nationales* (GEN).

4. The *Haut Conseil* report, Vol. 1 (1984, 313) lists the following state-owned corporations among the thirty-six first-category French industrial exporters: Renault, CGE, Thomson, SNIAS, Rhône-Poulenc, Usinor, Dassault, CEA, SNEA, PUK, S. Gobain, Vallourec (private, but 25% owned by Usinor), SNECMA, Sacilor, Matra, CDF-Chimie, Ato-Chimie, and Bull. Eighteen other first category exporters remained in the private sector.

5. Of books written by Crozier, the following discuss bureaucratization and domination by the system as a principal cause of decline and malevolence in contemporary France: *The Bureaucratic Phenomenon*; *The Stalled Society*; *Strategies for Change*; *Actors and Systems*. In *The Trouble with America* (1984, 118), Crozier writes that the same disease caused by "visceral attachment to centralized bureaucracy" is now overwhelming the United States and causing that nation's decline. Crozier diagnoses the United States' "serious disease" as "delirium of due process" and "legal madness."

CHAPTER 11. CENTRALIZED MANAGEMENT

1. The *OECD Economic Surveys 1986–1987: Germany* reports (1987, 18): "The consolidation efforts pursued over the last four years or so resulted in 1985 in a stabilisation of the *debt-to-GNP ratio* at a moderate level by international standards." They note a rapid increase in *Lander* debt from 28 to 33 percent in the early 1980s. German writers complain about these, in their opinion, high budgetary deficits, and German public opinion (in contrast, for instance, to Italian), expresses a strong disapproval for deficits. However, the survey evaluates German deficits as quite

moderate in comparison with those of other nations. Again, German writers complain that the subsidization of industries and agriculture is very costly. The survey reports (25) "subsidisation in Germany is not high compared to many other countries."

2. Webber (1983, 61) maintains that the close cooperation (at all levels) between the government and the organizations of both labor and capital, which distinguishes West Germany from the other large Western industrial states, is a major factor contributing to its stability. Riemer (1982), discussing the crisis management orchestrated by Schmidt under the Social Democratic–Liberal coalition in the late 1970s, argues that the Bundesbank played an exceptionally important role in maintaining economic stability by conducting an independent monetary policy free of short-range political objectives. Knott (1981), in a sense, complements Reuss's (1963) earlier analyses of West German financial *dirigiste* practices by discussing new developments—Western Germany's budgetary policies and other forms of financial management. See also Wallach (1985, 244–246), who expresses a somewhat different opinion.

3. The state's holding of VBA shares was reduced from 46% to 20%, VIAG from 100% to 60%; of Industrieverwaltungsgesellschaft from 100% to less than 50%.

4. For a detailed analysis of IRI, ENI, EFIM, EGAM, and EAGAT until the middle of the 1970s, see *The State Participation System in Italy* (Italy. Presidency of the Council of Ministers 1977). The subdivisions within these organizations are frequently changing.

5. The 1988 *Fortune* International 500 (August 1, 1988) lists IRI (sales, $41,270.0 million; net income, $146.5 million; employees, 422,000) on the third place in the list of the biggest industrial corporations outside the United States and ninth place in the world; ENI (sales, $24,242.5 million; net income, $483.6 million; employees, 119,152) as fifteenth in the list of the biggest industrial corporations outside the United States and twenty-sixth in the world. In contrast, the two largest Italian privately owned corporations reported proportionally much larger profits: Fiat (sales, $29,642.8 million; net income, $1,830.2 million; employees, 270,578) is eighth in the list of the biggest industrial corporations outside the United States and seventeenth in the world; Montedison, partially, but to a declined extent owned by the state-owned companies (sales, $10,636.2 millon; net income, $315.4 million; employees, 66,785) as forty-eighth in the list of the biggest industrial corporations outside the United States.

6. Are (1982, 54) makes the same point, i.e., "the greater a company's losses, the more credit it secured and vice versa. In respect of all companies, during the decade, self-financing covered 47% of the increase in net fixed assets. But for the public companies that coverage amounted to 26.3%, for the private firms 76.1%."

7. The 1988 *Fortune* (August 1, 1988) international list of 500 biggest industrial corporations outside the United States in 1987 includes nine biggest industrial corporations (total sales, $119,515.4 million; net income after sales, $3,045.9 million) in Italy (population 57 million), and nineteen such corporations (total sales, $68,335.4 million; net income after sales, $2,345.0) in Sweden (population over 8 million). IRI and ENI—giant state-owned corporations—are enumerated among Italian top corporations. Only one state-owned corporation—Procordia—is listed among the Swedish nineteen. Most of these corporations appeared on the list of 500 biggest only recently, which can be regarded as an indication that big privately owned multinationals are doing very well under Swedish nonconformist socialist rule. In contrast to Italian corporations, operating mostly in the domestic market, Swedish corporations produce most of their commodities for international markets (e.g., Volvo and Electrolux produce 70–90 percent of their output for international markets). They also employ sizable numbers of employees in foreign countries.

8. Another initiative of *Mitbestimmung*, instituting wider participation in

ownership, was favored by the Christian Democrats in the 1960s. Under this policy, advanced simultaneously as a denationalization program, workers were invited to obtain shares of state-owned companies in which they were employed in lieu of pay raises and other benefits. It was assumed that as "owners," the employees would develop a "more positive work attitude" and refrain from strikes and other "class conflict" activities. Advertised as an alternative to strictly capitalist or strictly state ownership, and supported by unions, the program was implemented in Volkswagenwerke, Preussag, and VEBA, but became unpopular after a short time.

9. On etatization in West Germany see: Ernst-Porksen (1984); *Die Zähmung des Leviathan* (1980); and *Zuviel Staat?* (1982).

CHAPTER 12. ETATIZATION AND NATIONALISM

1. According to other accounts (see *Canada Year Book* 1988, 21.7) the figures are different. The 1985 Canadian exports to the United States, as recorded by Canada (in billions of Canadian dollars) was $93.2. These exports were recorded in the United States as U.S. imports, valuing $94.2; reconciled data: $95.0. Canadian imports from the United States, as recorded by Canada, amounted to $74.6; recorded in the United States as U.S. exports, $64.5; reconciled data: $73.5. The trade balance according to the Canadian count was + $18.6; according to U.S. records, - $29.7 for the United States; reconciled data: Canada + $21.5. *In toto* reconciled data for the balance of trade in Canada's favor are, in 1981, + $3.4; 1982, + $12.1; 1983, + $14.4; 1984, + $20.0; 1985, + $21.5.

2. In 1982, of the capital invested in manufacturing, 51% was Canadian, 38% U.S., and 11% from other countries; in petroleum and natural gas, 55% was Canadian, 35% U.S., and 10% from other nations; in mining and smelting, 57% was Canadian, 31% U.S., and 12% from other nations.

3. In manufacturing, 43% was Canadian, 43% U.S.; in petroleum and gas, 25% Canadian, 59% U.S.; in mining and smelting, 42% Canadian, 45% U.S.

4. According to Malcolm, trying to please Canadian readers (1986, 191–193):

It is entirely possible today that some average American works in a skyscraper owned by Canadians in a downtown being redesigned by Canadians, processes office forms printed by Canadians, grabs a quick lunch in a restaurant owned by Canadians, buys a Canadian novel in a bookstore owned by Canadians, or watches construction of a new office tower being built by Canadians. After work he jumps on a railcar made by Canadians and powered by electricity from Canada to meet his wife in a car built in Canada from Canadian iron ore to drive on Canadian cement to his home constructed by Canadians with Canadian lumber, underwritten by Canadian financing, and heated by Canadian natural gas to watch Canadian football on a cable TV system owned by Canadians or to read a Canadian-owned magazine or Canadian-owned news-paper printed on Canadian paper.

This fictitious American family, which might well be protected by Canadian insurance companies, could listen to their favorite rock group, all Canadians. They might go out to dinner at a luxurious Canadian-owned hotel and then to a racetrack to watch Canadian Thoroughbreds run. On the weekends, if the weather coming down from Canada is nice, they could take in a Canadian-made movie with Canadian stars like Christopher Plummer, Donald Sutherland, Genevieve Bujold, or Margot Kidder. Or they might prefer to feed the Canada geese that moved into a nearby park or see an American movie about an all-American hero named Superman growing up in a most bucolic midwestern American small town that was really filmed in a Canadian small town. . . . Economically, Canada, the old colonial pussycat, doormat to foreigners plundering resources and profits, is fast becoming a voracious tiger, especially within the North American economic scene. . . . A new generation of aggressive savvy, and well-financed Canadian businessmen is confidently buying back large portions of foreign-controlled companies at home and simultaneously marching south with energetic business imagination and cunning into an essentially open United States market ten times the size of Canada's.

In my opinion, instead of "The Economy," this part of Malcolm's book should more appropriately have been called "The Canadian Imperialist Dream." Not even in Canada is it possible to experience such a wholesome Canadian life.

5. Ownership in this instance means principal ownership of 20 percent or more of shares.

6. The reader must be warned against reliability of these calculations and regard the paragraph rather as an example. The annual *Canadian Business 500* (1984) was selected because it seemed more suitable for the analysis than the more widely read *Financial Post*, also carrying lists of 500 principal corporations.

7. The number of recipients of old-age security, for instance, increased from 1,105,776 in 1966, to 1,957,288 in 1976, to 2,652,234 in 1986; the number of recipients of the guaranteed income supplement went up from 860,392 in 1971, to 1,087,113 in 1976, to 1,329,886 in 1986. For another set of figures and analysis of the "The Welfare State" see the *Report of the Royal Commission* (1985, 2: 545) and Ismael (1987).

8. Quebec developed an gigantic electricity generating hydrosystem and sells energy to New York and other states south of the border. However, to pay for the construction of new megastations in northern areas of the province, Quebec imposed higher taxes on citizens. Sasketchewan nationalized the potash industry.

CHAPTER 13. SOFT ETATIZATION

1. in 1981, Japanese plants employed 14,000 robots; 4,100 were employed in the United States, 2,300 in West Germany, 1000 in France, 600 in Sweden, and 500 in Great Britain (*New York Times*, December 13, 1981, Sect. 3: 1, citing *Daiva Securities America*, "Robot Industry Association" Wertheim & Co.).

2. As a result of well-developed preventive medicine, life expectancy in Japan is one of the highest in the world. In 1983, it was 74.20 years for males and 79.78 for females (see Sone 1985, 21). Because of the small number of unemployed, the Japanese government did not have to spend as much as other industrialized nations did on transfer payments to the unemployed. It was also spending proportionally less on welfare and on support for single female-parent families. Sone (1) writes with circumspection that though Japanese expenditure for social security as a proportion of GNP is still relatively small compared to other industrialized nations, "social security expenditures as a proportion of the general account in Japanese government has been a largest proportion for the last ten years." According to figures in his article, Japan's

health expenditure in 1984 was $500 per head (U.S.: $1,500), Japan had 128 doctors per 100,000 population (U.S.: 192), Japan's life expectancy (77 years) was longer than in the United States (75 years), Japanese infant mortality per 1,000 was 7 (U.S.: 12), instances of death from heart disease per 100,000 were in Japan 266 (U.S.: 435); the difference between Japan and Western Germany is even greater. He indicates that the expenditures on social security do not solve problems alone.

3. At present, Gorbachev's leadership is taking a different approach. Family is again proclaimed an important unit of social structure. The party expects the family to take part in socialization of individuals, and the individuals to support senior members of the family, partially relieving the state from this obligation. Pavlik Morozov, the boy declared a hero under Stalin, who reported his parents to the police for expressing anti-party opinions, was declared not worthy of that title by Gorbachev.

4. Johnson (1978, 27) discerns six types of public corporation in Japan: (1) direct government enterprises; (2) special legal entities, narrowly defined; (3) special legal entities, broadly defined; (4) auxiliary organs (*gaikaku dantai*), foundations, promotion associations, and so forth; (5) national policy companies, narrowly defined; (6) national policy companies, broadly defined. He defines their functions as follows (16):

> For one, they make loans to implement official industrial policies and to aid low productivity or declining sectors of the economy. They also spend funds to strengthen the industrial infrastructure or to develop resources. They help stabilize prices; they produce revenue; and they do research.

Only nationally important services, which the private sector regards as unprofitable, are operated by the state.

5. This financial practice began to change in the 1980s. More Japanese invest directly in the stock and the U.S. bond markets.

CHAPTER 14. THE NEW MORALITY

1. While it is true that the school, mass media, and peer group exerted then a greater influence than the family, community, and the Church, it is also true that this was a period when Western societies changed into consumer societies, and the population, at large, began to a greater degree to change their lifestyles in accordance to the dictates of the market. Supply determined demand, as economists say today.

2. See Yankelovich (1974).

3. According to the OECD (1971, 25) analytical report on development of higher education, enrolment after World War II increased. The figures for strictly university enrolment are lower. At first, after World War II, enrolment in non-university higher education increased rapidly; in the 1960s, enrolment in this type of institution began to decline, while university enrolment continued to increase.

4. Bell is not unique in this analysis. Other sociologists before him have described society as comprising several spheres of activity or coexisting orders of interaction. Parsons (see Parsons & Smelser 1957) and other functionalist theorists characterized society as consisting of four essential subsystems: the economy; the polity; institutions that preserve established patterns (i.e., culture); and what in some works was described as household, and in others as subsystems of integrative and socializing institutions. Mills (Gerth & Mills 1958) distinguished five institutional orders: political; economic; military; kinship; and religious. Mills (1956) then

described the power elite of society as being made up of the higher circles of three of these orders: the corporation chieftains; the warlords; and the political directorate.

5. See Yankelovich (1972, 169–170; Westhues, 1972).

6. Yankelovich's analysis is descriptive, but a "Do this and do not do that" list of the new rules in the "ethic of self-fulfilment" can be composed by extracting cases from the pages of his book. The rules are:

1. Seek self-fulfilment, not "a good family," "money," "social standing," and "responsibility." "Fulfillment is being my own person" (110–114; 146–150).
2. Be committed and concerned with causes, such as environmental deterioration, social justice, and the future of humanity.
3. Be creative (80–84).
4. "Bigness, newness, excess power and the other elements of conspicuous consumption are not as important as they once were" (38–42).
5. Hard work does not always pay. Do not make it the principle of your life. Yet, seek work that is challenging and interesting and do not engage in something solely because it pays (152–154).
6. Working in small groups and collectivities, based on collegial relationships, is better than working in large hierarchical structures (41–45).
7. Take advantage of available and abundant choices and freedoms in order to enhance your personal self-satisfaction (52–57).
8. Strive to balance your "emotional," "sexual," "material," and "intellectual" needs; and respond to new needs which arise as your "psychoculture" changes shape.
9. "Like sex in relation to love, the issue of money in relation to personal success is loaded with ambiguity" (56).
10. Search for your self beneath any artificial social roles imposed on you by the system (67–68).
11. Instead of acting out roles developed by society, design your own roles to fit your own, unique personality (75).
12. Be tolerant (87–88).
13. Do not get caught in the "rat race." Do not follow the Joneses (151–158).
14. Be yourself. Relax—wear casual dress, do not attribute great importance to codes, feel free, save competition for sports, enjoy modest aspirations (157–159).
15. *Your first duty is to yourself.* Do what you want to do (248).

7. Inglehart interprets the role of the mass media as "mixed." However, because the media do (11) communicate dissatisfaction, opposition to conventional values, alternative lifestyles, and dissonant signals, even when they are controlled by the "Establishment," the media, he writes, constitute some force of change.

8. In 1938, Mitchell reports, 75% believed that "for a woman to remain unmarried, she must be 'sick,''neurotic' or 'immoral'." In 1978, only a minority (26%) felt this way. The majority (60% in 1980) took a stand for the legalization of abortion on demand. In 1979, only 37% condemned premarital sex, compared to 85% in 1967. Most (56% in 1980, as compared with 33% in 1970) agreed that "both sexes have the responsibility to care for small children." Most (60% in 1977, in contrast to 26% in 1966) agreed that "the people running the country don't care what happens to me." In 1979, 75% of those interviewed agreed "that it is morally acceptable to be single and have children," 62% agreed "that interracial marriages are not morally wrong." Eighty two percent agreed "that it is not morally wrong for couples to live together even if they are not married." Only 21% wished for a return to standards of the past.

9. McCloskey and Zaller fail to recognize the affinity between capitalism and democracy. The fact is that only capitalist societies have effectively operated democratic systems. Although in theory, as Schumpeter did, one can envisage a noncapitalist, democratic, multiparty system, effective multiparty systems have not merged outside capitalist societies so far. "Democracy" (see Naess 1956) has been defined in many ways. Defined as a free-market system or equal-opportunity system in politics, the concept is quite compatible with the idea of capitalism. McCloskey and Zaller are right, however, that the idea has been recently frequently interpreted as a system of equality. In this sense it is, indeed, incompatible not only with capitalism, but with bureaucracy, organization, and achievable equity.

10. See Lipset and Schneider (1983, Ch. 5). The *New York Times* (February 16, 1986) reports, on the basis of surveys conducted in the United States and various European nations, that

> citizens of the leading Western European democracies trust their governments less than Americans trust theirs and are far less inclined to express pride in their countries. . . . According to surveys taken in late 1985, 49 percent of Americans said they trusted the Government in Washington to do what is right "all or most of the time." The comparable figure in West Germany was 41 percent, and in France and Italy 33 percent. In Britain and Spain, the figures were even lower. . . . In the United States, 87 percent said they were "very proud" to be an American. At the other extreme, only 21 percent of West Germans described themselves as "very proud" to be a German.

CHAPTER 15. IS ETATIZATION INEVITABLE?

1. In some instances the more traditional meaning of "development" is employed as well, however.

2. Little of historical significance seems to occur in such uneventful times. Societal and economic development stalls and the situation remains constant for a long time. The most notorious case of this kind occurred in fourteenth- and fifteenth-century China, at a time when Europe was moving into the "take-off period," into the modern industrial era. Elvin (1973, 298–315) labeled the Chinese policy an "equilibrium trap." He writes that China was so much affected by that policy, which generated "quantitative growth but qualitative stand-still" that, instead of becoming the leading and most industrialized nation in the world, it persisted without development for several centuries. Actually, it sank into "underdevelopment" from which it is presently trying to cure itself.

3. Marx and Engels attributed different meanings to the concept of "revolution" in different works. Discussing the revolutionary events during the nineteenth century, they employed the colloquial meaning of the word: "sudden and violent change of government" and the system of class domination. In a number of letters and works (*Grundsatze des Kommunismus,* by Engels; Marx/Engels, *Werke,* 4: 372; Engels' "Preface to the English Edition" of *Capital,* Vol. 1; *Aufzeichnung eines Interviews, das Karl Marx einem Korrespondenten der Zeitung 'The World' gewahrte,* Marx/Engels, *Werke,* 17: 641; *Capital* 1962, 3: 428), Marx and Engels write about the possibility of peaceful and gradual transformation of capitalism into socialism as a result of technological development, development of stock companies and cooperatives, and more intensive polarization within capitalist society. According to

the last-mentioned source (here quoted after Marx, Engels & Lenin 1967, 75):

> In stock companies, the function is divorced from capital ownership, hence also labour is entirely divorced from ownership of means of production and surplus labour. The result of the ultimate development of capitalist production is a necessary transitional phase towards the reconversion of capital into the property of associated producers, as outright social property. On the other hand, the stock company is a transition toward the conversion of all functions in the reproduction process which still remain linked with capitalist property, into mere functions of associated producers, into social functions.

In this sense, as Avineri writes (1970, 178; see also 36–38, 160, 202–204) the revolution was to consist in a dialectical negation of negation (*Aufhebung*) of capitalism. In this sense, in some writing, Marx and Engels employed the concept of revolution in a meaning close to the one conveyed by "transmutation" in this book.

4. Certain Hegelian pronouncements, from which Marx derived the concept of historical inevitability, can be deciphered as prognostications. While Hegel was attempting to discover the law and philosophy of history of the past, Marx, in contrast, discusses the past in order to predict the inevitability of the future.

5. Laquer (1982, 207) notes also that in 1943 there were 5 million cars in use in Western Europe. By 1957, this figure had trebled, and, in 1965, the number of cars on the roads of Western Europe reached a total of 44 million.

6. Braun (1984, 84–94), in an analysis of current technological development, discerns three concerns raised by writers discussing contemporary processes of change: (1) fear of unemployment; (2) fear of loss of skills; (3) fear of loss of privacy and freedom.

7. According to Harris Louis, Westin and associates survey of attitudes toward privacy (1981):

> three out of every four Americans now believe that the "right to privacy" should be akin to the inalienable American right to life, liberty and the pursuit of happiness. . . . One out of every three Americans believes that our society is very close to, or already like, the type of society described by George Orwell in his book 1984. . . . One of every two Americans (48%) is worried about how the Federal government will use the personal information it gathers on individuals.

Only half (50%) "are worried about whether the business community is using the personal information it gathers on individuals in a proper manner." Simons (1982), the author of a study developed with the National Computing Centre in Britain discussing the legislation enacted to protect privacy in different countries, reports that the public in that nation expressed similar feelings.

CHAPTER 16. THE NEW STATE

1. Schumpeter distinguishes between growth, occurring naturally and spontaneously, and development, which is organized and directed from above.

2. For close to a week the population was not evacuated from the area affected

by radiation, because local authorities waited for instruction from provincial, and provincial from Ukrainian, and Ukrainian from central authorities. Gorbachev and the politbureau acknowledged that the system is too closed, inoperative, and turgid, and, therefore, does not work well in a condition of sudden adversity when people in the field have to act without instructions. The local authorities had to be given more responsibility and freedom of control their affairs. *Glasnost* was the answer; it is also expected that it would stimulate production and economic initiative. This, as recent events in Armenia have proved, bear certain consequences, undesired by Soviet leaders.

3. In a report on *perestroika*, Flora Lewis writes (*New York Times*, Sect. 4, September 11, 1988) that the politbureau is now considering several projects of mixed economy. She writes that according to one recommendation, state control is to be limited to 20–25 percent of the GNP. Another 40–45 percent is to be put under indirect state control, exercised by tax and credit means. The rest is to become a free market. I doubt whether so radical a scheme of change can be put in practice; evidently, however, major changes are required.

Bibliography

DOCUMENTS AND STATISTICAL SOURCES

Annual abstract of statistics. 1981, no. 117. London: HMSO.

Annual abstract of statistics. 1983, no. 119. London: HMSO.

Annual abstract of statistics. 1988, no. 124. London: HMSO.

Annuaire statistique de la France. 1986, vol. 91. Paris: Institut national de la statistique et des études économiques.

Annuario statistico italiano. 1983. Roma: Istituto Centrale di Statistica.

A Study of UK nationalised industries. 1976. London: HMSO.

Background material and data on programs within the jurisdiction of the Committee on Ways and Means. 1984. Washington, DC: U.S. Government Printing Office.

The Budget in brief. Japan 1984. Tokyo: Budget Bureau, Ministry of Finance.

Budget of the United States government, 1987. 1986. Washington, DC: Office of Management and Budget.

Canada year book. 1985. Ottawa: Statistics Canada.

Canada year book. 1988. Ottawa: Statistics Canada.

Current population report: Consumer income 1977. March, 1979. Series P–60, no. 118. Washington, DC: U.S. Bureau of the Census.

Development of higher education, 1950–1967. 1971. Paris: OECD.

Economic outlook. 1984. Paris: Organization for Economic Cooperation and Development.

Employment: The challenge for the nation. 1985. (Cmnd 9474). London: HMSO.

The Europa year book. 1980. London: Europa Publications.

Facts and figures of Japan. 1982. Tokyo: Kinji Kawamura.

Federal credit programs. Special analysis F. 1982. Washington, DC: Office of Management and Budget.

The Federal Reserve System: Purpose and functions. 1979. Washington, DC: Board of Governors, The Federal Reserve.

Financial statement and budget report. 1985–1986. 1985. London: H.M.Treasury.

Flora, Peter, Franz Kraus, and Winfried Pfenning. 1987. *State, economy, and society in Western Europe 1815–1975. A data handbook*. Chicago: St. James Press.

Government finance statistics yearbook, 1984, vol. 8. Washington, DC: International Monetary Fund.

Government finance statistics yearbook, 1985, vol. 9. Washington, DC: International Monetary Fund.

Government finance statistics yearbook, 1986, vol. 10. Washington, DC: International Monetary Fund.

Government finance statistics yearbook, 1987, vol. 11. Washington, DC: International Monetary Fund.

Haut conseil du secteur public rapport. 1984. vol. 1. L'extension du secteur public: les objectifs et les réalisations, vol. 2. La question du secteur public: le suivi des activités. Paris: La Documentation Française.

Historical tables. Budget of the United States government: Fiscal year 1986. 1986. Washington, DC: Executive Office of the President. Office Management and Budget.

Instruments of monetary policy in the Federal Republic of Germany. Reprint from Monetary policy in the countries of the European Economic Community. 1971. Bonn: Deutsche Bunsdesbank.

Money income and poverty status of families and persons in the United States: 1984. (Advance Report, March, 1985). Current Population Reports. Series P-60, no. 149.

Mortimer, Harold E. 1982. The Depository institutions act of 1982. [DIDMCA]. Washington, DC: Practicing Law Institute.

National accounts of OECD countries 1964–81. 1983, 1985, vol. 1 and 2. Paris: Organization for Economic Cooperation and Development.

The Nationalised Industries. 1978. London: HMSO.

OECD economic surveys: United Kingdom. 1980. Paris: OECD.

OECD economic surveys: United Kingdom. 1986. Paris: OECD.

OECD economic surveys: United Kingdom. 1987. Paris: OECD.

OECD economic surveys: France. 1983. Paris: OECD.

OECD economic surveys: France. 1984. Paris: OECD.

OECD economic surveys: France. 1987. Paris: OECD.

OECD economic surveys: Germany. 1986. Paris: OECD.

OECD economic surveys: Germany. 1987. Paris: OECD.

OECD economic surveys: Italy. 1987. Paris: OECD.

Poverty profile. 1988. Ottawa: National Council of Welfare.

Report. Royal commission on the economic union and development prospects for Canada. 1985, vol. 1, 2, 3. Ottawa: Canadian Government Publishing Centre.

Report on the world current account discrepancy, 1987. Washington, DC: International Monetary Fund.

Ross, David P. 1980. The Canadian fact book on income distribution. Ottawa, Ont.: The Canadian Council of Social Development.

Schweitzer, Carl-Christoph et al. 1984. Politics and government in the Federal Republic of Germany: Basic documents. Leamington Spa, Eng.: Berg.

Special analysis F: The budget of the United States government, 1983. 1982. Washington, DC: Office of Management and Budget; Executive Office of the President.

Special analyses of the budget of the United States government. Fiscal year 1986. 1985. Washington, DC: Executive Office of the President, Office of Management and Budget.

Special analyses of the budget of the United States government. Fiscal year 1987. 1986. Washington, DC: Executive Office of the President, Office of Management and Budget.

The State participation system in Italy. 1977. Rome: Istituto Poligrafico dello Stato.

Statistical abstract of the United States. 1986. Washington, DC: Bureau of the Census.

Statistical handbook of Japan. 1981. Tokyo: Prime Minister's Office.

Statistical Survey of Japan's Economy. 1984. Tokyo: Economic & Foreign Affairs

Research Association.
Der Wissenschaftliche Beirat beim Bundesministerium der Finanzen. Entschliessungen, Stellungnahmen und Gutachten 1949–1973. 1974. Tubingen: J.C.B. Mohr (Paul Siebeck).
World Development Report. 1978. Washington, DC: World Bank.
World Development Report. 1980. Washington, DC: World Bank.
World Development Report. 1983. Washington, DC: World Bank.
World Development Report. 1985. Washington, DC: World Bank.

BOOKS AND ARTICLES

Abercrombie, Nicholas, and John Urry. 1983. *Capital, labor and the new middle classes*. London: Allen & Unwin.
Abraham, Neville. 1974. *Big business and government*. London: Macmillan.
Alexis, Marion. 1983. Neo-corporatism and industrial relations: The case of German trade unions. *West European Politics* 6, no. 1 (January 1983): 75–92.
Alford, Robert R., and Roger Friedland. 1985. *Powers of theory: Capitalism, the state, and democracy*. Cambridge: Cambridge University Press.
Anderson, Charles W. 1978. The political economy of Charles E. Lindbloom. *American political science review* 72, no. 3 (September 1978): 1012–1016.
Anderson, Gary M. 1987. The US federal deficit and national debt: A political and economic history. In *Deficits*, ed. James M. Buchanan et al. Oxford: Basil Blackwell.
Andrain, Charles. 1985. *Social policies in Western industrial societies*. Berkeley: Institute of International Studies.
Andrews, William G. 1982. *Presidential government in Gaullist France: A Study of executive–legislative relations 1958–1974*. Albany: State University of New York Press.
Andrews, William G., and Stanley Hoffmann, eds. 1981. *The Fifth Republic at twenty: The impact of the Fifth Republic on France*. Albany: State University of New York Press.
Anton, Thomas J. 1980. *Administered politics: Elite political culture in Sweden*. Boston and Hague: Martinus Nijhoff.
Apple, R. W., Jr. 1983. New stirrings of patriotism. *New York Times Magazine*, December 11, 1983.
Are, Giuseppe. 1982. Economic state control in Italy. *Survey* 26, no. 1 (Winter 1982): 49–64.
Ashford, Douglas E. 1983. Reconstructing the French 'État': Progress of the *loi Defferre*. *West European Politics* 6, no. 3 (July 1983) 264–270.
Auletta, Ken. 1982. *The Underclass*. New York: Vintage Books.
Avineri, Shlomo. 1970. *The Social and political thought of Karl Marx*. Cambridge: Cambridge University Press.
———. 1974. *Hegel's theory of the modern state*. Cambridge: Cambridge University Press.
Barber, Benjamin R. 1975. Justifying justice: Problems of psychology, measurement and politics in Rawls. *American political science review* 69, no. 2 (June 1975): 663–674.
Bardach, Eugene, and Robert A. Kagan. 1982. *Going by the book: The problem of regulatory unreasonableness*. Philadelphia: Temple University Press.
Barry, Brian. 1975. *The Liberal theory of justice: A critical examination of the principal doctrines in A Theory of justice by John Rawls*. Oxford: Clarendon Press.

Bartlett, Bruce, and Timothy P. Roth, eds. 1983. *The Supply side solution.* Chatham, NJ: Chatham House.

Baum, Warren C. 1958. *The French economy and the state.* Princeton, NJ: Princeton University Press.

Bawley, Dan. 1982. *The Subterranean economy.* New York: McGraw Hill.

Beck, Barbara. 1984. Down to earth: A survey of the West German economy. *The Economist* (February 4, 1984): 1–27.

Beck, Morris. 1981. *Government spending: Trends and issues.* New York: Praeger.

Beckhart, Benjamin Haggott. 1972. *Federal reserve system.* Washington, DC: American Bankers Association.

Bell, Daniel. 1978. *The Cultural contradictions of capitalism.* New York: Basic Books.

Bell, Daniel, and Irving Kristol. 1981. *The Crisis of economic theory.* New York: Basic Books.

Bendix, Reinhard. 1977. *Nation-building and citizens: Studies of our changing social order.* Berkeley: University of California Press.

———. *Max Weber: An intellectual portrait.* Berkeley: University of California Press.

Bendix, Reinhard et al., eds. 1968. *State and society: A reader.* Berkeley: University of California Press.

Bennet, James T., and Thomas J. Dilorenzo. 1983. *Underground government: The off-budget public sector.* Preface by Gordon Tullock, epilogue by William Simon. Washington, DC: CATO Institute.

Benoist, Jean-Marie. 1970. *Marx est mort.* Paris: Gallimard

Ben-Porath, Yoram; ed. 1986. *The Israeli economy: Maturing through crises.* Cambridge, MA: Harvard University Press.

Berger, Suzanne, ed. 1981. *Organizing interests in Western Europe: Pluralism, corporatism, and the transformation of politics.* Cambridge: Cambridge University Press.

Berle, Adolf A., and Gardiner C. Means. 1968. *The Modern corporation and private property.* New York: Harcourt, Brace & World.

Berlin, Isaiah. 1954. *Historical inevitability.* London: Oxford University Press.

Bernstein, Marver H. 1955. *Regulating business by independent commission.* Princeton, NJ: Princeton University Press.

Berrington, Hugh. 1983. Change in British politics: An introduction. *West European Politics* 6, no. 4 (October 1983): 1–25.

Bertalanffy, Ludwig Von. 1968. *General system theory: Foundations, development, applications.* New York: Braziller.

Beyme, Klaus Von. 1974. *Die politische Elite in der Bundesrepublik Deutschland.* Munchen: R. Piper.

———. 1985. The Role of the state and the growth of government. *International Political Science Review* 6, no. 1 (January, 1985): 11–34.

Birnbaum, Pierre. 1980. The State in contemporary France. In *The state in Western Europe,* ed. Richard Scase. London: Croom Helm.

———. 1982. *The Heights of power: An essay on the power elite in France,* with a new postscript. Tr. Arthur Goldhammer. Chicago: University of Chicago Press.

Black, Cyril et al. 1975. *The Modernization of Japan and Russia.* New York: Free Press.

Blades, Derek. 1982. *The Hidden economy and the national accounts.* Occasional studies. Paris: Economic Statistics and National Accounts Division. OECD.

Blinder, Alan S. 1980. The Level and distribution of economic well-being. In *The American economy in transition,* ed. Martin Feldstein. Chicago: University of Chicago Press.

Blocker, H. Gene, and Elizabeth H. Smith, eds. 1980. *John Rawls' theory of social justice: An introduction.* Athens, OH: Ohio University Press.

Bloom, Allan. 1975. Justice: John Rawls vs. the tradition of political philosophy. *American political science review* 69, no. 2 (June 1975): 648–662.

———. 1987. *The Closing of the American mind.* New York: Simon & Schuster.

Bock, Edwin A., ed. 1965. *Government regulation of business.* Englewood Cliffs, NJ: Prentice Hall.

Boissonade, Pierre. 1932. *Colbert: Le triomphe de l'étatisme: La fondation de la suprematié industrielle de la France. La dictature du travail.* Paris: Marcel Riviere.

Borcherding, Thomas E. et al. 1982. Comparing the efficiency of private and public production: The evidence from five countries. *Zeitschrift fur Nationalökonomie. Journal of Economics.* Supplement 2. New York: Springer Verlag.

Borins, Sanford F. 1972. The political economy of "the Fed." *Public Policy* 20, no. 2 (Spring, 1972): 175–198.

Borins, Sanford F., with Lee Brown. 1986. *Investments in failure: Five government corporations that cost the Canadian taxpayer billions.* Toronto: Methuen.

Bottomore, Tom. 1985. *Theories of modern capitalism.* London: Allen & Unwin.

Bowles, Samuel, and Herbert Gintis. 1986. *Democracy and capitalism: Property, community, and the contradictions of modern social thought.* New York: Basic Books.

Boyle, Charles et al. 1984. *People, science and technology: A guide to advanced industrial society.* London: Harvester Press.

Braun, Ernst. 1984. *Wayward technology.* London: Frances Pinter.

Briefs, A. Goetz. 1937. *The Proletariat: A challenge to Western civilization.* New York: McGraw-Hill.

Broad, C. D. 1923. *Scientific thought.* New York: Harcourt, Brace.

Brookes, Warren T. 1982. *The Economy in mind.* Foreword by George Gilder. New York: Universe Books.

Brooks, Harvey. 1980. Technology: Evolution and purpose. *Daedalus* 109, no. 1. Special issue: Modern technology: Problem or opportunity? (Winter 1980): pp. 65–81.

Bruce-Briggs, B., ed. 1979. *The New class?* New Brunswick, NJ: Transaction Books.

Buchanan, James M. et al. 1987. *Deficits.* Oxford: Basil Blackwell.

Burnham, David. 1983. *The Rise of the computer state.* Foreword by Walter Cronkite. New York: Vintage Books.

Burnham, James. 1962. *The Managerial revolution.* Harmondsworth, Eng.: Penguin.

Burton, J. 1979. *Trade union and inflation.* London: Macmillan.

Cameron, David R. 1978. The expansion of the public economy: A comparative analysis. *American political science review* 72, no. 4 (December, 1978): 1243–1261).

———. 1984. Social Democracy, corporatism, labour quiescence, and the representation of economic interest in advanced capitalist society. In *Order and conflict in contemporary capitalism,* ed. John H. Goldthorpe. Oxford: Clarendon Press.

Cameron, Rondo, ed. 1972. *Banking and economic development: Some lessons of history.* New York: Oxford University Press.

Cargill, Thomas F., and Gillian G. Garcia. 1982. *Financial deregulation and monetary control: Historical perspective and impact of the 1980 act.* Stanford, CA: Hoover Institution Press.

Carnoy, Martin, and Derek Shearer. 1980. *Economic democracy: The challenge of the 1980s.* White Plains, NY: Sharpe.

Carnoy, Martin et al. 1983. *The New social contract: The economy and government after Reagan.* New York: Harper & Row.

Carroll, Peter N., and David W. Noble. 1979. *The Free and unfree: A history of the United States.* Harmondsworth, Eng.: Penguin.

Castells, Manuel. 1980. *The Economic crisis and American society.* Princeton, NJ: Princeton University Press.

Cawson, Alan. 1982. *Corporatism and welfare: Social policy and state intervention in Britain.* London: Heinemann.

Cerny, Philip G., and Martin A. Schain, eds. 1981. *French politics and public policy.* Foreword by Stanley Hoffmann. London and New York: Methuen.

———. 1983. Democratic socialism: the Mitterrand presidency eighteen months on. *West European Politics* 6, no. 3 (July 1983): 197–215.

———. 1985. *Socialism, the state and public policy in France.* New York: Methuen.

Chamberlain, Neil W. 1980. *Forces of change in Western Europe.* London: McGraw-Hill.

Chandler, Alfred D. Jr. 1977. *The Visible hand: The managerial revolution in American business.* Cambridge, MA: Harvard University Press.

Chapman, John W. 1975. Rawls's theory of justice. *American political science review* 69, no. 2 (June, 1975): 588–593.

Charles, S. T., and A. L. Webb. 1986. *The Economic approach to social policy.* Brighton: Wheatsheaf.

Charlot, Jean. 1971. *The Gaulist phenomenon: The Gaulist movement in the Fifth Republic.* New York: Praeger.

Chevalier, Louis. 1973. *Labouring classes and dangerous classes in Paris during the first half of the nineteenth century.* Tr. Frank Jellinek. New York: Howard Fertig.

Chodak, Szymon. 1963. *Systemy partyjne Europy zachodniej.* Studia Socjologiczno-Polityczne, no. 9. Warsaw: PWN.

———. 1973. *Societal development: Five approaches with conclusions from comparative analysis.* New York: Oxford University Press.

———. 1983. Etatization: Its concept and varieties. In *Research in social movements, conflicts and change.* Research annual 5. Ed. L. Kriesberg. Greenwich, CN: JAI Press.

Clark, Rodney. 1979. *The Japanese company.* New Haven, CN.: Yale University Press.

Clarkson, Stephen. 1985. *Canada and the Reagan challenge.* Toronto: Lorimer.

Clecak, Peter. 1983. *America's quest for the ideal self: Dissent and fulfillment in the 60s and 70s.* New York: Oxford University Press.

Clemens, John. 1983. *Polls, politics and populism.* London: Gover.

Clément, Pierre M. 1861. *Histoire de la vie et de l'administration de Colbert.* Paris: Guillaumin.

———. 1892. *Histoire de Colbert et de son administration.* Paris: Libraires-editeurs.

Clement, Wallace. 1983. *Class, power and property: Essays on Canadian society.* Toronto: Methuen.

Coates, David. 1980. *Labor in power? A study of the Labour government 1974–1979.* London: Longman.

Coates, David, and John Hillard, eds. 1986. *The Economic decline of modern Britain: The debate between left and right.* Brighton: Wheatsheaf.

———. 1987. *The Economic revival of modern Britain: The debate between left and right.* London: Edward Elgar.

Coates, J. H. 1985. UK manufacturing industry: Recession, depression, and prospects for the future. In *Prospects for recovery in the British economy,* ed. F. V. Meyer. London: Croom Helm.

Cohen, Stephen. 1977. *Modern capitalist planning: The French model.* Berkeley: University of California Press.

Cole, Charles Woolsey. 1964. *Colbert and a century of French mercantilism*. 2 vols. Hamden, CN: Archon Books.

———. 1943. *French mercantilism*. New York: Columbia University Press.

Coleman, Richard P., and Rainwater, Lee. 1978. *Social standing in America: New dimensions of class*. New York: Basic Books.

Cooley, Charles H. 1956. *Social organization*. Glencoe, IL: Free Press.

Coser, Lewis A. 1967. *Continuities in the study of social conflict*. New York: Free Press.

———. 1969. *The Functions of social conflict*. New York: Free Press.

Cox, Andrew, and Noel O'Sullivan eds. 1988. *The Corporate state: Corporatism and the state tradition in Europe*. London: Elgar.

Cranston, Maurice. 1985. Britain in squalor. *American Spectator* 18, no. 5 (May 1985): 19–21.

Crick, Bernard, ed. 1981. *Unemployment*. London and New York: Methuen.

Creedy, John, ed. 1981. *The Economics of unemployment in Britain*. London: Butterworth.

Cross, Rod. 1982. *Economic theory and policy in the U.K.* Oxford: Martin Robertson.

Crozier, Michael. 1964. *The Bureaucratic phenomenon*. Chicago: University of Chicago Press.

———. 1973. *The Stalled society*. New York: Viking.

———. 1982. *Strategies for change: The future of the French society*. Tr. William R. Beer. Cambridge, MA: MIT Press.

———. 1984. *The Trouble with America: Why the system is breaking down*. Foreword by David Riesman. Tr. Peter Heinegg. Berkeley: University of California Press.

Crozier, Michael, and Erhard Friedberg. 1980. *Actors and systems: The politics of collective action*. Tr. A. Goldhammer. Chicago: University of Chicago Press.

Daedalus. 1979. Special Issue: *The State* 108, no.4 (Fall 1979).

Daedalus. 1980. Special Issue: *Modern technology: Problem or opportunity?* 109, no. 1 (Winter 1980).

Dahl, Robert A. 1971. *Polyarchy: Participation and opposition*. New Haven, CN: Yale University Press.

Dahrendorf, Ralf. 1982. *On Britain*. London: British Broadcasting Corporation.

———. 1987. Government, entitlement and growth. Interview of Ralf Dahrendorf. *Reporting from Russell Sage Foundation*. Occasional publication no. 10. (May 1987).

Daniels, Norman, ed. 1975. *Reading Rawls: Critical studies on Rawls's theory of justice*. New York: Basic Books.

Darwall, Stephen L. 1980. Is there a Kantian foundation for Rawlsian justice? In *John Rawls' theory of social justice: An introduction*, ed. H. G. Blocker and E. H. Smith. Athens, OH: University of Ohio Press.

De Gaulle, Charles. 1970. *Discours et messages*. 5 vols. Édition établié avec le concours de François Goguel. Paris: Plon.

———. 1971. *Memoirs of hope, renewal 1958–62, endeavour 1962–*. Tr. T. Kilmartin. London: Weidenfeld & Nicolson.

De Grazia, Raffael. 1984. *Clandestine employment*. Geneva: International Labour Office.

De Jasay, Anthony. 1985. *The State*. Oxford: Basil Blackwell.

Delorme, Robert. 1984. A New view on economic theory of the state: A case study of France. *Journal of economic issues* 18, no. 3 (September 1984): 715–744.

Derossi, Flavia. 1982. *The Technocratic illusion*. New York: Sharpe.

Derthick, Martha, and Paul J. Quirk. 1985. *The Politics of regulation*. Washington, DC: Brookings Institution.

Djilas, Milovan. 1957. *The New class.* New York: Praeger.

Dogan, Mattei. 1985. The Social-security crisis in the richest countries: Basic analogies. *International social science journal* 37, no. 1 (January 1985): 47–60.

Donner, Frank. 1980. *The Age of surveillance: The aims and methods of American political intelligence system.* New York: Knopf.

Doran, Charles F., and John H. Sigler, eds. 1985. *Canada and the United States.* Englewood Cliffs, NJ: Prentice Hall.

Downs, Anthony. 1960. Why the government budget is too small in a democracy. *World Politics* 12, no. 4 (July 1960): 541–563.

Dray, William H. 1964. *Philosophy of history.* Englewood Cliffs, NJ: Prentice Hall.

Durkheim, Émile. 1958. *Suicide.* Tr. John A. Spoulding and George Simpson. Glencoe, IL: Free Press.

———. 1966. *The Rules of sociological method.* Ed. E. G. Catlin. New York: Free Press.

———. 1984. *The Division of labor in society.* With an introduction by Lewis A. Coser. Tr. W. D. Halls. New York: Free Press.

Durkheim, Émile, and Marcel Mauss. 1971. Note on the notion of civilization. Tr. Benjamin Nelson. *Social Research* 38, no. 4 (Winter 1971): 807–813.

Dyson, Kenneth. 1984. The Politics of corporate crisis in West Germany. *West European Politics* 7, no. 1. (Winter 1984): 24–46.

Eads, George C., and Michael Fix, eds. 1984. *The Reagan regulatory strategy: An assessment.* Washington, DC: Urban Institute Press.

Ehrbar, A. F. 1980. How to save social security. *Fortune* 109, no. 5 (August 25, 1980): 34–39.

———. 1982. Social security: Heading for the wrong solution. *Fortune* 111, no. 12 (December 13, 1982): 113–120.

Einaudi, Mario et al. 1955. *Nationalization in France and Italy.* Ithaca, NY: Cornell University Press.

Elliot, Brian, and David McCrone. 1987. Class, culture and morality: A sociological analysis of the new conservatism. *Sociological Review* ,no. 3 (August 1987): 485–515.

Ellul, Jacques. 1964. *The Technological society.* Introduction by Robert Merton. Tr. John Wilkinson. New York: Knopf.

———. 1978. *The Betrayal of the West.* Tr. Matthew J. O'Connell. New York: Seabury.

———. 1980. *The Technological system.* Tr. Joachim Neugroschel. New York: Continuum.

Elvin, Mark. 1973. *The Pattern of the Chinese past.* London: Methuen.

Emi, Koichi. 1978. *Essays on the service industry and social security in Japan.* Tokyo: Kinokuniya.

The Empire strikes back: Race and racism in 70s Britain. London: Hutchison, in association with the Centre for Contemporary Cultural Studies, University of Birmingham.

Employment: The challenge for the nation. 1985. *Cmnd 9414.* London: HMSO.

d'Entrèves, Alexander Passerin. 1967. *The Notion of the state.* Oxford: Clarendon.

Erhard, Ludwig. 1962. *Presperity through competition.* London: Thames & Hudson.

Ernst-Porksen, Michael, ed. 1984. *Alternativen der Ökonomie—Ökonomie der alternativen.* Special Issue AS 104. Berlin: Argumenten.

Evans, Peter B. 1986. Transnational linkages and the economic role of the state: An analysis of developing and industrialized nations in the post-World War II period. In *Bringing the state back in,* ed. P. Evans et al. Cambridge: Cambridge University Press.

Evans, Peter B. et al., eds. 1986. *Bringing the state back in.* Cambridge: Cambridge

University Press.

Feige, Edgar L. 1979. How big is the irregular economy? *Challenge* 22, no. 5 (November–December 1979): 5–13.

Feigenbaum, Edward A., and Pamela McCorduck. 1984. *The Fifth generation: Artificial intelligence and Japan's computer challenge to the world.* New York: New American Library.

Feldstein, Martin, ed. 1980. *The American economy in transition.* Chicago, IL: University of Chicago Press.

Ferkis, Victor C. 1974. *The Future of technological civilization.* New York: Brazilier.

Fine, Ben, and Laurence Harris. 1985. *The Peculiarities of the British economy.* London: Lawrence & Wishart.

Fishkin, James. 1975. Justice and rationality: Some objections to the central argument in Rawls' theory. *American political science review* 69, no. 2 (June 1975): 615–629.

Flora, Peter, and Arnold J. Heidenheimer, eds. 1984. *The Development of welfare states in Europe and America.* New Brunswick: Transaction Books.

Flora, Peter, and Jens Alber. 1984. Modernization, democratization and development of welfare state in Western Europe. In *The Development of welfare states in Europe and America,* ed. P. Flora and J. Heidenheimer. New Brunswick: Transaction Books.

Foster, David. 1980. *Innovation and Employment.* Oxford: Pergamon Press.

Fraser, John. 1981. *Italy: Society in crisis, society in transformation.* Boston: Routledge & Kegan Paul.

Freeman, Roger A. 1981. *The Wayward welfare state.* Stanford, CA: Hoover Institution Press.

Friedan, Betty. 1983. Twenty years after "The Feminine mystique." *New York Times Magazine,* February 27, 1983.

Friedman, Kathi V. 1981. *Legitimation of social rights and the Western welfare state: A Weberian perspective.* Chapel Hill: University of North Carolina Press.

Fry, Geoffrey K. 1979. *The Growth of government.* London: Cass.

Fry, John A., ed. 1979. *Limits of the welfare state: Critical views on post-war Sweden.* Fornborough, Eng.: Saxon House.

Fukutake, Tadashi. 1974. *Japanese society today.* Tokyo: University of Tokyo Press.

Fukutake, Tadashi et al. 1981. *The Japanese Family.* Tokyo: Kinji Kawamura Foreign Press Center.

Furlong, William Barry. 1982. America's other budget. *New York Times Magazine,* February 21, 1982: 32–74.

Galbraith, John Kenneth. 1969. *The Affluent society.* Boston: Houghton Mifflin.

Gamble, Andrew. 1985. *Britain in decline.* London: Macmillan.

Ganssmann, Heiner. 1983. Marx without the labor theory of value? *Social Research* 50, no. 2. (Summer 1983): 278–304.

Garraty, John A. 1978. *Unemployment in history: Economic thought and public policy.* New York: Harper & Row.

Gatti, James F., ed. 1981. *The Limits of government regulation.* Foreword by Malcolm F. Severance. New York: Academic Press.

Gawson, Alan. 1982. *Corporatism and welfare: Social policy and state intervention in Britain.* London: Heinemann.

Geismar, Alain et al. 1969. *Vers la guerre civille.* Paris: Ed. et Publ. Premières.

Gersuny, Carl, and Warren I. Rosengren. 1973. *The Service society.* Cambridge, MA: Schenkman.

Gerth, H. H., and C. Wright Mills. 1958. *Character and social structure.* New York: Harcourt, Brace & World.

————. eds. 1967. *From Max Weber: Essays in sociology.* New York: Oxford

University Press.

Gibney, Frank. 1979. Japan: *The fragile super-power*. New York: New American Library.

Giddens, Anthony. 1983. *A Contemporary critique of historical materialism*. Berkeley: University of California Press.

Giddens, Anthony, and Gavin Mackenzie, eds. 1982. *Social class and division of labour*. Cambridge: Cambridge University Press.

Gilder, George. 1981. *Wealth and poverty*. New York: Basic Books.

Ginzberg, Eli, and Robert M. Solow. 1974. An Introduction to this special issue. *Public Interest* 34 (Winter 1974): 4–13.

Glastetter, Werner et al. 1983. *Die wirtschaftliche Entwicklung in der Bundesrepublik Deutschland 1950–1980*. Frankfurt: Campus.

Glucksmann, André, *Les maîtres penseurs*. Paris: Grasset.

Goffee, Robert and Richard Scase, eds. 1987. *Entrepreneurship in Europe*. London: Croom Helm.

Goldman Leventman, Paula. 1981. *Professionals out of work*. New York: Free Press.

Goldthorpe, John H. 1982. On the service class, its formation and future. In *Social class and division of labour*, ed. Anthony Giddens and Gavin Mackenzie. Cambridge: Cambridge University Press.

————. ed. 1984. *Order and conflict in contemporary capitalism: Studies in the political economy of Western European nations*. Oxford: Clarendon.

Goldwater, Barry. 1976. *The Coming breakpoint*. New York: Macmillan.

Goodman, David. 1978. Countdown to 1984: Big brother may be on schedule. *Futurist* 12, no. 8. (December 1978): 344–353.

Goodman, Walter. 1983. "Statecraft" abhors moral vacuum. Review of *Statecraft as Soulcraft* by George Will. *New York Times*. Reprinted in *Gazette* (Montreal, August 13, 1983).

Goubert, Pierre. 1970. *Louis XIV and twenty million Frenchmen*. Tr. A. Carter. New York: Vintage Books.

Gough, J. W. 1963. *The Social contract: A critical study of its development*. Oxford: Clarendon Press.

Gould, Inc. 1977. *Technology and overregulation: Or, why our standard of living might not get better*. Paper no. 10. Rolling Meadows, IL: Gould, Inc.

Grant, Wyn. 1982. British industrial policy: the problem and its perception. *Parliamentary affairs* 35, no.3 (Summer, 1982): 282–296.

Green, Diana. 1981. The Budget and the plan. In *French politics and public policy*, ed. P. G. Cerny and M. A. Schain. London and New York: Methuen.

Gregor, A. James. 1969. *The Ideology of fascism*. New York: Free Press.

Greider, William. 1987. *Secrets of the temple: How the Federal Reserve runs the country*. New York: Simon & Schuster.

Grossberg, Kenneth, ed. 1981. *Japan today*. Philadelphia: ISHI.

Grossman, Gregory, ed. 1970. *Essays in socialism and planning in honor of Carl Landauer*. Englewood Cliffs, NJ: Prentice Hall.

Guillaume, Henri. 1986. Implications of the new indicative planning. In *French industrial policy*, ed. William James Adams and Christian Stoffaes. Washington, DC: Brookings Institution.

Guzzardi, Walter, Jr. 1982. Reagan's reluctant deregulators. *Fortune* 111, no. 5 (March 8, 1982): 34–40.

Gutmann, Peter M. 1979. Statistical illusions, mistaken policies. *Challenge* 22, no. 5 (November–December 1979): 14–17.

Haberman, Clyde. 1988. Pricey Japan. *New York Times Magazine* (May 8, 1988): 42–43, 100.

Hague, Rod. 1983. Confrontation, incorporation and exclusion: British trade unions in collectivist and post-collectivist politics. *West European Politics* 6, no. 4 (October 1983): 130–163.

Haitani, Kanji. 1976. *The Japanese economic system*. Lexington, MA: Heath.

Halal, William E. 1986. *The New capitalism*. New York: John Wiley & Sons.

Hall, Peter. 1986. *Governing the economy: The politics of state intervention in Britain and France*. Cambridge, MA: Polity Press.

Hamel, Hannelore, ed. 1983. *Bundesrepublik Deutschland—DDR: Die Wirtschaftssysteme*. München: C. H. Beck.

Hanami, Tadashi. 1979. *Labor relations in Japan today*. Tokyo: Kadansha International.

Handelman, Stephen. 1988. *The Uncommon kingdom: Britain in the 1980s*. Toronto: Collins.

Hanley, David L. et al. 1984. *Contemporary France: Politics and society since 1945*. London: Routledge & Kegan Paul.

Hannay, N. Bruce, and Robert E. McGinn. 1980. The Anatomy of modern technology: Prologomenon to an improved public policy for the social management of technology. *Daedalus* 109, no. 1 (Winter 1980): 25–53.

Hansen, Susan B. 1983. *The Politics of taxation: Revenue without representation*. New York: Praeger.

Harrington, Michael. 1962. *The Other America: Poverty in the United States*. New York: Macmillan.

————. 1984. *The New American poverty*. New York: Holt, Rinehart & Winston.

Harris, Seymour E., ed. 1951. *Schumpeter: Social scientist*. Cambridge, MA: Harvard University Press.

Harrison, Reginald J. 1980. *Pluralism and corporatism: The political evolution of modern democracies*. London: Allen & Unwin.

Harrop, David. 1980. *America's paychecks: Who makes what*. New York: Facts on File.

Harsanyi, John C. 1975. Can the maximum principle serve as a basis for morality? *American political science review* 69, no. 2 (June 1975): 594–606.

Hartley, Anhony. 1987. The Remoulding of British politics, *Encounter* 69, no. 3 (September–October 1987): 3–10.

Hawkins, Christopher. 1983. *Britain's economic future*. Brighton: Wheatsheaf.

Hayward, Jack. 1986. *The State and the market economy*. London: Wheatsheaf.

Heaton, Herbert. 1948. *Economic history of Europe*. London: Harper & Row.

Heertje, Arnold, ed. 1981. *Schumpeter's vision: Capitalism, socialism and democracy after 40 years*. New York: Praeger.

Hegel, Georg. 1967. *Philosophy of history*. Tr. J. Sibree with a new introduction by C. J. Friedrich. New York: Colonial Press.

————. 1957. *The Philosophy of law*. Ed. J. Loewenberg. New York: Scribner's Sons.

Heidenheimer, Arnold J. 1984. Education and social security entitlements in Europe and America. In *The Development of welfare states in Europe and America*, ed. P. Flora and A. J. Heidenheimer. New Brunswick, NJ: Transaction Books.

Hemming, Richard, and Ali M. Mansoor. 1988. *Privatization and public enterprise*. Occasional Paper no. 56. Washington, DC: IMF.

Henderson, Nicholas. 1979. Britain's decline: Its causes and consequences. *The Economist* 7029 (June 2, 1979): 29–40.

Herman, Edward S. 1982. *Corporate control, corporate power*. Cambridge: Cambridge University Press.

Heydebrand, Wolf V. 1983. Technocratic corporatism: Toward a theory of occupational and organizational transformation. In *Organizational theory and public policy*, ed. Richard H. Hall and Robert E. Quinn. Beverly Hills, CA:

Sage.
————. Technocratic administration: Beyond Weber's bureaucracy. Paper delivered at the Fifth Max Weber Colloquium of Comparative Historical Sociology. October 1983.

Higgins, Joan. 1978. *The Poverty business: Britain and America*. Oxford: Basil Blackwell; London: Martin Robertson.

Higgs, Robert. 1987. *Crisis and Leviathan: Critical episodes in the growth of American government*. New York: Oxford University Press.

Hindley, Brian, ed. 1983. *State investment companies in Western Europe: Picking winners or backing losers?* New York: St. Martin's Press.

Hirsch, Fred. 1978. *Social limits to growth*. Cambridge, MA: Harvard University Press.

Hirsch, Joachim. 1980. Developments in the political system of West Germany since 1945. In *The State in Western Europe*, ed. Richard Scase. London: Croom Helm.

Hobbes, Thomas. 1969. *Leviathan*. New York: Washington Square Press.

Hoffmann, Stanley. 1974. *Decline or renewal: France since the 1930s*. New York: Viking.

————. 1988. Mitterrand: The Triple mystery. *French Politics and Society* 6, no. 2 (April 1988): 3–6.

Hoffmann, Stanley et al. 1963. *In Search of France*. Cambridge, MA: Harvard University Press.

Holland, Stuart, ed. 1972. *The State as entrepreneur: New dimensions for public enterprise: The IRI state shareholding formula*. London: Weidenfeld & Nicolson.

Hougan, Jim. 1975. *Decadence, radical nostalgia, narcissism and decline in the seventies*. New York: Morrow.

Howe, Irving, ed. 1983. *1984 revisited: Totalitarianism in our century*. New York: Harper & Row.

Hughes, Christopher. 1962. *The Parliament in Switzerland*. London: Cassell.

Hughes, James J., and Richard Perlman. 1984. *The Economics of unemployment: A comparative analysis of Britain and the United States*. New York: Cambridge University Press.

Hummel, Ralph P. 1977. *The Bureaucratic experience*. New York: St. Martin's Press.

Huntington, Samuel P. 1952. The Marasmus of the ICC: The commission, the railroads and the public interest. *Yale Law Journal* 61, no. 4, (April 1952): 467–509.

Hutber, Patrick. 1976. *The Decline and fall of the middle class—and how it can fight back*. London: Associated Business Programmes.

Ike, Nobutaka. 1974. Japan: *The new superstate*. San Francisco: Freeman.

Inglehart, Ronald. 1971. The Silent revolution in Europe: Intergenerational change in post-industrial societies. *American Political Science Review* 65, no. 4. (December 1971): 991–1017.

————. 1977. *The Silent revolution: Changing values and political styles among Western publics*. Princeton, NJ: Princeton University Press.

Inglehart, Ronald, and Jacques-René Rabier. 1985. The Withering away of Marx: Changing political cleavages in Western nations. Paper presented at the 18th IPSA World Congress. Paris.

Innis, Harold A. 1956. *Essays in Canadian economic history*. Ed. Mary Q. Innis. Toronto: Toronto University Press.

Inkeles, Alex. 1975. The Emerging social structure of the world. *World Politics* 27, no. 4 (July 1975): 467–495.

————. 1980. Continuity and change in the American national character. *Tocqueville Review* 2, no. 2–3 (Spring–Summer 1980): 20–51.

———. 1981. Convergence and divergence in industrial societies. In *Directions of change: Modernization theory, research, and realities*, ed. Mustafa O. Attir et al. Boulder, CO: Westview.

———. 1984. The Responsiveness of family patterns to economic change in the United States. *Tocqueville Review* 6, no. 1 (Spring–Summer 1984): 5–50.

Inkeles, Alex, and David H. Smith. 1974. *Becoming modern*. Cambridge, MA: Harvard University Press.

Ippolito, Denis S. 1978. *The Budget and national politics*. San Francisco: Freeman.

———. 1984. *Hidden spending: The politics of federal credit programs*. Chapel Hill: University of North Carolina Press.

Ismael, Jacqueline S. 1987. *The Canadian welfare state: Evolution and transition*. Edmonton: University of Alberta Press.

Jackson, John D. 1985. *Culture integration and culture unity—a dark problem: A comment on the ambiguity of Canadian culture*. 16th Annual Sorokin Lecture, University of Saskatoon, January 24, 1985.

Jacobs, Donald P. 1979. *Regulating business: The search for an optimum*. San Francisco, CA: Institute for Contemporary Studies.

Jahoda, Marie. 1982. *Employment and unemployment: A Social-psychological analysis*. Cambridge: Cambridge University Press.

Jamieson, Ian. 1980. Capitalism and culture: A comparative analysis of British and American manufacturing organizations. *Sociology* 14, no. 2 (May 1980): 217–245.

Janowitz, Morris. 1976. *Social control and the welfare state*. New York: Elsevier.

Jay, Peter. 1986. *Englanditis*. In *The Economic decline of modern Britain*, ed. D. Coates and J. Hillard. Brighton: Wheatsheaf.

Jencks, Christopher, and David Riesman. 1977. *The Academic revolution*. Foreword by Martin Trow. Chicago: University of Chicago Press.

Jenkins, Clive, and Barries Sherman. 1977. *The Collapse of work*. London: Methuen.

Jessop, Bob. 1982. *The Capitalist state: Marxist theories and methods*. New York: New York University Press.

Johnson, Chalmers. 1978. *Japan's public policy companies*. Stanford, CA: Hoover Institution.

———. 1982. *MITI and the Japanese miracle: The growth of industrial policy, 1925–1975*. Stanford, CA: Stanford University Press.

———, ed. 1984. *The Industrial policy debate*. San Francisco: Institute for Contemporary Studies.

Johnson, Paul. 1983. *Modern times: The world from the twenties to the eighties*. New York: Harper & Row.

Jones, Aubrey. 1985. *Britain's economy: The roots of stagnation*. New York: Cambridge University Press.

Jordan, Bill. 1985. *The State: Authority and autonomy*. Oxford: Basil Blackwell.

Joseph, Sir Keith. 1986. Solving the union problem is the key to Britain's recovery. In *The Economic decline of modern Britain*, ed. David Coates and John Hillard. Brighton: Harvester.

Kahn, Herman, and Thomas Pepper. 1979. *The Japanese challenge: The success and failure of economic success*. New York: Crowell.

Kanter, Rosabeth Moss. 1977. *Men and women of the corporation*. New York: Basic Books.

Katsenelinboigen, Aron. 1978. Studies in Soviet economic planning. *International Journal of Politics*. (Spring–Summer 1978): vii–xiii; 1–229.

Katzenstein, Peter J. 1984. *Corporatism and change: Austria, Switzerland, and the politics of industry*. Ithaca, NY: Cornell University Press.

———. 1987. *Policy and politics in West Germany: The growth of a semisovereign state*. Philadelphia: Temple University Press.

Keegan, William. 1984. *Mrs Thatcher's economic experiment*. London: Penguin Books.

Keene, Karlyn. 1984. A Conversation with Daniel Yankelovich. *Public opinion* 6, no. 6 (December–January 1984): 2–8.

Keller, Bill. 1988. New Soviet ideology boss rejects world struggle against West. *New York Times* (October 5, 1988); reprinted in *Gazette*, October 6, 1988.

Kelman, Steven. 1980. Occupational safety and health administration. In *The Politics of regulation*, ed. James Wilson. New York: Basic Books.

Keniston, Kenneth. 1968. *Young radicals: Notes on committed youth*. New York: Harcourt Brace Jovanovich.

———. 1971. *Youth and dissent: The rise of a new opposition*. New York: Harcourt Brace Jovanovich.

Keniston, Kenneth, and the Carnegie Council on Children. 1977. *All our children: The American family under pressure*. New York: Harcourt Brace Jovanovich.

Kesselman, M. 1985. The Tranquil revolution at Clochemerle: Socialist decentralization in France. In *Socialism, the state, and public policy*, ed. P. Cerny and M. Schain. London and New York: Methuen.

Keynes, John Maynard. 1947. *The General theory of employment, interest and money*. London: Macmillan.

King, Preston. 1967. *Fear of power: An analysis of anti-statism in three French writers*. London: Cass.

Kirtzner, Israel M. 1980. The "Austrian" perspective. *Public Interest*. Special Issue: *The Crisis in economic theory* (1980): 111–122.

Klein, Dieter. 1974. *Allgemeine Krise und staatsmonopolisticher Kapitalismus*. Berlin: Dietz Verlag.

Knott, Jack H. 1881. *Managing the German economy: Budgetary politics in a federal state*. Lexington, MA: Lexington Books.

Kojima, Kazuto. 1977. Public opinion trends in Japan. *Public Opinion Quarterly* 41, no. 2 (Summer 1977): 206-216.

Kolko, Gabriel. 1964. *Wealth and poverty in America: An analysis of social class and income distribution*. New York: Praeger.

Kriesberg, Louis. 1973. *The Sociology of social conflicts*. Englewood Cliffs, NJ: Prentice Hall.

Kuisel, Richard F. 1981. *Capitalism and the state in modern France*. Cambridge: Cambridge University Press.

Kuroda, Toshio. 1973. *Japan's changing population structure*. Tokyo: Ministry of Foreign Affairs.

Küster, Georg H. 1974. Germany. In *Big business and the state: Changing relations in Western Europe*, ed. Raymond Vernon. Cambridge, MA: Harvard University Press.

Kuznets, Simon. 1950. *Shares of upper income groups in income and savings*. Occasional Paper no. 35. New York: NBER.

Ladd, Everett Carl. 1984. Values: generations apart. *Public Opinion* 6, no. 6 (December–January, 1984): 21–36.

Lampert, Heinz. 1976. *Die Wirtschafts- und Sozialordnung der Bundesrepublik Deutschland*. Munchen: Gunter Olzog.

Landauer, Carl. 1983. *Corporate state ideologies: Historical roots and philosophical origins*. Berkeley: Institute of International Studies.

Laqueur, Walter. 1982. *Europe since Hitler: The rebirth of Europe*. Harmondsworth, Eng.: Penguin Books.

Lasch, Christopher. 1977. *Haven in a heartless world: The family besieged*. New York: Basic Books.

————. 1979. *The Culture of narcissism: American life in an age of diminishing expectations.* New York: Warner Books.

————. 1984. *The Minimal self: Psychic survival in troubled times.* New York: Norton.

Lasswell, Harold D. 1936. *Politics: Who gets what, when, how.* New York: McGraw-Hill.

Laufer, Heinz. 1974. *Der Föderalismus der Bundesrepublik Deutschland.* Stuttgart: Kohlhammer.

Laux, Jeanne Kirk, and Maureen Appel Molot. 1988. *State capitalism: Public enterprise in Canada.* Ithaca, NY: Cornell University Press.

Lavau, Georges et al., eds. 1983. *L'Universe politique des classes moyennes.* Paris: Fondation Nationale des Sciences Politiques.

Laxer, Gordon. 1985. Foreign ownership and myths about Canadian development. *The Canadian Review of Sociology and Anthropology*, 22, no. 3 (August 1985): 311–345.

Lebra, Joyce C. 1973. *Okuma Shigenobu: Statesman of Meiji Japan.* Canberra: Australian National University Press.

Lehmbruch, Gerhard. 1984. Concertation and the structure of corporatist networks. In *Order and conflict in contemporary capitalism*, ed. John H. Goldthorpe. Oxford: Clarendon Press.

Lekachman, Robert. 1976. *A History of economic ideas.* New York: McGraw-Hill.

————. 1976. *Economists at bay: Why the expert would never solve your problem.* New York: McGraw-Hill.

Lenin, Vladimir Il'ich. 1960. *Collected works*, vols. 27 and 32. Moscow: Foreign Language Publishing House.

————. 1969. *State and revolution.* Moscow: Progress.

————. 1978. Imperialism, the highest stage of capitalism. *Collected works*, vol. 22. Moscow: Progress.

Leonard, Herman B., and Elisabeth H. Rhyne. 1981. Federal credit and the "shadow budget." *Public Interest* 65 (Fall 1981): 40–58.

Leone, Robert A. *Who Profits? Winners, losers, and government regulation.* New York: Basic Books.

Leontiades, James C. 1985. *Multinational corporate strategy: Planning for world markets.* Lexington, MA: Heath.

Leontief, Wassily. 1979. Is technological unemployment inevitable?" *Challenge* 22, no. 4 (September–October 1979): 48–50.

Lewin, Moshe. 1974. *Political undercurrents in Soviet economic debate.* Princeton, NJ: Princeton University Press.

Lewis, W. Arthur. 1965. *Theory of economic growth.* New York: Harper & Row.

Lieberman, Sima. 1977. *The Growth of European mixed economies, 1945–1970.* Cambridge, MA: Schenkman.

Lindblom, Charles E. 1977. *Politics and markets: The world's political-economic systems.* New York: Basic Books.

Lindsay, Jack. 1954. *Civil war in England.* New York: Barnes & Noble.

Linton, Ralph. 1964. *The Cultural background of personality.* London: Routledge & Kegan Paul.

Lipset, Seymour Martin. 1972. The politics of American sociologists. *American Journal of Sociology* 78, no. 1 (July 1972): 67–104.

————. 1976. *Rebellion in the university.* Chicago: University of Chicago Press.

————. 1980. *The Third century: America as a post-industrial society.* Chicago: University of Chicago Press.

————. 1981a. *Political man: The social basis of politics.* Baltimore, MD: Johns Hopkins University Press.

————. 1981b. What happened to the proletariat? A Historic mission unfulfilled. *Encounter* 56 (June 1981): 18–34.

————. 1981c. The Limits of social sciences. *Public Opinion* 4. no. 5 (October–November, 1981): 2–9.

————. 1985, Canada and the United States: The cultural dimension. In *Canada and the United States*, ed. Charles F. Doran and John H. Sigler. Englewood Cliffs, NJ: Prentice Hall.

Lipset, Seymour Martin, and William Schneider. 1979. The Public view of regulation. *Public Opinion* 2, no. 1 (January–February 1979): 6–13.

————. 1983. *The Confidence gap: Business, labor and government in the public mind*. New York: Free Press.

Locke, John et al. *Social Contract*. With an Introduction by Sir Ernest Barker. London: Oxford University Press.

Lombardini, S. 1969. Italian fascism and the economy. In *The Nature of fascism*, ed. S. J. Woolf. New York: Vintage Books.

Louis Harris & Associates, Inc., and Alan F. Westin. 1981. *The Dimension of privacy: A national opinion research survey of attitudes toward privacy*. New York: Garland.

Lowi, Theodore J. 1969. *The End of liberalism: Ideology, policy, and the crisis of public authority*. New York: Norton.

Lukes, Steven. 1967. Alienation and anomie. In *Philosophy, Politics and Society*. Third Series. New York: Barnes & Noble.

Lutz, Vera C. 1965. *French planning*. Washington, DC: American Enterprise Institute for Public Policy Research.

MacAvoy, Paul W., ed. 1970. *The Crisis of the regulatory commissions: An introduction to a current issue of public policy*. New York: Norton.

Machin, Howard, and Vincent Wright, eds. 1985. *Economic policy and policy-making under the Mitterand presidency 1981–84*. London: Pinter.

Madden, Carl H., ed. 1977. *The Case for the multinational corporation*. New York: Praeger.

Malcolm, Andrew H. 1986. *The Canadians*. Toronto: Paperjacks.

Malinvaud, Edmond, and Jean-Paul Fitoussi. 1980. *Unemployment in Western countries*. Proceedings of a Conference held by the International Economic Association at Bischenberg, France. London: Macmillan.

Malraux, André. 1972. *Felled oaks: Conversation with de Gaulle*. Tr. Irene Clephane. New York: Holt, Rinehart & Winston.

Marcus, Alfred A. 1984. *The Adversary economy: Business responses to changing government requirements*. Westport, CT: Quorum Books.

Markovits, Andrei S., ed. 1982. *The Political economy of West Germany: Modell Deutschland*. New York: Praeger.

Marris, Robin, ed. 1974. *The Corporate society*. New York: Wiley.

Mars, Gerald. 1982. *Cheats at work: An Anthropology of workplace crime*. London: Allen & Unwin.

Marsh, Allan. 1975. "The Silent Revolution," value priorities and qualty of life in Britain. *American Political Science Review* 69, no. 1 (March 1975): 21–30.

Marsh, David. 1983. Interest group activity and structural power: Lindblom's Politics and Markets. *West European Politics* 6, no. 2. Special Issue on Capital and Politics in Western Europe. (April 1983): 3–13.

Marsh, Robert M. 1967. *Comparative sociology: A codification of cross-societal analysis*. New York: Harcourt, Brace & World.

Marshall, Byron K. 1967. *Capitalism and nationalism in prewar Japan: The ideology of the business elite 1868–1941*. Stanford, CA: Stanford University Press.

Marx, Karl. 1963. *Early writings.* Tr. T. B. Bottomore. London: C. A. Watts.

———. 1965. *Capital,* 3 vols. Tr. from the Third German Edition, Samuel Moore and Edward Aveling; ed. Frederick Engels. Moscow: Progress Publishing.

———. 1967. *Writing of the young Marx on philosophy and society.* Tr. and ed. Lloyd D. Easton and Kurt H. Guddat. Garden City, NY: Doubleday.

Marx, Karl, and Frederick Engels. 1968. *The Communist manifesto.* New York: International Publishers.

———. 1970. *The German ideology.* New York: International Publishers.

———. 1953. *Selected correspondence.* Moscow: Progress Publishing.

———. 1975. *Selected correspondence.* Moscow: Progress Publishing.

Marx, K., F. Engels, and V.I. Lenin. 1967. *On scientific communism.* Moscow: Progress Publishers.

Masuda, Yoneji. 1981. *The Information society as post industrial society.* Tokyo: Institute for the Information Society.

Maxwell, James A. 1968. *Fiscal policy: Its technique and institutional setting.* New York: Greenwood.

McClelland, David C. 1961. *The Achieving society.* Princeton, NJ: D. Van Nostrand.

McCloskey, Herbert, and John Zaller. 1984. *The American ethos: Public attitudes toward capitalism and democracy.* Cambridge, MA: Harvard University Press.

McCormic, Janice. 1983. Thorns among the roses: A year of the socialist experiment in France. *West European Politics* 6, no. 1 (January 1983): 44–64.

———. 1985. Apprenticeship for governing: An assessment of French socialism in power. In *Economic policy and policy-making under the Mitterand presidency 1981–1984,* ed. H. Machin and W. Wright. London: Pinter.

McKinney, John Clifford. 1966. *Constructive typology and social theory.* New York: Appleton-Century-Crofts.

McLellan, David. 1971. *Marx's Grundrisse.* London: Macmillan.

Melton, William C. 1985. *Inside the Fed: Making monetary policy.* Homewood, IL: Dow Jones-Irwin.

Meltzer, Allan H., and Scott F. Richard. 1978. Why government grows (and grows) in a democracy. *Public Interest* 52 (Winter 1978): 111–118.

Meny, Yves. 1985. Local authorities and economic policy. In *Economic policy and policy-making under the Mitterrand presidency 1981–1984,* ed. by H. Machin and W. Wright. London: Pinter.

Meyer, F. V., ed. *Prospects for recovery in the British economy.* London: Croom Helm.

Michael, Donald N. 1962. *Cybernation: The silent conquest.* Santa Barbara, CA: Center for the Study of Democratic Institutions.

Miliband, Ralph. 1969. *The State in capitalist society.* New York: Basic Books.

Miller, Arthur Raphael. 1971. *The Assault on privacy: Computers, data banks and dossiers.* Ann Arbor: University of Michigan Press.

Miller, Robert, and John Wood. 1982. *What price unemployment? An alternative approach.* London: IEA.

Mills, Charles Wright. 1956. *The Power elite.* London: Oxford University Press.

Minford, Patrick. 1987. Unemployment: Cause and cure. In *The Economic revival of modern Britain: The debate between left and right,* ed. D. Coates and J. Hillard. London: Elgar.

Mirow, Kurt Rudolf, and Harry Maurer. 1982. *Webs of power: International cartels and the world economy.* Boston: Houghton Mifflin.

Mishan, E. J. 1973. To grow or not to grow: What are the issues? *Encounter* 11, no. 5 (May 1973): 9–29.

Mitchell, Arnold. 1983. *The Nine American lifestyles: Who we are and where we are going.* New York: Macmillan.

Mitchell, Austin. 1983. *Four years in the death of the Labour Party*. London: Methuen.

Mitnick, Barry M. 1980. *The Political economy of regulation: Creating, designing and removing regulatory forms*. New York: Columbia University Press.

Mitterrand, François. 1982. *The Wheat and the chaff*. Introduction by William Styron. New York: Seaver Books.

Monsen, R. Joseph, and Kenneth D. Walters. 1979. State-owned business abroad: New competitive threat. *Harvard Business Review* (March–April 1979): 160–170.

————. 1983. *Nationalized companies: A Threat to American business*. New York: McGraw-Hill.

Mückl, Wolfgang J. 1982. Wie problematisch ist die Staatsverschuldung? In *Zufiel Staat?* Berlin: Kohlhammer.

Murray, Charles. 1984. *Losing ground: American social policy 1950–1980*. New York: Basic Books.

————. 1985. Helping the poor: A few modest proposals. *Commentary* 82, no. 5 (May 1985): 27–34.

Naess, Arne et al. 1956. *Democracy, ideology and objectivity*. Oslo: Oslo University Press.

Naisbitt, John. 1983. *Megatrends: The new directions transforming our lives*. New York: Warner Books.

Nakagawa, Yatsuhiro, and Nobumasa Ota. 1981. *The Japanese-style economic system*. Tokyo: Foreign Press Center.

Nash, Ronald H., ed. 1969. *Ideas of history*. Vol. 1. *Speculative approaches to history*. New York: E.P. Dutton.

Negandhi, Annant R., and Martin Welge. 1984. *Advances in international comparative management*. A Research Annual. Greenwich, CT: JAI Press.

Nell, Edward. 1983. On the conception of the state in macroeconomic theory. *Social Research* 50, no. 2 (Summer 1983): 401–427.

Nelson, Benjamin. 1968. Scholastic rationales of "conscience," early modern crisis of credibility, and the scientific–technological revolutions of the 17th and 20th centuries. *Journal for Scientific Studies of Religion* 7, no. 2 (Fall 1968): 157–177.

————. 1972. Communities, societies, civilizations: Postmillenial views on the faces and masks of time. In *Social Development: Critical Perspectives*, ed. Manfred Stanley. New York: Basic Books.

————. 1973. Civilizational complexes and intercivilizational encounters. *Sociological analysis* 34, no. 2 (Summer 1973): 79–105.

Nettl, J. P. 1967. Political mobilization: *A sociological analysis of methods and concepts*. London: Faber & Faber.

Nevin, Michael. 1983. *The Age of illusions: The political economy of Britain, 1968–1982*. London: Gollancz.

Newton, Ronald C. 1974. Natural corporatism and the passing of populism in Spanish America. In *The New corporatism: Social political structures in the Iberian world*, ed. F. B. Pike and T. Strich. Notre Dame, IN: University of Notre Dame Press.

Neymarck, Alfred. 1970. *Colbert et son temps*. Gèneve: Slatkine Reprints.

Noll, Roger G. 1971. *Reform in regulation*. Washington, DC: Brookings Institution.

Norling, Bernard. 1970. *Timelesss problems in history*. Notre Dame, IN: University of Notre Dame Press.

Norman, E. H. 1940. *Japan's emergence as a modern state*. New York: Institute of Pacific Relations.

Novak, Michael. 1982. *The Spirit of democratic capitalism*. New York: American

Enterprise Institute and Simon & Schuster.

Nozick, Robert. 1974. *Anarchy, state and utopia.* New York: Basic Books.

Nuechterlein, Jammes. 1983. George Will and American conservatism. *Commentary* 81, no. 4 (October 1983): 35–43.

Nutter, G. Warren. 1978. *Growth of government in the West.* Washington, DC: American Enterprise Institute.

Oakeshott, Michael. 1962. *Rationalism in politics.* New York: Basic Books.

O'Connor, James. 1973. *The Fiscal crisis of the state.* New York: St. Martin's Press.

———. 1974. *The Corporations and the state.* New York: Harper & Row.

Offe, Claus, 1972. *Strukturprobleme des kapitalistishen Staates.* Frankfurt a M.: Suhrkamp V.

———. 1983. The Attribution of public status to interest groups: Observations on the West German Case. In *Organizing interests in Western Europe,* ed. Suzanne Berger. Cambridge: Cambridge University Press.

———. 1985. *Contradiction of the welfare state.* Ed. John Keane. London: Hutchinson.

Ouchi, William G. 1982. *Theory Z.* New York: Avon.

Ozenda, Michel, and Dominique Strauss-Kahn. 1985. French planning: Decline or renewal? In *Economic policy and policy-making under the Mitterrand presidency 1981–84,* ed. H. Machin and W. Wright. London: Pinter.

Pachter, Henry M. 1975. *The Fall and rise of Europe.* New York: Praeger.

———. 1978. *Modern Germany.* Boulder, CO: Westview.

Panitch, Leo. 1977. *The Canadian state: Political economy and political power.* Toronto: Toronto University Press.

———. 1979. The Development of corporatism in liberal democracies. In *Trends toward corporatist intermediation,* ed. P. Schmitter and G. Lehmbruch. London: Sage.

Pareto, Vilfredo. 1963. *The Mind and society: A treatise on general sociology.* Ed. Arthur Livingston. New York: Dover.

Parry, Gerraint. 1985. Welfare state and welfare society. *Government and Opposition* 20, no. 3 (Summer 1985): 287–296.

Parsons, Talcott, and Neil J. Smelser. 1957. *Economy and society.* London: Routledge & Kegan Paul.

Pascale, Richard T., and Anthony G. Athos. 1981. *The Art of Japanese management.* New York: Simon & Schuster.

Pascall, Glenn. 1985. *The Trillion dollar budget: How to stop bankrupting America.* Seattle, WA: University of Washington Press.

Peacock, Alan et al., eds. 1984. *The Regulation game: How British and West German companies bargain with government.* Oxford: Basil Blackwell.

Perroux, François. 1983. *The New concept of development: Basic tenets.* London: Croom Helm.

Peterson. Peter G. 1982. Social security: The coming crash. *New York Review of Books* (December 2, 1982): 34–57.

———. The Salvation of social security. *New York Review of Books* (December 16, 1982): 50–58.

Pevzner, J. A., ed. 1985. *Gosudarstvenno-monopolisticheskoe regulirovanie v Iaponii.* (State-monopoly reulatory practice in Japan). Moskow: Nauka.

Peyrefitte, Alain. 1986. *The Trouble with France.* New York: New York University Press.

Pike, Fredrick B., and Thomas Stritch, eds. 1974. *The New corporatism: Social-political structures in the Iberian world.* Notre Dame, IN: University of Notre Dame Press.

Plattner, Marc F. 1979. The Welfare state vs. the redistributive state. *Public Interest*

55 (Spring 1979): 28–49.

Podbielski, Gisela. 1974. *Italy: Development and crisis in the post-war economy.* Oxford: Clarendon Press.

Podhoretz, Norman. 1980. The New nationalism and the 1980 elections. *Public Opinion* 3, no. 1A (February—March, 1980): 2–5.

Poggi, Gianfranco. 1978. *The development of the modern state: A sociological introduction.* Stanford, CA: Stanford University Press.

Polsby, Nelson. 1983. A Special kind of conservative. Review of *Statecraft as Soulcraft* by George F. Will. *Fortune* (July 25, 1983): 103–106.

Poole, Robert W., Jr., ed. 1982. *Instead of regulation: Alternatives to federal regulatory agencies.* Lexington, MA: Heath.

Porter, John. 1965. *The Vertical mosaic: An analysis of social class and power in Canada.* Toronto: University of Toronto Press.

Posner, M. V. 1967. *Italian public entreprise.* Cambridge, MA: Harvard University Press.

Poulantzas, Nicos. 1976. *Classes in contemporary capitalism.* London: NLB.

Prichard, J. Robert S. 1983. *Crown corporations in Canada: The calculus of instrument choice.* Toronto: Butterworths.

Pryke, Richard N. 1981. *The Nationalised industries: Policies and performance.* Oxford: Robertson.

Rae, Douglas. 1979. The Egalitarian state: Notes on a system of contradictory ideals. *Daedalus.* Special Issue: *The State* 108, no. 4 (Fall 1979): 37–54.

Raines, John Curtis. 1975. *Illusion of success.* Valley Forge, PA: Judson Press.

Rawls, John. 1971. *A Theory of justice.* Cambridge, MA: Belknap Press.

Ray, S. K. 1981. *Economics of the black market.* Boulder, CO: Westview.

Rees, John. 1971. *Equality.* London: Macmillan.

Rees, Merlyn. 1973. *The Public sector in the mixed economy.* New York: Barnes & Noble.

Rees, Ray. 1976. *Public enterprise economies.* London: Weidenfeld & Nickolson.

Reich, Charles A. 1972. *The greening of America.* New York: Bantam Books.

Reuss, Frederich Gustav. 1963. *Fiscal policy for growth without inflation: The German experiment.* Baltimore, MD: Johns Hopkins University Press.

Revel, Jean-François. 1977. *The Totalitarian temptation.* Tr. David Hapgood. Garden City, NY: Doubleday.

Rex, Martin. 1985. *Rawls and rights.* Lawrence, KS: University Press of Kansas.

Richardson, Jeremy, and Roger Henning, eds. 1984. *Unemployment: Policy responses of western democracies.* Beverly Hills, CA: Sage.

Riddell, Peter. 1983. *The Thatcher government.* Oxford: Robertson.

Riemer, Jeremiah M. 1982. Alterations in the design of model Germany: Critical innovations in the policy machinery for economic steering. In *The Political economy of West Germany,* ed. Andrei S. Markovits. New York: Praeger.

Riesman, David. 1954. *Individualism reconsidered and other essays.* Glencoe, IL: Free Press.

———. 1955. *The Lonely crowd: A study of the changing American character.* Garden City, NY: Doubleday.

Roberts, Paul Craig. 1984. *The Supply-side revolution: An insider's account of policymaking in Washington.* Cambridge, MA: Harvard University Press.

Roming, Michael J. 1983. Who's to say what they are worth? *New York Times,* September 18, 1983.

Roper, Burns W., and Thomas A. W. Miller. 1985. Americans take stock of business. *Public Opinion* (August–September, 1985): 12–15.

Rose, Richard. 1980. *Changes in public employment: A Multi-dimensional comparative analysis.* Paper no. 61. Glasgow: University of Strathclyde Press.

————. 1981. The Growth of government in the United Kingdom since 1945: A programme of research. Paper no. 94. Glasgow: Centre for the Study of Public Policy.

————. 1985. *How exceptional is American government?* Paper no. 150. Glasgow: Centre for the Study of Public Policy. University of Strathclyde Press.

Rosenthal, Glenda G., and Elliot Zupnick, eds. 1984. *Contemporary Western Europe: Problems and responses.* New York: Praeger.

Ross, George. 1980. Destroyed by the dialectic: Politics, the decline of Marxism, and the new middle strata in France. *Theory and Society* 16, no. 1. (January 1987): 7–38.

Rostow, Walt W. 1978. *The World economy: History and prospect.* Austin: University of Texas Press.

Roszak, Theodore. 1969. *The Making of a counter culture.* New York: Doubleday.

Rowe, J. Z. 1965. *The Public-private character of United States central banking.* New Brunswick, NJ: Rutgers University Press.

Rueschemeyer, Dietrich, and Peter Evans. 1986. The State and economic transformation: Toward an analysis of the conditions underlying effective intervention. In *Bringing the state back in,* ed. P. B. Evans et al. Cambridge: Cambridge University Press.

Rule, James et al. 1980. *The Politics of privacy.* New York: New American Library.

Sanford, Cedrick. 1977. *Social economics.* London: Heineman.

Sargent, J. A. 1899. *The Economic policy of Colbert.* London: Longmans, Green.

Savary, Julien. 1984. *French multinationals.* New York: St. Martin's Press.

Savas, E. S. 1982. *Privatizing the public sector: How to shrink government.* Chatham, NJ: Chatham House.

Scase, Richard. 1982. The Petty bourgeoisie and modern capitalism: A consideration of recent theories. In *Social class and the division of labour,* ed. A. Giddens and G. Mackenzie. Cambridge: Cambridge University Press.

Scase, Richard, and Robert Goffee. 1982. *The Entrepreneurial middle class.* London: Croom Helm.

Schaefer, David Lewis. 1979. *Justice or tyranny? A critique of John Rawls' "A Theory of justice".* Port Washington, NY: Kennikat Press.

Schmitter, Philippe C. 1975. *Corporatism and public policy in authoritarian Portugal.* Beverly Hills, CA: Sage.

Schmitter, Philippe C., and Gerhard Lehmbruch, eds. 1979. *Trends toward corporatist intermediation.* Beverly Hills, CA: Sage.

Schmoller, Gustav Friedrich Von. 1967. *The mercantile system and its historical significance.* New York: A. M. Kelley.

Schnitzer, Martin. 1974. *Income distribution: A Comparative study of the United States, Sweden, West Germany, the United Kingdom and Japan.* New York: Praeger.

Schumpeter, Joseph A. 1936. *The Theory of economic development: An inquiry into profits, capital, credit, interest, and the business cycle.* Tr. R. Opie. Cambridge, MA: Harvard University Press.

————. 1966. *Capitalism, socialism and democracy.* London: Unwin.

Scruton, Roger. 1984. *The Meaning of conservatism.* London: Macmillan.

Seeman, Melvin. 1959. The Meaning of alienation. *American Sociological Review* 24, no. 6 (December 1959): 783–791.

Sennett, Richard. 1978. *The Fall of public man: On the social psychology of capitalism.* New York: Vintage.

————. 1981. *Authority.* New York: Vintage Books.

Servan-Schreiber, Jean-Jacques. 1968. *The American challenge.* New York: Atheneum.

Severn, William. 1973. *The Right to privacy*. New York: Washburn.

Shepherd, William G. 1985. *Public policies toward business*. Homewood, IL: Richard D. Irwin.

Sheppard, Robert. 1988. $4.6 billion later, privatization gets tough. *Globe and Mail*, Report on Business. August 13, 1988.

Shonfield, Andrew. 1965. *Modern capitalism: The changing balance of public and private power*. New York: Oxford University Press.

Simmel, Georg. 1966. *Conflict and the web of group-affiliations*. Tr. Kurt Wolff and R. Bendix. Foreword by Everett C. Hughes. New York: Free Press.

Simon, Sir Ernest Darwin. 1939. *The Smaller democracies*. London: Gollancz.

Simons, G. L. 1982. *Privacy in the computer age*. Manchester, Eng.: NCC Publications.

Skidelsky, Robert, ed. 1977. *The End of the Keynesian era*. London: Billing & Sons.

Skocpol, Theda. 1979. *States and social revolutions*. Cambridge: Cambridge University Press.

———. 1986. Bringing the state back in: Strategies of analysis in current research. In *Bringing the state back in*, ed. P. B. Evans et al. Cambridge: Cambridge University Press.

Smelser, Neil J. 1968. *Essays in sociological explanation*. Englewood Cliffs, NJ: Prentice Hall.

———. 1976. *Comparative methods in the social sciences*. Englewood, Cliffs, NJ: Prentice Hall.

Smith, John. 1987. An Industrial strategy for Britain. In *The Economic revival of modern Britain*, ed. D. Coates and J. Hillard. London: Elgar.

Smith, Keith. 1984. *The British economic crisis*. Harmondsworth, Eng.: Penguin.

Smith, Stephen, and Susanne Wied-Nebbeling. 1986. *The Shadow economy in Britain and Germany*. London: Anglo-German Foundation.

Smith, Tom W. 1987. The Welfare state in cross-national perspective. *Public Opinion Quarterly* 51, no. 3 (Autumn 1987): 404-416.

Smith, Trevor. 1979. *The Politics of the corporate economy*. Oxford: Robertson.

Sobran, Joseph. 1983. George Will and the contemporary political conversation (properly understood). *American Spectator* 16, no. 10 (October 1983): 10–15.

Sone, Yasunori. 1985. Present problems and future prospects of Japanese welfare state. Paper presented at the 13th International Political Science Association World Congress. Paris.

Stark, Fortney H. 1983. Bring fair play to taxing of "perks." *New York Times*, September 18, 1983.

Stauffer, Robert B., ed. 1985. *Transnational corporations and the state*. Sydney, Australia: University of Sydney.

Stepan, Alfred. 1978. *The State and society: Peru in comparative perspective*. Princeton, NJ: Princeton University Press.

Stevens, Anne. 1980. The Higher civil service and economic policy making. In *French politics and public policy*, ed. Philip G. Cerny and Martin A. Schain. London and New York: Methuen.

Steward, James B. 1983. *The Partners*. New York: Simon & Schuster.

Stigler, George J. 1975. *The Citizen and the state*. Chicago IL: University of Chicago Press.

Stuart, Henry. 1981. *Informal institutions: Alternative networks in the corporate state*. New York: St. Martin's Press.

Suleiman, Ezra N. 1974. *Elites in French society: The politics of survival*. Princeton, NJ: Princeton University Press.

Surrey, Stanley S., and Paul McDaniel. 1985. *Tax expenditures*. Cambridge, MA: Harvard University Press.

Tawney, R. H. 1964. *Equality*. London: George Allen & Unwin.

Taylor-Gooby, Peter. 1985. *Public opinion, ideology and state welfare*. London: Routledge & Kegan Paul.

Thomson, David. 1969. *Democracy in France since 1870*. London: Oxford University Press.

Thurow, Lester C. 1980. *The Zero-sum society: Distribution and the possibilities for economic change*. New York: Basic Books.

Tilton, Timothy. 1979. A Swedish road to socialism: Ernst Wigforss and the ideological foundations of Swedish Social Democracy. *American Political Science Review* 73, no. 2 (June 1979): 505–520.

Toch, Josef. n/d. *Vergesellschaftung in Österreich*. Wien: Österreichischen Gewerkschaftsbundes.

de Tocqueville, Alexis. 1969. *Democracy in America*. Ed. J. P. Mayer. Tr. George Lawrence. Garden City, NY: Doubleday.

Toennies, Ferdinand. 1957. *Community and society (Gemeinschaft und Gesellschaft)*. Tr., with introduction by Charles P. Loomis. East Lansing, MI: Michigan State University Press.

Tolchin, Susan J., and Martin Tolchin. 1983. *Dismantling America: The rush to deregulate*. New York: Oxford University Press.

Tomison, Maureen. 1972. *The English sickness: The rise of trade union political power*. Foreword by Robert Carr. London: Tom Stacet.

Tongue, Williams W. 1974. *How we can halt inflation and still keep our jobs*. Homewood, IL: Dow Jones-Irwin.

Trout, Andrew. 1978. *Jean-Baptiste Colbert*. Boston, MA: Twayne.

Tsuji, Kiyoaki, ed. 1984. *Public administration in Japan*. Tokyo: University of Tokyo Press.

Tully, Shawn. Mitterrand's risky new right turn. *Fortune* (April 30, 1984): 163–170.

Tupper, Allan, and G. Bruce Doern. 1981. *Public corporations and public policy in Canada*. Montreal: Institute for Research on Public Policy.

Turner, Jonathan H. 1977. *Social stratification: A theoretical analysis*. New York: Columbia University Press.

Ulman, Lloyd, ed. 1973. *Manpower programs in the policy mix*. Baltimore, MD: Johns Hopkins University.

Useem, Michael. 1984. *The Inner circle: Large corporations and the rise of business political activity in the U.S. and U.K.* New York: Oxford University Press.

Vallier, Ivan, ed. 1973. *Comparative methods in sociology: Essays on trends and applications*. Berkeley: University of California Press.

Van Dyke, Vernon. 1975. Justice as fairness: For groups? *American political science review* 69, no. 2 (June 1975): 607–614.

Vercauteren, Paul. 1970. *Les sous-proletaires: Essai sur une forme de pauperism contemporain*. Paris: Editions "Vie Ouvrière."

Vernon, Raymond. 1977. *Storm over the multinationals*. Cambridge, MA: Harvard University Press.

Vernon, Raymond, ed. 1974. *Big business and the state: Changing relations in Western Europe*. Cambridge, MA: Harvard University Press.

Vogel, Ezra F. 1979. *Japan as number one: Lessons for America*. New York: Harper & Row.

Voltaire, François M. A. 1926. *The Age of Louis XIV*. Tr. M. P. Pollack. Preface by F. C. Green. London: Dent.

Wagener, Hans Otto. 1972. *Neue staatwirtschaftliche Funktionen bundeseigener Industriebeteiligungen*. Meisenheim am Glan: Anton Hain.

Wallach, H. G. Peter, and George K. Romoser, eds. 1985. *West German politics in the mid-eighties crisis and continuity*. New York: Praeger.

Wallis, W. Allen. 1976. *An Overgoverned society*. New York: Free Press.

Wanniski, Jude. 1978. Taxes, revenues, and the "Laffer curve." *Public interest* 50 (Winter 1978): 3–16.

———. 1983. *The Way the world works*. New York: Simon & Schuster.

Wattenberg, Ben J. 1984. *The Good news is the bed news is wrong*. New York: Simon & Schuster.

Weaver, Paul H. 1978. Regulating social policy and class conflict. *Public Interest* 50 (Winter 1978): 45–63.

Webber, Carolyn, and Aaron Wildavsky. 1986. *A History of taxation and expenditure in the Western world*. New York: Simon & Schuster.

Webber, Douglas. 1983. Combatting and acquiescing in unemployment? Crisis management in Sweden and West Germany. *West European Politics* 6, no. 1 (January 1983): 23–43.

———. 1983. A Relationship of "critical partnership"? Capital and the social-liberal coalition in West Germany. *West European Politics* 6, no. 3 (April 1983): 61–86.

Weber, Marianne. 1975. *Max Weber: A biography*. Tr. and ed. Harry Zohn. New York: Wiley & Sons.

Weber, Max. 1950. *General economic history*. Tr. Frank Knight. Glencoe, IL: Free Press.

———. 1956. *Staatssoziologie*. Berlin: Dunker & Humblot.

———. 1958. *The Protestant ethic and the spirit of capitalism*. Tr. Talcott Parsons. Foreword by R. H. Tawney. New York: Scribner's Sons.

———. 1958. *The City*. Tr. and ed. Don Martindale and Gertrud Neuwirth. New York: Free Press.

———. 1971. *Gesammelte Politische Schriften*. Ed. Johannes Winckelman. Tubingen: Mohr (P. Siebeck).

———. 1976. *The Agrarian sociology of ancient civilizations*. London: Frank.

———. 1978. *Economy and society*. vols. 1 and 2. Ed. Guenther Roth and Claus Wittich. Berkeley: University of California Press.

Weidenbaum, Murray L. 1976. *Business, government and politics*. Englewood Cliffs, NJ: Prentice Hall.

———. 1979. *The Future of business regulation: Private action and public demand*. New York: Amacon.

———. 1979. The high cost of government regulation. *Challenge* 22, no. 5 (November–December 1979): 32–39.

Weidenbaum, Murray L., and Robert De Fina. 1978. *The Cost of federal regulation of economic activity*. Washington, DC: American Enterprise Institute.

Weidenbaum, Murray L., and Michael J. Athey. 1984. What is the rust belt's problem. In *The Industrial Policy debate*, ed. Chalmers Johnson. San Francisco CA: Institute for Contemporary Studies.

Wellbank, J. H. 1982. *John Rawls and his critics: An annotated bibliogrphy*. New York: Garland.

Westhues, Kenneth. 1972. *Society's shadow: Studies in the sociology of counterculture*. Toronto: McGraw-Hill Ryerson.

Westin, Alan. 1967. *Privacy and freedom*. Foreword by Oscar H. Ruebhausen. New York: Atheneum.

White, Lawrence J. 1981. *Reforming regulation: Process and problem*. Englewood Cliffs, NJ: Prentice-Hall.

White, Theodore H. 1983. *America in search of itself*. New York: Warner Books.

———. 1985. The Danger from Japan. *New York Times Magazine* (July 28, 1985): 19–59.

Whyte, William H. 1963. *The Organization man*. Hammondsworth, Eng.: Penguin.

Wicclair, Mark R. 1980. Rawls and the principle of nonintervention. In *John Rawls' theory of social justice.* Ed. H. Gene Blocker and Elizabeth H. Smith. Athens, OH: Ohio University Press.

Wicklein, John. 1981. *Electronic nightmare: The new communications and freedom.* New York: Viking.

Wiener, Martin J. 1981. *English culture and decline of the industrial spirit, 1850–1980.* Cambridge: Cambridge University Press.

Wildavsky, Aaron. 1980. *How to limit government spending.* Berkeley: University of California Press.

———. 1984. *The Politics of the budgetary process.* Boston: Little, Brown.

Wilensky, Harold L. 1975. *The Welfare state and equality.* Berkeley: University of California Press.

———. 1976. *The "New corporatism," centralization and the welfare state.* London and Beverly Hills, CA: Sage.

Wiles, Peter. 1981. A Sovietological view. In *Schumpeter's vision: Capitalism, socialism and democracy after 40 years,* ed. Arnold Heertje. New York: Praeger.

Wilhelmsen, Frederick D. 1980. Modern man's myth of self identity. *Modern Age* 24, no. 1 (Winter 1980): 39–46.

Will, George F. 1983. *Statecraft as soulcraft: What government does.* New York: Simon & Schuster.

———. 1986. *The Morning after: American successes and excesses 1981–1986.* New York: Macmillan.

Will, Ian. 1983. *The Big brother society.* London: Harrap.

Williams, Philip M., and Martin Harrisson. 1971. *Politics and society in de Gaulle's republic.* London: Longman.

Wilson, James Q., ed. 1980. *The Politics of regulation.* New York: Basic Books.

Wilson, John. 1966. *Equality.* London: Hutchinson.

Wolff, Robert Paul. 1977. *Understanding Rawls: A reconstruction and critique of A theory of justice.* Princeton, NJ: Princeton University Press.

Woodsworth, David E. 1977. *Social security and national policy: Sweden, Yugoslavia, Japan.* Montreal, Ont.: McGill-Queen's University Press.

Wright, Erik Olin. 1985. *Classes.* London: Verso, New Left Books.

Yankelovich, Daniel. 1972. *The Changing values on campus.* New York: Washington Square Press.

———. 1974. *The New morality: A profile of American youth in the 70's.* New York: McGraw-Hill.

———. 1981. *New rules: Searching for self-fulfillment in a world turned upside down.* New York: Random House.

Young, Stephen, with A. V. Lowe. 1980. *Intervention in the mixed economy.* London: Croom Helm.

Die Zähmung des Leviathan. 1980. With contribution of H. Bonusand others. Baden-Baden, FDR: Nomos.

Zetterbaum, 1977. Equality and human need. *American political science review* 71, no. 3 (September 1977): 983–998.

Zuviel Staat? Die Grenzen der Staatstätigkeit. 1982. With contribution of Thomas Ellwein and others. Stuttgart, FDR: Kohlhammer.

Index